D0250280

INSIGHT GUIDES
SICILY

914.58049 SIC 2012
Sicily

$21.99
CENTRAL   31994014793696

APA PUBLICATIONS
Part of the Langenscheidt Publishing Group

✳ INSIGHT GUIDE
SICILY

Editorial

Project Editor
Siân Lezard
Series Manager
Rachel Lawrence
Publishing Manager
Rachel Fox
Picture Editor
Tom Smyth
Design Editor
Richard Cooke

Distribution

UK & Ireland
Dorling Kindersley Ltd
(a Penguin Group company)
80 Strand, London, WC2R 0RL
customerservice@dk.com

United States
Ingram Publisher Services
1 Ingram Boulevard, PO Box 3006,
La Vergne, TN 37086-1986
customer.service@ingrampublisher
services.com

Australia
Universal Publishers
PO Box 307
St Leonards NSW 1590
sales@universalpublishers.com.au

New Zealand
Brown Knows Publications
11 Artesia Close, Shamrock Park
Auckland, New Zealand 2016
sales@brownknows.co.nz

Worldwide
**Apa Publications GmbH & Co.
Verlag KG (Singapore branch)**
7030 Ang Mo Kio Avenue 5
08-65 Northstar @ AMK
Singapore 569880
apasin@singnet.com.sg

Printing

CTPS-China

© 2012 Apa Publications (UK) Ltd

All Rights Reserved

First Edition 1993
Fifth Edition 2012

ABOUT THIS BOOK

The first Insight Guide pioneered the use of creative full-colour photography in guidebooks in 1970. Since then, we have expanded our range to cater for our readers' need not only for reliable information about their chosen destination but also for a real understanding of that destination. Now, when the internet can supply inexhaustible (but not always reliable) facts, our books marry text and pictures to provide that much more elusive quality: knowledge. To achieve this, they rely heavily on the authority of locally based writers and photographers.

How to use this book

The book is carefully structured to convey an understanding of Sicily:

◆ The **Best of Sicily** section at the start of the book gives you a snap-shot of the island's highlights, helping you prioritise what you want to see and do.

◆ To understand the island today, you need to know something of its past. The **Features** section covers its people, history and culture in lively essays written by specialists.

◆ The **Places** section provides a full rundown of all the attractions worth seeing. The main places of interest are coordinated by number with full-colour maps. Margin notes provide background information and tips on how to save time and money.

◆ **Photo features** illuminate aspects of the island's archaeology, architecture and art.

◆ Photographs are chosen not only to illustrate geography and buildings but also to convey the moods of the island and the life of its people.

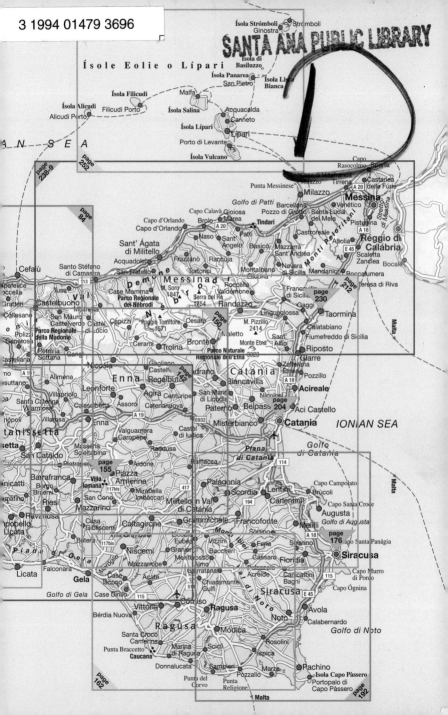

Map Legend

▰▰◻▰▰	Autostrada with Junction
▭ ▭ ▭ ▭	Autostrada (under construction)
▰▰▰▰	Dual Carriageway
▬▬▬	Main Road
▬▬▬	Secondary Road
▭▭▭	Minor road
▬▬▬	Track
▬ ▪ ▪	International Boundary
▬ ▬ ▬	Province Boundary
▭ ● ▭	National Park/Reserve
▭ ▭ ▭	Ferry Route
✈ ✈	Airport
† ⳨	Church (ruins)
†	Monastery
▟ ▛	Castle (ruins)
∴	Archaeological Site
∩	Cave
★	Place of Interest
⌂	Mansion/Stately Home
※	Viewpoint
⚑	Beach
▬▬	Autostrada
▬▬	Dual Carriageway
▬▬	Main Roads
▬▬	Minor Roads
▭▭	Footpath
▬▬▬	Railway
▬▬▬	Pedestrian Area
▬▬▬	Important Building
▬▬▬	Park
❶	Numbered Sight
⛌	Bus Station
❶	Tourist Information
✉	Post Office
⊞	Cathedral/Church
☾	Mosque
✡	Synagogue
⚑	Statue/Monument
▯	Tower
⸸	Lighthouse

LEFT: Temple of Concord in
the Valley of the Temples.

papers, travel documentaries and magazines such as *National Geographic*, and spends a large chunk of the year travelling around Italy.

In compiling the earlier editions of this book, Lisa found herself intrigued by the clash between the legendary immutability of Sicily and the apparent striving for change, particularly among the young.

Those were darker times, and she's now delighted to report that a sunnier Sicily is emerging, from "Mafia-free" holidays and the return of "stolen" art treasures to the revival of Ragusa, Siracusa and southeastern Sicily, the resurgence of Palermo, and the revitalisation of Sicilian wines.

Added to the mix are chic boutique hotels, Slow Food cookery courses, new walking trails through nature reserves, cruises around the Aeolian islands, and helicopter flights over Mount Etna. Sicily has never been more beguiling.

Insight Guide Sicily was proofread by **Neil Titman** and indexed by **Helen Peters**.

CONTACTING THE EDITORS

We would appreciate it if readers would alert us to errors or outdated information by writing to:

Insight Guides, P.O. Box 7910, London SE1 1WE, England.
email: insight@apaguide.co.uk

NO part of this book may be reproduced, stored in a retrieval system or transmitted in any form or means electronic, mechanical, photocopying, recording or otherwise, without prior written permission of *Apa Publications*. Brief text quotations with use of photographs are exempted for book review purposes only.
Information has been obtained from sources believed to be reliable, but its accuracy and completeness, and the opinions based thereon, are not guaranteed.

www.insightguides.com

◆ The **Travel Tips** listings section provides full information on transport, hotels, restaurants, shopping and activities, from culture and festivals to hiking and watersports. Information can be located quickly by using the index printed on the back cover flap – and the flaps are designed to serve as bookmarks.

The contributors

This edition of *Insight Guide Sicily* was commissioned by **Siân Lezard** and edited by **Cathy Muscat**.

The book was largely written and revised by **Lisa Gerard-Sharp**, a writer with a special interest in Italy. An award-winning British journalist, Lisa contributes to national news-

LEFT: view over the town of Noto.

Maps

THE BEST OF SICILY: TOP ATTRACTIONS

Sicily has something for everyone. The temples and other remains of ancient civilisations – Greek, Roman, Arab-Norman – are breathtaking, but the dramatic scenery, the vibrant cities, the food and the seductive way of life are just as appealing

△ **Explore Mount Etna**. Europe's largest active volcano can be reached by cable car, with a hike to the craters up the basalt-encrusted slopes or a trail-bashing jeep ride up to the ragged summits; you can even ski on Mount Etna. *See page 222.*

△ **Let your spirits soar in the Riserva dello Zingaro**. Set on the rugged coastline between Scopello and San Vito Lo Capo, this is Sicily's most successful nature reserve, with walks, beaches, birdlife and cosy guesthouses nearby. *See pages 48 and 101.*

▷ **Succumb to Sicilian Baroque in the Val di Noto**. This Unesco World Heritage site in southeastern Sicily embraces a cluster of cities where the Baroque architecture is often matched by the rugged scenery beyond. *See pages 21 and 192.*

◁ **Be a time traveller in the Valley of the Temples**. Agrigento's Greek temples are as fine as any ancient ruins remaining in Greece. February's almond blossom festival is a lovely time to visit. *See page 122.*

▷ **Get the *granita* habit**. Flavoured with fruit, almonds or coffee, these Sicilian sorbets are often eaten for breakfast, with sweet brioche. The best haunts include the Bam Bar in Taormina and Caffè Sicilia in Noto. *See pages 199 and 230.*

▽ **Admire Palermo's Arab-Norman heart**. From the Moorish, red-domed churches to the royal palace and the Cappella Palatina to the pleasure dome of La Zisa, these exotic monuments evoke *The Arabian Nights*. *See pages 64–6, 75 and 94–5.*

◁ **Visit a wine estate for a tasting**. Whether a grand estate such as Florio in Marsala or the organic Sirignano Wine Resort near Alcamo, this is a great experience, possibly including lunch or even a cookery course. *See pages 45 and 286.*

△ **Go island-hopping around the Aeolian Islands**. Vulcano boasts a smouldering volcano, as does Stróm-boli; Salina is sleepy and family-friendly; Panarea is chic; remote Alicudi is the land that time forgot. *See pages 251–9.*

▷ **Relish the mosaics at the Villa Romana**, a superb villa in Piazza Armerina, with some of the most extensive and beautiful Roman mosaics ever known, even if ongoing restoration means parts may be closed. *See page 154.*

▽ **Clamber over castles**. Sweep away the cobwebs by visiting great medieval castles, including those in Sperlinga, Cáccamo, Catania, Enna, Erice and Siracusa, generally built by the Normans or the Swabians. *See page 95.*

THE BEST OF SICILY: EDITOR'S CHOICE

From churches to beaches, scenery to street food, temples to towns... here, at a glance, are our recommendations, plus some tips that even Sicilians won't always know

BEST SICILIAN EXPERIENCES

- **Train around the volcano**. Dramatic sightseeing on the Circumetnea Railway, which circles the base of Etna on a four-hour trip from Catania or Taormina, with a stop at Randazzo. See page 215.
- **The Alcántara Gorge adventure**. Gola dell'Alcántara, near Taormina, is a wild gorge carved by the river. You can simply walk the gorge path or hire waders or wetsuits – the water is freezing. Buses from Taormina and Catania. Avoid Sundays. See page 217.
- **Hiking and eating in the Madonie mountains**. Follow limestone paths through meadows and woodlands of cork and holm to medieval villages and Slow Food feasts. See page 90.
- **To the islands by sea**. Ferries and hydrofoils sail from Palermo, Cefalù and Milazzo to islands off the Tyrrhenian coast – **Vulcano**, **Lípari** and **Salina** are closest. Sail to the **Egadi Islands** from Trápani. (Travel agents can organise trips from Catania, Messina and Taormina.) See page 264.
- **The *passeggiata***. The classic early evening stroll, with ices or *aperitivi*; an especially engaging experience in Alcamo, Cefalù, Noto, Ortigia, Ragusa Ibla, Scicli, Taormina, Trápani and, in summer, Mondello and the beach resorts.

TOP TOWNS

- **Cefalù**: charming medieval seaside resort and gentle introduction to Sicily, with its great cathedral and leisurely pace of life. See pages 89–90.
- **Erice**: the island's moodiest medieval town is lovely in any season, even swathed in winter mists. See pages 99–100.
- **Noto**: Sicily's most stunning Baroque city is a luminous stage set which lures you in to play a part. See pages 192–5.
- **Palermo**: both a glorious assault on the senses and the glittering summation of Arab-Norman Sicily. See pages 61–79.
- **Ragusa (Ibla)**: steeped in atmosphere, yet arguably the island's most civilised and hospitable centre. See pages 160–5.
- **Siracusa (Ortigia)**: Sicily's most lyrical city, especially in soporific Ortigia, an island apart. See pages 177–87.
- **Taormina**: chic hotels and cosmopolitan confidence make the resort a seductive retreat from Sicilian intensity. See pages 229–37.

Top Left: *passeggiata* at twilight on Piazza Aprile in Taormina.
Below: view over Ragusa Ibla in the south of the island.
Right: golden sandy beach in Ragusa Province.
Far Right: seafood stew, just one of many culinary highlights.

THE FINEST CHURCHES

- **Palermo**: the **Cappella Palatina** (Palatine Chapel) with its Byzantine and Arab-Norman mosaics. *See page 65.*
- **Palermo**: the **Oratorio di San Lorenzo**, near Piazza Marina. Grandiose Baroque with wonderful stuccowork by Serpotta. *See page 73.*
- **Monreale: Duomo**. Like the Capella Palatina in Palermo, but much bigger, Monreale Cathedral is a glittering tapestry of mosaics, which are matched by stunning mosaics in the cloisters. *See page 83.*
- **Cefalù: Duomo**. The mystical Arab-Norman cathedral is a candidate for Unesco World Heritage listing, as is Monreale. *See page 89.*
- **Siracusa: Duomo**. A Sicilian hybrid: a Greek Temple of Athena converted into an early Christian church, but later remodelled in exuberant Baroque style. *See page 184.*

ABOVE: Greek temple at Selinunte. **LEFT:** Madonna and Child statue in Monreale Cathedral near Palermo.

BEST BEACHES

- **San Vito Lo Capo**, near Erice, is acclaimed for its wild scenery and peacefulness. *See page 101.*
- **Mondello, Cefalù** and **Isola Bella** are over-popular but a perfect introduction to the Sicilian beach scene. *See pages 77, 89 and 234.*
- **Vendìcari**, south of Siracusa, boasts unspoilt beaches in a nature reserve, with even wilder beaches near **Capo Pàssero**. *See page 195.*
- **The islands**: lovely, diverse, often volcanic, the beaches on Ustica, the Egadi and the Aeolian Islands are in demand. *See pages 92, 111 and 251.*
- **Ragusa Province** has some of Sicily's best beaches. *See page 173.*

TOP TEMPLES

Sicily has more ancient Greek temples than Greece. The best are:

- **Agrigento**: ancient Akragas, the most hedonistic city in Greek Sicily, is the island's most celebrated ancient site. Set in the Valley of the Temples is the world's largest temple. *See pages 122–6.*
- **Segesta**: Trápani province. The majestic Doric temple stands in solemn isolation facing Monte Barbaro. *See page 102.*
- **Selinunte**: Trápani Province. A glorious setting for a ruined city founded around 650 BC but ravaged by the Carthaginians. *See page 107.*
- **Mózia**: Trápani Province. Not a temple but the site of a Carthaginian city on an island in the Stagnone lagoon. *See page 104.*

BEST STREET FOOD

- ***Sfinciuni***: slightly spicy Sicilian pizza with anchovies, oregano and breadcrumbs.
- ***Arancini***: deep-fried rice balls filled with meat or vegetables and bought from market or street stalls.
- ***Pane e panelle***: deep-fried chickpea fritters served in a warm sesame bun.
- ***Pani ca' meusa***: veal spleen sandwich, a Palermitan special for those with strong stomachs.
- **Fishy snacks**: from *calamari fritti* to seafood nibbles such as clams, oysters, sardines or even boiled octopus.

ONLY IN SICILY

- **Sicilian Baroque**. Palaces and churches created in a sumptuously theatrical style, characterised by fantasy and ornamentation. Noto might be the best-preserved Baroque town, but neighbouring Scicli, Ragusa and Módica are also superb, rebuilt after the 1693 earthquake. Catania and Acireale are also Baroque gems, as are the Serpotta oratories in Palermo.
- **Puppet theatre**. Puppet shows are a Sicilian tradition. Their stories are based on the adventures of the brave knights of Charlemagne (Carlo Magno), with the moral: the importance of honour and chivalry. The best in Palermo is Mimmo Cuticchio. *See pages 200 and 282.*
- **Classical drama**. Theatres at classical sites often return to their original function, with Greek drama

from May to July. Watch the Classics at Siracusa, Segesta, Taormina, Catania and Morgantina (www.teatriantichidisicilia.org). *See page 282.*
- **Easter festivals**. Nothing is as it seems in Sicily as the festivals are often a fusion of Christian and pagan rites, such as Prizzi's Dance of the Devils, depicting the battle between Good and Evil. *See page 138.*
- **Caltagirone pottery**. Famous for its ceramics since ancient times, Caltagirone *majolica* is unmistakable, painted in blue, green and yellow. The other two important ceramics centres on the island are Sciacca and Santa Stefano di Camastra (just outside Cefalù). *See page 201.*

Above: Caltagirone vase. **Left:** Roman mosaic – one of the Ten Maidens – in the Villa Romana del Casale. **Below:** the sun-baked mountains of Parco delle Madonie in the northwest of the island.

THE BOLDEST LANDSCAPES

- Many of the best landscapes are designated parks, such as the **Riserva dello Zingaro** *(see pages 48 and 101),* but may embrace mountains, volcanoes, coastline, "minor" islands and lagoons.
- **Mount Etna's volcanic park**: including the vast gullies of the Valley del Bove on the southeastern flank, created by the collapse of an ancient caldera. *See pages 224–5.*
- **Le Saline**: Tràpani's saltpans, with windmills and piles of "white gold". An arresting sight, best seen between May and September. *See page 104.*
- **Parco delle Madonie**: set in the sun-baked mountains south of Cefalù, with villages built on vertiginous slopes. *See page 90.*
- **Lo Stagnone**: north of Marsala, Sicily's largest lagoon is a mysterious place, home to Punic **Mózia**. *See page 104.*
- **Rock canyons**: the best are **Pantálica** *(page 197),* **Ispica** *(page 171),* **Alcántara** *(page 217)* and in the **Monti Iblei**, near Ragusa *(page 165).*

THE BEST OF PALERMO

- The **Palazzo dei Normanni** houses the Sicilian Parliament and the Royal Apartments. Don't miss the **Cappella Palatina** with Byzantine and Arab-Norman mosaics.
- **Markets**
  Great for atmosphere, and for the freshest food for picnics. **Ballarò** is the liveliest, surpassing the more established **Vuccirìa** and the **Capo** which is good for clothes.
- **Churches**
  The Norman **cathedral** containing royal tombs and a small museum.
  San Giovanni degli Eremiti. While the dreamlike La Martorana is under restoration, focus on San Giovanni, another Arab-Norman church, with a cloistered oriental garden.
  Convento dei Cappuccini. Gruesome catacombs containing 8,000 mummified Palermitans.

- **Museums and Opera**
  Museo Archeologico Regionale. This is one of the richest archaeological collections in Italy.
  Palazzo Abatellis. The 15th-century palace is home to the Galleria Regionale della Sicilia, with medieval sculptures as well as Renaissance paintings by Antonello da Messina.
  Teatro Massimo. A vast but elegant neo-classical and Art Nouveau opera house that was the setting for a compelling massacre in *The Godfather* series.
- **Gardens**
  Orto Botánico. One of Europe's leading botanical gardens, and now marking the start of a delightful seafront stroll that runs to the Foro Italico and the revamped port.
  Parco della Favorita. Lovely park laid out by the Bourbons.
  See pages 61–79.

ABOVE: Teatro Massimo, Palermo.

THE SWEETEST DESSERTS

- *Cannoli*: crunchy, rich, ricotta-filled sweet pastries studded with candied fruit and chocolate.
- *Cassata*: made from sweetened ricotta, candied fruit, almond paste and sponge cake.
- *Gelati*: Sicilians claim to having invented ice cream and make some of the best.
- *Granita*: sorbet made with fresh fruit or coffee and often served with a brioche.
- *Frutta alla Martorana*: invented by nuns, with marzipan moulded into convincing recreations of fresh fruit.

MONEY-SAVING TIPS

Lap up the culture.
Free churches. Most churches are free and superb, only hampered by restricted opening times (often closed 1–5pm). Many major sights now offer good-value **combined tickets**. These include a ticket for the temples and archaeological museum in Agrigento, and, in Palermo, a combined ticket for the Palazzo dei Normanni (Royal Palace) and another for five major churches (www.teso ridelalloggia.it, tel: 091 843 1605).

Stay in the countryside.
Economise on price, not atmosphere, by staying just outside the major centres, for instance in the olive oil-producing hills of Chiaramonte Gulfi rather than in Ragusa itself. The island's farm-stays *(agriturismi)* have improved dramatically and are generally delightful and good value. Book with specialist operators, such as Sunvil (www.sunvil. co.uk, tel. +44-020 8568 4499).
Travel by train and bus.
Although painfully slow, Sicilian trains are superb value (see www.trenitalia.

com and www.raileurope.co.uk). Several cheap but atmospheric services include the **Circumetnea** around the base of Etna (www.circumetnea.it, tel: 091 541 250) and the **Treno del Barocco**, which operates special services to the Baroque cities near Ragusa from spring to autumn (www.fsitaliane. it, tel: 0932 759634).

Buses are generally good value and more reliable than the trains. Ask at bus stations for schedules and maps to help with exploring. You'll be surprised how far you can go.

A VOLCANIC HERITAGE

Sicily's complex history has produced
an island with a unique character – proud,
introspective, enigmatic and irreverent

Sicily may be Italian, but the islanders are Latin only by adoption. They may look back at Magna Graecia or Moorish Sicily but tend to be bored by their exotic past. Mostly, they sleepwalk their way through history, as if it were a bad play in a long-forgotten language. Floating not far beneath the surface is a kaleidoscope of swirling foreignness against a backdrop of Sicilian fatalism.

This is the legacy of a land whose heyday was over 700 years ago. It is most visible in the diversity of architectural styles, brought together under one roof in a remarkable mongrel, Siracusa Cathedral.

The Greeks' lessons in democracy fell on stony ground: the Sicilians responded with a race of full-blooded tyrants. The Mafia showed equal disdain for democratic niceties: their shadowy state within a state became more effective than the pale, public model. Poor Sicilians knuckled under or emigrated, often flourishing on foreign soil. Until recently, most landed, educated Sicilians declined public office, preferring private gain to public good. As the Prince says in Lampedusa's *The Leopard*: "I cannot lift a finger in politics. It would only get bitten."

This is the deadly product served by Sicilian history. As the writer Leonardo Sciascia says: "History has been a wicked stepmother to us Sicilians." Yet it is this heritage of doom, drama and excess that draws visitors to an island marooned between Europe and Africa.

Recently, a renaissance of sorts has been under way, including a refusal to support the Mafia in many quarters. Sicily has also revamped its image, with restored historic centres, reopened museums and re-energised cities. Superb wine estates, seductive farmstays, stylish villa holidays, Sicilian cookery courses and guided nature trails are also part of the dazzling new landscape.

Goethe, too, found Sicily intoxicating, from the classical temples and Etna's eruptions to the volcanic Sicilians themselves. "To have seen Italy without seeing Sicily", he wrote, "is not to have seen Italy at all – for Sicily is the key to everything." ❏

PRECEDING PAGES: seller at the fish market in Catania; woman working at a bakery in Mazara del Vallo, Trápani. **LEFT:** wedding guest in Siracusa. **ABOVE:** painted cart in Palermo.

THE SICILIANS

Brooding, fatalistic and passionately pessimistic – or
celebratory, sensitive and overwhelmingly hospitable?
The Sicilians are a mass of apparent contradictions

Sicilians have a reputation for being brooding, suspicious and unfathomable. Closer
contact reveals stoicism, conservatism and
deep sensibility. This contradictory character
does not match the sunny Mediterranean
stereotype of *dolce far niente*, but outsiders may
nonetheless encounter overwhelming hospitality, boundless curiosity and smothering friend-
ship on the slimmest of pretexts.

In 1814 the British Governor of Sicily was
perplexed that "Sicilians expect everything to be
done for them; they have always been so accus-
tomed to obedience." His Sicilian minister argued
for absolutism: "Too much liberty is for the Sicilians what would be a pistol or stiletto in the hands
of a boy or a madman." Critics claim that Sicilians
remain sluggish citizens, subsidy junkies with little sense of self-help. Sicilians reply that power
and prestige lie elsewhere. History has taught
them to have no faith in institutions.

*Campaigning Sicilian journalist Giuseppe
Fava once said of his beloved island:
"The inability to structure society is the
Sicilian tragedy."*

The meaning of family

In the face of this, the traditional responses are
emigration, resignation, complicity or with-
drawal into a private world. Though emigration
has been the choice of millions, most Sicilians
choose to stay but avoid confrontation with
the shadow-state of patronage and the Mafia.

They prefer to live intensely, but in private. As a
result, their world is circumscribed by the family, the bedrock of island life.

Palermo is emblematic of the retreat from the
world and also of an ambivalence about class. It
goes against the grain of Sicilian sentimentality
to admit that the middle classes have fled the
historic centre in droves to settle in safe leafy
villages or in the suburbs. Optimists point to a
gradual return of the middle classes to the *centro storico*, with one square held up as a shining
example, a socially mixed island which could
be the city's salvation. But elsewhere, gentrification looks a long way off. Arab and African
immigrants occupy derelict buildings by the

port while hovels lurk in the shadow of splendid mansions. The Sicilian upper classes lead such a separate lifestyle that a social vacuum is inevitable. In rural Sicily, the divide is further consolidated by education, Mafia affiliation and isolation.

> *Appearances matter in Sicily: the word azzizzare (to beautify) comes from the Arabic; orfanità is Spanish-Palermitan dialect for looking good; spagnolismo (Hispanicism) means seeming better than you are.*

Yet within a cocoon of personal loyalty to friends and family, individuals cultivate their patch. In a traditionally oppressed culture, one's word is one's bond; lives have depended on *parole d'onore*, so promises must be kept. But in the eyes of a pessimistic or powerless individual, betrayal can happen only too easily, sparked off by a casual rebuff. Any rejection of hospitality is seen as a betrayal. As a Palermitan lawyer says: "For us, hospitality is a joy and a duty with obligations on both sides. A refusal is not just rude but fuels our *complessi di tradimento* [betrayal complex]."

Princely hospitality

The joy, of course, comes when the fortress doors are opened and through that chink appears a prince, welcoming you to a courtly scene straight out of Lampedusa's *The Leopard*, that Sicilian masterpiece of decline and fall. Sicily nurtures the seductive illusion that you are a treasured guest rather than a common tourist. But it may not be an illusion: Sicilian hospitality is legendary, as suffocatingly sweet as the local *cassata* sponge cake.

Particularly in Palermo and Ragusa, many leading families have decided to open their ancestral homes – and even their hearts – to the general public. Conte Federico, who welcomes guests to his Palermitan palace, embodies this spirit. The unaffected count, who can trace his lineage back to the great Emperor Frederick II of Sicily, enchants guests with an evening of

feasting and fantasy in princely proportions, including opera sung by his soprano wife. Before cocktails by candlelight in the Arab-Norman tower, fortunate guests can stroll through the staterooms and admire the suits of armour in the knights' hall. Dinner is based on exotic recipes dating from when Sicily was under Arab-Norman rule, and the centre of civilised Europe (*see page 268*).

Elsewhere, life has moved on, and the princess herself may be turning down your bedsheets (even princesses need to keep a roof over their heads, and count the cost of cleaning priceless chandeliers and portable altars). But the generous Sicilian spirit remains the same.

And this is true of the welcome in the simplest farmstay in the Madonie mountains. Whether a sumptuous palace with a Baroque ballroom or a boutique wine resort near Alcamo, these are genuine homes, and the pleasures are deeply domestic.

Not that hospitality is ever a simple commercial transaction in Sicily. The truest hospitality comes to foreigners whose slightest friendly gesture is rewarded with fresh pastries, a bunch of just-picked grapes, the keys to a long-closed church, or an insistence on a tour of an obscure archaeological site. Possibly all at once. It is delightful, even when the offers bear no relation to what you wanted.

LEFT: local man in Mazara del Vallo.
RIGHT: men near the fish market in Catania.

Foreign fusion

The story of private virtues and public vices is linked to Sicily's hybrid past. As the writer Gesualdo Bufalino says: "The Greeks shaped our sensitivity to light and harmony. The Muslims brought us a fragrance of oriental gardens, of legendary *Thousand and One Nights*; but they

> Sicilian proverbs reflect a dog-eat-dog society: "whoever makes himself a sheep will be eaten by a wolf" and "to the docile dog, the wolf seems ferocious."

also sowed in us a fanatical exaltation and an inclination to deceit and voluptuousness. The Spanish gave us hyperbole and haughtiness, the magnificence of words and rites, the magnanimity of our code of honour, but also a strong taste of ashes and death." Even today, the Arab west is overladen with inscrutability, Spanish manners and ceremony, while the Greek east is more democratic, with closer links to the Italian mainland. Sicily's miscegenation lives on in the language. *Cristiani* (Christians) is a generic word for people, just as *turchi* (Turks) refers to heathens.

Sicily's Baroque architecture is another hybrid – Spanish, Roman and Sicilian fusion, reflected in the islanders' Baroque temperament. As writer Stefano Malatesta says: "Everything's Baroque, excessive and eccentric: look at the lavish, multicoloured food, the decadent nobles, the elaborate courtesy, the contorted human relationships, the fine 18th-century minds, tinged by arrogance and aimlessness."

In Ragusa's Duomo, celebrity chef Ciccio Sultano concurs: "my cooking is voluptuously Baroque because I am Baroque: I never remove anything from my recipes but just pile on more."

A passion for the present

Despite their Baroque spirit and the burden of the past, Sicilians have a passion for the present. Thanks to a heightened sense of history, the islanders attach supreme importance to time. They see themselves as volatile forces of nature, as violent as Etna, but imbued with a sense of the sacred. Spirituality is expressed in spontaneous church services led by lay women. In festivals, classical polytheism merges with Christianity. But the everyday intimacy of the relationship with God implies a chatty equality and an acceptance of Him in any guise.

Lampedusa's *The Leopard* is illuminating in unravelling this state of being Sicilian: "Sicilians never wish to improve for the simple reason that they believe themselves perfect. Their vanity is stronger than their misery. Every invasion by outsiders upsets their illusion of achieved perfection, and risks disturbing their self-satisfied waiting for nothing at all."

Still, this melancholic immutability is enlivened by a zest for life best felt in Palermo's Ballarò market, the haunt of artisans and students, housewives and bootleggers. Ballarò is raucous and exotic, with spicy scents and sounds that transport you back to Moorish times. As local actress Teresa Mannino admits, "In Sicily everything screams – the people, the seagulls, even the sea itself."

But the best advice on fathoming the Sicilian maelstrom comes from fashion designer Domenico Dolce, of Dolce & Gabbana fame, who is passionate about his native land: "Don't go to Palermo with an itinerary, go with an open heart." ❑

LEFT: woman in Catania.

The New Sicily

Change is in the air and is cause for cautious celebration, from the resurgent southeast to urban regeneration and rural renewal across the island

A gainst the odds, Sicilian renewal is under way, even if it would be foolhardy to speak of a Sicilian renaissance: the island is too flawed and fatalistic for that. Still, the Sicilians have a talent for turning the painful past into something of beauty, with the *coppola storta* ("twisted cap") a testament to this talent. The cap, the traditional symbol of a lowlife *mafioso*, is now a cult design object, seen as reclaiming a "true" Sicilian identity. Similarly, land expropriated from the Mafia has been reborn as wine estates for the common good. And once feared symbols such as Palermo's palace of the Inquisition have been turned into telling museums. It's symbolic but also part of the redemption of Sicily.

Known as "an island within an island", the Val di Noto is currently the most dynamic part of Sicily. The locals attribute its unspoilt countryside, entrepreneurial spirit and escape from the tentacles of the Mafia to good fortune. When the Spanish kings ruled Sicily, the west was divided into vast estates run by absentee barons while the southeast was handed over to the local gentry who cherished their small estates. Partly as a result, in Noto, Módica, Ragusa, Scicli and Siracusa, the Unesco-listed Baroque gems in the Val di Noto, regeneration has taken root, with the cities looking increasingly splendid.

The picture is less rosy in Piazza Armerina, where the restoration of the fabulous Villa Romana is proving more challenging. Neighbouring Aidone has a fine new museum, showcasing Sicilian-Greek treasures "recuperated" from the Getty collection in Malibu. Elsewhere, the island abounds in Unesco World Heritage sites, with Palermo's Arab-Norman treasures currently awaiting listing, even if Palermo's Cappella Palatina has never looked more glittering. On the west coast, Trápani has revamped its historic centre and coastal promenade, while Mazaro del Vallo deserves praise for its Dancing Satyr Museum and vibrant Kasbah. Just along the coast is Marsala's magnificent Punic Ship Museum and Trápani's restored saltpans.

In the top resort of Taormina, both the Grand Timeo and San Domenico are standard bearers for Sicilian luxury. The moody former monastery of San Domenico has

acquired its second Michelin star, while the revamped Grand Timeo enjoys Taormina's finest views, with Mount Etna snow-capped or spouting molten lava. In Siracusa, Scicli, Ragusa and Palermo chic boutique hotels vie with palatial B&Bs.

In the countryside, a glut of gorgeous *agriturismi* (farmstays) and wine resorts now offer a lovely alternative to villa-living, especially when run by an effusive owner. For a very reasonable price, you can find a Slow Food farmstay overlooking a timeless scene of dry-stone walls and ancient olive groves. Not so much "new Sicily" as "old Sicily" reclaimed. ❑

RIGHT: moto taxi tour in Noto.

THE SHAPING OF SICILY

The island's warring tribes were subdued by the Romans, whose seven centuries of dominance were followed by a succession of foreign powers, including the Greeks, Germans, French, Spanish and Habsburgs. Although it became part of Italy in 1861, Sicily is in many ways un-Italian

Sicilian history is a cavalcade of invasion by ancient tribes. The Sicani, Siculi, and Elymni were the first. Then came the Carthaginians and Greeks, the Romans, Arabs, mercenaries and slaves, Vandals, Goths, Saracens, Normans and Spaniards. Most remained for long periods, adding rich layers to Sicily's extraordinary fusion of genes and culture.

The islanders were not great shapers of their own destiny but the powers of their subversiveness and survival were substantial. When invaded and occupied, they proved themselves to be a ball and chain around the neck of each conqueror.

The key to power

In days when the known world was limited to the lands lining the Mediterranean, the boundaries were Phoenicia (today's Lebanon) and the Straits of Gibraltar. Carthage was only 160km (100 miles) away, in Tunisia. Sicily was not only

In response to invasion, the Sicilians were sullen, slothful and uncooperative – a millstone dragging its rulers into futile conflict while leaving the Sicilians themselves free to live in their own luxurious private theatre.

in the centre, but it divided "the world" into two. Ancient superpowers could dominate one

LEFT: mosaic-adorned cloisters of Monreale Cathedral.
RIGHT: Venus Anadiomene, a Roman copy of a Greek original, held in the Museo Archeologico, Siracusa.

side or the other but in order to control both, they had to possess Sicily.

Although not a large island, Sicily was big enough for enemies like the Phoenicians and Greeks to occupy separate parts yet never quite big enough to be a power in its own right, even though Siracusa (Syracuse) was once considered the greatest city in Europe. The island was always at the mercy of larger forces swirling around its shores and dragged into almost every major Mediterranean war. However, three indigenous groups with separate cultures and languages were established: the Elymni (Elymians) in the northwest, the Sicani (Sicans) in the west and the Siculi (Sicels) in the east.

When the Phoenicians arrived, they occupied northwestern Sicily and welcomed the resident Sicani as neighbours. They fortified their settlements like Solunto and Panormus (Palermo) only when their livelihood was threatened by Greek expansion. On the island of Motya (modern Mózia), their base for attacking the Greeks, there were sensationalist aspects of their culture, such as sacred prostitution and human sacrifice. Numerous jars of charred babies imply that Motya was a grim place. The balance of power swung from Siculi to Sicani and back again. But since Sicily is named after the Siculi race, it is clear that they ultimately triumphed, in name at least.

THE NAME SICILY

The Siculi who gave their name to Sicily came from Liguria in the 13th century BC. According to Thucydides, they "defeated the Sicani in battle, drove them to the south and west of the island, and renamed it Sicily instead of Sicania." These seafarers and farmers were gradually Hellenised by Greek settlers on the east coast. However, in settlements like Siracusa, the Siculi were reduced to serfdom. They were seldom granted Greek citizenship, though a few were elevated from the status of barbarians (that is, non-Greeks), to persons qualified to marry Greeks – the ultimate accolade. Sicily abounds with Siculi settlements, with the best one at Ispica.

> *The Sicilian Greek colonies were ruled by "tyrants", a term that originally meant men who seized power instead of inheriting it – an early form of today's dictators.*

Enter the Greeks

When Sicily formed part of Magna Graecia (Greater Greece) it had a population of more than 3 million – greater than Athens and Sparta combined. The islanders spoke Greek and practised Greek art. Agriculture flourished, and the island became the granary of the Mediterranean.

But none of this was evident when the Greek migrants first arrived. Nor were they aware that there were Phoenician settlements on the western shore. The first colony on the east coast was Naxos (734 BC). Then came Zankle (Messina), Leontinoi (Lentini) and Katane (Catania). In the south, with settlers from Rhodes and Crete, were Gela, Akragas (Agrigento), Selinunte and Heraclea Minoa. Syrakusai (Siracusa), the greatest colony, was founded by Corinthian Greeks.

Sicily's first taste of the battles ahead occurred in 480 BC, when the Carthaginian commander Hamilcar invaded Sicily with 300,000 mercenaries aboard 200 galleys and 3,000 transport ships. He besieged Himera (Términi Imerese) by land and sea, prompting the tyrant Theron to appeal for help from Gelon, the tyrant of Siracusa. Gelon responded with 50,000 men and 5,000 cavalry and 150,000 Carthaginians were slain in the ensuing battle.

Athens intervenes

Sicilian cities were always ready to fight and, when Selinunte and Segesta quarrelled, Selinunte asked Siracusa for help, so Segesta approached Athens. After Segesta offered to cover the costs of military aid, Athens fell for Segesta's creditworthiness and did battle on its behalf *(see box page 26)*.

The battle for control of Siracusa's great harbour took place in 413 BC, with Greeks fighting Greeks. The Athenians were humiliated. Their generals were executed and the 7,000 captured troops were lowered 30 metres (100ft) into stone quarries, into a hell which was stifling hot by day and freezing at night. After 10 weeks, those who survived were sold as slaves.

Naturally, the Sicilian Greeks went back to fighting among themselves, thus triggering a second Carthaginian invasion. Hannibal, the eldest son of Hamilcar, had a score to settle with the city where Hamilcar died. In 409 BC he arrived with a powerful force and razed Selinunte to the ground. Then, at Himera, he sought personal vengeance with a massacre: 3,000 male survivors were taken to where Hamilcar had died, tortured and offered as sacrifices to the memory of the dead general.

A year later, Hannibal attacked Akragas. But, while digging trenches, the Carthaginians had

forging a treaty between Siracusa and Carthage. Then he changed the course of history by making an alliance with the newly expanding Mediterranean superpower: Rome.

Rome and Byzantium

In 264 BC the Punic Wars triggered momentous changes in Sicily. Sandwiched between the rival powers of Rome and Carthage, it was a battleground. Popular images of the Punic Wars are dominated by Hannibal's crossing the Apennines with elephants to attack Rome, but the first rounds were fought in Sicily, bringing the island firmly within the Roman Empire.

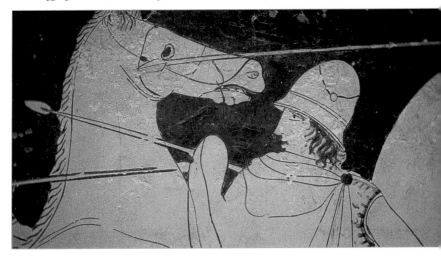

exposed corpses and a plague swept through the camp, killing Hannibal. The city eventually fell after an eight-month siege.

After blaming Siracusan generals for the defeat, in 405 BC a spirited demagogue, one Dionysius, came to power and ruled efficiently for 38 years, to be followed by Timoleon (345–336 BC), who restored a democracy of sorts. The next ruler was Agathocles (315–289 BC), who returned to the bellicose old days, seizing remaining Carthaginian land. Finally Hieron II (265–215 BC) brought a measure of stability,

Rome's takeover was methodical. First, Akragas (Agrigento) fell in 261 BC and 25,000 of its inhabitants were sold into slavery. Then Panormus (Palermo) and Selinunte and, ultimately, after a two-year siege, Siracusa. The island became Rome's first province (as opposed to being incorporated in the Republic) because it was deemed too Hellenised, too Greek in its culture. So Greek language and traditions prevailed. The next 50 years saw revolts by slaves which were brutally curbed.

In common with the rest of the Empire, the Sicilians became recognised Roman citizens in AD 212 – the island was now an extension of Italy. It acquired a reputation as a Roman

LEFT: Perseus slays Medusa, from Temple C at Selinunte.
ABOVE: detail from vase, Museo Archeologico, Gela.

resort, beloved by the likes of Caligula. A tantalising glimpse of Sicily as the playground of rich Romans can be seen in the Villa Romana at Casale *(see page 154)*.

Mosaics show a phantasmagoria of bathing, dancing, fishing, hunting, wine-pressing, music and drama – a vision of earthly paradise a wealthy, contented pagan would see while relaxing on holiday.

Vandals and Goths

Then Sicily exploded under the onslaught of the unmitigated louts of Western history – the Vandals. Having been expelled from Germany, they planned to use Sicily as a springboard back to Europe. But Sicily, like Rome and the rest of Italy, fell to yet another Germanic race, the Goths. As Italy grew too chaotic to remain the seat of the empire, the emperor decamped to Constantinople, or Byzantium, as the Eastern Empire was named. In time, his Byzantine general Belisarius was ordered to invade Sicily to reclaim Greek heritage; the Sicilians sighed with relief. But joy was premature. Emperor Constans II proceeded to seize property, tax extortionately and sell debtors into slavery. It was a slave who redressed the balance in AD 668. While Constans was being soaped in his bath, the slave picked up the soap box and brought it down on the emperor's head.

Visitors to Byzantine Sicily noted the women's love of ornament. Their jewels were a testament to the skills of Byzantine goldsmiths and a worldly counterpoint to shimmering church mosaics. Byzantine art is well served here even today, with cupolas emblazoned with austere Greek bishops and inscrutable saints. Classical naturalism ceded to Eastern stylisation and realism was replaced by decorative patterns and abstraction.

Arabs and Normans

During the Byzantine period, Sicily was the target of frequent piratical raids by Syrians, Egyptians and Moors from North Africa. As early as AD 652, Saracens from Kairouan (Tunisia) made incursions into the island. Then, in 827, came the fully fledged Arab invasion.

A fleet of 100 ships was despatched, with 10,000 troops, mainly Arabs, Berbers and Spanish Muslims. The Arabs slowly gained a foothold and, in 878, Siracusa, Sicily's first city for 1,500 years, fell. It now took second place to Palermo, as Christianity did to Islam, and Greek to Arabic. Palermo Cathedral was converted into a mosque and resounded to Muslim prayers for nearly 250 years. There was an influx of Arab settlers known as Saracens, a term that encompassed Arabs, Berbers and Spanish Moors.

As virtually an independent emirate, Sicily played a privileged role as a bridge between Africa and Europe. Trade flourished and taxation was low. The tolerant regime allowed subjects to abide by their own laws. Despite freedom of worship, Christians freely converted to Islam: there were soon hundreds of mosques in Palermo. As well as Arabs from Spain, Syria and Egypt, there were Berbers, Black Africans,

SEGESTA'S CUNNING RUSE

The Athenians were tricked into funding Segesta's war with Selinunte in 413 BC. Segesta misrepresented its wealth with a show of splendour at the temple of Aphrodite on Mount Eryx (Erice). The Athenian ambassadors enjoyed sumptuous banquets, eating off gold and silver plates. So awed were they that they had no hesitation in recommending ships be put at the disposal of Segesta. What the Athenians didn't know was that the temple treasures were fakes. The gold and silver plate was borrowed from the Siculi, as was the silver bullion. But the fraud was never exposed and the 250 ships that sailed from Piraeus with 25,000 men was the largest ever Greek armada.

Jews, Persians, Greeks, Lombards and Slavs. Western Sicily prospered.

Sicilian conservatism made for a smooth transition from Byzantine to Islamic architec-

> *The Arab domination enhanced Byzantine art and architecture. The emirs employed Byzantine craftsmen so earlier decorative patterns and stylisation suffused Islamic art. A thousand years of Greek-infused values could not be so easily erased.*

the concentration of power there. The Norman Hautevilles, Christian freebooters, needed no encouragement.

The Norman conquest

In 1068, Count Roger and his elder brother, Robert Guiscard, a fortune-hunting Norman knight, defeated the Arabs at Misilmeri, then during the siege of Palermo in 1072. Robert urged his men on to seize the city, which was "hateful to God and subject to devils".

The great Palermo mosque was quickly reconsecrated to Christ. Robert magnanimously shared the Sicilian spoils with Count Roger (also known as Conte Ruggero and King

ture. Although many churches were converted into mosques, the Arabs happily encased Byzantine art and symbolism in Islamic ornamentation. Christian and Islamic symbolism were conveniently fused.

Already a presence in Italy, the Normans were dismissed as "wolves" by the Arabs, who singled out their ferocity, barbarism and native cunning. Nonetheless, the "wolves" were invited to invade western Sicily by the emirs of Catania and Siracusa, as they were disgruntled by

Left: Roman fresco, Palermo's archaeology museum.
Above: the Saracens at the assault of Messina, from Jean Skylitzes' *Byzantine Chronicles*.

Roger I). He was an autocratic ruler, buttressed by the Byzantine concept of divine rule but, under Arab influence, was transformed from a foolhardy crusader and rough diamond into a cultured figure.

Arab influence did not wane with the Norman conquest. The Normans recognised Saracen superiority in culture and commerce, so welcomed Muslim courtiers and merchants. Most Arabs retained their castles, palaces and lands as well as their social prestige. Arab craftsmanship was prized in the conversion of mosques to cathedrals while their administrative skills, erudition and poetry were appreciated at court *(see box page 28)*.

Count Roger died in 1101, leaving Sicily governed by his widow until the coronation of his son, Roger II, in 1130. Revelling in glory, this Roger spent lavishly on palaces, mosques, gardens and education. As the richest king in Christendom, he indulged his love of Arab art and culture. He also patronised astronomers and astrologers, Koranic scholars and Sicilian poets. This charismatic king was well versed in three languages. His cosmopolitan court was home to French *jongleurs* and balladeers who followed the itinerant Norman knights.

As in Arab times, this liberalism decreed that "Latins, Greeks, Jews and Saracens be judged according to their own laws". Norman French, Greek, Arabic and Latin were all spoken. Even so, cultural and economic pressures led the Arabs gradually to retreat inland, away from the coastal cities.

> *In between empire-building, Frederick I of Sicily founded a school of Sicilian poetry, wrote a book on falconry and studied science, pondering such questions as the workings of Mount Etna and the precise location of hell.*

Only the Normans were granted fiefdoms, and the rise of the baronial class was the most dubious Norman legacy. But these rugged kings also bequeathed an efficient administration and a relatively liberal regime. In its day, this melting pot of racial talent made for Christendom's most culturally creative society.

From Bad to Good

Roger was succeeded by William I, posthumously nicknamed "the Bad" because he aroused jealousies by being "more a Mohammedan than a Christian in belief, in character and in manners". He lived like an Arab emir in a palace that contained a bodyguard of black slaves and a harem under eunuch management. His lifestyle was a matter of taste, not faith, because he had no qualms about raiding the Muslims in North Africa on behalf of the Pope.

His son, William the Good, was only 14 when crowned in 1166, and his reign was guided by Walter of the Mill, the English Archbishop of Palermo and architect of Palermo Cathedral. The English connection was strengthened when William II married Joanna, King Richard the Lionheart's sister. Richard raided Messina while on his way to the Crusades but presented Tancred, William's successor, with Excalibur, King Arthur's sword, a fitting tribute to the end of a legendary line of warrior kings.

Emperors, kings and viceroys

The death of William the Good in 1189 without an heir sent the succession reeling back to the House of Hohenstaufen (the Swabians) which produced the Prussian kings and Holy

ARAB ENLIGHTENMENT

On their arrival the Arabs instigated land reforms and encouraged the spread of smallholdings. Their reverence for water created the fountains, baths, reservoirs and storage towers still visible today, including in La Ziza in Palermo. Mining techniques were improved. Sulphur, lead, silver, antimony and alum were refined. They cultivated citrus fruits and introduced sugar cane, cotton, mulberries, palms, melons, pistachio nuts, papyrus and flax. Ice from Mount Etna was used to make sorbets and sherbets, while sea salt was dried at Trápani. They introduced coral and tuna fishing. Nor did the Islamic faith deter these sophisticated Arabs from planting *zubbibbu* grapes for wine.

Roman Emperors. Apart from a few interludes, Norman and Spanish blood would reign over Sicily until 1860.

After Roger's line petered out, Henry VI, the Holy Roman Emperor, moved in. Next was his son, Frederick I of Sicily, who was, confusingly, crowned Emperor Frederick II. Born in Palermo of a Norman mother, he never considered himself Sicilian yet was known as a "baptised Sultan", thanks to his predilection for a *seraglio* and Saracen pages. Despite the Arabian lifestyle, however, Muslims were discriminated against and rural settlements gave way to baronial estates – and complex fortifications running from Messina to Siracusa.

foreign yoke, it led to the War of the Vespers. It all began when the Easter Monday procession in Palermo was joined by French soldiers from Charles's garrison. The festive mood turned to silence as Sicilian men were searched by the French troops for concealed weapons. As the bell called the faithful to Vespers, the French captain ordered his men to search the women too. "He himself laid hands upon the fairest, and pretending to look for a knife upon her, he thrust his hand out to her bosom." She fainted in the arms of her husband, who let out the ringing cry: "*Moranu i franchiski*" (Death to the French), and the French officer was struck down dead at the feet of the woman he had insulted.

Successors such as Charles of Anjou called themselves king of Sicily, using the title as an adornment as they pursued greater ambitions abroad. Backed by the pope, Charles plundered the island and taxed so punitively that rebellion hung in the air. Charles moved his capital from Palermo to Naples.

The Easter rebellion in 1282, the most significant uprising in Sicily's history, was both a patriotic insurrection and a revolt against feudalism. But far from freeing Sicilians from a

The incident led to a riot which, with the encouragement of the local aristocracy, became an all-out revolt. The uprising spread from Palermo throughout Sicily, and in the massacre that followed no Frenchman was safe. The nobles of Palermo invited Peter II of Aragon to intervene on their behalf, and the Spaniard readily agreed, taking the title king of Sicily while promising to respect the freedom of Sicilians. Charles withdrew and French influence on the island ended.

Friction between the Spaniards in Sicily and the Normans in Naples frequently erupted into open warfare until 1372, when Naples agreed to Sicilian self-rule provided that the Sicilian ruler paid an annual tax to Naples and recognised the

LEFT: the Normans vanquishing the Saracens, sculpted on the cathedral of Mazara del Vallo. **ABOVE:** the court of Frederick II, *Stupor Mundi*.

dominance of the pope. This was submission under the guise of independence. Under the rule of a series of viceroys, the island was little more than a source of revenue for Spain, and was drained to fund the Reconquista and wars against the Turks.

A pawn in the game

After Charles II died in 1700, Sicily could do little but sit back and watch as the Wars of the Spanish Succession made Sicily little more than a bargaining chip tossed between contending European powers. The Treaty of Utrecht of 1713 awarded the island to the northern Italian House of Savoy.

THE SPANISH INQUISITION

After 1487 the Inquisition was powerful in Sicily. (Palermo boasts the newly restored Palazzo Chiaramonte, a severe palace that became the seat of the Inquisition with, carved on the prison walls, *pane, pazienza e tempo*, an appeal for bread, patience and time. Outside, heretics were burned.) The Spanish spy system used a grim police force to expel all Jews. Intellectual and cultural life suffocated. The system enforced the nobles' loyalty to the Spanish crown and supported baronial privileges. But, tied to feudalism, the peasants reverted to banditry. Now popularly perceived as honourable, brigandry was the breeding ground for the birth of the Mafia.

Victor Amadeus, Duke of Piedmont-Savoy and the new king, arrived in an English ship, Britain having decided that Sicily should be given to a weak Italian power rather than the stronger Austrian Habsburgs who still retained Naples. The Sicilian nobility hoped the new king would restore the glitter of the Spanish court and were nonplussed when he appeared in clothes made of undyed wool.

The king's survey of the economy underlined how far Sicily had degenerated. Why were there so many unemployed people in Palermo when agriculture was crying out for labour? Agriculture had dwindled so seriously that cereals had to be imported. Tax collection was put out to commercial tender, and the highest bidder unleashed a private army of thugs to recoup the cost.

In 1718 the Spanish invaded to recover their former land. The Sicilians, smarting under the Italian king's austerity measures, welcomed the 20,000 troops. Sicilian grandees brought their Spanish finery out of mothballs. The war climaxed at Francavilla, the biggest battle on Sicilian soil since Roman times. The victorious Habsburg emperor became king of Sicily.

His rule was short. Another Spanish fleet arrived in 1734 and, in a bloodless coup, took Sicily back. Sicily was yet again joined to Naples, under Charles of Bourbon, the Spanish infante. Then, when he succeeded to the Spanish throne in 1759, he handed it over to his son Ferdinand, whose reign lasted 66 years.

After Nelson's defeat of the French fleet in 1798, Ferdinand felt emboldened to attack French forces in Italy, but was forced to flee to Palermo under Nelson's protection. The king rewarded Nelson with the dukedom of Bronte, an estate near Mount Etna. Britain retained an interest in Sicily, if only to prevent Napoleon from moving in. In 1806, Ferdinand IV invited Britain to take over Sicily's defence – which made Sicily richer than it had been for centuries. British subsidies encouraged mining and reduced unemployment. While Ferdinand went on hunting trips, the real governor was William Bentinck, the British commander.

Britain could never decide what to do with Sicily. In the event, an Austrian reconquest of Naples meant that Britain withdrew and in 1816, the kingdom of the Two Sicilies was created. The kingdoms of Naples and Palermo were unified and Ferdinand became their king. Immediately he abolished the Sicilian flag and took to his court in Naples. Four years later, during the St Rosalia celebrations, Palermo rose against him, a rebellion only put down after the arrival of 10,000 Austrian troops.

Palermo again provided the flashpoint for a revolt in 1848. In the aftermath, the king offered a liberal constitution, but this was rejected in favour of an independent Sicily. The Bourbon flag was replaced by the Tricolour.

Garibaldi intervenes

That was the backdrop to another revolt in Palermo in 1860, which spurred Giuseppe the island from Bourbon rule in the name of the Piedmont House of Savoy.

Garibaldi's skill at guerrilla warfare and the growing support from the Sicilian peasantry ensured the victory over 15,000 Bourbon troops at Calatafimi. Within days, Garibaldi occupied Palermo and proclaimed himself dictator of the island, ruling on behalf of Vittorio Emanuele of Piedmont.

In a plebiscite, Sicilians voted almost unanimously for unification of Italy. This meant the end of Garibaldi's brief dictatorship and the assumption of power by Count Camillo Cavour in Turin. To many Sicilians, this fate sounded more like annexation than union.

By the end of the 19th century, emigration seemed the only escape from poverty. Many villages lost their menfolk to America, Argentina and Brazil. In a single year, Sicily lost 20 percent of its population.

Garibaldi to choose Sicily as the starting point for his unification of Italy. On 11 May he arrived at Marsala with 1,000 men to liberate

LEFT: Garibaldi's troops taking Palermo in May 1860.
ABOVE: Messina after the earthquake in 1908.

Under the Italian flag

Union with Italy under King Vittorio Emanuele II brought little but poverty, abortive uprisings and mass emigration. The new parliamentary system ushered in democracy of a sort, but as only 1 percent of the island's population was eligible to vote, few could see much improvement. Economically, the island's fortunes went from poor to poorer. There were abortive uprisings which were savagely repressed. In the last decades of the 19th century, the only escape from poverty seemed to be emigration.

The 20th century began ominously with the 1908 Messina earthquake which killed up to 84,000 people and destroyed thousands of homes. Then the conquest of Libya in 1912 was followed by World War I, taking a toll on the Sicilian economy. In 1934, swept along by Benito Mussolini's rhetoric in Rome, a plebiscite showed that only 116 Sicilians out of 4 million rejected Fascism.

Il Duce's master-plan was to industrialise the influential north and use Sicily as the provider of raw materials. He also planned to bring the Mafia to heel. Initially the Mafia were all for Mussolini; not so when he despatched Cesare Mori, an expert in uprisings, to eradicate the scourge. Various Dons were rounded up, while the carrying of firearms was forbidden. Mussolini announced that the Mafia had been elimi-

nated, the murder rate, he said, had dropped from 10 a day to only three a week. The net result was to drive the criminal families deeper underground.

Then, as the tide turned in World War II, the Allies chose Sicily as the landing stage for the war against Hitler in Europe. The coast was defenceless, air cover minimal and, even had there been good roads, most of the artillery was still horse-drawn. The US 7th Army under General Patton landed at Gela in July 1943 while British and Canadian forces tackled the east coast. The German and Italian forces scrambled across the Straits of Messina. Once more, Sicily came under foreign control.

After the war

In 1946, Italy's new government granted Sicily autonomy in areas such as agriculture, mining and industry. In elections it would be a contest between Christian Democrats on the one hand and Socialists and Communists on the other.

The balance of power lay in the hands of prominent *mafioso* Don Calógero Vizzini. For the Mafia, the issue was merely one of choosing political partners that would facilitate the allocation of building licences, import permits and state contracts. Don Vizzini made his choice: the Christian Democrats doubled their number of seats and were comfortably installed as the majority party for the next 40 years. Subsequent demands for government action against the Mafia fell on curiously deaf ears.

As for the faltering economy, Gulf Oil struck lucky near Ragusa in 1953 and later near Gela. Suddenly the island was key to Italy's oil industry and by 1966 one of several refineries was handling 8 million tons of crude a year. The petroleum industry attracted its chemical derivatives; gas was discovered, and Sicily at last commanded the power to make industrialisation practicable.

Relative prosperity started to filter through to the island, with the per capita income quadrupling compared with the 1950s. And the tourism industry ground into gear, as did the wine industry. Life had begun to get sweeter. Or possibly only bitter-sweet, which is a more Sicilian concept, born of centuries of distilled disappointment. ❑

THE MAFIA MEETS THE ALLIES

The Mafia played an unexpectedly important role in the Allied conquest of Sicily, and Vito Genovese, wanted for murder and other crimes by police in the United States, turned up as a liaison officer attached to a US army unit. Unwittingly, the Allies helped restore the Mafia's authority in Sicily and so erased Mussolini's only solid achievement: his bringing of the country's criminal families under control. In the absence of the previous Fascist administrators, the army invited a likely-looking candidate, Don Calógero Vizzini, to take on the job without looking into his background. He had been locked up by Mussolini as one of the most undesirable *mafiosi*.

LEFT: Benito Mussolini, who won Sicily to his cause.

Sicily Today

Sicilian society has been shaken out of its torpor. But it is an ambivalent awakening, reflecting Lampedusa's famous line: "Everything must change so that everything can stay the same"

Today, that oft-quoted line from Lampedusa's *The Leopard* could be paraphrased as: "Some things have changed, but some things remain the same." What hasn't changed is that Sicily seems to veer between stasis and crisis, currently concerning refugees. Even before the revolutions in North Africa, Sicily was struggling to cope with the influx of refugees, first Albanians, then Tunisians and Libyans. As the "back door to Europe", Sicily's coastline has been assailed by boatloads of Tunisians, with over 20,000 washed up on the shores of Lampedusa after Tunisia's president was overthrown in 2011.

What hasn't changed is that jobs are scarce, and looking out for oneself, and one's clan, is a matter of survival. Under-employed and undercapitalised, many people piece together a livelihood from a variety of jobs. The eternal Sicilian dilemma is whether to stay in the beloved homeland, and suffer economically, or to seek success abroad. Sicily's challenge is to convince its young that they have a future. Sadly, the *disfattista* temperament, full of destructive criticism, is brought to bear on new initiatives.

But what *has* changed is the Sicilian mindset, bringing stirrings of civic responsibility and the awakening of legions of "ordinary heroes". Sicilian heroes tend to be dead, ideally martyred like St Agata, while state-sanctioned heroes like the murdered anti-Mafia Judge Falcone are honoured too late. Any hero trying to change the system is scorned with the

ultimate insult: *"Idu nu du è"* (he's a nobody). Yet Sicily is full of unsung heroes. The grassroots association Addiopizzo fights against the payment of the *"pizzo"*, protection money widely paid to the Mafia. Founded in 2004, it burst onto the scene with the slogan, "A people who pay the *pizzo* are a people without dignity" plastered all over Palermo. Since then, over 800 businesses have signed up.

Using an Addiopizzo map, anyone can patronise shops, bars, restaurants and B&Bs that are standing up to the Mafia. There was another step forward when Confindustria, the national business associa-

tion, announced that it would expel members caught paying the *"pizzo"*. Civic-minded Sicilians also support Libera Terra shops and cooperatives, which sell pasta, oil, cheese and wine produced from confiscated Mafia lands.

These small but significant steps still mark the start of a grassroots movement in favour of civil society. But as a respected Palermo publisher said: "We Sicilians have always been subjects, never citizens. The awakening of a civic consciousness is new: give us time to learn how to become citizens." Sicily is still due its renaissance. ❑

RIGHT: father and daughter in Palermo.

DECISIVE DATES

20000–10000 BC
Old Stone Age settlers live in caves on Monte Pellegrino and the Egadi Islands.

2000–1000 BC
Bronze Age Sicilians trade with Mycenaean Greeks.

*c.***1250 BC**
The Siculi (Sicels), Sicani (Sicans) and Elymni (Elymians) settle.

*c.***860 BC**
Carthaginians (Phoenicians from North Africa) establish trading sites at Panormus (modern Palermo), Solus (Solunto) and Motya (Mózia).

*c.***734–700 BC**
Naxos, the first Greek colony in Sicily, is founded, followed by colonies at Siracusa, Megara Hyblaea, Gela, Selinus (modern Selinunte) and Akragas (Agrigento).

5th century BC
Height of Greek civilisation in Sicily. Siracusa rivals Athens in power and prestige.

480 BC
Gela, Akragas and Siracusa defeat the Carthaginians at the battle of Himera.

409–407 BC
Carthage sacks Selinus, Himera, Akragas and Gela. Plague forces Carthaginians to withdraw.

264–241 BC
First Punic War. Sicily is the battleground as Romans wage war on Carthaginians.

Rome and Byzantium
212 BC
Siracusa falls to the Romans; the island is ruled by Rome.

2nd century AD
Spread of Christianity in Sicily.

395
Sicily is part of the Western Roman Empire.

535
The Byzantines conquer Sicily, which is now under Emperor Justinian.

652
First major Arab raid on Sicily.

Arabs and Normans
831–78
Palermo falls to the Saracens (Arabs). Arabs capture Messina, Modica, Ragusa and Enna. Siracusa is taken by storm and destroyed.

965
Sicily under Arab control. Palermo second in size only to Constantinople.

1061
The Normans land in Sicily: they struggle against the Arabs.

1072
Norman Count Roger de Hauteville takes Palermo "for Christendom".

1091
Noto, the last major Muslim stronghold, falls to the all-conquering Normans.

1130
Count Roger's son, Roger II, becomes king of Sicily.

1198–1250
Emperor Frederick II rules Sicily.

1266
Charles of Anjou is crowned king of Sicily.

1282
The Sicilian Vespers. Popular Sicilian uprising against the French.

Spanish Rule

1302
The Aragonese begin 200-year domination.

1442
Alfonso V, king of Aragon, reunites Naples and Sicily and takes the title king of the Two Sicilies.

1502
The Spanish crown controls Sicily.

1513
The Spanish Inquisition arrives in Sicily.

1669
Etna erupts, destroying Catania.

1693
Massive earthquake strikes the east.

1713
Treaty of Utrecht. Victor Amadeus II of Piedmont-Savoy made king of Sicily.

1720
Austrian viceroys rule Sicily.

1734–1860
Spanish Bourbons rule Sicily through viceroys.

FAR LEFT BOTTOM: Greek ruins at Selinunte. LEFT MIDDLE: portolan chart of Sicily. ABOVE: Ferdinand I, king of the Two Sicilies, in 1816. RIGHT: Mount Etna erupting in 2002 as seen from the air.

1759
Kingdom of Naples and Sicily passes to Ferdinand IV.

1806–15
British occupation of Sicily.

1814
English-owned distilleries in Marsala begin producing a sherry-like wine.

1816
The kingdom of the Two Sicilies is created under the Bourbons.

Revolution and Unification

1848–9
Sicilian Revolution.

1860
Garibaldi forces the Bourbons off Sicily.

1861
Sicily joins kingdom of Italy.

1908
Messina destroyed by an earthquake.

1915
Italy joins the Allies in World War I.

1943
Sicily is invaded by Allies in World War II.

Modern Sicily

1951–75
One million Sicilians emigrate, especially to the US.

1968
Disastrous earthquake in the Belice Valley.

1986
The Mafia maxi-trials indict hundreds.

1992
Mafia assassinate two judges. Mount Etna erupts.

1995
Giulio Andreotti, seven times prime minister of Italy, is brought to Palermo to face charges of collaborating with the Mafia.

2002
Etna erupts. Days later, Strómboli also erupts.

2006
Mafia boss Bernardo Provenzano is caught after 43 years in hiding.

2011
Etna erupts repeatedly. Berlusconi forced out.

2012
Comiso airport opens for low-cost flights.

BUILDING FOR POSTERITY

The ancient Greeks, who held sway in Sicily, left the island with an unrivalled heritage of noble public buildings and domestic architecture

Of the three great ancient civilisations that held sway in Sicily, the Greeks left the most enduring architectural legacy. The Carthaginians' buildings and artefacts were largely destroyed by Greeks – an exception being the remains at Mózia, including fine pebble mosaics. And little remains of Roman temples and public buildings – ironically because of Rome's more sophisticated building technology.

Where the Greeks built with solid stone, the Romans used cement within brick casings and faced buildings with a veneer of high-quality stone or marble. Once this was plundered by later generations, the cement and brick soon crumbled. The most enduring Roman remains include indestructible amphitheatres built into hillsides (e.g. Siracusa) and lavish additions to Greek buildings (e.g. the theatre at Taormina).

The Greeks built most of their public buildings in the Doric style, with simple, austere lines and a perfect harmony of proportion. The earliest large-scale temple (575 BC) can be found at Siracusa. Its imposing design was reproduced, with variations, over two centuries at Himera, Segesta, Akrakas (Agrigento) and elsewhere, but most splendidly at Selinunte, where at least nine majestic temples were built in the period from 580 to 480 BC.

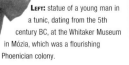

LEFT: statue of a young man in a tunic, dating from the 5th century BC, at the Whitaker Museum in Mózia, which was a flourishing Phoenician colony.

ABOVE MIDDLE: the Temple of Olympian Zeus at Agrigento once had 38 of these colossal *telamones* (giants) set on its outer wall acting as supporting columns.
ABOVE: a Doric temple, ruins of the ancient Greek city of Egesta, now known as Segesta.

ABOVE: Segesta's Greek theatre (3rd century BC). The tiers of seats face west, towards the Bay of Castellamare.

REMAINS TO BE SEEN

Sicily's archaeological museums showcase civilisations ranging from the Phoenicians to the Greeks and Romans.

Palermo's revamped Museo Archeologico contains Carthaginian and Egyptian treasures, Roman sarcophagi and sculptures, notably a huge Emperor Claudius enthroned like Zeus, as well as magnificent friezes from Selinunte *(see page 69)*.

Siracusa's museum houses a hugely diverse collection, featuring sensual statues, gruesome theatrical masks, huge burial urns and poignant sarcophagi *(see page 181)*.

Agrigento's equivalent includes intriguing Bronze Age finds, beautifully painted Attic vases, Hellenistic statuary, and Roman tombs and mosaics. The highlight is a huge *telamon* from the Temple of Zeus *(see page 124)*.

Newer museums with stunning exhibits include: Aidone ("the stolen Aphrodite"; *see page 158*); Marsala (the Punic ship; *see page 105*); and Mazara del Vallo (the *Dancing Satyr, see page 106*).

ABOVE: Greek pottery on display in Aidone's museum.

BELOW: the Temple of Concord is one of the best-preserved Greek temples anywhere. It was built around 430 BC.

ABOVE: the theatre at Taormina was built by Greeks for drama, but later enlarged by the Romans, who used it for circus games.

THE MAFIA

With its tradition of private justice and its code of
silence, the Mafia has long seemed impervious
to justice – but increasing public indignation means
that the tide may be turning

"If we can eliminate Cosa Nostra then the
country can grow: a Sicily without the Mafia
will be a Sicily that can start to develop
again," declared prosecutor Ignazio De Francisci.
Speaking after the arrest of Gaetano Riina, head
of the Corleone Mafia in 2011, the prosecutor
could allow himself a glimmer of optimism.
Gaetano had taken over from his notorious
brother, Godfather Toto Riina, who was arrested
in 1993 after 23 years on the run. Despite an
entrenched Mafia culture in Corleone, the prosecutor put his faith in the people: "It's not the
same town it was five or 10 years ago – civil
society has taken enormous steps forward."

The revulsion of Sicilians to the 1992 murders of Mafia-fighting judges Giovanni Falcone
and Paolo Borsellino has weakened the Mafia's
grip on public opinion, its greatest weapon, and
dented the age-old code of loyalty (*omertà*). A rise
in civic responsibility, tougher laws and greater

The Mafia earns over €130 billion a year –
around 10 percent of GDP – illicit income
acquired from arms-dealing, drug-trafficking,
prostitution, protection rackets and the
embezzlement of European Union funds.

police determination have driven Sicily's *mafiosi*
underground. But the cause is far from won.

Murky beginnings

The origins of what is arguably Italy's biggest
blight and its second-largest company can be
traced to medieval times and a mysterious
religious sect, the Beati Paoli, whose hooded
members lurked, armed with pikes and swords,
in underground passages beneath the streets
of Palermo. The modern Mafia took shape in
the early 19th century, in the form of brotherhoods, formed to protect Sicilians from corruption, foreign oppression and feudal malpractice.
Criminal interests quickly seeped in, and before
long the brotherhoods were feeding on the misery from which they pretended to defend their
members.

Between 1872 and World War I, poverty
forced 500,000 Sicilians to emigrate, mostly to
the Americas. There, many joined brotherhoods

based on those back home, and the foundations of Cosa Nostra were laid.

In 1925, Mussolini, appalled at the Mafia's new importance as a surrogate state, sent his prefect Cesare Mori to Sicily, and two years later victory was proclaimed for Mori's heavy-handed tactics. But Mori was also a threat to powerful agrarian *mafiosi*. Soon Sicily's landed interests struck a deal with the Fascists, and Mori left the island. In return, the agrarian *mafiosi* saw to it that Sicily's supposedly more criminal urban Mafia were almost wiped out. But the criminals won a reprieve in 1943, when they were given the job of clearing the way for the Allied invasion. Fearing that war between the US and Italy would damage their interests, Italian-American mobsters such as Lucky Luciano had struck a deal with US authorities in 1940. In return for their help, they were to be left alone. Local *mafiosi*, armed with weapons taken from captured Italian troops, were installed by the Allies as mayors of key Sicilian towns.

After the war, organised criminals began supporting Sicily's pro-separatist movement, backed by agrarian interests. Together with the authorities, the Mafia joined in the suppression of banditry, which had made inroads into its territory during the Fascist blitz.

Gangland massacres

In 1957 the American and Sicilian mafias met in Palermo's Grand Hotel et des Palmes for a summit, called to create the *Cupola* or Commission, and to establish the Sicilians' heroin franchise. The result was a criminal organisation with a clear pyramid structure.

The island's *mammasantissima* also had the satisfaction of securing the import and distribution of all heroin in the United States. It was known as the Pizza Connection since pizza parlours were a cover for money-laundering. Sicily emerged as a strategic centre for drugs, arms and international crime, confirming the shift of the Mafia's economic centre of gravity from the country to the city.

In the early 1980s a Mafia war left Palermo's streets strewn with blood and the Corleone-based clan undisputed victors. In response to charges of government complicity, a crackdown

on the Mafia was launched. Thousands of suspects were rounded up and an anti-Mafia pool of magistrates, which included Giovanni Falcone and Paolo Borsellino, was assembled. One "maxi-trial" resulted in 18 life sentences.

> *It is unrealistic for the state to eradicate the Mafia without tackling the social conditions that fuel it, ranging from poverty to high youth unemployment and stagnant economic growth.*

Murdering the magistrates

In spite of their success, the anti-Mafia pool of magistrates was mysteriously disbanded in 1988. Falcone moved to Rome as Director of Penal Affairs and lobbied for a force with powers similar to the American FBI. In May 1992, he was on the point of being nominated *super-procuratore*, its head, when the Mafia took their revenge. As he drove with his wife, Judge Francesca Morvillo, along the *autostrada* from the airport to Palermo, their car passed over a remote-controlled mine. The two judges and their three-man escort were killed instantly, their cars reduced to twisted burning metal, and a huge crater blown in the motorway. Today, the Falcone memorial is one

LEFT: Lucky Luciano, who forged links between the Sicilian and American mafias. RIGHT: off to court in one of the 1980s maxi-trials.

of the first sights to greet visitors driving from Palermo airport, itself renamed in honour of the heroic magistrates.

Two months later, fellow-magistrate Paolo Borsellino, Falcone's boyhood friend and obvious successor, became another "illustrious corpse". He had just arrived at his mother's home when an 80kg (175lb) bomb in his car was detonated, also killing his five bodyguards.

The terror continued in 1993 with bombs in Milan and Rome that killed bystanders and devastated churches; an explosion at Florence's Uffizi gallery destroyed minor masterpieces. But the Mafia had miscalculated. The assassinations of the two Palermo judges and the attempt to destroy the nation's cultural treasures only served to tighten the resolve of the Italians and their government against the Mafia.

End of the untouchables

In 1995 Giulio Andreotti, seven times prime minister and one of Italy's most respected elder statesmen, was accused of being a protector and friend of the Mafia in return for votes. Although he was acquitted, the message was clear to *mafiosi* and politicans alike: henceforth no one could be considered "untouchable". Even media tycoon Silvio Berlusconi, until recently the Italian prime minister, faces persistent charges of Mafia collusion, which he stoutly denies.

In response to changing circumstances, the Mafia has gone to ground, not murdering but money-laundering, or focusing on arms-dealing, extortion and property speculation. As the old Mafia guard languishes in jail, a more sophisticated organisation, based on "old Mafia values", has filled the power vacuum. The new-generation gangster is likely to be as ruthless on the stock exchange floor as on the streets of Palermo. No one could pretend that Cosa Nostra has disappeared. It is simply mutating, a Sicilian leopard – only with slightly less distinctive spots.

Public revulsion

But in society, there has been a shift in public attitudes towards silent acquiescence. Ever the cynic, Falcone called himself "simply a servant of the state *in terra infidelium*" (the land of disbelievers). But finally the believers are in the majority. Where once *mafioso* activity was seen as revolt against the state, justified by centuries of foreign oppression, today the population is less tolerant, particularly the young. The confiscation of Mafia property continues apace, and there is a genuine grassroots movement calling for change (*see page 33*). The revelations of political complicity at the highest level have destroyed any fanciful notion that the Mafia somehow represented the private citizen against the forces of authority.

While there is no doubt that Sicily still harbours some dangerous criminals, they can no longer rely on support, or even consent, from most Sicilians. The *mafiosi* haven't gone away, but they are no longer untouchable. ❑

THE BEDSHEET PROTEST

In Sicily the murder of the magistrates in 1992 sparked a popular backlash against the Mafia's excesses. On the evening of Falcone's assassination, three Palermo sisters and their daughters hung bedsheets with anti-Mafia slogans from the balconies of their neighbouring apartments. Soon other Palermitans joined in. The bedsheet protest caught on until it seemed that most of Palermo was making a personal stand against the Mafia. As anti-Mafia mayor Leoluca Orlando said later, "On certain days, you could look up at an apartment building and see where the Mafia Don lived – it was the apartment without a sheet hanging from the window."

LEFT: children take part in an anti-Mafia demonstration.

Sicily in the Movies

Sicily is a gift to film directors –
both intensely visual and an
island of extremes, it is a place
of passion, where life and death
embrace

Hollywood's infatuation with the glamour of gangsterland is legendary, especially in the assured hands of Francis Ford Coppola. In movies, the Mafia capital, Corleone, lends its jagged rocks and sullen populace to *The Godfather* trilogy, while the mountains around Montelepre, once the home of Salvatore Giuliano, Sicily's Robin Hood, echo to the sound of banditry.

The island's first international success was Visconti's *La Terra Trema* (*The Earth Shook*, 1947) based on Giovanni Verga's *I Malavoglia*, a tale of poverty and destiny in a fishing community. Naturally, the cast were real fishermen with impenetrable Sicilian accents. Then came *Stromboli: Terra di Dio* (1950), a chronicle of torrid passion between a Lithuanian refugee and a fisherman, an affair as doomed as the brooding melodrama of the movie.

Later, while Francesco Rosi's *Salvatore Giuliano* (1961) told the tragic tale of Sicily's greatest folk hero with the grandeur of a Greek myth, Visconti's glorious 1963 epic, *The Leopard*, exuded impeccable lushness, faded grandeur and decadence.

By 1984 the Italian mood was changing. Set in rural Sicily, the Taviani brothers' *Kaos* was a chaotic universe of legends and lost loves, of mother love and ties with the land. Then *Cinema Paradiso* (1988) brought a nostalgic slice of history following the arrival of the Talkies in small-town Sicily seen through the eyes of a young projectionist, and six years later, *Il Postino* (*The Postman*), shot on the island of Salina, told a 1950s tale of a fisherman's son who delivers mail to exiled Chilean poet Pablo Neruda. Over time, he develops an appreciation

of poetry (which helps him win the heart of the local beauty) and of Communism (which finally gets him killed).

But the most recurring popular theme in the Sicilian film canon is the Mafia. Leonardo Sciascia's anti-Mafia fiction inspired many Italian directors with strong plots and moral dilemmas, starting in 1968 with *Il Giorno della Civeta* (Day of the Owl). But true commercial successes, heretically, were American: Coppola's *The Godfather* trilogy, inspired by Mario Puzo's novel concerning Mafia wars in the 1950s, allowed Marlon Brando to play the Godfather with relish. The three movies' atmos-

phere made for operatic intensity; indeed *Part III* (1990) climaxed at Palermo's Teatro Massimo during Mascagni's foreboding opera, *Cavalleria Rusticana*.

More recently, German director Margarethe von Trotta's *Il Lungo Silenzio (The Long Silence)* dealt with anti-Mafia magistrates and won applause from Mafia widows, while *Nuovomondo (New World)* by Emanuele Crialese (2006) focused on the eternal Sicilian dilemma: whether to stay or leave. His latest, *Terranuovo* (2011), portrays Sicily as the "Promised Land" for desperate North African immigrants washed up on Linosa.   ❑

RIGHT: the lavish ballroom scene in *The Leopard*.

FOOD AND WINE

Sicily's exotic past, volcanic soil and teeming seas
combine to produce a powerful, opulent cuisine,
now matched by increasingly impressive wines

One of Sicily's best-kept secrets is its cuisine. Only a few Sicilian dishes, like the sweet-and-sour aubergine side dish known as *caponata* or the ricotta-filled *cannoli*, have crossed the Straits of Messina to find fame and fortune abroad.

The Greek colonists who arrived in the 8th century BC were astonished at the fertility of Sicily's volcanic soil, and Siracusa soon became the gastronomic capital of the classical world. By the 5th century BC the city had produced the first cookbook written in the West, Mithaecus' *Lost Art of Cooking*, and the first school for chefs.

The Arab legacy

The Arabs brought innovative agricultural and culinary techniques and introduced crops that enriched Sicilian cooking; citrus, rice and aubergines became staples. They also made Sicilian

On the coast, the sea sets the agenda – it may be a classic insalata di mare (seafood with oil, lemon and herbs), pesce spada affumicato (smoked swordfish) or a dish of thumbnail-sized fried cuttlefish.

cuisine sweet and spicy. Cane sugar was introduced, as was the Middle Eastern taste for sumptuous sweets – still a classic Sicilian trademark.

By the end of the Saracen occupation, the mould of Sicilian cooking had been set. The Normans employed Arab chefs and, until the Renaissance, Sicily exported pasta, sugar,

confectionery and citrus to northern Italy. But while the Spanish brought chocolate and tomatoes from the New World and French chefs were fashionable in the 19th century, Sicilian cuisine reflected class lines.

The poor survived on bread and wild greens; the aristocracy lived on lavish "baronial cuisine". It was left to the emerging *borghesia* to create contemporary Sicilian cooking: extravagant festive dishes, and simpler daily fare, always dedicated to exalting the extraordinary flavours of the produce.

ABOVE: fresh fish. **RIGHT:** seafood couscous.
FAR RIGHT: market produce.

The Sicilian menu

Restaurant starters: As *antipasti*, the classic dishes are *sarde a beccafico*, sardines rolled in breadcrumbs, with a pine-nut and currant filling, baked with bay leaves, or *involtini di melanzane*, stuffed aubergines in tomato sauce. In the mountain towns of the Madonie and Nebrodi, rustic *antipasti* include salami, cow's-milk cheeses (*caciotta* and *caciocavallo*), sheep's-milk cheeses (such as *tuma*) and wild mushrooms *sott'olio*. Sicily's finest cheese is arguably a mature Ragusano DOP, from the Monti Iblei hills near Ragusa.

Pasta: Most Sicilians feel pasta to be the proper first course. Under Arab rule, Sicily was the first place to produce dried pasta on a commercial

lamb and pork. Beef is best stuffed and braised in tomato sauce or skewered and grilled (*involtini alla siciliana*). But fish and seafood predominate in Sicily, whether as a main course (*pesce spada alla griglia*, grilled swordfish, or *tonno alla marinara*, tuna with olives, capers and tomatoes) or as a starter. Western Sicily's exotic *pasta con sarde* was invented in the 9th century by Arab army cooks who used whatever was at hand: sardines, saffron, pine nuts, dried currants and sprigs of wild fennel. In the east, a potent sauce of anchovies and breadcrumbs is still popular (*anclova e muddica*). In another dish, grated smoked tuna roe mixed with olive oil and parsley is poured over spaghetti.

scale. Today's best-loved dish is *pasta con le melanzane*, known in eastern Sicily as *pasta alla Norma* (after Bellini's operatic heroine). Here, tomatoes, basil, fried aubergines and a sprinkling of salted ricotta melt into a magical blend. Pasta can also be paired with *fritella*, a spring sauté of new peas, fava beans and tiny artichokes, or simpler combinations garnished with sautéed courgettes.

Couscous: In the Trápani area, where the Arab influence is strongest, a local version of couscous, steamed in a fish broth, supplants pasta. This is best tasted during the vibrant September Couscous Festival at San Vito lo Capo.

Fish and meat: The mountain pastures of the Madonie and Nebrodi produce exceptional

STREET FOOD AND MARKETS

Sicily has a long tradition of delicious snacks, especially in Palermo and Catania: chickpea fritters (*panelle*), potato croquettes (*crocche di patate*) and fried rice balls filled with meat and peas (*arancini*) provide a movable feast. In the same cities, the food markets serve up gastro-porn at its most deadly: writhing octopus, slithery eels and swordfish glisten on ice blocks; beyond are barrels of olives and lemons, bunches of basil and mint, sacks of oriental spices and trays of almond-encrusted pastries. In Palermo, Antica Focacceria (*see page 73*) provides a taster of street food, as do stalls in Ballarò market and Franco u Vastiddaru (corner of Piazza Marina and Via Emanuele).

Vegetables: *Melanzane alla parmigiana* (aubergine baked with parmesan), a Sicilian invention, reigns supreme. Equally fine is *peperonata* (sweet roasted peppers), or orange and fennel salad, a legacy of the Arabs, or artichokes fried, stuffed, roasted on coals, or braised with oil, parsley and garlic. Or bright-green cauliflower cooked with anchovies, cheese, olives and red wine. The interior boasts a survivor from classical times: *maccu*, a purée made from dried fava or broad beans flavoured with oil and wild fennel seeds.

Sweets: Choice becomes hardest towards the end of a meal. Sicilians have had a passion for sweet pastries since Arab times, and for ice cream since the 18th century *(see box below)*.

Surprising wines

"Sicilian wines encompass the spirit of 20 civilisations" claims wine buff Bruno Pastera. Certainly, Sicilian wines have a great pedigree, dating back to Phoenician and Greek times, but traditionally underperformed. With their prodigious amounts of sugar, they were despatched north for blending, to bump up the strength of better-known wines. More recently, there has been a full-scale return to producing serious drinking wines using native grape varieties.

Best known is Marsala, in the west of Sicily, still mistakenly synonymous with sickly-sweet liqueurs, but the best (known as *Vergine* or *Riserva*) are excellent, dry, smooth sherry-like wines.

SWEET DREAMS ARE MADE OF THIS

The most famous dish of Arab descent is *cassata siciliana*, the spectacular, exceedingly sweet gateau filled with ricotta cream and decorated with almond paste and candied fruit. "As beautiful as *cassata*" is high praise in Palermo. Instead, Sicilian artisanal ice cream comes in a bewildering array of flavours, from pistachio to pine nut, marzipan to ricotta.

Then there are Sicilan pastries. From the chewy *mustazzoli* biscuits or the nut-and-fig-flavoured *buccellato* to the opulent Arab tradition of *cannoli*. For centuries, the chief pastry cooks were nuns: Palermo alone had more than a score of convents, each famous for a particular sweet. A few convents still sell their pastries, including an atmospheric

one in Mazara. Instead, in Erice, the tradition is carried on by women who learned their trade in convent orphanages.

On All Souls' Day, Sicilian children traditionally awake to find sugar dolls and baskets of fruit at the foot of their beds, left there by "the souls of their forefathers". The fruit is made of marzipan, known as *pasta reale* or *martorana*, one of Sicily's most delightful culinary traditions. Nowadays, *martorana* is readily available all year round, and designed to resemble fruit, though visitors with more salacious tastes may be transported by other versions, the nuns' sweet triumphs: virgins' breasts *(minni di vergini)* or chancellors' buttocks *(fedde del cancelliere)*.

Marsala might be Sicily's most famous wine but the island abounds in award-winning wines. Veronica Bonelli, sommelier at Sicily's finest hotel, the Grand Timeo in Taormina, sums up

From Marsala and Malvasia dessert wines to Bordeaux-style Mount Etna wines, from floral white to full-bodied red Nero d'Avola and cherry-coloured Cerasuolo di Vittoria – reputable estates include Gulfi, Hauner, Marchesi di Gregorio, Passopisciaro, Planeta, Regaleali and Tenuta di Donnafugata.

the wine scene: "The west is better known, especially Nero d'Avola near Ragusa, and important wine-growing areas around Alcamo and Menfi, but there are also exciting wines coming from Mount Etna and the volcanic islands, such as the powerful but balanced wines made by the Hauner estate on Vulcano and Salina."

Even if modern Sicilian winemaking depends on merit alone, some of the best original estates were founded by the local nobility. The emblematic Regaleali estate, south of Palermo, is owned by the Conte Tasca d'Almerita, but has expanded to include estates on Mount Etna, as well as on the island of Mózia, near Marsala, and on the island of Salina. Given this range, the estate produces Rosso del Conte, a structured Nero d'Avola; Nozze d'Oro, a blend of native Inzolia and Sauvignon; dessert wines on Salina; and Etna wines based on the indigenous Nerello Mascalese varietal.

New-wave Etna wine-growers, such as the Passopisciaro estate in scenic Castiglione della Sicilia, use Nerello Mascalese to make award-winning Bordeaux-style reds. Instead, Catarratto and Inzolia are two native grape varieties that make superior whites, including dry, delicately floral wines around Alcamo. As for dessert wines, on the island of Pantelleria they favour Moscato, called Zibibbo, trained as low bushes against the incessant winds. The island of Salina has a similar tradition but with Malvasia rather than Moscato vines; the Carlo Hauner estate is recommended.

LEFT: family in front of a display of *martorana*, fruit-shaped marzipan sweets . **RIGHT:** at the bar.

Wine resorts

These are wine estates where you can usually stay, dine, or do a cookery or wine-tasting course. Just outside Alcamo, the Sirignano Wine Resort is a delightful organic estate run by the Marchese de Gregori. Guests stay in converted farm workers' cottages on the estate, and sample the marquess's superb wines over meals cooked by an outstanding chef.

Other fine wine resorts include La Foresteria dell'Azienda Planeta, near Menfi, and Capofaro Malvasia on Salina, owned by the aristocratic Tasca d'Almerita family, who were one of the first to offer wine and cookery courses on their estates (*see page 286*). ❏

THE MARSALA MERCHANTS

Marsala, produced around the town for which it is named, was created by 18th-century English merchants as an alternative to port. By 1773, John Woodhouse, originally a soap merchant, had found a way of both improving the taste of the wine and making it last longer. The fortified wine soon found favour with Nelson's fleet, with sailors at sea rewarded with a glass at sunset. Merchant Benjamin Ingham opened a rival winery in 1806, followed by Vincenzo Florio in 1833. Marsala, made by strengthening a base wine with grape brandy and ageing the result, rivals top sherries, Madeiras and ports. Marsala's seafront warehouses make good stops for wine-tasting (*see page 106*).

WILD PLACES

From mountains to volcanoes, nature reserves to marine parks, specks of islands to slithers of beaches, Sicily's wild places are slowly winning over adventurous travellers

"**A**t Francavilla, we hike up the hill to the ruined Norman castle, from where there is a fabulous view across the Arab citrus orchards and the Greek citadel of Castiglione to the stately, smoking, snow-capped bulk of Mount Etna." Nigel, a guide with Ramblers Worldwide, enthuses over how a simple hike in Sicily embraces several civilisations and scenery that stays with you for ever.

Sicily has increasing appeal for active visitors, whether you're looking for a speedy helicopter ride over Mount Etna or a Slow Travel walking holiday in the Madonie mountains. From salt-pans to steaming fumaroles, the island offers bewildering choice. The diversity of landscape is unmatched by other Mediterranean islands and, what's more, you can combine several experiences on the same day. At a stretch you could even ski Etna in the morning and sun yourself on the beach in the afternoon. More typically, you

THE WILD AND WINDY AEOLIANS

The Aeolian Islands form a dazzling archipelago of seven volcanic islands, and represent one of Sicily's most compelling wild attractions. Named after Aeolus, the god of the winds, these elemental islands still exude an otherworldly air. The mustard-tinted radioactive waters and shores are buffeted by the choppiest seas in the Tyrrhenian. The senses are bombarded by a kaleidoscope of colours, from black swirling sand dunes to the rusty red seams of iron and aluminium sulphates. Elsewhere, the sprinklings of white pumice stone contrast with glittering black volcanic rock, while deep-green capers throw bronze-coloured beaches into relief.

For drama, it is difficult to compete with the volcanic activity on Strómboli's seething crater. Other natural wonders include hot springs on Lípari and Panarea, with fumeroles, holes emitting volcanic gases, bubbling underwater on Vulcano and Strómboli. Apart from pyrotechnics, the archipelago also promises sapphire-coloured seas and a dramatic coastline.

On Vulcano, the Gran Cratere marks the start of a fairly arduous ascent of the eerie main crater. An hour's walk across black sands leads to the moonscape of the volcanic crust and a startling sense of the acrid vaporous emissions. Climbing up the crater is a rite of passage for many visitors.

may be wading through a volcanic river gorge in the morning and wading through Greek mythology in the afternoon, enthralled by the wild setting of Selinunte. What also sets Sicily apart is that a "nature trip" is often a voyage back into Sicilian history as well as geography.

Dipping into lagoons, islands and marine reserves

South of Trápani. the moody **Stagnone lagoon** embraces the Phoenician island of Mózia, stretching to the ancient salt marshes of the **Saline di Trápani**. These mysterious shallow lagoons are now protected so the tradition of salt extraction will survive, along with the solitary windmills.

you can also explore the underwater sea world of sponges, corals and fish, or follow a sub-aqua archaeological trail in search of Roman wrecks or amphorae. Sub-aqua and marine biology courses are on the rise, helped by the accessibility of Ustica via hydrofoil and ferry services from Palermo (*see page 263*).

For adventure-lovers, the **Aeolian Islands** are the most dramatic in Sicily, shaped by volcanic eruption and wind erosion. Strómboli, in particular, is a byword for pyrotechnics. The Aeolians also represent a paradise for ecologists, with geophysicists intrigued by seismic phenomena and molten lava brews. Nor can visitors fail to be impressed by the pervasive

The three **Egadi Islands**, only 30 minutes by hydrofoil from Trápani, are ringed by caves, creeks and miniature beaches. The clarity of the water and variety of marine life make swimming, sailing and diving a joy. Footpaths lead to secluded areas, but be prepared for rocky scrambles.

Closer to Palermo, **Ustica** is a well-established reserve and centre for marine studies. The rugged coastline is riddled with caverns and coves, partly accessible along coastal paths. On Ustica

LEFT: Sicilian wall lizard *(Podarcis waglerianus)* on the Aeolian island of Panarea. **ABOVE:** people walking on the rim of Vulcano's crater.

ANIMALS OF THE ISLAND

Though some creatures such as the wolf have vanished, the crested porcupine is still resident, as are the red fox, hare, wild cat, pine marten, weasel and edible dormouse. Among the island's eight species of bat are the mouse-eared bat and the rare Kuhl's pipistrelle and Savi's pipistrelle. Reptiles include the common green lizard, black snake, dark green snake, grass snake and viper, and nocturnal geckos attracted by any outside light. The shy land tortoise is around, but hard to spot with its excellent camouflage. In fresh water you may see the European pond turtle. Amphibians include the common toad, edible frog, tree frog and painted frog.

sulphurous smells and subaqueous burblings, phenomena matched by weirdly lovely lavic rock formations.

Exploring parks and nature reserves

Sicily is also blessed with an array of protected places that attract both serious hikers and Sunday cyclists. The **Parco dello Zíngaro** is the showcase Sicilian nature reserve *(see box)*.

East of Palermo, the **Parco delle Madonie** flaunt the most beguiling peaks, often dubbed "the Sicilian Alps." Wooded, mountainous slopes are topped by medieval hamlets and, in winter, the odd ski resort. **Parco dei Nebrodi**, east of the Madonie, is Sicily's largest designated park, covering the mountainous region from Santo Stefano di Camastra to the foot of Etna. Swathed in ancient beech and oak forests, the Nebrodi are a popular place for horse-riding.

The **Vendicari** salt marshes south of Siracusa appeal to both beach-lovers and birdwatchers. Autumn or winter sees waders and ducks sharing the sheltered waters with flamingos, storks and egrets. Full immersion in nature often means full immersion in ancient history.

West of Siracusa lie protected gorges lined with prehistoric necropolis. The **Necropoli di Pantálica** and Valle dell'Anapo accommodate extraordinary Bronze Age cave dwellings and

RISERVA DELLO ZÍNGARO – SICILY'S MODEL NATURE RESERVE

The Riserva dello Zíngaro (tel: 0924 35108, www.riservaz ingaro.it) is a Sicilian success story. Commonly known as Lo Zíngaro, it is both a glorious nature reserve sloping down to the sea and an emblem of Sicilian pride. In 1980, in response to plans to carve a main road through this pristine coast, a massive outcry from environmentalists mobilised public opinion and legislation was swiftly passed, securing the future of parks and reserves in Sicily.

Sandwiched between the mountains and the sea, the reserve boasts a Caribbean-style beach, secret coves and rocky headlands – complemented by artfully distressed stone cottages and ancient tuna fisheries. The Tonnara di Scopello, where tuna was processed until 1984, is one of the most evocative sights in Sicily. The fishery and bay are framed by majestic stack rocks and a medieval watchtower. Well-marked walking trails include one running from the scenic fishing hamlet of Scopello to Tonarella, an easy 6km (4-mile) hike. En route, walkers are torn between the drama of the promontory plunging into the sea and the scent of wild fennel, which often finds its way into *pasta con le sarde*, pasta with sardines. With a cosy atmosphere and an array of rustic apartments, Scopello and San Vito lo Capo make homely bases. Raptors love it here too: the reserve is home to peregrine falcons, golden eagles, kites and Bonelli's eagles.

walks along the Anapo River Valley, alongside dramatic gorges and canyons.

The **Parco dell'Etna**, enveloping Etna's dramatic mountain and crater, can be explored on an afternoon jaunt or on organised treks, including the five-day Grande Traversata Etnea. On the

Follow your guide's advice in choosing the right Etna trail as, depending on volcanic activity, Etna can be a damp squib smelling of rotten eggs or prove the most dramatic memory of your stay.

lower slopes, lush citrus groves and bananas give way to pine groves and, finally, to volcanic terrain where only hardy flowers like the Etna violet can survive the extremes of temperature.

Wild family fun

When temples pall and tempers fray, nothing beats a trip up **Mount Etna** to astound fractious children. Although Sicily does have theme parks, such as **Etnaland**, nothing compares with the real thing. Etnaland, with its suspended cableway and water park, delivers only a token nod to the elemental surroundings. Instead, **Etnavventura**, set on the southern flanks of Mount Etna, offers more contact with nature. Best of all, it's an adventure park conveniently close to the cable car at Rifugio Sapienza, so can be seamlessly combined with an educational (ssh) ascent of Etna *(see page 215)*.

Leave the car at **Rifugio Sapienza** and then chug up the cable car, some 2,500 metres (8,200ft) above sea level, marvelling at the mounds of lava. A jeep transfer then winds its way to the summit, crunching through a barren lunar landscape. If the crunch of clinker is too tame for teenagers, then opt for a guided Etna hike or helicopter tour *(see page 222)*.

Also in eastern Sicily, close to Etna, is the **Golea dell'Alcántara**, another unmissable experience for youngsters at ease with rushing water. Carved into rock-hard basalt, this 20-metre (66ft) -deep lava-stone gorge is the creation of one of Mount Etna's ancient eruptions. Teenag-

ers will enjoy wading in the freezing waters, but the tougher canyoning experience (in a hired wetsuit) is only suitable for those over 16.

On the Palermo side of Sicily, in the Madonie mountains, the **Parco Avventura Madonie** is the island's best adventure playground. On offer are rope-ladder-walking, tree-climbing, cable slides, mountain-biking, hiking and horse-riding through the woods *(see page 92)*. The park provides a similar experience to Etnavventura, plus you can pre-book a picnic lunch.

Nor do the archaeological sites need to be a challenge if approached in the right way. **Selinunte** is probably the most child-friendly classical site *(see page 107)*. ❑

Left: beach in the Riserva dello Zíngaro.
Right: flamingos on the saltpans at Nubia.

BIRDS WORTH SPOTTING

More than 150 species of birds, both migratory and nesting, have been logged on the island. The notable predators include the golden eagle and the peregrine falcon, but they are not the only birds of prey sustained by the island's numerous small mammals and lizards: you may see Bonelli's eagles, red kites, marsh harriers, European sparrowhawks and a variety of owls. Besides the familiar blackbirds, crows, robins, skylarks and thrushes, you may spot the hoopoe, red-billed chough, nuthatch, coal tit, Sicilian long-tailed tit, redstart, blackcap, greenfinch, quail and cirl bunting. On summer evenings swifts, swallows and martins join the bats swooping round the terraces.

PLACES

A detailed guide to Sicily and its islands,
with principal sites clearly cross-referenced
by number to the maps

Sicilian scenery is dramatic, sometimes harsh but seldom graceless. Today this granary of ancient Rome contains citrus groves, pastureland and vineyards as well as endless vistas of wheatfields. Away from the coast, an intriguing volcanic hinterland unfolds with wild mountains, gorges and sweeps of rich ochre-coloured earth.

Between Catania and Messina, Mount Etna's smoking plumes hover above the ski slopes, citrus farms, vineyards and nonchalant villages that climb the volcano's skirts.

To most visitors, sophisticated yet elemental Taormina is the acceptable face of Sicily, a place of undiluted pleasure where culture shock is absent. On the northern coast is Cefalù, Taormina's rival resort, and a cocooning retreat after the intense capital, Palermo. Outside these cosmopolitan pockets, the adventure begins. The souks and inlaid street patterns of Mazara del Vallo would not be out of place in Morocco. The perfect medieval town of Erice is a shrine to pagan goddesses. The island of Mózia reveals its Phoenician port and sacrificial burial grounds. Built to intimidate the gods, the Greek temples of Agrigento, Segesta and Selinunte are a divine reflection of Magna Graecia. The Romans responded to the Greeks with the vivid mosaics of Piazza Armerina as an imprint of a sophisticated culture.

Then, in Palermo, Cefalù and Monreale are cathedrals and churches that testify to Byzantine craftsmanship, Arab imagery and Norman scale. Elsewhere, Moorish palaces, Swabian castles and domed churches offer reinterpretations of this inspired Sicilian hybrid. To top it all, Baroque explodes in the architectural fireworks of Noto, Siracusa, Scicli and Ragusa, seductive cities in the newly revitalised southeast.

Sicily is to be explored and, while the island's rich architectural heritage beckons, the beaches, volcanic islands, wine routes and wild places are equally compelling. But the sun-baked island would be diminished without Sicilian hospitality, whether in a simple farmstay or in a family-owned palazzo run by princely hosts. The welcome can be as sweetly enveloping as *cassata*, the island's legendary dessert.   ❏

PRECEDING PAGES: view of the Aeolian Islands from Vulcano; Teatro Massimo, Palermo.
LEFT: driving through Ragusa Ibla. **ABOVE RIGHT:** mosaic in Monreale Cathedral.

Sicily

0 — 20 km
0 — 20 miles

N

Genova, Livorno
Napoli

Cagliari, Tunis
Cagliari, Livorno
Tunis

Ísola di Ustica · Ustica

T Y R R H E

Capo Gallo
Ísola delle Fémmine
Partanna-Mondello
Golfo di Palermo
Punta Ráisi
Terrasini
Cinisi
Carini
Palermo
Capo Zafferano
Bagheria
Golfo
Términi I.
Tér
Ime

Capo San Vito
San Vito lo Capo
Mácari
Punta del Saraceno
Custonaci
Castelluzzo
Castellammare
Balestrate
Golfo di Terrasini
Monreale
Villagrázia
Piana degli Albanesi
A 19
E 90

Ísole Égadi
Ísola di Lévanzo
Trápani
Érice
Castellammare
A 29
E 90
113
Álcamo
Segesta
San Giuseppe Jato
Partinico
Bolognetta
Baucina
Cefalà Diana
Cáccа
Ísola Maréttimo
Maréttimo
Lévanzo
Favignana
Ísola Favignana
Marausa
Ísole dello Stagnone
Granatello
Trápani
Vita
Calatafimi
Campóreale
San Cipirello
Palermo
121
Montemaggiore
Belsit
Mezzojuso
Vicari

Tunis

Salemi
Ciávolo
Aquila
Gilbellina Nuova
Poggióreale
Roccamena
Corleone
Lercara Fríddi
Valle
A
Marsala
Petrosino
Castelvetrano
Partanna
Santa Margherita di Bélice
Contessa Entellina
Prizzi
Castronuovo di Sicília
Val
Prat

Capo Feto
Mazara del Vallo
Campobello di Mázara
Selinunte
Porto Palo
Menfi
Sambuca di Sicília
Chiusa Scláfani
Palazzo Adriano
Bivona
Búrgio
San Giovanni Gémini
Muss
Casteltérmini
189
Capo Granitola
Calamónaci
Sciacca
Caltabellotta
Cianciana
San Biagio Plátani
Raca

Capo San Marco
115
Ribera
Cáttolica Eraclea
Raffadali
Aragona
Fav
Bonsignore
Montallegro
Capo Bianco
Agrigento

Siculiana
Punta Grande
Porto Empédocle
Agrigento
Valle dei
Cannatello
Punta Blanca
Pa
Monte

M E D I T E R R A N E A N   S E A

Pantelleria
Trápani
Pantelleria
Ísola di Pantelleria
M. Gibele
700
Punta Limarsi
Polacca
Punta

Linosa, Lampedusa
Porto Empédocle
Í. di Lampione
Ísole Pelágie
Lampedusa
Ísole di Lampedusa
Í. di Linosa
Linosa

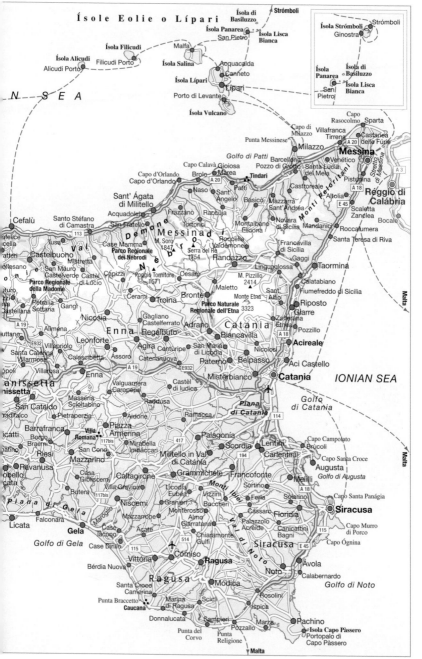

Ísole Eolie o Lípari

Ísola di Basiluzzo
Ísola Panarea
San Pietro
Ísola Lisca Bianca
Strómboli

Ísola Filicudi
Malfa
Ísola Salina
Acquacalda
Canneto
Ísola Alicudi
Alicudi Porto
Filicudi Porto
Ísola Lípari
Lípari
Porto di Levante

N SEA

Ísola Vulcano

Ísola Strómboli
Strómboli
Ginostra
Ísola Panarea
San Pietro
Ísola di Basiluzzo
Ísola Lisca Bianca

Capo Rasocolmo
Sparta
Villafranca Tirrena
Castanea delle Fúrie
Punta Messinese
Golfo di Patti
Milazzo
Capo di Milazzo
Venético
Messina
Stretto di Messina
Barcellona Pozzo di Gotto
Santa Lucia del Mela
Pistunina
Reggio di Calábria
Capo Calavà
Gioiosa Marea
Brolo
Tindari
Patti
Castroreale
Altolia
Scaletta Zanclea
Bocale
Santa Teresa di Riva

Cefalù
Santo Stéfano di Camastra
Capo d'Orlando
Capo d'Orlando
Naso
Sant'Ágata di Militello
Acquadolci
San Fratello
Frazzanò
Raccúja
Sant' Angelo
Basicò
Mazzarrà Sant'Andréa
Novara di Sicilia
Mandanici
Roccalumera

Tusa
Case Mamma
Parco Regionale dei Nébrodi
M. Soro 1847
Serra del Ré 1754
Tortorici
Montalbano Elicona
Roccella Valdémone
Francavilla di Sicilia
Gaggi
Taormina

Castelbuono
Mistretta
San Mauro
Castelverde
Castèl di Lúcio
Cúpizzi
Poggio Tornitore 1571
Cesarò
Randazzo
Linguaglossa
Calatabiano
Fiumefreddo di Sicilia
Riposto

Parco Regionale della Madoníe
Petralia Sottana
Gangi
Cerami
Troina
Bronte
M. Pizzillo 2414
Maletto
Sant'Alfio
Zafferana Etnea
Giarre
Pozzillo

Nicosia
Gagliano Castelferrato
Adrano
Parco Naturale Regionale dell'Etna
Monte Etna 3323
Catania
Biancavilla
Nicolosi
Acireale

Allmena
Enna
Regalbuto
Centúripe
San Maria di Licodia
Paternò
Belpasso
Aci Castello

Villapriolo
Leonforte
Ássoro
Caterinanuova
Misterbianco
Catania

Santa Caterina
Villarmosa
Calascibetta
Enna
Valguarnera Caropepe
Castèl di ludica

IONIAN SEA

anissetta
nissetta
San Cataldo
Masseria Scïoltabino
Pietraperzia
Raddusa
Ramacca
Piana di Catania
Golfo di Catania

radifalco
Barrafranca
Borgo
Braemi
Villa Romana
Aidone
Piazza Armerina
Mirabella Imbáccari
Palagónia
Scordia
Lentini
Carlentini
Capo Campolato
Brúcoli

icatti
nafino
Riesi
San Cono
Mazzarino
Militello in Val di Catánia
Francofonte
Meilli
Augusta
Golfo di Augusta

Ravanusa
bello
cata
Casa Gibliscemi
Villa Gravina
Caltagirone
Grammichele
Sortino
Ferla
Solarino
Capo Santa Panágia

Piana di Gela
Butera
Niscemi
Licodía Eubéa
Graníeri
Vizzini
Buccheri
Cássaro
Floridia
Siracusa

Licata
Falconara
Gela
Case Iacono
Mazzarrone
Acate
Monterosso Almo
Giarratana
Palazzolo Acréide
Canicattini Bagni
Capo Murro di Porco

Golfo di Gela
Case Dirillo
Chiaramonte Gulfi
Siracusa
Capo Ógnina

Vittoria
Cómiso
Ragusa
Noto
Ávola
Calabernardo
Golfo di Noto

Bérdia Nuova
Ragusa
Módica
Rosolini
Íspica

Santa Croce Camerina
Marina di Ragusa
Scicli
Pachino
Ísola Capo Pàssero
Portopalo di Capo Pàssero

Punta Braccetto
Caucana
Donnalucata
Sampieri
Punta del Corvo
Punta Religione
Pozzallo
Marza

Malta

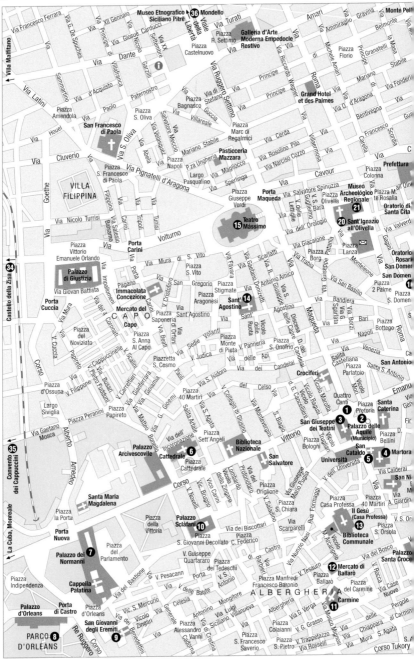

Palermo

0   200 m
0   200 yds

Via del Mare
Via Galileo Ferraris
uzzo
Via Galvani
Via Sammuzzo
rco Crispi
Via Patuano
Via Alessandro Volta
Piazza XIII Vittime
rta iorgio
Via Filippo Patti
azza Giorgio enovesi
Molo Sud
Via Castello
Castell a Mare
CM.8
Giorgio Genovesi
Via Bivona
Alessandro Castello
Via Barilai
Via S. Sebastiano
Via Tonda
Via Cianciolo
Tavola
Mercato Ittico
Piazza Castello

Golfo di

Palermo

Piazza Fonderia
V. Cesarini
Via F. Matera
Via Cala
Piazza Tarzana
Porta Carbone
La Cala
Piazza Cap. di Porto
Porta Felice
CIRIA
Cassari
Via Chiavettieri
Santa Maria della Catena **19**
Piazza S. Spirito
Cala
Corso Via Bottai
Via del Parlamento
Oratorio di San Lorenzo **29**
Via Vittorio Emanuele
Piazzetta Dogana
Piazza Marina **26**
Museo Internazionale delle Marionette **32**
Palazzo Butera **31**
Mura delle Cattive
Foro Italico (Umberto I)
VILLA
ntica acceria ancesco
San Francesco d'Assisi **28**
Santa Maria dei Miracoli
V. Merlo
Palazzo Mirto **27**
Piazza S. Francesco d'Assisi
Palazzo Chiaramonte **25**
V. de' Franchi
V. Butera
V. Niscemi
A
MARE
Cassa armio
alascibetta
Galleria d'Arte Moderna (GAM) **30**
Via Resuttana
V.IV Aprile
Vicolo P.all'alloro
Palazzo Lanza Tomasi
La Pietà
Salita alle Mura di Cattive
Porta Dei Greci
Via Alloro
Via Scopari
V.Lungarini
V.S. Carlo
Via Aragona
Paternostro
P. Ce Prevosti
Vicolo Castro
C. dell'Alloro
Via di Blasi
Via del Sciarra
Galleria Regionale (Palazzo Abatellis) **24**
Via Alloro
La Gancia
Piazza Spasimo
Savona
Santa Teresa
Piazza della Kalsa
Teatro Politeama Garibaldi
Via Schiavuzzo
Via Francesco Riso
Piazza S. Eumo
della Vetreria
Via S. Teresa
Piazza Ventimiglia
Vicolo del Pallone
Lincoln
Cecilia
Divisi
V.Maestro d'Acqua
V.Aragona
Via Garibaldi
Via Filippo
L A   K A L S A
Lo Spasimo **+**
Cervello
tta i ese
Palazzo Aiutamicristo **23**
La Magione **22**
Piazza Rivoluzione
Piazza Magione
dello Spasimo
Porta Reale
Abramo
Foro Italico (Umberto I)
V. Monte Santo
Gorizia
Via della Pace
Via G. Filangieri
Via Magione
Via C. Pardi
Roma
Via Milano
Corso
Via Manzoni
Via Abramo
Lincoln
Porta Castro Filippo
ORTO BOTÁNICO **33**
VILLA GIULIA
ste
Porta Garibaldi
V. Rosario Gregorio
Via A. di Rudinì
Via Paci
Antonio Ugo
Archirafi
Piazza Giulio Cesare
V. Balsamo
V.P. Randazzo
V.M. Cipolla
Via Tiro a Segno
Stazione Centrale
San Giovani dei Lebbrosi
Mille
↓ Bagheria

N

PALERMO

Love it or loathe it, Palermo pulls a punch, with the ongoing restoration of the city centre hailed a success – so let an array of Arab-Norman architecture and exotic street food dazzle your senses

Palermo

Palermo is both an essay in chaos and a jewel-box of a city: no map does justice to the city's confusion. Sicily's capital is a synthesis of bombsites and beauty, with sumptuous Arab-Norman and Baroque splendour interspersed with an intriguing Moorish muddle. Indeed, Palermo is not merely a crucible of Mediterranean culture but of world culture, given its history of conquest by Phoenicians, Romans, Byzantine Greeks, Arabs, Normans and Spaniards. As a result, the Spanish grid system is subverted by Moorish blind alleys, while domed churches may resemble mosques. Even the Palazzo dei Normanni, the royal palace, is built on Punic walls, but looks Moorish, Byzantine and Baroque by turns.

As a complex city culture that knows many masters, Palermo is, by nature, secretive yet seductive. Many masters, past and present, have been corrupt or neglectful. The cosmopolitan city was devastated during the Allied invasion of Italy when, in 1943, Allied bombs shattered the port and historic centre. Afterwards, the Mafia, in league with corrupt politicians, stepped in, accepting funds

from Rome and, later, the European Union, for the rebuilding of the *centro storico*, only to siphon off the money for their own pleasures.

Public attitudes only changed with the Mafia murders of magistrates Giovanni Falcone and Paolo Borsellino in 1992 *(see page 39)*. Palermitans experienced a wave of revulsion, and citizens were no longer willing to be silently dominated by the Mafia. After a period of political stagnation, a feeling of hope now permeates the air as the Sicilian authorities combat

Main attractions

CHIESA DELLA MARTORANA
CATTEDRALE (CATHEDRAL)
PALAZZO DEI NORMANNI
SAN GIOVANNI DEGLI EREMITI
BALLARÒ MARKET
ORATORIO DEL ROSARIO DI SAN DOMENICO
MUSEO ARCHEOLOGICO REGIONALE
PALAZZO ABATELLIS (GALLERIA REGIONALE)
PIAZZA MARINA
ORTO BOTÁNICO (BOTANICAL GARDENS)
CASTELLO DELLA ZISA
CONVENTO DEI CAPPUCCINI

LEFT: Ballarò market.
RIGHT: Il Gesù, also known as Casa Professa, Sicily's first Jesuit church.

corruption with some success. A citizen-led anti-Mafia movement and new civic pride seems to have taken root, despite a compromised city administration. *(For details on 'Mafia-free' tours, see page 286).*

The historic centre

Palermo is divided into four sections by the **Quattro Canti** , the crossroads at Piazza Vigliena, where "four corners of the city" are formed by two great arteries, **Via Maqueda** and **Corso Vittorio Emanuele**, the main street, built over a Phoenician road. The corners, embellished with Baroque stonework and fountains, are hard to appreciate amid the roar of traffic and the clatter of horses' hooves.

Northwest of Corso Emanuele is the **Capo** quarter and southwest the **Alberghería**. Northeast of Via Roma is the **Vucciria** and southeast lies the **Kalsa**. Each quarter reveals a picturesque clutter of mansions, markets and forbidding Baroque churches with luminous interiors.

Just along from Quattro Canti is **Piazza Pretoria** ❷, dominated by the Fontana Pretoria. This Baroque square

Statues adorning Piazza Pretoria.

BELOW RIGHT: Porta Nuova.

was once disparagingly nicknamed **Piazza della Vergogna** (the Square of Shame) because of its abundance of flagrantly nude statues that make up the 16th-century Tuscan fountain. More than 30 near-naked nymphs, tritons, gods and youths surround its vast circular basin. Allegedly, the local nuns chopped off the noses of many of the naked men (but stopped short of castration). The statues were recently restored and ornamental railings added to prevent further mishaps.

Adjoining the square is the **Palazzo delle Aquile**, the remodelled town hall, with eagles decorating the exterior. The towering presence here, however, is **San Giuseppe dei Teatini** ❸ (Mon–Sat 7.30am–11am, 6pm–8pm, Sun 8.30am–1pm), whose opulent interior exudes a Baroque spirit, beginning with the majolica-encrusted cupola. During the 17th and 18th centuries the church was theatrically decorated with multicoloured marble and with eight massive columns in grey marble to support the dome, which is emblazoned with a fresco of the *Triumph of Sant'Andrea Avellino* (1724) by Borremans.

Getting around

The historic centre, where you'll be spending nearly all your time, is best tackled on foot – driving is stressful and parking a problem. The hop-on-hop-off sightseeing buses are a useful way of getting your bearings and handy when tiredness sets in.

Taxis are best telephoned, or found at taxi ranks or outside big hotels (check the meter is switched on).

A horse-drawn carriage *(carrozza)* may be tempting but both you (and the blinkered horses) may be exposed to heavy traffic, summer heat and pollution.

City Sightseeing Palermo: "hop-on-hop-off" tours in red, open-top double-decker buses (24-hour ticket €20, half-price after 2pm) with night tours in summer too, and bus links to Monreale. For information on routes and tariffs, visit www.palermo.city-sightseeing.it.

Taxis: Autoradio Taxi: tel: 091 513 311. Radio Taxi: tel: 091 225 455.

Carriages: Pick up a horse-drawn carriage from outside the Teatro Massimo (from €50).

Transport network: information on city buses and parking, www.amat.pa.it.

On neighbouring Piazza Bellini the campanile of **Chiesa della Martorana** ❹ (closed for restoration until 2013) stands tall alongside the three small red domes of San Cataldo. La Martorana was established in 1143 by George of Antioch, an admiral whose successes brought such fortune to Norman Sicily that Roger II honoured him with the title emir. (The church was originally called Santa Maria dell'Ammiraglio, or St Mary of the Admiral, in his honour.) Greek Byzantine craftsmen made the splendid mosaics. In the cupola is *Christ Pantocrator Blessing from the Throne*; elsewhere, with angels and apostles, are scenes from the Ascension, the Annunciation, the Birth of Christ and Roger II crowned king by Christ. It is one of the most beautiful Norman churches in Sicily, but may have been even finer had not the nuns from the nearby convent demolished and altered much of it. Their Order, founded by Eloisa Martorana, was given the church in 1233, but Mussolini returned it to the Greek Orthodox community in 1935 as their cathedral.

The triple-domed church of **San Cataldo** ❺ (Mon–Sat 9.30am–2pm, 3.30–7pm, Sun 9am–2pm; charge) is one of the last sacred buildings built in the Arab-Norman style. If the interior appears plain, it is probably only because of comparison to its gilded neighbour, La Martorana. Subdued light reveals the three domes supported by squinches and piers; the Fatimid capitals are so delicate they appear to float. The mosaic floor and lattice windows are original; in the crypt are sections of Palermo's ancient Roman walls.

The Cattedrale

West from Quattro Canti, Corso Vittorio Emanuele leads away from the port towards the cathedral, separating the Albergheria and Capo quarters. This main thoroughfare was once known as Via Cassaro Vecchio, *vecchio* being old and *cassaro* derived from *qasr*, Arabic for castle.

The **Cattedrale** ❻ (Mon–Sat 7am–7pm, Sun and public hols 7am–1pm, 4–7pm; www.cattedrale. palermo.it) is a Sicilian hybrid: mentally erase the incongruous dome

TIP

Pastry shops *(pasticcerie)* sell delicious handmade marzipan confections designed to look like peaches, oranges, pears, prickly pears and apples. They are usually known as *frutti alla martorana*, because it was the Benedictine nuns in the convent that took over Palermo's La Martorana church in 1233 who first created them. The convent no longer exists, but the marzipan lives on.

BELOW: Piazza Pretoria.

Antonello Gagini, a marble sculptor like his father Domenico, is considered the finest Renaissance sculptor in Sicily. Between 1510 and 1536 he and his studio sculpted in marble, terracotta and stucco. Among his many masterpieces in Palermo is the Madonna della Scala *(1503) in the cathedral.*

and focus on the desert-coloured stone, sculpted doorway and Moorish decoration, and the geometric Arab-Norman apses behind the cathedral. It was begun in 1185 on the site of a basilica that replaced a mosque in the 9th century. The cathedral was the work of an Englishman, Walter of the Mill, who went on to become Archbishop of Palermo in 1168. The mosaic over the portal came from the original Byzantine church while, on the left-hand column, an inscription from the Koran came from the original mosque.

The Baroque interior is a cool shell, a wan setting for six **royal Norman tombs** that include that of Roger II, the first king of Sicily (d. 1197) and Frederick II (d. 1250), emperor of Germany and king of Sicily. Borne by crouching lions, the sarcophagi are made of rare pink porphyry and sculpted by Arab masters, the only craftsmen who knew the technique in Norman times. In the nave are statues of saints by Antonello Gagini *(see margin)*. The treasury contains royal mantles and the crown of Constance of Aragon (d. 1222), bedecked with

jewels. Constance was 24 when she married Emperor Frederick II, age 14. In the crypt are 23 tombs, many of them Roman.

The Palazzo dei Normanni

Beyond the cathedral on the Corso is **Piazza della Vittoria**, with a garden sheltered by palm trees and a triumphal gate, the **Porta Nuova**, erected in 1535 to celebrate Charles V's victory in Tunisia. Also here is the **Palazzo dei Normanni** ❼, the eclectic royal palace and centre of power since Roger II converted the original 9th-century Arab towered castle into his residence, an Arab-Norman palace. It houses the city's greatest site, the superb **Cappella Palatina** (Palatine Chapel).

Now the seat of the Sicilian Parliament, this cube-shaped palazzo has walled gardens overgrown with orchids, papyrus, banyan trees, *ficus beniamine*, as well as dwarf palms, whose leaves are reputed to take 50 years to grow, and African kapoks, said to be a favourite with monkeys in their natural habitat because they store water in their barrel-like trunks. As the main building was turned into

BELOW: Palermo's Cattedrale.

the home of the **Sicilian Regional Assembly** in 1947, its visiting hours are limited (usually Fri–Mon 8.30am–5.30pm but check on www. fondazionefedericosecondo.it; charge).

Cappella Palatina

Leading off a lovely loggia is the superb **Cappella Palatina** (Mon–Sat 8.30am–5.30pm; charge), the royal chapel built for Roger II between 1130 and 1140. He ensured each of the religions in his kingdom – Muslim, Catholic and Greek Orthodox – was represented within the chapel. The interior displays glittering mosaics on the dome and apse, recalling the life of Roger II as well as Christian themes. These include sumptuous Biblical scenes incorporating the Annunciation, the Raising of Lazarus, the Building of the Ark, the Nativity and the Destruction of Sodom. The inlaid floors, marble walls, columns and candle holders and a 3-metre (10ft) tall paschal candlestick, richly decorated with animals carved in white marble, were made by Romans, while Arab craftsmen created the exquisitely carved and

painted wooden ceiling; it portrays Christian paradise (as seen through Muslim eyes) with naked maidens surrounded by Normans prudishly clothed and crowned with haloes. The *muqarna* ceiling is remarkable, made by master-craftsmen from Syria, Iraq and Libya. Where else can you see Persian octagonal stars meet Islamic stalactites with palm trees and peacocks while men play chess, hunt and drink amid entwined dancers and female musicians? Unique in a Christian church, it is a composition of ineffable oriental splendour.

On the top floor of the palace are the **Royal Apartments**, mostly decorated in Bourbon style, reflecting the tastes of the Spanish viceroys. The **Sala da Ballo** has a fine view to the sea. However, the loveliest rooms are Arab-Norman, especially the **Sala di Re Ruggero** (1140) with its splendid mosaics of hunting scenes. More recently revealed sections include the **Mura Puniche**, the Punic walls and postern – the oldest part of the palace – and the **Chiesa Inferiore**, mistakenly called the crypt as it lies below the Cappella Palatina, but actually the

The Palazzo dei Normanni, dating back to the 9th century, is home to the Sicilian Parliament.

BELOW LEFT: the exquisite Capella Palatina.

Crucible of culture

Palermo is a bewildering jumble of periods and styles. A Phoenician colony existed here from the 8th century BC, perched on the water's edge and sheltered by mountains, but it was only after Palermo fell to the Arabs in AD 831 (having been under Roman rule since 254 BC) that it came into its own. By the 9th century the city flourished as a great centre of scholarship and art, the home of Jewish and Lombard merchants, Greek craftsmen, Turkish and Syrian artisans, Persian artists and African slaves. It had the most multiracial population in Europe. Under Arab rule, there were 300 mosques, and the city was ringed by pleasure palaces like La Zisa and hunting lodges like La Cuba. By 1091 Norman rule coincided with Palermo's own golden age, one of expansion, enlightenment, prosperity and cultural riches, incorporating Greek, Roman and Arab traditions.

Under the Spanish rule that followed, the Moorish city was remodelled along grand Baroque arteries. Yet behind the grand Quattro Canti crossroads that divide the city into four *quartieri* (districts), the old Moorish maze continues to swirl with crooked alleys, lively markets and cosmopolitan chatter.

The multicoloured dome of San Giovanni degli Eremiti.

BELOW: cloisters of San Giovanni.

Lower Church, used for ceremonies and burials in Arab-Norman times.

Through Porta Nuova is Piazza Indipendenza, Palazzo d'Orleans and the **Parco d'Orleans ❽** (Mon–Fri 9am–1pm, 3–6pm, Sat–Sun 9am–1pm), lush gardens belonging to the Palazzo, the official residence of the Sicilian president. Mothers play here with children, men play cards and office-workers eat ice creams sandwiched in buns, a Palermitan speciality.

The Albergheria Quarter

South of Corso Emanuele, the Albergheria Quarter was once the home of Norman court officials and rich merchants from Pisa and Amalfi. Although many dilapidated houses are home to illegal immigrants, a sense of community prevails over scenes of urban decay.

The romantic **San Giovanni degli Eremiti ❾** (Tue–Sun 9am–1pm, 2–6.30pm; charge), with its distinctive five red cupolas, lies just south of the royal palace on Via dei Benedettini, at the western edge of the Albergheria Quarter. It illustrates the Arab influence favoured when its con-struction was begun by Roger II in 1132, a year after he had been elected king. Built over a Benedictine mon-astery founded in 581, this Moorish spot reveals Arab squinches, filigree windows and elegant Norman clois-ters overgrown with jasmine, citrus, mimosa and pomegranate. Its recent restoration and new route stress hith-erto neglected aspects, from the well and concealed cistern to the secret underground river.

Arab architectural motifs haunt **Palazzo Sclafani ❿**, a fortified medi-eval palazzo north of San Giovanni, built in 1330 by one of the most pow-erful feudal families.

Further east, on Piazza del Car-mine, is the fabulously domed church of **Carmine ⓫** (Mon–Sat 9am–10.30am, Sun 9.30am–noon) with fine paintings and majolica. This is the heart of **Ballarò market ⓬**, a noisy haunt of artisans and stu-dents, housewives and bootleggers. Currently Palermo's liveliest daily market, it is raucous, authentic and sprawling, with the hurly-burly of the exotic food stalls clashing with the second-hand clothes stalls *(for more on street food, see page 43)*.

Sicily's first Jesuit church, **Il Gesù ⓭** (Mon–Sat 10am–1pm, 4–7pm; Sun 8am–12.30pm), is on Piazza Casa Pro-fessa. Also known as Casa Professa for its learned Jesuit origins, its interior is beautifully decorated with colourful marble, sculptures, tritons and cher-ubs. It has been restored after being damaged in World War II.

The Capo Quarter

The battered *Capo quartiere* lies north of the cathedral. Since its origins as the slave traders' quarter, the Capo has been isolated, historically the poorest area of the city. It is a maze of alleys, but the centrepiece, masked by market stalls, is the church of **Sant'Agostino ⓮** (Mon–Sat 7am–12pm, 4pm–6pm, Sun 7am–12pm), the sober remains of a medieval

monastery, adorned with crests of the powerful Chiaramonte and Sclafani dynasties. Their crests and some lava mosaics decorate a delicate late 13th-century portal surmounted by a 14th-century rose window. Inside are gilded stuccoes by Giacomo Serpotta (*c.*1711), matched by charming 16th-century cloisters and a small garden.

This warren of streets conceals restored churches such as the **Immacolata Concezione** on Via Porta Carini, but others lie derelict. Some have been put to new uses like San Marco, which is now a care home. These streets are the setting for the **Capo market**, an inexpensive source of food, clothes and household goods.

Within walking distance of the market, northwards on Via Maqueda, historic Capo gives way to 19th- and 20th-century Palermo with **Teatro Massimo** ⓰, the city's vast opera house, dominating Piazza Verdi (tours: Mon–Sat 10am–2pm, unless there's a rehearsal; for opera tel: 091 605 3111; www.teatromassimo.it). The well-restored building, first opened in 1897, was designed by Palermo's illustrious Giovanni Battista Basile in eclectic rather than neoclassical style. The portico, graced by Corinthian columns, is of Greek inspiration, while the cylindrical shapes of the building and the cupola owe more to Roman ideal. Inside, the grandiose main staircase is Baroque while the decor, rich in floral motifs, is decidedly Art Nouveau.

On Via Magliocco, just east of Piazza Verdi, is the **Pasticceria Mazzara**, a celebrated café and pastry shop linked to literary figures such as Tomasi di Lampedusa (*see panel page 131*).

The Vucciria Quarter

The name of this quarter is a corruption of the French *boucherie*, thanks to the quantity of meat traditionally on sale in the **Vucciria market**. The stalls straggle along alleys from Via Roma to **San Domenico** ⓰ (Tue–Sun 9am–1pm), a Baroque church with an impressive facade that has its foundations in the 1300s but was altered around 1636 by the Dominican Order. In the 18th century, the Spanish viceroys tried to impose order on Palermo's most chaotic market but failed dismally. Little has

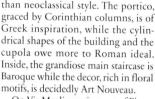

On the lovely piazza beside the Teatro Massimo are two kiosks designed by Battista Basile's son Ernesto; they are in the Art Nouveau style that he used for much of his work in Palermo.

BELOW LEFT: Ballarò market. **BELOW:** Teatro Massimo.

TIP

The city is known for its bustling markets. The winding lanes of the Ballarò, the Vucciria and the Capo are reminiscent of an Arab souk. Some stalls will grill fish, squid and octopus while you wait *(for more on street food, see page 43)*. Keep exploring and you find everything is available, from clothes to bootleg DVDs and CDs.

changed and the names of the surrounding streets echo the old local trades: silversmiths, ironmongers, pasta makers, shoemakers. The colourful stalls display capers and pine nuts, spices and sun-dried tomatoes, endless varieties of meat and sausages and bootleg tapes, and are particularly charming as night falls and the red awnings are illuminated. However, the success of Ballarò market means that the Vucciria market truly bustles only on Saturdays.

If the Vucciria palls, leave the market and consider a drink in the faded *belle époque* grandeur of the **Grand Hotel et des Palmes** at 398 Via Roma. Wagner reputedly completed *Parsifal* in a gilded salon here in 1882, while the wartime Mafia boss, Lucky Luciano, later held court in the dining room.

Behind the church of San Domenico, on Via Bambinai, a doll makers' street that has stayed close to its roots by selling Christmas crib figures as well as votive offerings, is a Baroque jewel, the **Oratorio del Rosario di San Domenico ⑰** (Mon–Sat 9am–1pm, www.tesoriodellaloggia.it). It is a theatrical chapel created by the mas-

ter in stuccowork, Giacomo Serpotta *(see page 81)*, with putti playing cellos amidst seashells, eagles and allegorical exotica. The altarpiece, the *Madonna of the Rosary*, is the work of Van Dyck (c.1624) and considered one of the finest in Sicily and Italy.

Just around the corner, on Via Valverde, lies another celebrated oratory, **Oratorio di Santa Cita ⑱** (Mon–Sat 9am–1pm), reached through lush gardens. The oratories were places where nobles gathered, centres for charitable works as well as for displays of personal status and wealth. In Santa Cita, Serpotta's ravishing stuccowork depicts the *Intercession of the Virgin in the Battle of Lepanto* with all of the boats exquisitely differentiated.

La Cala

Beyond the chapel is **La Cala**, the scruffy portside edged by Via Cala. Fishing boats bob against a backdrop of bombed palazzi whose cellars house immigrant families. However, regeneration is gradually seeping into this semi-derelict quarter with the restoration of churches, like **San Giorgio dei Genovesi** (Mon–Sat 9am–1pm),

BELOW: tango dancing is popular on summer evenings in the city.

A night out in Palermo

A night out might begin on the rooftop of **Rinascente**, Palermo's smart new department store on Via Roma, where cool Palermitans sip cocktails while watching the facades on Piazza San Domenico turn from tawny to violet. Then it might be time to move on to **Caffè Spinnato** (Via Principe di Belmonte) for tasty morsels before heading to the opera at **Teatro Massimo** (Piazza Verdi, tel: 091 605 3111, www.teatromassimo.it). If a laidback evening takes precedence over high culture, then many Palermitans will choose the seductive **Kursaal Kalhesa**, close to the revitalised seafront (Foro Umberto I 21, tel: 091 616 2282, www. kursaalkalhesa.it), for Arab-tinged fusion food in a jasmine-scented courtyard.

which is now an exhibition centre. The transformation of La Cala and the old port area is the city's biggest project in coming years, including the **Castello a Mare**, the newly reopened archaeological zone on the far side of the bay. This area suffered most from bomb damage in World War II, and the city was moved further from the sea by an accumulation of falling masonry, which is gradually being removed. The striking site, which includes crumbling Arab bastions, is now used for concerts and events.

Sandwiched between the port and Piazza Marina *(see page 72)* is **Santa Maria della Catena ⓭** (Mon–Fri 9am–1pm), a well-restored 15th-century church with an early Renaissance portico at the top of a flight of stairs. The church was named after the medieval chain *(catena)* that sealed the harbour in times of war. Inside, a 16th-century *baldacchino* covers a charming 14th-century fresco of *The Madonna and Child*.

Piazza Olivella

From the port, if you retrace your steps to Via Roma and turn into Via Bara, you come to **Piazza Olivella**, part of a charming artisans' quarter of puppet-makers, pastry shops and inns. The grand Baroque church of **Sant'Ignazio all'Olivella ⓴** (closed Wed morning; Mon–Sat 9–10am, 5–6pm, Sun 9–10am) begun in 1598 but with a 17th-century facade, has some fine pictures.

Adjoining the Olivella church is the **Museo Archeologico Regionale ㉑** (reopening in 2012 after refurbishment). This is the essence of classical Sicily encased in a late Renaissance monastery, with artefacts that illustrate the region's glorious historical roots, from prehistoric times to the Roman era. There are inscrutable Egyptian priestly figures found near Mózia *(see page 104)*, and anthropomorphic sarcophagi stare out of Semitic faces and square bodies. In a large cloister is a tangle of lush vegetation and a lily pond.

The museum's most important treasures are in the fabulous **Sala di Selinunte**, including carved stone reliefs (the *metopes*) that were set above the columns at Selinunte in about 470 BC *(see page 107)*. The

Detail of Intercession of the Virgin in the Battle of Lepanto.

BELOW LEFT: yachts in La Cala. **BELOW:** getting married in Sant'Ignazio all'Olivella.

EAT

Fried pizza (as opposed to traditional oven-baked pizza) is available across Sicily, but *sfincione di Palermo* belong to the city. Here the pizza dough is leavened with cheese, then covered in a sauce of onion, tomatoes, cheese and anchovies and baked in an oven. After a while it is fried, breadcrumbs are scattered over it and it is returned to the oven to continue baking. Not for dieters.

friezes depict deities, such as Athena protecting Perseus as he tussles with Medusa; Hercules slaying dwarves or battling a Cretan bull; Zeus marrying a frosty Hera on Mount Ida; Actaeon turning into a stag. Other highlights are the terracotta votive offerings from Selinunte; as well as the celebrated bronze ram that once stood over the gate of Castello Maniace in Siracusa.

The Museo Archeologico also displays an Etruscan collection with sculptures and painted terracotta works from the 6th to 5th centuries BC uncovered in Chiusi (Tuscany). Superb Greek vases of the same period depict the *Myth of Tripolemus* and the *Battle of Athena against the Giants*. There are also casts of engravings from Addaura on nearby Monte Pellegrino and a Roman mosaic showing Orpheus enchanting wild beasts.

La Kalsa Quarter

In Arab times the Kalsa Quarter was where the emir lived in splendour, and in the Middle Ages it became the chosen district for the homes of wealthy merchants. The word *kalsa*

comes from the Arabic *khalisa*, meaning "pure" or "chosen".

Little of this purity shows today. La Kalsa may be picturesque, but it is impoverished, having been badly damaged during World War II as it fringes the harbour. When Mother Teresa's mission settled close to bomb-struck Piazza Magione, wealthy Palermitans were horrified to be lectured by an Albanian nun, even one incarnating sainthood. Her message was that since Palermo was as poor as the Third World, charity should begin at home. The message, however, seems to have struck a chord since the area is being slowly regenerated with a cheery materialism heralded by new bars, especially close to the delightfully gentrified **Piazza Marina** *(see page 72)*.

This seemingly abandoned corner of Palermo houses a wonderful Norman church as well as the late Mother Teresa's nuns and the church of **Santa Teresa alla Kalsa** (Tue–Sun 7am–11am, 4–7pm).

On neighbouring Piazza Magione, Moorish filigree windows and blind arcading announce the ancestry of **La Magione** ㉗, (Mon–Sat 9am–noon, 3–6.30pm, Sun 9.30am–12.30pm). This imposing Cistercian church was founded in 1151 but was then presented to the Imperial Teutonic Order by Henry VI in 1197. Norman architecture predominates, with a gracious interior complemented by a 14th-century altar and painted Crucifix. The delicate cloisters (Mon–Sat 9am–7pm, Sun 9am–1.30pm) contain a 15th-century fresco of the Crucifixion. Around the church is a charming garden of palm trees, a prelude to a walk around the Orto Botánico, the neighbouring botanical gardens.

On Piazza Magione is a memorial to the magistrate Giovanni Falcone, assassinated by the Mafia in 1992 and, to one side of the piazza, is **Teatro Politeama Garibaldi** (1861), a small theatre seemingly saved from

BELOW: La Kalsa.

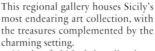

ruin. Just east of Piazza Magione, in the honeycomb heart of the Kalsa, is **Lo Spasimo** (normally daily 9am–11pm, but temporarily closed after a wall collapsed; tel: 091 616 1486). This evocative entertainment complex is set in a former 16th-century monastery. Jazz concerts are held in the cloisters and the roofless church, which, given a sultry, starry night and swaying palms, creates a romantic, Moorish atmosphere.

Via Magione leads into Via Garibaldi with, among the palazzi, **Palazzo Aiutamicristo** ㉓, a Catalan-Gothic mansion built in 1490 containing a loggia and porticoed courtyard. It was along Via Garibaldi, and that is now Corso dei Mille, that Giuseppe Garibaldi made his triumphant advance into Palermo on 27 May 1860.

The Regional Art Gallery

Just east, Via Alloro, the city's patrician centre in the Middle Ages and the principal street in the Kalsa, leads to **Palazzo Abatellis** (1488), a grand Catalan-Gothic mansion that is home to the **Galleria Regionale** ㉔ (Tue–Fri 9am–6pm, Sat–Sun 9am–1pm).

This regional gallery houses Sicily's most endearing art collection, with the treasures complemented by the charming setting.

Newly refurbished, the gallery has a clearer, more compelling layout, which only adds to its charm. Set off a Renaissance courtyard and loggia, over two floors, the collection offers a journey back through Sicilian art, showcasing paintings and sculpture from the 15th and 16th centuries. The highlights include a serene bust of *Eleanor of Aragon* by Francesco Laurana, engaging Gagini sculptures by a Sicilian master and a haunting *Annunciation* (1476) by Antonello da Messina, Sicily's greatest painter of the 1400s.

The undoubted masterpiece is the powerful 15th-century *Triumph of Death*, with a skeleton archer as the grim reaper of Death riding on a spectral horse, cutting a swathe through wealthy bishops, nobles and fair maidens. Here, Death shoots only at those who do not want to die because they are enjoying life to the full; he ignores the poor and disabled, who pray for divine intervention and a release from their earthbound

The cloisters of Palazzo Aiutamicristo.

BELOW LEFT: interior of La Magione.

Princely pastimes

As a Spanish vassal, Sicily indulged in conspicuous consumption on grandiose city palaces. The foreign viceroys sold feudal privileges and titles to fill their coffers and inflate the numbers of the aristocracy. Under the Neapolitan Bourbons, Palermo's population doubled and the city boasted more palaces than in the entire British Empire. Yet Palermo is oddly democratic, with all classes living hugger-mugger in the historic centre. Many palazzi have remained temples to Sicilian secrecy, but others have opened their ornate portals to prying eyes, and their ballrooms to privileged parties. Beyond the Baroque courtyards are Gothic loggias and Moorish watchtowers, restored private chapels and Rococo staterooms.

You can now stay in several castle-like palaces in Palermo, including with Conte Federico *(see page 268)*. Other palatial homes can be visited, including Palazzo Alliata di Pietragliata (Via Bandiera 14, tel: 091 325 323) or the ancestral home of Tomasi di Lampedusa (groups only, tel +333 316 5432). Apart from beguiling "private" visits, the patrician owners may offer recitals and classical concerts, cookery courses and tastings on ancestral wine estates.

Antonio di Francesco's 14th-century Madonna with Child *at Palazzo Abatellis.*

BELOW: *Triumph of Death* fresco at Palazzo Abatellis.

troubles. The subject is macabre but strangely compelling.

Next to the gallery is the austere **La Gancia**, originally the 15th-century church of **Santa Maria degli Angeli** (currently closed). On display are works by Antonello Gagini, Pietro Novelli and Giacomo Serpotta.

Palazzo Chiaramonte

A short walk away is **Palazzo Chiaramonte** ㉕ (Fri–Sun 10am–6pm but subject to change; charge), a baronial palace built by the Chiaramonte dynasty in 1307. It became the palace of the Spanish viceroys and then the seat of the Inquisition from 1605 to 1782. Carved on the grim prison walls inside is a poignant plea for *pane, pazienza e tempo* (bread, patience and time). Heretics and dissenters were burned to death outside, but so too were artists and intellectuals, damned as subversives. Commonly known as Lo Steri, the building was restored for the Chancellor of Palermo University but is also a fascinating museum.

A formidable inner courtyard leads to the Inquisition prisons, which are covered in pleas and etchings. Off the first-floor loggia is the Sala Magna (Great Hall), where the Spanish viceroys met, and which is adorned with a superb medieval coffered ceiling.

Other highlights include the Chiesa di Sant'Antonio Abate, a Gothic gem once linked to the palace by an overhead passageway and, incongruously, *Vucceria*, Guttuso's languid depiction of Palermo's best-known market.

Piazza Marina

Alongside Palazzo Chiaramonte is **Piazza Marina** ㉖, originally a muddy inlet that silted up and was reclaimed in Saracen times. Since then the square has witnessed the shame and glory of city history. It was used by the Aragonese for weddings and jousts and, because it was close to the prisons, for public executions too. In the centre is Giardino Garibaldi. As it is the only gentrified square in the old quarter, the locals are self-consciously proud of its shady park and well-tended banyan trees. The square holds a bric-a-brac market on Saturday afternoons and Sunday mornings. Across the square is the charming Renaissance church of **Santa Maria dei Miracoli** (Mon–Fri 9am–5pm, Sat 9am–1pm).

Close by, on Via Merlo, is **Palazzo Mirto** ㉗, an unprepossessing palazzo with a delightful interior. This Palermitan palace may be the embodiment of the "voluptuous torpor" described in *The Leopard*, but is far from unique. In 1982 the palace and its contents were donated to the state by the descendants of the Princes of Lanza Filangri, whose ancestors have lived in the palazzo since the 17th century.

Now a museum (Tue–Fri 9am–6.30pm, Sat–Sun 9am–1pm; charge), the palazzo provides an insight into how a grand family lived and lays bare the eclectic tastes of the Palermitan aristocracy in the 18th century. Below *trompe l'œil* ceilings are Louis

XVI chairs, rustic panelling, heroic tapestries, crib figures and, of course, a personal altar. A chinoiserie salon has lacquered oriental cabinets, porcelain and pagoda-style seats.

St Frances and St Lawrence

A little further along Via Merlo, across from Palazzo Mirto, is **San Francesco d'Assisi ㉘** (daily 7am– 11am, 4.30–6.30pm), one of Palermo's loveliest Gothic churches, its austerity softened by a beautiful portal and delicate rose window. It was damaged during World War II but well restored. The nave (1255–77) is edged with 14th-century chapels and eight statues by Serpotta (1723).

Nearby, on Via Immacolatella, is the **Oratorio di San Lorenzo ㉙** (daily 10am–6pm; charge). The interior is a whimsical yet overwrought extravaganza of stucco by Giacomo Serpotta. The masterpiece is based on the lives of Saints Francis and Lawrence, with every surface awash with cheeky cherubs and lavish allegories. One of Caravaggio's last paintings, a *Nativity*, hung over the altar but was stolen in 1969.

Opposite the church of San Francesco, at 58 Via Paternostro, is **Antica Focacceria di San Lorenzo** *(see page 78)*, a legendary inn with battered bow windows matched by marble slabs and a gleaming brass stove. This period piece has a reputation for rustic snacks like *panini di panelle* (fried chickpea squares) and, an acquired taste, *pani cu' la meusa* (tripe served in a bun). The owner was also the first Palermitan restaurateur to challenge the notion of paying the *pizzo*, extortion money, and won, helping to lend support for the anti-Mafia Addio-pizzo movement *(see page 33)*.

Modern Art Museum

From here, walk to neighbouring Via Sant'Anna and the **GAM ㉚** (Galleria d'Arte Moderna, Tue–Sun 9.30am– 6.30pm, tel: 091 8431605, www.galleriadartemodernapalermo.it).

Set in a lovely Catalan mansion and former convent, this stylish museum covers such movements as neoclassicism and Romanticism, especially through Sicilian art. The museum has the added attraction of a good restaurant.

TIP

"A people who pay the *pizzo* (protection money) are a people without dignity" runs the slogan. Support a good cause by taking home local organic produce (such as wine, chickpeas, sun-dried tomatoes) by shopping at the Bottega dei Sapori (tel: 091 322 023, www.liberaterra.it) on Piazza Castelnuovo 13, Palermo. It's part of Libera Terra, an anti-Mafia association which farms land confiscated from the Mafia *(see page 33)*.

BELOW: banyan tree in Piazza Marina.

A display at the Puppet Museum, where puppet shows are put on throughout the year.

The revitalised seafront

Until very recently, Palermo turned its back on the sea and the stark waterfront was lined with shoddy stalls. But now a 2km (1¼-mile) trail known as the **Passeggiata a Mare**, the promenade along Foro Italico, has brought the locals back to the seafront. Palermitans either stroll along, admiring the headlands and one another, or lounge on funky, marble-clad beds dotted along the shore.

Much of this area was reduced to rubble by Allied bombing during the war, including **Palazzo Butera** ③, eulogised by Goethe. Once Sicily's grandest palace, it is now often used for receptions or as a film set (tel: 091 611 0162). As part of the ongoing regeneration of the waterfront, the council has restored the terraced **Mura delle Cattive** below Palazzo Butera. Decorated with statues, this was nicknamed "Wall of the Nasty Women" in honour of the sour-faced widows and spinsters who once glowered at lovers strolling by. In the 18th century, this was the place for illicit evening assignations on the pretence that the terrace had fine views over the seafront to Monte Pellegrino and that the heat here was less oppressive.

The marina below was Palermo's grand seafront in the heady days of the *belle époque* and was both a public parade and chance for louche encounters. Now known as **Foro Italico**, this area fell into decline until the creation of the promenade. The waterfront walk now features landscaped gardens popular with joggers and sunbathers, and stretches all the way to Villa Giulia and the Orto Botánico, the botanical gardens.

Off Via Butera, in Piazzetta Niscemi, is the Puppet Museum, **Museo Internazionale delle Marionette** ② (Mon–Fri 9am–1pm, 3.30–6.30pm, Sat 9am–1pm; charge), with a collection of around 3,000 puppets from Palermo, Catania and Naples, as well as from Africa and the Far East. Puppet shows are staged there throughout the year, as are children's puppet-making activities.

Instead, off Foro Italico, close to the elegant **Porta Reale** (1786), is **Villa Giulia** (daily summer 8am–8pm, winter 8am–5pm) with an attractive garden and the **Orto Botánico** ③

Leopard changing its spots?

Although endlessly fascinating, Palermo is also gritty, chaotic and fatalistic about the future, so hardly provides the perfect blueprint for urban regeneration. Yet after a long slumber, the city is being revitalised, albeit on a small scale. The celebrated Serpotta oratories have been restored, along with other significant churches and museums, including Palazzo Abatellis, one of the island's major art collections. Churches and museums are being revamped, with the archaeological museum due to reopen shortly. Exotic monuments such as the Palazzina Cinese folly and the Moorish palace of La Zisa have also been restored. Palermo's seafront, for so long neglected, has finally been given back to its citizens, with a proper promenade and gardens. Elsewhere, increased pedestrianisation would bring some peace to the historic centre, but so far there have only been tentative small-scale experiments, as in Via Principe di Belmonte, a popular spot for cocktails. Cautious experiments in hectic areas such as Via Roma have not been expanded. In a city which gave birth to *The Leopard*, a hymn to nostalgia and decadence, it would be foolish to expect a leopard to change its spots, but the leopard is certainly flexing its muscles.

(daily summer 9am–8pm, until 6pm in winter; charge). These delightful botanical gardens are dotted with pavilions, sphinxes and a lily pond and enlivened by bamboo and bougainvillea, banyans and magnolias, pineapples and petticoat palms.

The western suburbs

Beyond the Capo Quarter, off Via Guglielmo Buono, is **Piazza Zisa** and one of the most impressive examples of Arab-Norman secular architecture in Sicily. It is purely Islamic in its inspiration. In Norman times palaces encircled the city "like gold coins around the neck of a bosomy girl", – the vivid description by the Arab poet Ibn Jubayr. None were finer than those in the ruler's private hunting reserves. The poet's words evoke the pleasure dome of **Castello della Zisa** (daily 9am–6.30pm; charge; take the Line B bus there).

Begun in 1160 by William I, and known as La Zisa (from the Arabic for magnificent), this was to be a place of joy and splendour. An Arabic inscription by its entrance conjures up earthly paradise within. The palace later became a fortress and grand residence before returning to its Moorish roots. Now restored, with the Moorish gardens recently reinstated, La Zisa is magnificent once more.

An Arab arch leads to a palace built on the site of a Roman villa so that it could exploit an existing aqueduct. Devoted to water, the Arabs installed a system of canals, feeding water from the aqueduct into a charming fountain in a vaulted vestibule which, in turn, fed a pond outside. In fact, La Zisa's most charming spot is the vestibule, adorned by honeycomb vaults, the fountain and a glorious mosaic of peacocks and huntsmen. On the top floor, the hall was originally an atrium with the side rooms thought to have formed the harem.

South of La Zisa, screened by walls, is **La Cuba** (Mon–Sat 9am–6.30pm, Sun 9am–1pm; charge), the final piece of the Moorish jigsaw. Once domed, this disappointing pavilion lies along Corso Calatafimi, but in Arab times was set in a lake within the luxuriant grounds of La Zisa. In *The Decameron* Boccaccio set a story of illicit love in this "sumptuous villa" which is

EAT

Watermelon custard, *crema di anguria*, is a fragrant Sicilian speciality. The sweet red pulp of watermelon is mixed with a little sugar, corn starch and jasmine water, then heated to a creamy consistency. As it cools, pieces of candied pumpkin and plain chocolate are mixed into the custard. It's served chilled. In Palermo many sweet pastries are filled with this, often called *gelu di miluni*.

BELOW: Orto Botánico.

Art Nouveau frescoes adorn the Villa Igiea, a seaside hotel.

Below: in the Convento dei Cappuccini.

now, although partly restored, a ruin marooned in an army barracks.

The **Convento dei Cappuccini** ㉟ (daily Mar–Oct 9am–1pm, 3–5.30pm, Nov–Feb 9am–noon, 3–5.30pm; charge), the Capuchin friars' convent with its grim catacombs, lies on Via Cappuccini midway between La Cuba and La Zisa. In macabre Sicilian style, corpses of the clergy, nobles, lawyers and the bourgeoisie were mummified here from the 16th century to 1881. In these galleries embalmers have stored over 8,000 dearly departed souls. Many are hung on walls, dressed and grimacing at visitors.

North and Conca d'Oro

Travelling northward towards the chic resort of Mondello, you come to the city outskirts and the legendary "golden shell", the **Conca d'Oro** plain, carved between coast and mountains. This should be carpeted with marigolds and citrus groves, but land speculation and corruption have ensured that Palermo's countryside is mostly encased in concrete, with environmental laws circumnavigated by unscrupulous builders.

Villa Igiea, Palermo's de luxe seaside hotel on the east coast, is a survivor, a fine example of the city's Art Nouveau era. Ernesto Basile, son of the architect of the Teatro Massimo, designed it for the entrepreneurial Florio family who chose this terraced setting overlooking the sea. The Art Nouveau dining room is a harmonious composition of elegant cabinets, functional furnishings and ethereal frescoes.

On the northern outskirts, the road leads to Palermo's park, the former hunting grounds of the **Parco della Favorita** (daily) at the foot of Mount Pellegrino; this was purchased by the exiled Bourbon king Ferdinand in 1799 to make his exile from Naples more bearable. His domineering consort, Maria Carolina, conceived of the **Palazzina Cinese** (daily 10.30am–4.30pm, www.casinacinesepalermo.it) as a Petit Trianon to rival the creation of her sister, Marie Antoinette. Recently restored, this oriental folly combines Chinese decorative motifs with Gothic and Egyptian flourishes.

Next door is **Villa Niscemi** (Sun 9am–12.30pm, Mon–Sat from 9am by arrangement; tel: 091 740 4822), whose fate seems assured as an entertainment centre. The villa was used as Giuseppe di Lampedusa's model for Tancredi's home in *The Leopard*. Owned by a noble family who came to Sicily with the Normans, the villa blends elegance with rustic charm.

Di Lampedusa's own ancestral home, **Villa Lampedusa** (daily 9am–12.30pm), built in 1770 but bought by the Principe around 1845, is also nearby and well signposted. *(For information on how to visit this and other Lampedusa sites, see "On the trail of* The Leopard*", page 131.)*

Also here is the **Museo Etnografico Siciliano Pitrè** (Mon and Fri 4–6pm, Wed–Thur 9am–noon), which houses an ethnographic collection that illustrates Sicilian life, customs and folklore. There are costumes, painted carts, musical instruments and carriages,

including a model of the 18th-century carriage designed to transport a statue of Santa Rosalia *(see right)*.

From the coast, a scenic road climbs Monte Pellegrino, the city's holy mountain, passing citrus groves and shrubland. In the sandstone slopes, the **Grotto di Adduara caves** (closed) have revealed prehistoric drawings carved into the walls. It is a beautiful location, crowded at weekends with cars and picnickers. From the terraced slopes, sweeping views span the bay of the Conca d'Oro.

On the mountainside the **Santuario Santa Rosalia** (currently closed) is a shrine to Palermo's revered patron saint. According to legend, Rosalia renounced the world on the death of her father, becoming a religious recluse in this hermitage, where she died in 1166. In 1624, while Palermo was in the throes of a deadly plague, Rosalia appeared to a visitor on the mountain asking him to search for her remains in the cave and give her a Christian burial. Her grave found, she was disinterred and her relics carried in procession into Palermo where the plague miraculously ceased. Such was the spread of religious devotion to her that within a year a chapel with its cavern sanctuary was established in her honour, a place of pilgrimage. Mountain views and souvenir stalls are the additional rewards for trailing up to this sanctuary.

Mondello

Set in the lee of Monte Pellegrino is the fashionable resort of **Mondello** ㊱, easily reached from Palermo by bus from Viale della Libertà. The resort, pioneered by the Bourbons, began as a tuna-fishing village but was turned into a garden suburb in the 1890s and reached its heyday in the interwar years. Even if the Art Nouveau villas are now engulfed by ribbon development, Mondello has a certain charm. It remains a popular meeting place for Palermitans who come to the lido to swim, socialise and dine on fresh fish.

The centre of attraction is the striking Art Nouveau pier. Other attractions are slight but seductive, from summer sea breezes to a ruined medieval watchtower, as well as cool beach clubs and the chic Alle Terrazze restaurant on the pier: Palermo at its most docile.   ❏

The Museo Pitrè contains the towering 18th-century Carrozza di Santa Rosalia, which was towed by teams of mules through Palermo's streets on 15 July, the feast day of Santa Rosalia. On board were garlanded maidens, musicians with their instruments and, beneath a cupola surrounded by winged angels, a huge statue of the saint.

BELOW: Mondello at night.

Isola delle Femmine and Terrasini

Further along the coast, away from Mondello on the A29, are two more resorts. Isole delle Femmine is best avoided. It may face an island of the same name, but is surrounded by an industrial zone and the sea is often polluted. Terrasini, however, overlooks the Golfo di Castellamare and is a former fishing village with sandy beaches and clean sea. It has three museums: Antiquarium (Piazza Falcone-Borsellino) with ancient finds from the sea, Museo Etnografico (Via Carlo Alberto della Chiesa) with a folklore collection and Museo di Storia Naturale (Via Cala Rossa), a natural history museum. (Usually open all year, Mon–Sat 9am–12.30pm.)

BEST RESTAURANTS, BARS AND CAFÉS

Prices for a three-course dinner per person and a half-bottle of house wine:
€ = under €20
€€ = €20–35
€€€ = €35–70
€€€€ = over €70

Palermo

Sicilian chefs used to be snapped up by starry establishments abroad, but many of today's culinary talents are now showcasing their talents at home. Although the real culinary renaissance is in the southeast of the island, Palermo's restaurants are increasingly creative while remaining true to themselves. Even so, many still fall into the categories of "fancy" or "folkloristic". Around Piazza Marina, the shabby-chic La Kalsa Quarter has a range of distinctive bars and restaurants. The best street snacks (see page 9) are also in the wider historic area, including the Ballarò and Vucciria markets, so make sure you try these. In summer, the dining scene moves to the beach at Mondello.

Al Covo de' i Beati Paoli
Piazza Marina 50
Tel: 091 616 6634
www.alcovodeibeatipaoli.com €€
With tables set out on Palermo's prettiest piazza, this is a pleasant spot in summer. The pizzas are good, but service can be slow. Dinner only.

Al Santa Caterina
Corso Vittorio Emanuele 256
Tel: 091 662 9018 €€
Varied menu, including good pizzas. Book a balcony table overlooking the Corso. Closed Wed.

Antica Focacceria San Francesco
Via Paternostro 58
Tel: 091 320 264
www.afsf.it €
Not to everyone's taste but it is quaint, boisterous (especially at lunch) and rough and ready. The place for trippa (tripe), arancine, panini and focaccia. It does also serve "non-street" food, but that would be missing the point. Closed Tue Oct–May.

Antico Caffè Spinnato
Via Principe di Belmonte 107 €
In a chic, pedestrianised zone, this is where the smart set gather for aperitivi. The Spinnato group are known for their superb ice creams, cassata and cannoli served here and at **Al Pinguino** (Via Ruggiero Settimo 86) and **Il Golosone** (Piazza Castelnuovo 22).

A'Vucciria
Via dei Chiavettieri 7
Tel: 091 331 127 €€
Excellent seafood served in the heart of the market. Also try the pasta specials, especially spaghetti a'vucciria. By Piazza Marina. Closed Thur.

Basile
Via Bara 76
Tel: 091 335 628 €
Near the Teatro Massimo, this lunch-only place is chaotic but good value. Choose from a range of daily, mainly meaty specials, then pay at the counter and collect your meal. Closed Sun.

Biondo
Via Carducci 15
Tel: 091 583 662 €€
Warm and welcoming trattoria. Best known for its mushroom dishes when in season. Closed Wed and Aug.

La Cambusa
Piazza Marina 16
Tel: 091 584 574 €€
A recently refurbished restaurant passionate about serving the freshest seafood.

Cocoa
Porta Chiesa dei Cocchieri
Tel: 091 252 5602 €€
A refreshing change from hardcore Palermitan street food, as these dishes are distinctly light and ungutsy yet still typical. A sophisticated jazz ambience.

Cucina Papoff
Via Isidoro La Lumia 32
Tel: 091 586 460
www.cucinapapoff.com €€€
Refined yet imaginative Sicilian cuisine in an Art Nouveau setting. Friendly atmosphere. Try the fish and u maccu, broad beans with fennel. Closed Sat lunch, Sun and Aug.

Gigi Mangia
Via Principe di Belmonte 104
Tel: 091 587 651 €€
Trattoria with delicatessen (that delivers food and wine worldwide). Patronised for its delicious vegetarian appetisers and Il colonnello va a Favignana, a pasta dish with tomatoes, herbs and bottarga (tuna roe). Closed Sun.

GourmArt
Piazza Sant'Anna 21
Tel: 091 843 1608 €€
Inside the Modern Art Gallery (GAM), the museum restaurant goes to town on fish, including seafood salad.

Kursaal Kalhesa
Foro Umberto I 21
Tel: 091 616 2282
www.kursaalkalhesa.it €€
An exotic night out at this special restaurant, wine bar, bookshop and concert venue in the heart of the Kalsa. In the upstairs restaurant tuck into the Arab-tinged fusion food. Downstairs, prop up the bar with cool young Palermitani, or sip Nero d'Avola in the garden, where the heady perfume of night-blooming jasmine fills the air. Open Tue–Fri, noon–3pm, 6pm–1.30am; Sat–Sun noon–1.30am.

Osteria dei Vespri
Piazza Croce dei Vespri 6
Tel: 091 617 1631

www.osteriadeivespri.it. €€€
A Michelin-starred spot in a lovely sheltered square, with outdoor tables in summer. The cooking is creative Italian, matched by a superb wine list. Closed Sun.

Peppe Giuffre'
Rinascente
Via Roma 255
Tel: 091 601 7881 €–€€
Mediterranean cooking in the rooftop food hall of the stylish new Rinascente department store. Also Obik, a mozzarella bar. Food hall open daily until midnight.

Le Pergamene
Piazza Marina 48
Tel: 091 616 6142 €€
Reliable restaurant serving meat, fish, varied antipasti and pizzas.

Primavera
Piazza Bologni 4
Tel: 091 329 408 €€
Set close to the cathedral, with tables on the piazza. Traditional fare, with pasta con le sarde (fresh sardines), pasta con i broccoli and grilled calamari. Closed Sun dinner and Mon.

Questione di Gusto
Via Principe di Scordia 104
Tel: 091 328 318 €€€
Bustling trattoria near the market, hence excellent antipasti (especially roasted vegetables) and fresh fish. Spaghetti vongole e cozze (with mussels and clams) is recommended, as are the grilled meats. Closed Fri.

Regine
Via Trápani 4
Tel: 091 586 566
regine@ristoranteregine.it €€€€
Sicilian specialities abound, especially the antipasti (look for peperoni ripieni alla palermitana, stuffed sweet peppers Palermo-style). Closed Sun and Aug.

Santandrea
Piazza Sant'Andrea 4
Tel: +334 999
www.ristorantesantandrea.eu €€€
Set a stone's throw from the Vucciria market in the lively Kalsa area, this gourmet trattoria is perfect for an alfresco dinner. Try the seafood antipasti feast and the pasta dishes, notably the pappardelle with capon, artichokes and fennel. Service is hit and miss. Evenings only. Closed Sun.

La Scuderia
Viale del Fante 9
Tel: 091 520 323
www.lascuderia.snc.it €€€€
An established and popular spot in the Parco della Favorita, praised for its mastery of Sicilian cuisine. Closed Sun and Aug.

Tonnara Bordonaro
Tel: 091 637 2267
www.kursaaltonnara.it €€
Set in a converted tuna fishery in Arenella, on the edge of town, this is an inviting spot in summer, with a boat-shaped bar in the courtyard and a restaurant that embraces a lovely terrace and sea views. Try the risotto, tuna or swordfish carpaccio. Live music.

With its Liberty villas and lidos, the seaside resort of Mondello has a fashionable summer dining scene. Most trattorie have outdoor terraces with sea views.

Addaura Reef
Lungomare Cristoforo Colombo 3021
Tel: 091 455 167
www.addaurareef.com €€
On the coastal road west of Palermo, out towards Mondello, this is where cool Palermitani come to get a tan and take a dip. By day, enjoy a Med-fusion lunch. As dusk falls, the cool beach bar becomes even cooler, with cocktails and grazing on the sushi and sashimi buffet. Open May–Sept daily, 9am–late.

Bye Bye Blues
Via del Garofalo 23
Tel: 091 684 1415
info@byebyeblues.it €€
On the road into Mondello, this place is known for the freshest produce, especially fish, so do book. Closed Tue and Nov.

Charleston le Terrazze
Via Regina Elena
Tel: 091 450 171 €€€€
Set in an Art Nouveau beach establishment, this gracious spot is particularly good for fish. Book ahead. Closed Wed Nov–Apr and early Jan–early Feb.

Trattoria Sympaty
Via Piano di Gallo 18
Tel: 091 454 470 €€€
A charming trattoria with a nautical theme; showcases fish and seafood. Closed Fri at dinner and end Nov–mid-Dec.

Primafila
Via Saputo 8
Tel: 091 868 4422 €€€
Welcoming establishment close to the waterfront. Tables outside. Traditional Sicilian fare. Closed Mon and Nov.

La Ruota
Via Lungomare
Tel: 091 868 5108 €€
A trattoria with grilled fish as its speciality. Open all year.

RIGHT: fish dish from Charleston le Terrazze.

A FLOWERING OF FLAMBOYANCE

The earthquake of 1693 wiped the architectural slate clean in many Sicilian cities and gave free rein to the new, ornate tastes of the ruling class

The Baroque of the 18th century was a golden age for Sicilian architecture, a tantalising game of silhouettes and perspectives, an opportunity for wild ornamentation, with sculpted cornices, fanciful balconies and flowing staircases.

Roberto Ando, the Palermitan film director, believes Baroque as "a paradigm of Sicily – tortuous, eccentric, secretive, the endless search for a form".

In Palermo, *spagnolismo*, the love of ostentation, found its natural soulmate in baroque taste. Urban planning led to grandiose squares and fancy streets. Convents, churches and oratories sprang up in the historic centre, and city palazzi competed for attention. Balconies and cornices were adorned with angels, nymphs, gargoyles and grimacing monsters.

The capital's church of San Giuseppe dei Teatini exudes a Baroque spirit, as does the stucco-encrusted Immacolata and the well-restored Casa Professa. As for palaces, Palermo boasts Palazzo Mirto, both a Baroque world and a showcase to the Sicilian nobility.

In Bagheria, villas acquired opulent staircases and marble-encrusted ballrooms. The distinguished Baroque cities of Ragusa and Módica indulged in spatial experiment, theatrical vistas flanked by flights of steps. In Noto, Baroque meant spaciousness, symmetry and loftiness. It is a stage set of a city, sculpted in golden stone, exuding a sense of *joie de vivre*.

ABOVE: marble carving of a cherub in the church of Santa Chiara, Noto.

RIGHT: statue of San Marziano on the Duomo, Siracusa; he was the first bishop of the city.

Above: the ceiling of Il Gesù, Sicily's first Jesuit church, is decorated in flamboyant Baroque style.

THE PLASTER MASTER

Giacomo Serpotta, born in Palermo in 1656, was a genius in stucco, who elevated Sicilian plasterwork from a craft to an art. His most breathtaking creations can be seen today in several of Palermo's well-restored oratories.

In the Vucceria market area, itself a manifestation of the restless Baroque spirit, Serpotta's lavish Oratorio del Rosario di San Domenico combines frothy statues of the Virtues with a joyful abundance of capering cherubs. The neighbouring Oratorio di Santa Cita is another masterwork. A host of exuberant angels and cherubs clamber over walls and window frames; allegorical statues seem to float in space, while an intricate stucco panel depicting a sea battle in relief employs metal wire for the ships' rigging. Closer to Piazza Marina, Serpotta's Oratorio di San Lorenzo has a fragile beauty bordering on the overblown, every creamy surface festooned with allegorical stucco figures.

Plan your independent (or guided) Serpotta tour online, through the association that manages the Serpotta masterpieces (www.tesoridellaloggia. it, tel. 091 843 1605, oratories open mornings only).

Right: the dazzling concave-convex exterior of San Giovanni in Scicli is matched by an equally impressive interior. The whole town of Scicli, in Ragusa province, is a Baroque gem.

Above: detail from the Fountain of Orion in Messina, sculpted by Giovanni Angelo Montorsoli in 1547.

PALERMO PROVINCE

Leave the bustling capital to explore Monreale's glittering Arab-Norman cathedral, the remote Madonie mountains, the brooding heartland that was home to the Mafia, and the island of Ustica

utside **Palermo ❶** is a province of extreme light and shade, of exuberant festivals and shimmering cathedrals. This was once the Mafia heartland, with gulleys and mountain lairs nurtured by the mythology of banditry and poverty. Now, as the small towns begin to flourish again, the spiritual isolation that made this a wild province is evaporating.

Monreale

These remote rural pockets feel far away from the Moorish voluptuousness and sophistication of **Monreale ❷**, 8km (5 miles) from the capital. In the words of a Sicilian proverb: "He who goes to Palermo without seeing Monreale leaves a donkey and comes back an ass."

Certainly, its sumptuous cathedral is the apogee of Arab-Norman art. The **Duomo di Monreale** (summer Mon–Sat 8am–6pm, Sun 8am–10am, 3.30–5.30pm, winter Mon–Sat 8am–12.30pm, Sun 8am–10am, 3.30–5.30pm) and Benedictine monastery were built by William II, *c.*1183, on a hill overlooking the Conca d'Oro. Flanked by square bell towers, the cathedral dedicated to the Assump-

tion is not instantly awe-inspiring, yet its details are exquisite. An arched 18th-century Romanesque portal frames a greenish bronze door decorated with Biblical scenes by Bonanno da Pisa (1185). The portal displays sculpted bands of garlands, figures and beasts alternating with multicoloured mosaics. To the left, a Gagini porch shelters another bronze door, by Barisano da Trani (1179), inspired by the delicacy of Byzantine inlaid ivory. The apses are Sicily's most opulent: interlacing

Main attractions

MONREALE
   (DUOMO DI MONREALE)
PIANA DEGLI ALBANESI
CORLEONE
SOLUNTO
VILLA PALAGONIA (BAGHERIA)
CASTELLO DI CÁCCAMO
CEFALÙ
PARCO REGIONALE
   DELLE MADONIE
   (MADONIE MOUNTAINS)
CASTELBUONO
USTICA

LEFT AND RIGHT: cloisters and interior of the stunning 12th-century cathedral at Monreale.

Column detail in Monreale.

limestone and lava arches, sculpted as delicately as wood.

Monreale drew craftsmen from Persia, Africa, Asia, Greece, Venice, Pisa and Provence. The glistening gold interior fuses Arab purity of volume with Byzantine majesty. The shimmering (restored) mosaics are unequalled anywhere.

In the apse the *Christ Pantocrator*, about 6 metres (20ft) tall, is an authoritarian God presiding over the Madonna, angels and saints. Look for Thomas à Becket, who entered sainthood after Henry II of England had him murdered. (Henry was William's father-in-law.) Above the royal throne is a mosaic of *Christ Crowning William the Good*, a tribute to the king whose world embraced concubines, eunuchs and black slaves. Other delights include Cosmati paving, Roman capitals incorporating busts of Ceres and Proserpine, and a gilded ceiling whose rafters resemble the spines of beautifully bound books.

The garden cloisters (daily 9am–6.30pm; charge) express William's love of Islamic art and are the most sumptuous 12th-century cloisters in the world. Every second pair of white marble columns has a vivid zigzag mosaic pattern spiralling up the shaft. Many sculptures echo the mosaics but add a personal note, including the name of a mason, or musicians playing Sicilian instruments. The *Allegory of the Seasons*, an enchanting marble composition, depicts tree-planting and pig-killing. In one corner, a loggia creates a chiaroscuro effect with a glorious, slightly phallic fountain. Shaped like a palm tree trunk, the shaft is crowned by lions' heads.

After raucous Palermo, Monreale exudes provincial calm, and while the town is probably an anticlimax after seeing the cathedral's mosaics, a stroll offers a chance to savour the pedestrianised centre, with its crumbling Baroque churches and shops selling ceramics or fine ices. The **Chiesa del**

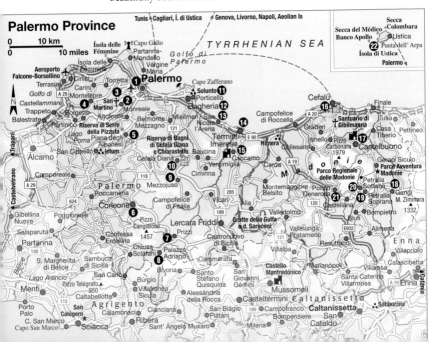

Palermo Province

Monte has stuccowork by Serpotta while the church of **Madonna delle Croci**, set higher on the hill, offers a last lingering view from the cathedral to the coast.

Bandit country

In the lushly mountainous landscape towards **Boccadifalco** is the hill resort of **San Martino delle Scale** with the Benedictine **Abbazia di San Martino** ❸ (Mon–Sat 9am–noon, 4.30–6.30pm, Sun 9–11am, 5–6.30pm). Reputed to have been founded by St Gregory the Great in the 6th century, the abbey was destroyed and rebuilt a number of times over the centuries. Now part convent, part school, it is known for its monumental staircase, monastic library and 18th-century paintings, including Marabitti's *St Martin and the Beggar*. The surrounding pine forests are a cool escape in summer.

A short distance away is **Montelepre** ❹, of which John Addington Symonds wrote in 1873: "The talk was brigands and nothing but brigands." This was especially true on the eve of World War II, when the tragic outlaw and local folk hero Salvatore Giuliano reigned over these desolate crags. If Mafia chroniclers are correct, this is still bandit country, and beyond the boulder-strewn countryside little seems to have changed since Giuliano's day. The medieval heart of Montelepre remains enmeshed by scruffy alleys and courtyards coiled around the Chiesa Madre.

Neighbouring **Partinico** is a byword for urban poverty. In the 1950s Danilo Dolci, known as Sicily's Gandhi because of his dedication to the poor, chose benighted western Sicily to set up his centres in an attempt to improve local conditions and expose the power of the Mafia. His work undimmed, he died unnoticed in poverty in 1997.

Piana degli Albanesi ❺, along the SS624, appears suspended above a lake. Lush pastures are encircled by hills, once home to 15th-century Albanian settlers. The community moved here in 1488 after Turkish troops invaded their homeland. Since then, generations have kept their customs and Orthodox faith in this cheerful town. Marriages and funerals, Epiphany and Easter are times for Byzantine rites leavened with enough folklore to draw visitors in. The community speaks Albanian at home; signs are in Albanian as well as Italian. Local cuisine is a cultural stew: *stranghuie* (gnocchi), *brumie me bathé e thieré*, a filling bean casserole, or *dash*, castrated ram, Albanian-Greek style.

It was at Portella della Ginestra, just above the artificial lake of **Lago Piana degli Albanesi**, that Salvatore Giuliano gunned down 11 Piana citizens in 1947. Whether Giuliano was forced to shoot by the Mafia or was deceived by his own treacherous lieutenant is still unclear.

Corleone

Corleone ❻, perched along the rural SS118, is enfolded in desolate hills and high verdant plains, is

Two very different movies relate the story of the local bandit Salvatore Giuliano. Michael Cimino's 1987 The Sicilian embraces the romantic "Robin Hood" view. But Francesco Rosi's 1962 documentary-style Salvatore Giuliano offers much greater insight into the social and political forces of the late 1940s.

BELOW: Monreale's cloisters.

TIP

Don't waste time in Corleone trying to follow in the footsteps of the Corleone clan in *The Godfather* movies. The town was too developed by the early 1970s for director Francis Ford Coppola's taste and the Sicilian scenes were shot in Sávoca *(see page 247)*.

dominated by the Castello, a rocky outcrop topped by a Saracen tower. A prison until 1976, it is now home to Franciscan friars who take their vow of poverty seriously. Below, the rooftops are stacked in a chromatic range of greys. At first sight, Corleone fails to live up to its infamous reputation as the cradle of the Mafia. It was from here, after all, that Mafia boss Toto Riina ruled before moving to Palermo where he went into hiding until his arrest in 1993. Bravely, the town has changed the name of its central piazza to Falcone-Borsellino, to honour the anti-Mafia magistrates gunned down by the Mafia. It also opened a **Mafia Museum** in 2000 – far more of a neutral documentation centre than a Disneyland experience. The town was established in 1237 and its **Chiesa Madre** contains 16th–17th-century wooden statues and stalls.

To the southeast lies the medieval town of **Prizzi** ❼ with its sloping chequerboard of rust-tiled roofs. The town is celebrated for its bizarre traditional Easter festival known as the *ballo dei diavoli* (dance of the devils). Dating back to Sicani times,

the dance depicts the eternal struggle between Good and Evil, winter and spring, Christianity and paganism. The gap-toothed devil masks are primitive but menacing, while the atmosphere of ritualised violence appears to echo Mafia lore.

The neighbouring village of **Palazzo Adriano** ❽, 10km (6 miles) southwest, encapsulates the rivalries of these provincial backwaters. Two sombre churches share the main square in mutual antipathy: the Orthodox **Santa Maria dell'Assunta** scorns the Catholic **Santa Maria del Lume**. Ironically, the square starred in the warmly evocative movie *Cinema Paradiso*. From here, the route back to the coast passes the hilltop village of **Mezzojuso** ❾, snug in the Ficuzza woods. Like many others, the village has mixed Albanian and Arab ancestry and religious frictions. **Annunziata**, the Catholic church, is overshadowed by the Orthodox **San Nicola**, home to lovely Byzantine icons.

Nearby, **Santa Maria delle Grazie** houses frescoes and the finest iconostasis in Sicily, while the adjoining monastery displays precious Greek

BELOW: view of Corleone.

manuscripts and miniatures. **Cefalà Diana** ⑩, just north, is firmly in the Arab camp, with a tumbledown castle and the island's best-preserved Moorish bathhouse.

East of Palermo

From the capital to Cefalù, the coast curves past fishing villages and coves to Capo Zafferano and the ruins at **Solunto** ⑪ (Mon–Sat 9am–5.30pm, Sun 9am–1pm; closed Mon; charge). Set on majestic cliffs, the ruins are less impressive than the wild location. The solitary ruins were originally Solus, one of the earliest Phoenician trading posts on the island, until destroyed by Dionysius of Siracusa in 398 BC as he tried to clear Sicily of all non-Greeks. Later, it was taken by invading Carthaginians who invited Greeks to return, thus Hellenising the settlement. Then in the First Punic War, in 254 BC, it fell to Rome, only to be abandoned during the 3rd century AD. The highlights among the extensive ruins are the floor mosaics (including Leda and the Swan) and a luxurious villa dwelling with a colonnaded peristyle. From the *agora* there are stunning views of the Casteldaccia vineyards, an ancient castle and the coastal resort of Cefalù. Beyond the wizened olive trees and battered boulders are charming swimming spots near the lighthouse on the cape. **Porticello**, on the shore just below Solunto, is a straggling fishing village popular with Palermitans for a seafood Sunday lunch.

Bagheria

Just inland is **Bagheria** ⑫, 15km (9 miles) from Palermo, which developed during the *Ottocento* (19th-century) vogue for ostentatious summer villas surrounded by orange trees but declined during the 20th century due to unbridled land speculation. These patrician villas are mostly in late Renaissance style, with grand staircases and a central body flanked by sweeping concave wings. The U-shaped

lower wings were reserved for servants, with underground chambers (*stanze del scirocco*) used by the patricians as retreats from the humid summer heat. The villas were encircled by French formal gardens.

While views of cement works often mar the pastoral idyll, some villas are pitiful wrecks, others retain their grandeur. A fine example is **Villa Cattolica** (Tue–Sun, summer 9am–1pm, 3–7pm; closed Mon). Built around 1737, it houses the **Museo Guttoso**, a bizarre collection of contemporary paintings and the tomb of Renato Guttoso (1912–87), one of Sicily's best-known modern painters. A sculptor friend made him a surreal blue tomb to match the sky, a capsule of kitsch among the cactus and lemons.

But the strangest villa of all is the **Villa Palagonia** (daily 9am–1pm, 3.30–5.30pm; www.villapalagonia.it) (*see box page 88*).

Términi Imerese

Further east, 8km (5 miles) outside Términi Imerese, is **San Nicola l'Arena** ⑬, a picturesque fishing village with a 15th-century crenellated

The Saracen castle at Cefalù was an important stronghold on the Palermo–Agrigento road.

BELOW: ruins at Solunto.

Stirring statue of Giuseppe la Masa in Términi Imerese.

castle overlooking the harbour. Now a nightclub, the castle belongs to aristocrats from Palermo. Beside it is a solid brick *tonnara* (tuna fishery), a reminder that the coast was devoted to tuna fishing until recently.

Términi Imerese 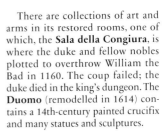 itself is an unfortunate jumble of industry, resort and classical ruins. However, the upper town remains fairly unspoilt, with a 17th-century **cathedral** (the statue of Jesus in one of the chapels has real hair) and the **Museo Civico** (Tue–Sat 9am–1pm, 4–6.30pm, Sun 9am–1pm), which has an art collection and archaeological finds. Just east of town is an impressive Roman aqueduct set in a wild olive grove.

Inland is **Cáccamo** 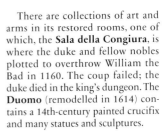, a dramatic 12th-century castle (daily 9am–1pm, 3–7pm; charge), one of the most important Norman strongholds in western Sicily and undoubtedly the province's best-preserved castle. It was the base of the local dukes of Cáccamo until sold to the Region in 1963. The towers, battlements and ramparts look convincingly medieval, even if parts were redesigned during the Baroque period.

There are collections of art and arms in its restored rooms, one of which, the **Sala della Congiura**, is where the duke and fellow nobles plotted to overthrow William the Bad in 1160. The coup failed; the duke died in the king's dungeon. The **Duomo** (remodelled in 1614) contains a 14th-century painted crucifix and many statues and sculptures.

Himera

The site of ancient **Himera** (daily 9am–6pm, charge), founded as a colony of Zancle (Messina) in 648 BC, is nearby, east of Términi Imerese, in an industrial zone near Buonfornello. Himera was the scene of the 480 BC defeat of the Carthaginians by Theron of Agrigento and his brother Gelon of Siracusa, when the advance of the Carthaginian leader Hamilcar, determined to rid Sicily of all Greeks, was thwarted. Hamilcar perished in the defeat but in 409 BC his son Hannibal returned with a stronger force and devastated the city. There are ruins of a Doric temple and traces of houses, as well as an extensive museum containing findings from the site.

Villa Palagonia

This villa, built in 1715 by Tommaso Maria Napoli, is famous for its crumbling interior with cracked mirrors and its garden full of grotesque statues of monsters, dwarfs, tormented souls and fantastic animals. Most, it is said, were created by the surreal imagination of the wealthy Prince Palagonia and are said to represent his faithless wife's lovers. Beside the main entrance, two gargoyles with gaping mouths were used to extinguish the footmen's torches. A flamboyant double staircase ascends to the *piano nobile*, with the salon's mirrored ceiling representing the sky. Engraved over the door is the message: "Mirror yourself in these crystals and contemplate the image of human frailty."

Cefalù

A return to the coast at **Cefalù** ⓰ is a chance to visit the province's great counterpoint to Monreale Cathedral. Sitting snugly below the massive hill of **La Rocca**, Cefalù is the west coast's rival to Taormina. The consensus is that, although Taormina has better hotels, nightlife, sophistication and atmosphere, Cefalù is equally picturesque, but more peaceful, family-friendly and better-provided with beaches. What's more, the resort makes a safe haven from which to explore gritty Palermo.

The cathedral, or **Duomo** (daily 8am–noon, 3.30–6.30pm), was built in 1131 by Roger II with a bold twin-towered façade and a triple apse with blind arcading. (The king confidently had a porphyry sarcophagus made for himself, but he and the sarcophagus are now in Palermo Cathedral as he died before this cathedral was completed.) Inside, a severe nave is flanked by 16 ancient columns with Roman capitals surmounted by Gothic arches. A sense of majesty is created by the concentration of other-worldly mosaics in the presbytery and over the altar. A superbly compassionate *Christ Pantocrator* in the apse holds an open book with Greek and Latin Biblical text (John 8:12): "I am the light of the world, he who follows me will not walk in darkness." Other highlights are the Norman font and the open-timber roofs which bear traces of the original Arab-Norman paintings.

Out of season, **Piazza del Duomo** is a delightful suntrap with a view of the cathedral at the foot of steep cliffs running up to the fortifications. The square is also framed by the Corso, a Renaissance seminary and a porticoed **palazzo**. Here, the Caffè Duomo is the place for an *aperitivo*. Cefalù's **old port,** tangibly Moorish and home to Tunisian fishermen, has been a backdrop in countless films, including *Cinema Paradiso*.

A warren of alleys leads west from **Corso Ruggero** and reveals Renaissance facades, Gothic parapets and mullioned windows overlooking tiny courtyards. An underground spring bubbles up in the arcaded Arab baths, sited at the bottom of curved steps. **Via Porto Salvo** passes

TIP

Cefalù makes an appealing base for exploring the Madonie Park on its doorstep, but for more of a sense of the mountains and the gentle pace of life, stay around Castelbuono (see page 91).

BELOW: Términi Imerese.

Cefalù Cathedral dominates the town.

BELOW: Cefalù beach.

battered churches and flourishing craft shops. In summer, the town is a delightful tourist trap with quaint craft boutiques selling ceramics and gold jewellery, matched by sophisticated restaurants. **Porta Pescare**, one of the surviving medieval gates, opens onto a creek, beach and boatyard. In the evening, the seafront, bastion and Corso become a parade devoted to the dual pleasures of a *passeggiata* and a *gelato*.

From Piazza Duomo, a steepish hill leads down to **Museo Mandralisca** (daily 9.30am–12.30pm, 3.30–7pm; charge). Apart from several Madonnas, this is a dusty collection, except for Antonello da Messina's *Portrait of an Unknown Man* (*c.*1460). The painting once served as a door to a pharmacy cabinet on the island of Lipari where an assistant, unnerved by the sneering expression, scratched the unknown man's face.

Above the medieval town is **Rocca**, where the original Arab town was sited, with sweeping views over Cefalù and the sea. After the Norman conquest in 1063, the populace left the looming crags for the port below.

Salita Saraceno leads up three tiers of city walls to the restored fortifications of the crumbling stone castle, revealing traces of a pool, fountain, cistern and prison. Nearby is the so-called **Tempio di Diana**, *c.*4th century BC, built over an earlier cistern.

The Madonie mountains

Cefalù is the gateway to the delightful Madonie mountains and their designated regional park, the **Parco Regionale delle Madonie** (tel: 0921 684 011; www.parcodellemadonie.it). Thanks to tourism based on outdoor pursuits like hiking and horse-riding, the Madonie region has largely escaped grinding poverty and rural emigration. In summer, well-signposted *agriturismi* (farmstays) make an appealing way of exploring the area.

Compared with the neighbouring Nebrodi mountains, the **Monti Madonie** range is higher (Pizzo Carbonara 1,979 metres/6,495ft), more accessible and more open to tourism. Unlike a lot of Sicily, the Madonie range has not been scarred by deforestation or urban blight. **Piano Cervi** and **Monte San Salvatore** are riddled with aqueducts and streams. Majestic firs have grown on these rugged ridges since the Ice Age and were used to create the roof of Monreale Cathedral. In the remoter regions, wild cats and eagles still roam.

Drives in the Madonie mountains tend to be off-the-beaten-track adventures to lofty medieval villages straight out of a Sicilian Spaghetti Western. Fortunately, the hairpin bends tend to end in a Slow Food inn or in the perfect spot for a picnic. Yet unlike most Sicilian regional parks, the Madonie are pretty accessible without a car, and trails are better marked than elsewhere, with buses running from Cefalù, Castelbuono and Petralia. Cefalù makes the best base for beach-lovers, but otherwise the Madonie villages are some of the prettiest in Sicily, and well-suited to pony-trekking too. But to explore fully, a car is best. For tours, contact the **Parco delle Madonie** directly *(see tip right)*.

Rural route

After Cefalù, coastal olive groves give way to pine woods and valleys before the venerated sanctuary of **Gibilmanna** comes into view. The 16th-century **Capuchin monastery** contains an underrated museum of rural life and sacred art (daily, summer 9.30am–12.30pm, 3.30–7pm, winter 9am–1pm, 3–5pm).

Isnello, 7km (4 miles) south, a winter ski resort, has a ruined Byzantine castle overlooking majolica-encrusted spires and limestone cliffs.

A vastly superior feudal castle towers over **Castelbuono** ⊕, 12km (7 miles) east, a civilised, prosperous, well-kept place that could be mistaken for Tuscany. Castelbuono lobbied successfully to be an exit point from the Palermo–Messina motorway. As such, it is reaping the benefits in the weekend influx of visitors drawn to the lively atmosphere, well-restored

churches and welcoming restaurants. The 15th-century castle (Tue–Sun 9am–1pm, 4–8pm; charge) is austere but with a pleasant chapel.

The rural route follows the SS286 south to **Geraci Siculo** (22km/14 miles) and then winds up to **Gangi** ⊕, a tortoise-shaped town with a crumbling watchtower that is now a hard-working rural centre. On the second Sunday in August, in a custom dating back to the days of Demeter, sheaves of wheat tied with red ribbons decorate the streets for a harvest celebration, the *Sagra della Spiga*.

More surreally Sicilian is the sight awaiting unsuspecting visitors to Gangi's parish church. The **Chiesa Madre** now displays a crypt of the village's finest mummifed priests (Sun only 10am–noon, 4–6.30pm).

Petralia Soprana

Follow the SS120 west and the jagged skyline of **Petralia Soprana** ⊕ comes into view. This seemingly prosperous town, set on a spur, has covered passageways leading to a belvedere with bracing views, marred only by a vast car park on stilts. The **Chiesa Madre**

TIP

A day trip offered by travel agents from Palermo and Cefalù visits mountain enclaves and fortified villages linked to the feudal Ventimiglia dynasty. There are also buses from Cefalù to the towns and villages. A car is best, however. For tours contact the **Ente Parco delle Madonie**, Corso Ruggero 116 (tel: 0921 684 011; www.parco dellemadonie.it).

BELOW: village perched on a ridge in the Madonie mountains.

The Sicilian Alps

Known as "the Sicilian Alps", the Madonie offer some of the island's more accessible walking country, matched by some of the best rural inns. Hiking through the foothills of the Madonie mountains means limestone trails scuffed by wild boar and views over vertiginous slopes to the Tyrrhenian Sea. Every inviting hamlet seems to have its own precipitous hillside, ruined Norman fortress and luminous Madonna. Walkers tread paths dotted with porcupine quills en route through woodlands of cork and holm oak, myrtle and beech. For company, there are grazing goats, soaring eagles, lizards on sun-baked rocks, peregrine falcons and wizened peasants in flat caps.

was built in the 1300s by the Ventimiglia family. Half-hidden down alleys are striking mansions and watchtowers.

Petralia Sottana  (the lower town), nestling in the wooded hillside, also exudes a quiet ease. Now a mountain resort, this former Norman citadel has Romanesque, Gothic and Baroque churches. The **Chiesa Matrice** is perched on a *belvedere* and swathed in mist; inside is a precious Arabian candelabra.

Families might want to head to an exciting adventure playground nearby. Set in the Madonie, it's known as the **Parco Avventura Madonie** (Località Gorgonero, Petralia Sottana, tel: 0921 856 253; daily 9am–6.30pm year-round but call to book Oct–May; www.parcoavventuramadonie.it).

The road west to **Polizzi Generosa** passes *masserie*, feudal farmsteads that were as self-sufficient as most villages. The **Chiesa Madre** has a 16th-century Flemish triptych and Venetian organ. Polizzi is a trekking centre which, in season, sustains walkers with pasta and asparagus (*pasta cu l'asparaci*).

Petralia Sottana rises out of the misty Madonie mountains.

BELOW: in Castelbuono.

From here, the fast A19 returns to the coast, as does the winding route via the ski resort of **Piano Battaglia**.

Ustica

The lovely island of **Ustica** ⓩ, 60km (37 miles) from Palermo, is connected daily to the city by hydrofoil and ferry services (1 hour and 2½ hours respectively) and can be visited on a day trip. It is extremely popular with swimmers and nature-lovers, but serious divers or underwater photographers will choose to make the island their base.

Ustica is Sicily's best-established and best-preserved marine reserve. The rugged coastline is riddled with caverns and coves, partly accessible along coastal paths, and below its clear waters is an explosion of colour and life that includes corals, sea sponges and anemones as well as barracuda, bream, scorpion fish and groupers.

The volcanic, black, turtle-shaped island turns itself into a riot of colour in spring when wild flowers are abundant; true landlubbers can enjoy visits to the ruins of a Saracen castle (a long climb), the church of **San Bartolomeo** with its colourful ceramic saints, and call in at the small **museum**, open in summer only, which contains items found in the surrounding sea. A walk around the island will take about four hours, covering 10km (6 miles).

One of the pleasures is an excursion from **Cala Santa Maria**, ideally on a glass-bottomed boat in order to view the marine reserve. There are 10 grottoes, too, mostly on the eastern side of the island, with **Grotta Azzurra** as azure as it sounds, with its cave 100 metres (330ft) long.

For information about marine reserve sites and boat trips contact **Centro Accoglienza per la Riserva Marina** (tel: 091 844 9456). For scuba information contact **Mare Nostrum Diving** (tel: 330 792 589; booking@ marenostrumdiving.it). ❑

BEST RESTAURANTS, BARS AND CAFÉS

Prices for a three-course dinner per person and a half-bottle of house wine:
€ = under €20
€€ = €20–35
€€€ = €35–70
€€€€ = over €70

Monreale

Antica Forneria Tusa
Via Pietro Novelli 25
Tel: 091 640 4513 €
A bakery that hasn't changed its recipe for bread for well over a century.

Bricco e Bacco
Via B D'Aquisito 13
Tel: 091 641 7773 €€
Regulars come for the good-quality meat and reliable wine list.

Dietro l'Angolo
Via Piave 5
Tel: 091 640 4067 €€
A brief stroll from the Duomo, this restaurant has a lovely terrace with great views. The pasta dishes are reasonably priced, and there are set menus. Closed Tue.

Principe di Corleone
Contrada Malvello
Tel: 091 846 2922
wwwprincipedicorleopne.it €
As part of a local wine and food foray in Palermo Province, visit this wine estate and do a tasting.

Riccardo III
Contrada Pezzingoli
Tel: 091 414 237 €€
Characteristic place inside an old stable with

a varied menu. Fri–Sun only. Closed Aug.

Taverna del Pavone
Vicolo Pensato 18
Tel: 091 640 6209
www.tavernadelpavone.eu
€€–€€€
Cosy inn in a 17th-century building. On the menu are such traditional dishes as *caponata, cacciocavallo* cheese and sardines, Sicilian-style. Closed Mon.

Castelbuono

Fratelli Fiasconaro
Piazza Margherita 10
Tel: 0921 677 132
www.fiasconaro.com €
Sweets and pastries made using manna or chocolate.

Nangalarruni
Via della Confraternite 10
Tel: 0921 67142
www.hostariananangalarruni.it €
Noted chef Giuseppe Carollo celebrates the best ingredients in the Madonie mountains, from mushrooms to pork, organic vegetables, sheep's cheese, and sweet pastries. The meal might be washed down with wine from the Santa Anastasia estate in the hills below town.

Cefalù

La Botte
Via Veterani 6
Tel: 0921 424 315 €€
Small, charming, with tables outside in warm weather. Varied menu,

meat and fresh fish. Closed Mon.

La Brace
Via XXV Novembre 10
Tel: 0921 423 570
www.ristorantelabrace.com €€€
Impressive cooking for a simple trattoria. Booking essential. Closed Mon & Tue lunch.

Kentia
Via Bordonaro 26
Tel: 0921 423 801 €€€
Known for its charm, cuisine and garden. Sample the *scaloppine ai funghi* and *panzerotti di magro.* Closed Tue and Jan.

Magno
Via Belvedere 4
Tel: 0921 923 348 €€
Traditional trattoria right by the Duomo.

Ostaria del Duomo
Via Seminario 5
Tel: 0921 421 838 €€€
Lovely open-air location overlooking the cathedral. Seafood specialities. Authentic *caponata, penne* and *carpaccio di tonno,* tuna carpaccio. Open Mar–Nov.

Lo Scoglio Ubriaco
Via Corso Ortolani di Bordonaro 2
Tel: 0921 423 228 €€
A terrace overlooks the harbour, so you can watch the fishing boats while enjoying *spaghetti al cartoccio* (baked spaghetti). Closed Tue (except in summer).

Vecchia Marina
Via Vittorio Emanuele 73
Tel: 0921 420 388 €€€

Terrace overlooks the fishermen's beach. Try the *casareccie con gamberi e carciofi* (home-made pasta with prawns and artichokes). Closed Tue and Jan.

Gangi

Tenuta Gangivecchio
Gangivecchio
Tel: 0921 644 982
www.tenutagangivecchio.com €€
A former monastery outside Gangi that is a charming hotel with the best Sicilian cuisine.

Gibilmanna

Fattoria Pianetti
Contrada Gratteri
Tel: 0921 421 890
www.fattoriapianetti.com €€
An *agriturismo* on the hillside. Excellent cooking with home-grown organic produce.

Isnello

Piano Torre
Park Hotel, Piano Torre
Tel: 0921 662 671
www.pianotorreparkhotel.com €€€.
This charming hotel at the heart of the reserve has an excellent restaurant with a varied Sicilian menu. Closed Mon.

Ustica

Da Bruschetto
Piazza Umberto 1
Tel: 091 844 9795 €€
One of the best seafood restaurants on Ustica. Open Easter–end Sept.

THE ARAB-NORMAN LEGACY

Moorish domes, Norman cloisters, shimmering mosaics, honeycomb ceilings and fanciful geometry are just a few of the eclectic features that evoke Arab-Norman Sicily

Arab-Norman rule coincided with Palermo's golden age, when the city was ringed by pleasure palaces such as La Zisa. Named after *aziz*, Arabic for splendid, this Moorish palace is a testament to Arabian craftsmanship, with stalactite vaults, latticework windows, a tiered fountain, and a wind chamber to protect the emir's family from the enervating scirocco.

Instead, the Cappella Palatina represents a Sicilian fusion of Byzantine, Arab and Norman civilisations. The ceiling is unique in a Christian church, a composition of ineffable oriental splendour. The Normans asked Arab craftsmen to portray paradise, and they obliged with naked maidens which the Normans prudishly clothed and crowned with haloes. Still, the roof remains a paradise of the senses: Persian octagonal stars meet Islamic stalactites.

Under Arab rule, the citizens of Palermo acquired a love of Islamic ornamentation that has never left them. Monreale Cathedral is also covered in a shimmering tapestry of mosaics, a tribute to a king whose world view embraced concubines, eunuchs and black slaves.

This fusion of styles is typified by Cefalù Cathedral: the raised choir represents an Oriental element whereas the gold firmament behind Christ is Byzantine. But a Norman font guarded by leopards symbolises King Roger's Hauteville dynasty.

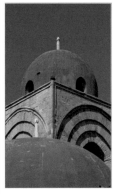

LEFT: the red-domed San Giovanni degli Eremiti in Palermo was a Byzantine basilica converted into a mosque, so Arab squinches, filigree windows and Norman cloisters are all present.

BELOW: Cefalù Cathedral was built in 1131, just 40 years after the Normans had conquered Sicily, and is a fine example of the fusion of Arab and Norman styles. The Byzantine mosaics inside are stunning.

LEFT: the roof of San Pietro monastery in Marsala.

NORMAN CASTLES

The Normans planted their realm with castles in Romanesque and Gothic styles, inspired by Northern architecture, but often subverted by Moorish and Byzantine models, as in Palermo's Palazzo dei Normanni. From Cáccamo to Enna, Norman castles are one of the glories of Sicily. In the Arab-Norman citadel of Troìna, the loftiest town in Sicily, and the first Norman diocese, Count Roger and his wife were besieged by Saracens in 1064. The couple escaped by classic Norman cunning: while their enemies were lulled into a drunken stupor, the Normans scurried along secret vaulted passages that burrow deep under the castle.

But neighbouring Sperlinga is Sicily's finest Norman castle, dating from 1082. After the bloody Sicilian Vespers in 1282, Sperlinga became the Angevins' last stand. The castle was besieged but the French forces within held out for more than a year, protected by a system of trap doors that deposited invaders in underground pits. The only access is still a staircase hewn out of the rock. Switchback paths climb to the summit and crenellations with sweeping views over oak woods and olive groves.

Above: cloisters at Museo Regionale Pepoli in Trápani, which holds an eclectic collection of Sicilian paintings and sculpture.

Above: Norman soldiers depicted on the cloisters at Monreale Cathedral, one of the greatest examples of Norman architecture in the world.

TRÁPANI PROVINCE

Western Sicily is the most seafaring part of the island, famous for its North African atmosphere, nature reserves, endless beaches and, above all, its remarkable ancient sites and treasures

A s the least definable yet most varied province, the Provincia di Trápani is a collection of contradictions. This seafaring region represents a swathe of ancient Sicily, from Phoenician Mózia to Greek Selinunte, medieval Erice and Arab Mazara del Vallo. The landscape spans saltpans, vineyards, woods and coastal nature reserves.

Trápani

In ancient times Drepanon (hence **Trápani ❶**) was the port of Eryx (*see Erice, page 100*), famous in the Mediterranean for its wealth and magnificent temple of Venus, goddess of fertility. As a seafaring power, its history lay at the heart of the Mediterranean world.

As the capital of the province, Trápani commands the commerce of the seas: its **Stazione Maríttima** off Piazza Garibaldi is an embarkation point for the Egadi Islands (*see page 111*) and the remoter island of Pantelleria (*see page 115*), as well as Sardinia, Naples and Tunis.

Trápani's traditional industries of coral, tuna fishing and salt production linger on, and it is said the town may also be a Mafia money-laundering centre – a rumour borne

out by the city's countless small banks. Successful but culturally moribund was the consensus – until recently, when the citizens realised that, with careful restoration, the historic seafront could be the equal of any city. And realised that pedestrianisation and revamped churches were not just good for the soul but good for business too.

Visually, Trápani is appealing from a distance: a patchwork of shallow lagoons bounded by thin causeways. In summer, drying in the sun, there

Main attractions
TRÁPANI
ERICE
RISERVA DELLO ZÍNGARO
SAN VITO LO CAPO
SEGESTA
SALTPANS AT NÚBIA
MÓZIA
MARSALA
MAZARA DEL VALLO
SELINUNTE
CAVE DI CUSA

LEFT: temple at Selinunte.
RIGHT: Trápani harbour.

An elaborately decorated Madonna (gold-plated copper, coral and pearl) dating from the 18th century at the Museo Regionale Pepoli, Trápani.

are also heaps of salt roofed with red tiles. Close up, the promontory with the old town now has an easy charm, with its 11th-century Spanish fortifications matched by a regenerated seafront. The romantic promenade can certainly rival any in Sicily. The salty port also offers *cuscusu* (fish soup) and lobster in boisterous fishermen's haunts.

After a snack of *arancini* rice balls at Bettina (Via di Torrearsa 110), stroll along the **Mure di Tramontana**, the ancient Spanish bastions. Literally overshadowed by the massive Tramontana walls, the once unsavoury fishing quarter has been transformed into an atmospheric promenade back into Trápani's seafaring past. From **Piazza Mercato del Pesce**, the former fish market, a leisurely walk leads along the sea walls to the **Bastione Conca**. En route to the bastion are views of both the bay and the fishermen's cottages. From here, the historic district comes into

view, dwarfed by Monte San Giuliano looming beyond. If not tempted by the beach, reached via Porta Osuna, then carry on to the **Torre di Ligny** (Mon–Sat 10am–noon, 5–8pm), a fortress built in 1671. Freshly restored, the fortress overlooks the archaeological zone and the open sea. Softly illuminated, it now makes a romantic evening stroll, a fact not lost on Trápani's young lovers.

The rest of Trápani's sights are not monumental but more than occupy a morning before taking a ferry to the outlying islands. Centred on Via Giudecca, the small Jewish Quarter has a faded charm epitomised by the **Palazzo della Giudecca** while on the tip of its promontory is the **Torre di Ligny** once more. **Via Torrearsa**, facing the grandiose Palazzo Cavarretta, marks the start of a stroll taking in Baroque churches, palaces and inviting bars, including on lively **Via Garibaldi**, the main street. The cathedral area is newly pedestrianised,

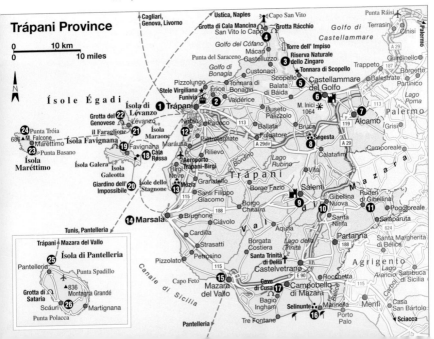

while Baroque churches are being restored. On Via Generale Giglio the church of **Purgatorio** (1683) boasts a fine dome and the 18th-century wooden statues of the **Misteri** that are borne aloft in a moving Good Friday procession.

Prosaically, the impetus for the city's resurgence is linked to the rise of low-cost flights, but a new city pride is also part of the story. Mercantile Trápani might yet become cultural Trápani.

Sanctuary of the Madonna

About 3km (2 miles) north of the old town is **Santuario dell'Annunziata** (daily 8am–noon, 4–7pm), a Carmelite church founded in 1315 but rebuilt in 1760. This sanctuary of the Madonna is considered Trápani's main monument. Its charms are a Baroque bell tower, a Gothic rose window and a doorway decorated in a zigzag pattern. Inside is a rococo nave and a cluster of exotic domed chapels. Dedicated to fishermen, the frescoed **Cappella dei Pescatori** (1481) embraces Byzantine and Moorish elements, as well as a Span-ish diamond-point design. Behind the high altar is the lavish **Cappella della Madonna**, with sculptures by Antonino Gagini and the revered statue of the Madonna di Trápani by Nino Pisano, crowned in jewels. This venerated Madonna is credited with miraculous powers.

The **Museo Regionale Pepoli** (Mon–Sat 9am–1.30pm, Wed, Fri, Sat 3pm–7.30pm; charge) is the city's eclectic museum, housed in the former convent adjoining the cathedral. Off the cloisters lie Gagini sculptures, important Sicilian paintings and craftsmanship in the form of coral cribs and gilded figurines, enamelled Moorish lamps and majolica tiles. Gaudiest of all is a coral crucifix by Fra Matteo Bavera, with a salmon-coloured Christ against an ebony and mother-of-pearl cross.

Erice

Just north is a more peaceful base than Trápani for exploring – and staying. In spring, the winding road climbs past views of acacia, wild gladioli and waxy lemon blossom to the legendary Mount Eryx (today's

TIP

The Trápani Card is a useful combined ticket giving discounts on museums (such as the Salt Museum) and other attractions. Book through the tourist office.

BELOW: Trápani street scene.

Where ecology counts

Trápani Province is the most Arab and Phoenician in its ancestry and, as such, it has garnered a reputation for being somewhat lethargic and morally compromised. Yet environmentally it is often at the forefront. Trápani takes a stand against pollution, land speculation and the destruction of coastal saltpans. Here, both windmills and marshes are protected, as is the lagoon around Mózia, off Marsala, and the trailblazing reserve of Lo Zíngaro (see page 101). It was Trápani that launched *pescaturismo* (fishing tourism), offering visitors excursions with fishermen in order to discover aspects of the coast, its marine parks and the beguiling tuna fisheries here and on the Egadi Islands.

Erice bell tower.

BELOW:
Pasticceria Maria.

Monte San Giuliano). Swathed in seasonal mists or in a carpet of flowers, **Erice ❷**, perched at 750 metres (2,460ft), is an exquisite, tiny medieval walled town. The Carthaginian walls survive, rough-hewn slabs inscribed with Punic symbols, while nearby is the charming Quartiere Spagnolo, the 17th-century Spanish bastion.

As ancient Eryx, this mystical city was founded by the Elymni (Elymians), the mysterious settlers of Segesta who worshipped the Mediterranean fertility goddess known as Astarte to the Elymni and the Phoenicians, as Aphrodite to the Greeks and as Venus to the Romans.

The entrance to the town is **Porta Trápani**, a medieval gate leading directly to the **Chiesa Madre** (daily 8.30am–12.30pm, 3–6pm), with its 15th-century porch and a bell tower that began as a watchtower. Despite the profusion of churches within the walls, it is the views from the gardens of the **Villa Balio** on the summit of the hill that justify a pilgrimage. Below stretch ragged turrets, wooded groves and vineyards; a tapestry of saltpans and sea slip all the way to

the turtle-shaped Egadi Islands and to Cap Bon in Tunisia. As the English poet Fiona Pitt-Kethley concluded: "If you want a good view, go up Eryx, not Etna."

On a rocky outcrop is the **Castello di Venere** (daily 9am–to sunset, Oct–March; closed Mon). Inside the crenellated Norman walls is the site of the fabled **Tempio di Venere**, now the battered marble remains of a temple, beside a well. **Castello Pepoli**, with its neo-Gothic medieval tower, adds to the scene but is not open to the public.

Virgil compared Eryx to Greece's Mount Athos for its altitude and spiritual pre-eminence. Not that Erice remains a sanctuary today. Its orphanages and convents have become ceramics and carpet shops or nightclubs and chic restaurants. Still, behind this public face lies a private Erice, one of wall-hugging cobbled alleys, grotesque Baroque balconies, votive niches and secret courtyards. In keeping with Arab traditions, such courtyards were where women and children could sit in private, working or chatting by the well. Erice is a par-

Sweet indulgence

Erice has a name for exceedingly sweet pastries based on almonds and dried fruits. As in Palermo with its *martorano* marzipan confections, *dolci ericini* were originally made by novice nuns in a closed convent. But in 1975 this convent closed, and locals lament that the sweets are not as home-made as they once were. However, Maria Grammatico, who learnt her craft in the convent, vies for the title of Sicily's best bakery with her **Pasticceria Maria** on Corso Vittorio Emanuele. (Her rival is Caffe Sicilia in Noto.) Apart from *pasta reale* (exotic marzipan treats), her sweets have such poetic names as *sospiri* (sighs) and *belli e brutti* (beauties and beasts).

adox. In winter it resembles a windy Umbrian hill town, yet in summer it bursts with tourists and bijou boutiques recalling the Côte d'Azur.

Riserva dello Zíngaro

This coast was once noted for its rich tuna-fishing grounds, and surviving *tonnare* (tuna fisheries) are being restored, both here and on the Egadi Islands. The coastal road passes the traditional **Tonnara di Bonagia** before reaching the **Riserva dello Zíngaro ③**, a superb reserve set on a rocky headland pierced with sheltered coves and bays, and home to buzzards and falcons as well as palms, carobs and euphorbia. Many trails criss-cross the reserve, including the *sentiero della costa*, a coastal footpath that runs for 11km (7 miles) from Scopello to San Vito lo Capo, roughly a five-hour walk.

On the headland lies **San Vito lo Capo ④**, a burgeoning resort noted for its fine coast, sandy beaches, fish restaurants and heady couscous festival. The northern entrance to Lo Zíngaro lies 11km (7 miles) southeast, just before the ruined Torre dell'Impiso. The coastal road south skirts the reserve, passing more ruined towers, primeval mountains, shepherds' huts, tuna fisheries and ragged rock formations at sea. The changing coastline continues to Castellammare, with the rugged journey made by boat, on horseback or on foot.

Scopello ⑤, which is 10km (6 miles) before Castellammare, marks the southern entrance to the reserve and makes a lovely lunch stop in one of the rustic seafood trattorie. This fishing village is based around a *baglio*, an imposing medieval farmstead. Paths lead to the attractive bays of Cala Bianca, Cala Rossa and Baia Guidaloca and views dominated by the **Tonnara di Scopello** (9am–12.30pm summer only), the most scenic tuna fishery in Sicily. Beyond lies the bay and a shingle

beach, topped by a couple of Saracen towers, designed to combat piratical invasions.

A leisurely four-hour marked trail begins in the south, beyond **Galleria di Scopello**, and hugs the coast, passing coves and beaches, until it meets the road at Uzzo, in the northern end of the reserve.

Castellammare del Golfo

Castellammare del Golfo ⑥, an overgrown fishing village, enjoys panoramic views across the gulf and, from the port, a boat ferries visitors to Lo Zíngaro nature reserve (tel: 0924 35108). The sweet, pastel-coloured cottages and idyllic harbour with its trattorie belie the town's bloody past as a Mafia haunt. In the 1950s, around 80 percent of the male population had been to jail and the internecine Mafia warfare led the port to become the chief embarkation point to the US.

Gavin Maxwell lived among the tuna fishermen in the 1950s, recording their destitution and illiteracy in his book *Ten Pains of Death* (1958). Even then, there was a clash between

TIP

In spring, the Riserva Naturale dello Zíngaro is a magnet for birdwatchers. Bird types include Bonelli's eagle, the Sicilian rock partridge, the peregrine falcon, the buzzard, the kestrel and the red kite.

BELOW: view of Punta del Saraceno from Erice.

EAT

Cuscus alla Trapanese is the region's great fish couscous, with sea bass, sea bream, red mullet, grouper, mussels, clams and prawns. The fish are cleaned and boned; shells are removed. Stock is made with the trimmings plus onion, celery, carrot and parsley. After lightly frying the fish with garlic, it is added to the filtered stock. The couscous is prepared in a steamer and then covered with pieces of the fish, some stock, and a pinch of chopped chilli.

BELOW: Castellammare del Golfo.

old and new lifestyles: "From my eyrie in the castle I watched Castellammaresi women come down to the sea to bathe and swim fully dressed in their everyday clothes, and to meet, while so floundering, bronzed visiting nymphs in bikinis and snorkels."

Alcamo

From Castellammare consider a 13km (8-mile) detour east to **Alcamo ❼**, a confident, quietly prosperous wine town that provides a charming taste of small-town Sicily. After visiting the **Chiesa Madre**, call in to the medieval **Castello dei Conti di Modica** to see the castle's **Enoteca** (tel: 0924 22301), a new wine museum and tasting centre. From here, wine-lovers can make their way to drinks at **La Barrique** (Piazza Mercato), lunch at **La Baita** or a wine and food pairing experience at the wonderful **Sirignano Wine Resort** *(see page 109).*

Segesta

In rolling countryside south of Castellammare lies **Segesta ❽** (daily 9am–1 hour before sunset; charge), one of the most romantic classical

locations. The site can also reached along the A29 from Trápani.

The vast, largely unexcavated city of **Egesta** (today's Segesta) is believed to have been founded by the Elymni in the 12th century BC. The settlers claimed to be refugees who escaped the fall of Troy, but some scholars believe them to be an iconoclastic tribe of Iberian-Ligurian descent. Elymnian writings found at Segesta are in an unfathomable language nonetheless written in the Greek alphabet. However, the Trojan link could explain their hatred of the Greeks, an enmity that led to their role in the razing of their rival nation at Selinunte in 409 BC. (Segesta itself was sacked by Siracusa in 307 BC when nearly 10,000 residents were killed and the rest sold as slaves.)

Crowning a low hill on the edge of a ravine is a great Hellenic monument, the roofless **Doric temple** that lacks a *cella* (inner chamber) and fluting on its 36 columns, but is no less lovely for that. No one knows to which god the temple was dedicated, or if it was ever completed. It appears

to have been abandoned, unfinished, around 420 BC.

A regular shuttle bus takes visitors to the next level on **Monte Barbaro** 3km (2 miles) away with its theatre built in the 3rd century BC. (Only the fittest should attempt the 30-minute climb on foot.) Well preserved, the theatre measures 63 metres (207ft) in diameter and has 20 rows of seats facing the fabulous view of the Golfo di Castellammare. Greek plays are staged here in summer.

The earthquake zone

In 1968 a major earthquake struck western Sicily, including Calatafimi, Salemi, Partanna and Gibellina. Over 50,000 people were left homeless and many still live in makeshift accommo-dation. The reasons for this are unclear but would appear to involve bureau-cratic inefficiency and yet another curi-ous disappearance of funds earmarked for the project. **Salemi ⑨**, a benighted hilltop town, is the most intriguing of the earthquake spots, with its black-ened medieval alleys and crumbling churches. Just east lies **Gibellina Nuova ⑩**, a would-be futuristic new town built after the earthquake flat-tened the original city, 18km (11 miles) to the west. **Ruderi di Gibellina ⑪**, the rubble of a devastated city, has been left as it fell in 1968.

The North African coast

South of Trápani is the so-called North African coast, closer to Tunisia than to mainland Italy. It is known for its saltpans, reflecting an industry that has flourished since Phoenician and Roman times thanks to ideal conditions: low rainfall, regular tides and the absence of estuaries that would dilute the salinity. Salt was the mainstay of the local economy between the 14th and 17th centuries. Today's **Via del sale** (the salt road) stretches from Trápani to the Sta-gnone Lagoon, embracing Mózia and Marsala. It takes in stretches of salt-pans and newly renovated windmills, with the brackish lagoons home to wild ducks, grey herons, common puffins and African cranes. As a result, this coastal area has become a designated nature reserve dedicated to the workings of the saltpans and the passage of migratory birds.

Pre-Punic pottery masks at the Whitaker Museum in Mózia.

BELOW LEFT: saltpans at Núbia. **BELOW:** Doric temple at Segesta.

In 397 BC, the Greek tyrant Dionysius, laying siege to Motya, was trapped in the lagoon by a Carthaginian fleet supporting the islanders. He built a road of logs, 4km (2½ miles) long, across the land between the lagoon and the sea and his ships were pushed across the land on rollers. It was a clever plan; the Carthaginian fleet was destroyed and Dionysius killed the islanders or sold them into slavery.

Saltpans and lagoons

At **Núbia** ⑫, only 5km (3 miles) out of Trápani, is the **Museo delle Saline** (Tue–Sat 9am–noon, 3–6pm), a working museum which demonstrates the ancient salt industry in action. (In March sea water is drawn into the saltpans where it evaporates in the sun. By July the salt is dry enough to be harvested into pyramids, covered with tiles, and allowed to dry out before being taken away for cleansing and packaging.)

Further south, a stretch of saltpans and shallow lagoons embraces the marshy **Saline dello Stagnone**, the largest lagoon on Sicily's coastline. Poetic views across the shallow saltpans are intensified at sunset. On the coast is a newer, well-organised salt museum, **Mulina Salina Infersa** (daily 9am–8pm), housed in a converted windmill.

Mózia

From a small jetty here a ferry crosses the lagoon to the **island of Mózia** ⑬, Sicily's chief Punic site (boats run 9.30am–6.30pm summer, until 4pm in winter). A submerged Phoenician

BELOW: ferry to Mózia.

causeway just below the surface links the island to the shore, but this is now impassable.

Mózia, first known as Motya, looms on the far side of the Stagnone lagoon, its largest island. As Motya, it was established as a Phoenician colony in the mid-8th century BC, set within a ring of ramparts and towers, and protected by a landward bastion. When the Phoenicians founded a colony, Lilybaeum (Marsala), as their new home, Motya fell into total neglect. It was bought, centuries later, by the Marsala wine merchant Joseph Whitaker (1850–1936), who made the excavations his life's work. As Mózia was never again colonised, Whitaker discovered a secret city more complete than Carthage.

The ruins of Motya are still only partially excavated, but the remains of the city walls, cemetery and small man-made harbour, the **cothon**, are visible. There is also a **tophet**, dedicated to the goddess Tanit, where the Phoenicians reputedly sacrificed their first-born children. Ruins of mosaic-encrusted houses include the **Casa dei Mosaici** with a black and white pebble floor depicting lions attacking a bull. The well-restored **Whitaker Museum** contains pre-Punic pottery and nearly 1,000 burial urns. One particular treasure is a remarkably fine Greek statue from the early 5th century BC of a sinuous youth, possibly a charioteer, known as *The Man in a Tunic*.

Marsala

Marsala ⑭ occupies the next cape, 10km (6 miles) south, and takes its name from the Arabic Marsa-al-Allah, harbour of God. The view of Capo Boeo, the most western point of Sicily, was enjoyed by refugees from Mózia in 396 BC when it became Carthaginian **Lilybaeum**, the best-defended Punic naval base in Sicily, and the only city to resist Greek expansion westwards. (Marsala, in turn, has given

its name to a famous dessert wine produced in the local vineyards.)

Marsala is an engaging place with a mix of chic wine bars and traditional seafood inns, reflecting its role as a cosmopolitan port. But overladen as it is with impressive Roman, Hellenistic and Punic remains, the faintly Moorish flavour is just one strand. In that, Marsala is quintessentially Sicilian.

In the heart of the old town is the **cathedral** dedicated to **St Thomas di Canterbury**, built on the site of a church dedicated to St Thomas à Becket. Close to the cathedral on Via Giuseppe Garraffa is the small **Museo degli Arazzi** (Tue–Sat 9am–1pm, 4.30–6pm, Sun 9.30am–1pm; charge), containing 18 richly coloured Flemish tapestries given to the church in 1589 by the Archbishop of Messina.

Spread over the promontory are the ruins of **Lilybaeum (Lilibeo)**, presented through Baglio Anselmi (a former distillery) in the **Museo Archeologico** (Sun–Tue 9am–1pm, Wed–Sat 9am–7pm; charge). These historic Marsala warehouses display finds from Mózia and Lilybaeum, including Roman mosaics, striking

Hellenistic funerary monuments and a superb **Punic ship** reconstructed after its discovery by English archaeologist Honor Frost and recovery from the Stagnone Lagoon in 1971. At 35 metres (115ft) long, the war galley was manned by 68 oarsmen. For some unexplained reason its original iron nails have not rusted.

Close by are the remains of a Roman villa at the **Insula Romana di Capo Boeo** (Sun–Tue 9am–11.30am, Wed–Sat also 2.30–4.30pm), a reminder that this was once the most important Roman city in Sicily, with ongoing excavations leading to the opening of new sites. One such is the **Ipogeo di Crispia Salvia** (Sat 9am–1pm, booked through the Baglio Anselmi or tel: 0923 952 535), an underground chamber frescoed with funerary banqueting scenes.

On the seafront is the **Cantine Florio** (*see box page 106*), one of the most typical of the Marsala distilleries, mostly set in *bagli*, imposing walled estates. The Florio are Sicily's greatest entrepreneurs, but the amber-coloured dessert wine was pioneered by British wine merchants

Garibaldi Gate, Marsala.

BELOW: Marsala Cathedral.

DRINK

Marsala wine comes in different "flavours", most sweet, though Marsala all'Uovo (with egg yolks) is sweetest of all. The dry Marsala Secco, served chilled, is a pleasant *aperitivo*, while Marsala Vergine, matured for at least five years, is considered best of all.

(see page 45). The Florio museum even flaunts the illicit bottles sent to the USA during Prohibition, when Florio cunningly labelled the alcohol as seasoning or medicinal tonic.

Mazara del Vallo

From Marsala, the coastal road passes saltpans and marshes north to Trápani or south to **Mazara del Vallo ⓯**, a place of moods rather than specific sights. The fishing port feels like a North African souk and indeed flourished under Arab rule. A ragged **Norman castle** overlooks the seafront and palm-filled park, while the **Norman cathedral** has been given a Baroque veneer and contains two dramatic Roman sarcophagi. The main portal depicts Count Roger vanquishing a Muslim infidel.

Yet Christian sights are underpinned by a Moorish sensibility, Sicilian-style, especially in the fishing quarter. Overlooking the port, the dilapidated Norman-Byzantine church of **San Nicolò Regale** boasts crenellations and Roman mosaics.

Since the town is now home to one of Italy's largest fishing fleets,

the Mazaro river is packed with trawlers all the way to the fish market. **Via Pescatori** is full of Tunisian fishermen, but the women are hidden away. Behind lies the Kasbah, the Tunisian Quarter, an intriguing den of arcaded, tapering alleys and backstreet charm. **Piazza Bagno** has a hammam with baths and massage. Nearby are a ritual butcher's and several Tunisian cafés with North Africans smoking *chicha* bubble pipes. The Tunisian trawlermen, the backbone of the local fishing fleet, are made to feel welcome. The mayor has made restoration of the Kasbah a priority, with courtyards increasingly decorated with colourful mosaics. But a Christian mood reasserts itself in the **Chiesa di San Michele**, a blaze of gold, and the adjoining **Convento di San Michele**, where nuns from a closed order make some of the best Sicilian pastries (ring the bell and speak softly through the grille).

A couple of squares south, on Piazza Plebescito stands the **Museo del Satiro** (daily 9am–6.30pm), a delightful new museum dedicated to the *Dancing Satyr*, a Greek bronze dredged up

BELOW: fishmonger in Mazara del Vallo.

Marsala tasting tour

After seeing Marsala, visit the seafront *bagli* (wine warehouses) for a Marsala tasting or try the wines in **La Bottega del Carmine** (Via Caturca 20, tel: 0923 195 4446), a chic wine bar. The history of Marsala is intriguing, with the wine business founded by 18th-century English merchants. The most historic estates are **Cantine Florio**, Lungomare Via Florio (Mon–Fri 9am–1pm, 3–5.30pm, Sat 9am–1pm, tel: 0923 781 111, www.cantineflorio.com) and **Pellegrino** (daily, book, Via del Fante 39, tel: 0923 719 911, www.carlopellegrino.it). The only producer not swallowed up by a mega brand such as Martini is **De Bartoli** (daily, Contrada Samperi 292, Marsala, tel: 0923 962 093, www.marcodebartoli.com).

by a Mazara trawler. Now restored, the young satyr is dancing himself into an orgiastic state for eternity.

The seafront is the mayor's next project, with a marina planned on one side and a proper beach on the other. Decent sandy beaches are currently a 10-minute drive away at **Tonnarella**.

Selinunte

As the most westerly Hellenic colony, 30km (19 miles) east of Mazara, **Selinunte** ⑯ was a pocket of Greece in the part of Sicily under North African control. Set in a richly arable plain on the edge of the sea, the ancient city was founded in 650 BC by colonists from Megara Hyblaea. It took its name from *selinon*, Greek for the wild celery that grew here in abundance. By the 5th century BC it had become a prosperous city with great temples and two harbours, where the rivers Modione and Cottone that then framed the site reach the sea. At that time Selinunte and the city of Siracusa were allied in

their hatred of powerful Carthage (in today's Tunisia) but, in 409 BC, when the Carthaginians attacked the city with the help of the people of Segesta, it was ransacked and destroyed. The city never fully recovered, and when in 250 BC it was again attacked, the population decamped and resettled at Lilybaeum (Marsala). However, an aerial view of Selinunte's collapsed columns reveals that they fell like dominoes, evidently the result of an earthquake, not man's destruction.

Surprisingly for Sicily, the huge **archaeological site** (daily 9am–5pm, until 4pm in winter; charge) is not overshadowed by building but left in splendid isolation, flanked by two rivers and the ancient ports, both silted up. The oldest temples, named alphabetically Ⓐ, Ⓑ, Ⓒ and Ⓓ, lie in the acropolis, while the main temples Ⓔ, Ⓕ and Ⓖ were built on the eastern hill.

A curious entrance directs visitors from the ticket office and car park

Selinunte is probably the most child-friendly classical site: the mystical setting and the sprawling ruins prompt enthusiastic scrambling over fallen pillars, with the electric train on hand for when tiredness sets in. Marinella beach lies beyond the ruins, perfect for parents to watch the children play while they tuck into a lobster lunch.

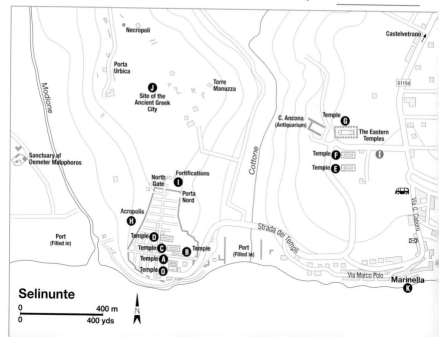

Selinunte

0 ——— 400 m
0 ——— 400 yds

N

Temple remains at Selinunte.

through tunnels in sandbanks to the reconstructed **Temple E** that was possibly dedicated to Hera (Juno) wife of Zeus, queen of heaven. Its lovely sculptures are in the Museo Archeologico in Palermo, much to the chagrin of locals who would like the *metopes* and friezes to return, especially the statue of the *ephebe*, a noble youth, which was unearthed by a local farmer.

Temple F, the oldest on the hill, is the most damaged of the trio, dedicated, perhaps, to Athena, goddess of war, while **Temple G**, probably dedicated to Zeus (Apollo), is now a vast heap of rubble with one restored raised column. Each column in this temple was built using stone drums weighing 100 tons and remained incomplete. Fragments of their painted stucco have been unearthed.

Sited within a walled enclosure, the **acropolis** retains some original **fortifications** . The 5th-century BC **Temple O** is barely visible, with only the *stylobate* (platform) remaining, while **Temple A** is equally elusive.

On the knoll of the hill is the conspicuous **Temple C**, dated at around mid-6th century BC. The largest temple of all, it appears to have been dedicated to Apollo, the great Olympian god. When the columns collapsed in an 8th-century earthquake they flattened a Byzantine village that had grown around them. The columns were rebuilt into a towering colonnade in 1927. Only the platform remains of **Temple B**, while **Temple D** has its platform and some blocks from the columns.

North of the acropolis is the **Ancient City** , and on either side of it lies an unexcavated necropolis. Selinunte is a tragic yet hauntingly lovely spot. The sight and sound of the waves merge with squabbling magpies and fast yellow-back lizards. In cracks of the ruins grow aromatic wild fennel, parsley, mandrake, acanthus and beds of yellow flowers. It is deeply therapeutic.

A lengthy visit to the sprawling site can be followed by a swim along the sandy coast. Framed by temples, the seafront at **Marinella** is lined with lively restaurants.

Ancient quarries

Between Selinunte and Castelvetrano a road leads to **Campobella di Mazara**, a wine-producing town. Further on are the **Cave di Cusa** , the ancient quarries that provided the stone to build Selinunte. Set 4km (2½ miles) south of Campobella di Mazara, this charming rural site, overrun with wild flowers, is always open (daily, times vary). Huge column drums lie chiselled, as if ready to be transported to Temple G at Selinunte, 18km (11 miles) away, before being abandoned.

The fascination lies in the complex mechanics of construction. Old sketches show how half-carved capitals were levered and pillars were hauled to Selinunte in carts. The poignancy lies in the fact that all work stopped the moment Selinunte was destroyed. The vanquished city just disappeared under the sands. It is yet to be excavated. ❑

BEST RESTAURANTS, BARS AND CAFÉS

Prices for a three-course dinner per person and a half-bottle of house wine:
€ = under €20
€€ = €20–35
€€€ = €35–70
€€€€ = over €70

Trápani

Ai Lumi
Corso Vittorio Emanuele 75
Tel: 0923 540 922
wwwailumiit €€
An atmospheric spot in converted stables serving traditional cuisine. B&B too. Closed Nov.

Caupona Taverna di Sicilia
Piazza Purgatorio 32
Tel: 0923 546 618
www.cantinasiciliana.it €€
Superb seafood: try the caponata di pesce.

P & G
Via Spalti 1 (by Villa Margherita park)
Tel: 0923 547 701 €€
Casual seafood place serving Trápani classics like neonata (baby sardines), pizzas and couscous. Closed Mon.

Paradiso
Lungomare D. Alighieri 22
Tel: 0923 22303 €€€
A highly regarded inn specialising in neonata, spaghetti ai ricci (spaghetti with sea urchins) and tuna. Book. Closed Sun.

Safina
Piazza Umberto I 35 (opposite the railway station)
Tel: 0923 22708 €€
Huge portions at low prices. Closed Wed in winter.

Trattoria del Porto
Via A Staiti 45
Tel: 0923 547 822 €€
A family-run trattoria in the port area with seafood specialities and outdoor tables.

Alcamo

La Baita
Via P Palermo 106 – Contrada Turchi
Tel: 0924 25554
www.la-batia.it €€
Set in a former convent, this hotel-restaurant combines ambience and engaging service with authentic Sicilian cuisine. Subtle antipasti segue into mains that are equally strong on meat and fish dishes, as well as pizza, with cannoli for dessert.

Sirignano Wine Resort
Contrada Sirignano
Tel: 091 251 5281 €€
Set among rolling vineyards, this appealing wine resort is home to a remarkable chef who creates delicate reinterpretations of Sicilian dishes. Combine lunch with a wine-tasting.

Erice

Moderno
Via Vittorio Emanuele 67
Tel: 0923 869 300
www.hotelmodernoerice.it €€€
Classic Sicilian cooking. Charming terrace with panoramic views. Closed Mon in quiet season.

Monte San Giuliano
Vicolo San Rocco 7
Tel: 0923 869 595
www.montesangiuliano.it €€
Very good traditional Trapanese cuisine. Try the involtini di melanzana (stuffed aubergine rolls).

Pasticceria Maria Grammatico
Via Vittorio Emanuele 14
Tel: 0923 869 390
www.mariagrammatico.it €€€
Traditional Sicilian pasticceria. Closed Mon.

La Pentolaccia
Via Guarnotti 17
Tel: 339 486 2432
www.ristorantelapentolaccia.it €€
Former monastery. Fish and couscous specials. Good choice of local wines. Closed Tue.

San Vito lo Capo

Alfredo
Contrada Valanga 3
Tel: 0923 972 366 €€€
Good seafood. Known for pasta dishes with bottarga (cod roe). Closed Mon.

Tha'am
Via Abruzzi 32
Tel: 0923 972 836 €€€
Arab influences show in the decor and dishes. Closed Wed Oct–May.

Marsala

Delfino
Lungomare Mediterraneo 672
Tel: 0923 751 076
www.delfinobeach.com €€€
On waterfront 4km (2½ miles) from centre. Great seafood. Closed Tue except Apr–Oct.

Divino Rosso
Via XI Maggio
Tel: 0923 711 770
divinorosso@libero.it €€
Fabulous selection of wines sold by the glass. Excellent meat and fish dishes. Book for dinner. Closed Feb and Mon.

Trattoria Garibaldi
Piazza Addolorata 36
Tel: 0923 953 006 €€
Good seafood dishes.

Mazara del Vallo

Alla Kasbah
Via Itria 10
Tel: 0923 906 126 €€–€€€
Good local spot for fish couscous. Closed Mon.

Al Pesciolino d'Oro
Lungomare San Vito 109
Tel: 0923 909 286
www.alpesciolinodoro.it €€
Seafood of all kinds. Closed Thur.

Del Pescatore
Via Castelvetrano 191
Tel: 0923 947 580
www.ristorantedelpescatore.com €€€.
Try the swordfish and spicy pasta dishes. Closed Mon.

Selinunte

Pierrot
Via Marco Polo 108 at Marinella
Tel: 0924 46205
www.ristorantepierrotselinunte.it €€€.
Emphasis on seasonal fish. Closed Tue in winter.

THE EGADI ISLANDS AND PANTELLERIA

As the easiest offshore islands to visit, the Egadi attract summer crowds, but out of season they offer peace and traditional charm. Much further south lies Pantelleria, Sicily's island close to the shores of North Africa

As a short ferry ride from Tràpani, the archipelago of the Egadi Islands (Ísole Égadi) are deservedly popular. Set in a marine reserve, Favignana, Lévanzo, and Maréttimo are a paradise for sailors, scuba-divers and fans of tuna fish. Today, fishing and tourism keep the economy alive, and the recent restoration of the tuna fishery has given the island of Favignana a new focus.

Cave drawings

The Egadi have 15,000 years of history, and the caves of Favignana and Lévanzo contain traces of the islands' prehistoric settlers. In Lévanzo, cave drawings in the Grotta del Genovese etched 12,000 years ago show bulls and deer as well as hunting men. It is thought the archipelago was once part of a land bridge linking Africa to Italy.

The islands were the springboard for the Arab conquest of Sicily and the great traders, the Phoenicians, then settled here and remained until despatched by the Romans. Over the centuries the Saracens and the Normans followed, then the Aragonese and, finally, the Genoese. The Normans and Aragonese fortified the

Egadi, while the Spaniards encouraged the growth of a coral industry.

After Spain sold the islands to Genoese bankers in 1637, the economy took off and reached its peak under the entrepreneurial Florio family in the early 19th century, when both tuna and tufa (volcanic rock) were exported.

Favignana

At 20 sq km (8 sq miles), **Favignana**, home to around 4,400 people, is the largest and most populous island.

Main attractions

TONNARA DI FAVIGNANA
DIVING OFF PUNTA MARSALA
LÉVANZO BOAT TOUR
GROTTA DEL GENOVESE
WALKING ON MARÉTTIMO
CYCLING ON FAVIGNANA AND PANTELLERIA
PANTELLERIA'S DAMMUSI HOUSES
MOSCATO PASSITO WINES
MUD BATHS

LEFT: the port at Maréttimo island, a paradise for divers.
RIGHT: Favignana, the largest of the Egadi Islands.

TIP

Book an archaeology-themed walking or cycling tour of Favignana with Ancilla Finazzi (tel: 3898 048 028) or check other walks with the tourist office (Largo Marina 14, tel: 0923 545 511).

Ancient tufa-quarrying remodelled the landscape until it was brought to a standstill in the 1950s by the high cost of extracting and transporting the rock.

The island is a homage to stone, its slopes dotted with tufa houses. Even cliffs and caves represent a pleasing spectrum of ochre, russet and cream-coloured rocks. However, if cyclists heading for one of the coves stop to peer over the roadside stone walls, they will discover an abundance of sunken gardens. These sheer stone walls, overgrown with wild fennel and capers, give shelter from the sweeping sea winds to the orange and lemon trees, as well as the figs and tomatoes planted below on the floor of the abandoned quarries. Other quarries were carved at the very edge of the sea too, so that the tufa could be loaded directly onto the boats transporting it to the mainland. Stone from the maze-like **Cala Rossa** helped build many cities in Sicily and North Africa. The chiselled walls and eroded geometry of the seaside quarries make Cala Rossa a popular spot for picnics and swimming.

In the bustling medieval town of **Favignana** , to one side of the ferry quay in the **port**, near where the ferry docks, stand beautiful vaulted warehouses in which the big black-bottomed tuna boats, the long nets and huge anchors are stored during the winter. The still waters of the harbour reflect the tiled roofs and stone smokestacks of the **Tonnara di Favignana**, a former tuna cannery, which closed in the 1990s (all processing is now carried out in Trápani). Previously known as Tonnara Florio, this masterpiece of industrial archaeology has recently been converted into a heritage museum covering the tuna business (Tue–Sun 10am–1pm, closed in winter; tel: 0923 808242).

Palazzo Florio, built in 1876, was once the home of the tuna tycoon Ignazio Florio. Today it contains the tourist office (tel: 3385 366 075), town hall and a cultural centre. The palazzo and the statue of Ignazio Florio in **Piazza Europa** recall the island's heyday. In Florio's time, a day's catch could be as high as 10,000 fish. Today, it has shrunk to under 2,000 a month because of overfishing. Even so, the

Below: Cala Dogana, the port at Lévanzo.

tuna industry survives, with traditional techniques allied to hi-tech sonar detection, used to spot the shoals.

If tuna is on your mind, call into **Sapori di Mare** (Via Roma 23) to dine on tuna prepared 50 different ways, from tuna *caponata to* sweet and sour tuna.

Also in town is **Forte San Giacomo**, a fortress built by Roger II in 1120, later converted into a Bourbon prison in 1837, and today housing a maximum-security prison for some of Sicily's finer mafiosi.

Palaeolithic caves

Eastwards along the shore is **Punta San' Nicola**, awaiting excavation of its caves that were inhabited in Palaeolithic times, **Bagno delle Donne** (once the women's baths), and **Cala Rossa** where the sea was said to have turned red in 241 BC during a bloody battle between the Carthaginians and Romans. Also in the east, in the Bue Marina area, see the **Giardino dell'Impossibile** ❷⓪ (daily 4–7.30pm; tel: 0923 921 501) botanical and tropical gardens "impossibly" thriving in an ancient tufa-stone quarry.

Lévanzo

The smallest island, and the one closest to the mainland, bears witness to the islanders' bond with the sea. Much of the coast is still inaccessible, except by boat. The port of **Lévanzo** ❷⓵ (or **Cala Dogana**, because the Customs offices are here) consists of a handful of houses with rooms to let, a couple of small hotels, several cafés and trattorie.

Its one tarred road turns into a dirt track as it leaves town and winds along a gentle valley between the peaks of the Pizzo del Mónaco and the Pizzo del Corvo. The stony slopes are covered with *macchia mediterranea*, arid-looking grey-green scrub that turns lush with the winter rains and blooms in spring.

At the head of the valley the track forks: the left-hand path zigzags down the steep coast towards the sea, leading to the **Grotta del Genovese** ❷⓶, a deep cavern overhanging the rocky shoreline. It is Lévanzo's greatest treasure. If the sea is calm and the wind right, you can reach the grotto by boat, combining a visit to see the ancient carvings with sailing and

View of the Egadi Islands from the mainland.

Diving in Sicily

Marine caverns, reefs, rainbow-coloured sponges, ancient wrecks and archaeological sites are all part of the Sicilian diving experience. Although Ustica is, by common consent, an experienced diver's first choice, all the offshore marine reserves offer good diving. The Egadi Islands' crystalline waters teem with marine life and are popular with snorkellers as well as divers. On the island of Favignana, snorkelling and scuba-diving enthusiasts appreciate the waters off Punta Marsala, Punta Fanfalo and Punta Ferro, including the underwater cavern between Scoglio Corrente and Cala Rotonda.

Serious divers or underwater photographers might wish to make the island of Ustica their base *(see page 92)*. As Sicily's best-established marine reserve, Ustica's waters reveal an explosion of colour, from corals, sea sponges and anenomes to barracudas, breams, scorpion fish and groupers. Deep-sea archaeological excursions also explore wrecks and inspect amphorae in their original sites on the seabed. Ustica can be visited on a day trip from Palermo.

But even the top resorts should be able to set up a customised diving or snorkelling experience. From Taormina, the most popular dives are around Isola Bella and reveal octopus, schools of fish and a selection of corals.

The beautiful Blue Grotto dive (at a depth of 16 metres/52ft) showcases colourful corals and eels lurking in craggy walls. Far more challenging is the dive to the so-called "Roman temple" (at a depth of 26 metres/85ft), the result of a shipwreck over 2,000 years ago. These ghostly white marble columns were intended for a temple at Taormina until the Roman ship came to a sticky end off Capo Taormina.

The Great Tuna Massacre

The cruel ritual is both a gory tradition and a gruesome spectacle that survives despite conservationists' concerns and the contravention of conventions on driftnet fishing

Tuna fishing is rooted in the Sicilian psyche. Nowhere is this more so than in Favignana, where it is considered the sea's ultimate challenge to man, as well as the island's traditional livelihood. The tuna's only predators are the killer whale, the Mako shark and man, and their ritual death here at the hands of fishermen is both gruelling work and a disturbing spectacle.

The season lasts from May to mid-June, with the ritual *mattanza*, the traditional method of tuna slaughter, as the inexorable fate of the passing shoals. The fast-swimming tuna hunt off the coast of Norway but spawn in the Mediterranean's warm waters. Shoals circle Favignana where they are captured in a system of huge chambered nets *(tonnare)* introduced by the Arabs in the 9th century. Buoys mark out a 100-metre (330ft) rectangle; up to 10km (6

miles) of nets are suspended between the floats. Halfway along lie five antechambers. The innermost section is the *camera della morte*, the death chamber 30 metres (100ft) deep. At dawn, or when the winds are right, the helmsman leads the fleet in prayers, aided by an image of the Madonna. The 60-strong crew sings and chants the *cialoma* in guttural tones. Entreaties are uttered by the *rais*, a Moorish title given to the chief fisherman, who travels in a separate boat and constantly checks the entrance to the *camera della morte*.

The black boats encircle the nets. When the *rais* decides that the currents are right, the shoal is steered into the death chamber and the gate closed. As it fills with fish, the floating death trap sags, like a heavy sack. To the command of *"Tira, tira!"* (pull, pull!) the net is pulled tight. The *rais* chants the fateful battle cry. Each verse of this blood-thirsty sea shanty has a chorus of *"Aiamola, aiamola"*, perhaps derived from *Allah! Che muoia!* (Allah, may it die!).

As the net is drawn in to the length of a football pitch, the fish circle frantically in the *sarabanda della morte*, the dance of death. The chanting stops and the slaughter begins. The frantic fish are harpooned and caught behind the gills with long pole-gaff hooks to be dragged onto the boats. Some of the tuna are man-sized.

As the silvery fish are pierced, the frothing water is stained red. It takes a frenzied 15 minutes and a sea of vivid red to slaughter about 200 tuna, although some die of heart attacks or over-oxygenation. With true Sicilian logic, the tuna's breeding grounds also become their tragic end. ❑

Top: drawing of the annual *mattanza* on the wall of a shop in Favignana. **Left:** dividing up the tuna.

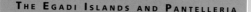

swimming from a craft hired at Cala Dogana (or book with the custodian of the *grotta:* Signor Natale Castiglione at Via Calvario 11, near hydrofoil quay; tel: 0923 924 032).

The **rock carvings** are prehistoric and were not found until 1949. Etched into the soft stone about 10,000 years ago, they include impressions of human dancers and wild animals in naturalistic poses. More recent ones of men, women and fish were created about 5,000 years ago.

Most of the rest of the island is inaccessible, and there are only a few inlets for swimming.

Maréttimo

The most mysterious, mountainous and greenest of the Egadi Islands, Maréttimo lies to the west, separated from its sister islands by a stretch of sea rich in sunken treasure. Here lie the remains of the Carthaginian fleet destroyed by the Romans in 241 BC.

The little port of **Maréttimo** ㉓ has no hotel, but manages with a few serviced apartments and enthusiastic B&B arrangements. Peace and natural beauty are what draw visitors here. Scuba-divers come to explore the 400 caves and grottoes scattered along the coast; plant-lovers study the Mediterranean vegetation at its purest. The rest simply want to relax, swim in the aquamarine waters, or take three-hour trips in the brightly coloured traditional boats around the coast.

Ambitious visitors will climb up to survey the island from **Monte Falcone** (686 metres/2,250ft). An easier walk is an excursion to **Case Romane**, not houses but ruined Roman fortifications not far from the village. (From the port follow directions to Pizzeria Filli Pipitone.) Beside the ruins is a crumbling Arab-Norman chapel.

An alternative hike leads north along the cliffs and cuts across an isthmus to **Punta Tróia** ㉔, a rocky promontory dominated by a Saracen castle. Originally a watchtower,

the castle was enlarged by Roger II and converted by the Spanish into its present form, with an underground cistern that later did service as a dreaded prison. But such sombre thoughts quickly float away on this restful, thyme-scented island.

In summer, hikers should always carry bottled water with them. On these parched islands, water is more precious than wine.

Pantelleria

Pantelleria is closer to Tunisia's Cap Bon, 70km (44 miles) away, than to Sicily, which is 110km (68 miles) distant, and is reached on a six-hour ferry crossing from Trápani, or by air. At 83 sq km (247 acres), it is the largest island off Sicily, with a population estimated at 7,600. The island's evocative name probably derives from the Arabic "daughter of the winds", after the winds that can buffet this rocky outpost, even in August. The island is dotted with *dammusi* – cube-like, low-domed houses – and surrounded by terraces used for growing capers or grapes; even the vines are trained low to protect them from the winds. The

DRINK

Pantelleria is famous for its sweet raisins and for its wines, especially *Moscato di Pantelleria* produced from its sweet moscato grape, Zibibbo. The wine made from raisins is *Passito*, usually highly scented with almonds.

BELOW: Punta Tróia, Maréttimo.

TIP

You can bring a car on the *traghetto* (ferry) from Trápani. However, on Pantelleria it's easier to rent a moped or use the bus service between the town and Scauri and Tracino. Bicycles and motorscooters can also be rented in town. The tourist office is on Via San Nicola (tel: 0923 911 838).

landscape is dramatic and relatively bleak but enlivened with hot springs, jagged rocks and coves instead of beaches. Many mainland Italians, especially from Milan (like fashion designer Giorgio Armani) have summer retreats here.

Pantelleria town

Pantelleria town ㉕ was bombed heavily during the Allied forces invasion of Sicily in World War II, so charm is in short supply. But the island itself has a lively air as well as an exoticism encapsulated by the white-cubed houses and restaurants that serve fish couscous.

Pantelleria was originally founded as a trading post by the Phoenicians. Its small harbours provided excellent protection for the small ships of the day. The island was captured by Rome but eventually – after the Vandals and Byzantines – it was the Arabs who claimed it and introduced farming.

A rewarding hike or a bus ride from Pantelleria town to the port of **Scáuri** ㉖ on the southern coast passes the traditional domed, white-washed *dammusi* houses, framed by terraced vineyards, small settlements and expanses of blackened, lava-stone landscape. The dry-stone walls enclose citrus groves and often appear to have hardy, locally bred donkeys peering over them.

The route also passes strange Neolithic dome-shaped funerary monuments, known as *Sesi*, conceivably built by early settlers who arrived here around the 18th century BC. Little is known of the *Sesi* people; it is assumed they came from Tunisia on foot before the Mediterranean Sea developed. They built circular domed structures using the island's volcanic rock, similar in shape to the *dammusi*. At Mursia their village with *Sesi* structures was protected by walls. Its name, Alta Mura, means High Wall.

Hot springs and mud baths

The island's volcanic origins are visible in the presence of lava stone, basalt rock, hot springs, *stufe* (volcanic steam vents) and a landscape pitted with small *cuddie* (baby spouts), which are extinct volcanic craters. On **Monte Grande** (836 metres/2,743ft), near the hamlet of Bugebera, lies a lake in an old crater full of warm, bubbling, sulphurously brown waters, known as **Specchio di Venere** (Venus's mirror) and used by local bathers to cure myriad ills. The water here can reach 50°C (122°F) because of a hot spring. **Bagno d'Acqua** is another small lake inside a former crater, and visitors are drawn to it too, in order to cover themselves with beautifying volcanic mud.

As for coastal scenery, the craggy shore is studded with coves, with rocks shaded from red through green and black. For swimmers and divers, the absence of beaches is compensated for by the privacy occasioned by secluded coves and hot springs, and by the quality of the underwater landscape, with sightings of ancient wrecks as well as sea sponges and coral. In fact, the great excursions on the island are a tour in a car or by boat. By boat is better. ❑

BELOW: *dammusi* house on Pantelleria.

BEST RESTAURANTS, BARS AND CAFÉS

Prices for a three-course dinner per person and a half-bottle of house wine:
€ = under €20
€€ = €20–35
€€€ = €35–70
€€€€ = over €70

Unlike on the Aeolian Islands, the Egadi rarely represents creative cuisine or fashionable dining, but there's always good seafood to be had in traditional trattorie.

Favignana

La Bettola
Via Nicotera 47
Tel: 0923 921 988 €€
Simple, inexpensive trattoria. No frills, but with a wide selection each day of tuna and swordfish dishes. Closed Thur.

Egadi
Via Cristoforo Colombo 17
Tel: 0923 921 232
www.albergoegadi.it €€€
Popular hotel restaurant renowned for its fish, especially tuna. Closed Oct–Mar.

Il Nautilus
Via Amendola 6, Porto
Tel: 349 182 2815 €€
Excellent tuna carpaccio and *spaghetti con tonno e gamberi* (with tuna and prawns). The inexpensive set menu includes spaghetti with shrimps and capers and tomatoes.

El Pescador
Piazza Europa 38, Porto
Tel: 0923 921 035 €€€
Run by a fishing family who take the pick of the fresh catch. Simple cooking, the speciality is spaghetti with fresh tuna and capers. Closed Wed (except summer) and Feb.

La Tavernetta
Piazza Madrice 62
Tel: 0923 921 939 €€€
Local specialities given star treatment. Excellent fish. Book.

Lévanzo

Paradiso
Via Lungomare 8
Tel: 0923 924 080 €€
Simple hotel restaurant overlooking the sea. Closed Oct–Mar.

Pensione dei Fenici
Via Calvario 18
Tel: 0923 924 083 €
Pensione with a restaurant on the terrace. Closed Oct–Jan.

Maréttimo

Onda Blu
Piazza Umberto
Tel: 0923 923 102 €
Pasta with wonderful sauces, grilled vegetables, fish, all served at tables on the square. Open summer only.

Le Rose dei Venti
Punta S Simone 4
Tel: 0923 923 249
www.isoladimarettimo.it €

Family hotel with a modest restaurant serving excellent fresh fish as well as lobster. Closed Nov–Mar.

Pantelleria

Il Cappero
Via Roma 33
Tel: 0923 912 601 €€
By the port, and a popular place for simple dishes; fish too, of course. And pizza. Closed Mon.

Gabbiano Azzurro
Via Trieste 5
Tel: 0923 911 909 €
Cheap and cheerful establishment. Closed Fri.

I Mulini
Via Kania 12, Contrada Tracino
Tel: 0923 915 398
imulini@galactica.it €€€

A charming old windmill typical of the countryside, adapted with enthusiasm. Good local cooking; garden tables in summer months. Very popular, so booking essential. Dinner only. Closed Tue. Open Easter–end Oct.

La Nicchia
at Scauri Bassa
Tel: 0923 916 342 €€
Pizzeria and ristorante where specialities are fish and couscous. Some tables outside. Dinner only. Closed Wed. Open Easter–end Oct.

Zabib
Porto di Scauri
Tel: 0923 916 617 €€€
Good restaurant, open only for dinner.

RIGHT: seafood platter.

AGRIGENTO AND THE VALLEY OF THE TEMPLES

The classical splendour of the Valley of the Temples makes this Sicily's most visited ancient sight, overshadowing Agrigento itself

Siracusa may have been the most powerful city in Greek Sicily but **Agrigento** (known as Akragas to the Greeks, Agrigentum to the Romans) was the most wealthy and luxurious, a city that reached from the acropolis high on the ridge down to the blue sea below. It was first settled by people from Gela in 580 BC, attracted there by the abundance of springs and the prospect of a dreamy, well-fortified site. It was Benito Mussolini who, in his campaign to unify Sicily and all Italy under one flag, changed its name to Agrigento.

Exploring Agrigento

At first sight, little remains of the ancient splendour. Not that the "modern" city is wholly poor, or even modern. Beneath the charm-less muddle is a fascinating urban mix. The medieval core is a maze of Moorish streets and substandard housing while, in contrast, the new quarter overlooks the temples in an attempt at bourgeois chic, but one that went horribly wrong when landslides, aggravated by overcrowd-ing and shoddy building, killed many in 1966.

Even so, don't be dismayed. Resto-ration is under way in Agrigento, and the summer festival season is magi-cal. Even the image of a parasitical city living off its past glories can be dispelled by a starlit night, a heady southern Sicilian wine and a dinner of grilled swordfish as an alternative to tuna.

If you are in the Agrigento area only for a day, head straight for the **Valle dei Templi** (Valley of the Temples, *see page 122*) and restrict your visit to the town of Agrigento

Main attractions
CHIESA DI SANTO SPIRITO
SANTA MARIA DEI GRECI
CATACOMBE (CATACOMBS)
TEMPIO DELLA CONCORDIA
TEMPIO DI HERA
TEMPIO DI CASTORE E POLLUCE (DIOSCURI)
SAN NICOLA
MUSEO ARCHEOLOGICO REGIONALE
HELLENISTIC-ROMAN QUARTER
THE TEMPLES AT NIGHT
GIARDINO DI KOLYMBETRA

LEFT: Igor Mitoraj bronze in the Valley of the Temples.
RIGHT: ruins of Castor and Pollux Temple with Agrigento in the background.

Agrigento's crest.

itself for dinner and an evening stroll. Parking problems, poor public transport, the scattered nature of the archaeological sites and their relative distance from the city, make it inconvenient to combine the city and the temples, even for meals.

If not staying close to the Valle dei Templi, take a picnic lunch to avoid the coach party options on site. The **tourist office** is at Via Empedocle 73 (tel: 0922 20391).

City sights

Above Via Atenea, Agrigento's pedestrianised main shopping street as well as the entrance to the historic quarter, stands the **Chiesa di Santo Spirito ❶**, the church of a fine Cistercian abbey founded in 1290. Often known as the **Badia Grande**, it is the finest church in the city. It is a complex of cloisters, chapter house and refectory in Chiaramonte style (*see margin note opposite*). The church has a Gothic portal and rose window, plus a panelled ceiling and Baroque interior with stuccoes attributed to Serpotta. The vaulted Gothic dormitory leads to a chapter house with mullioned windows and a bold portal, all emboldened with Arab-Norman geometrical motifs.

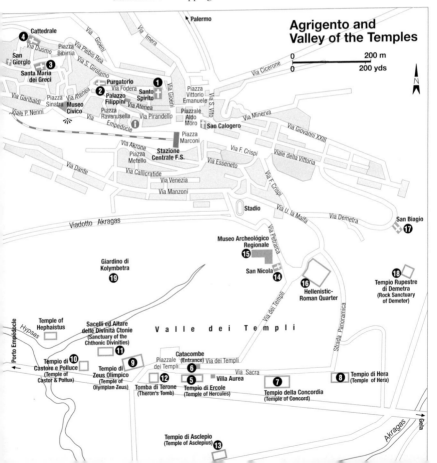

The sacristan in the house opposite will gladly open the church for a tip, while the Cistercian nuns sell sweet almond and pistachio pastries shaped like snakes, shells and flowers. Faced with such delights, the French writer Dominique Fernandez was torn between the "Baroque opulence" of the architecture and the "Arab unctuousness" of the cakes. The cakes won.

The historic quarter

Dominating Piazza Purgatorio, off Via Atenea, is the 17th-century church known simply as the **Purgatorio ❷**, built on an ancient sacred site, but better known for its riot of Baroque allegorical stuccowork by Serpotta.

To the left of the church, a stone lion guards an entrance to the ancient underground drinking water and drainage system. Created in the 5th century BC, these were known as one of the wonders of the ancient world. Linked to the underground chamber beneath San Nicola church *(see page 126)*, the system used conduits and cisterns to channel water to the city. There are plans to open the chambers to the public and create a copy of a

Roman food store complete with a lava-stone grinding mill.

Further west is **Santa Maria dei Greci ❸**, a Norman church set among Agrigento's alleyways, in the heart of the medieval quarter. A Chiaramonte Gothic portal leads to a Norman nave, a coffered ceiling and some Byzantine fragments. Below ground is the greatest surprise: the church is constructed around a 5th-century Greek temple dedicated to Athena. A narrow gallery contains the bases of six fluted Doric columns, the remains of the temple peristyle and stereobate. The sanctuary spans Greek and Christian cults: tradition has it that St Paul preached here.

On Via del Duomo is the 14th-century cathedral, the **Cattedrale ❹**, which surmounts a ridge and incorporates Arab-Norman, Catalan-Gothic and Baroque elements, from Catalan blind arcading to a Norman bell tower. The Norman-Gothic nave boasts an inlaid, coffered ceiling while the graceful Baroque stuccowork in the choir contrasts with a severe Gothic chapel.

Further south, on Via Atenea, the newly restored Baroque **Palazzo**

The Chiaramonte, the dominant feudal dynasty of the 14th century, gave its name to the Catalan-Gothic architectural style, in which fortresses doubled as palaces, with decorated facades, vaulted rooms and lavish painted ceilings. The best of these tower houses had an austere beauty.

BELOW: the cathedral at Agrigento.

Agrigento's lurid past

The city abounds in classical anecdote regarding its fabled wealth. For example, the tyrant of Akragas kept wine in reservoirs hacked out of solid rock; each giant cellar contained 4,000 litres (900 gallons). And returning Olympic heroes were welcomed by cavalcades of chariots drawn by white horses, which were legendary in the Greek world. One ruler of this sybaritic city supposedly burned his enemies alive in a large bull made of bronze.

The people, it was said, "built for eternity but feasted as if there were no tomorrow". The city rivalled Athens in the splendour of its temples, but in its hedonistic lifestyle Akragas was the Los Angeles of the ancient world.

Temple of Hercules in the Valley of the Temples, built in 520 BC.

Filippini is a shining example of Agrigento's renewed commitment to culture.

Even more uplifting is the way the classical city stages open-air performances of drama in tribute to Persephone. The modern city responds with *passeggiata* along tree-lined **Viale della Vittoria**. From this road there are some excellent views of the Valley of the Temples. At the far end is the medieval church of San Biagio and the Sanctuary of Demeter.

Valle dei Templi

It is here, for a fleeting moment, that the classical world comes alive. The Valley of the Temples is not really a valley but a string of Doric temples that stand imposingly on a ridge south of the city facing the sea. An ideal first glimpse of the temples is by night, during a drive along the **Strada Panoramica** and **Via della Valle dei Templi**. The temples glow in the dark countryside, radiating a sense of cohesion, security and serenity. This crest of temples was designed to be visible from the sea, both as a beacon for sailors and to show that the gods guarded

BELOW RIGHT: Temple of Concord, the best-preserved Greek temple in the world.

the sacred city from mortal danger.

An early start guarantees enough solitude to slip back into the classical world. But unless you plan to view the Tempio della Concordia (the Temple of Concord, *see opposite*) from the elegant restaurant in Villa Athena, come armed with a picnic. Otherwise, the on-site snack bar could bring you back to the present times with a bump.

Piazzale dei Templi, the entrance to the main temples, was once the *agora* (market place) and is still alive to the ancient trading spirit. The local guides operate a monopoly, refusing to allow unauthorised rivals to present the archaeological park, and small boys often demand money to protect tourists' cars from unknown dangers, a feature of many Sicilian sites. The archaeological park falls into two sections: the enclosed **Western Zone** (daily 8.30am–7pm; June–end August evening visits by request until 10pm) and the unenclosed **Eastern Zone** (open access), which is best viewed in the early morning or late afternoon – or perhaps from afar when it is flood-lit at night.

Safeguarding Sicilian treasures

Sicilian treasures are probably safer than they have ever been, with recent success stories all over the island. The Sicilian Ministry of Culture has instituted a long-term collaborative venture with California's Getty Museum to favour the exchange of priceless treasures. Agrigento is a prime beneficiary, lending its Greek marble *Kouros (The Agrigento Youth)* and another Attic masterpiece, in return for significant American loans and assistance. The Getty is also installing anti-earthquake protection to the Agrigento museum.

Instead, Aidone has recovered its *Venus*, and other treasures, which ended up in the Getty Museum in Malibu. After incontrovertible proof linking it to Morgantina, the *Venus* returned to Sicily in 2010, and has set a precedent regarding the recovery of stolen treasures, including the drawing up of new anti-trafficking legislation *(see page 158)*.

The picture is not so rosy at the Villa Romana, where the priceless Roman mosaics have suffered from flood damage, vandalism and political wrangling. Although damage and discoloration have occurred, the Unesco-listed mosaics are finally being restored in line with international curating standards *(see page 155)*.

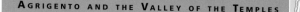

The Eastern Zone

The first treasure visible in the Eastern Zone is the **Tempio di Ercole ❺** (Temple of Hercules). Built in 520 BC in Archaic Doric style, this is the oldest temple, second in size here to the Temple of Zeus and of roughly the same proportions as the Parthenon in Athens. It once had a gorgeous entablature emblazoned with lions, leaves and palms, but now it presents an almost abstract puzzle. Although much is in ruins, Alexander Hardcastle performed a truly Herculean task by re-erecting eight columns in 1924.

Villa Aurea, which is set in olive and almond groves beside the former Golden Gate, once belonged to Hardcastle, the Englishman who devotedly excavated the site. The grounds are riddled with catacombs and water cisterns, which run under rocks and orchards the length of the classical site. A path on the left leads to the **catacombs ❻**, which emerge in a necropolis on the far side of the villa. Now excavated and well lit, the passages cut through the rock and reveal a cross-section of tombs and fossilised bones.

Arches link circular rooms *(tholoi)* containing circular honeycomb cells stacked high with shelf-tombs. Though the oldest tombs here date from the 4th century BC, the main Roman *necropoli* lie just to the south, while Greek burial grounds are scattered around the city.

At the end of the Via Sacra lies the **Tempio della Concordia ❼** (Temple of Concord), abutting ancient city walls. After the Theseion in Athens, it is the best-preserved Greek temple in the world. The pastoral surroundings are at odds with the temple's bloody history: on this bulwark thousands were slain in battle against Carthage. Dating from 430 BC, the temple was saved from ruin in the 6th century by being converted into a church. The peristyle was sealed by dry-stone walls, and the *cella* opened to form twin naves, although sadly the *metopes* and pediment were destroyed.

The tapering columns tilt inwards imperceptibly, creating an ethereal grace and airiness that belie the weighty entablature. A further refinement is that the fluted columns have different spacing, narrowing towards

TIP

The **Festival of Myth** takes place in Agrigento in summer and features classical and pop concerts in the Valley of the Temples (tel: 0922 32888, www.ilsestante. net). In February the temples provide a striking backdrop for the annual **Almond Blossom Festival** (Sagra del Mandorlo) and international folk festival. There are parades, shows, crafts exhibits and a chance to listen to anything from Filipino groups to Scottish pipe bands.

BELOW: Temple of Concord at night.

CLASSICAL GLOSSARY
A cella is the inner room of an ancient Greek or Roman temple.
A metope is the space between two ornamental triglyphs on a Doric frieze.
A peristyle is a series of columns surrounding a temple or court.
An entablature is the upper part of a temple, resting on pillars or columns.
A telamon is a male sculpture used as a supporting pillar.

BELOW: bronze sculpture among the catacombs in the Valley of the Temples.

the corners. They were originally coated with glazed marble dust to protect the flaky sandstone, then painted with vivid polychrome scenes, predominantly bright blue or blood-red. Now lichen-coated, the temple still represents sheer perfection in line. The only jarring image is the distant cityscape with its high-rise apartment buildings and cemetery but, seen though a heat haze, even that shimmers obligingly. The temple is transformed by light: locals say that one has not lived until seeing Concord changing with the seasons, at dawn and sunset, dusk and moonlight.

Restoration of the temples is ongoing, with the jury still out as to whether damaged sections of the temples should be replaced by replicas, and the originals moved to the city's well-designed archaeological museum. Even if certain sections have been moved, it might be the only solution.

Commendable cultural initiatives are under way, such as the evocative summer music festivals and contemporary sculpture exhibitions. Sculptors of the stature of Igor Mitoraj have been invited to display their works in the Valley of the Temples. Mitoraj's recent exhibition, a "conversation" between contemporary man and the gods of classical myth, was a superlative example of what to aspire to.

The **Tempio di Hera ❽** (Temple of Hera) surmounts a rocky ridge which formed part of the city ramparts. Known as Juno to the Romans, Hera was protector of engaged and married couples. Fittingly, hers is held to be the most romantic of temples, set "high on the hill like an offering to the goddess". Yet Zeus's sister and wife was perceived as a bloodthirsty goddess, to be appeased by sacrifice at an altar beside the walls. Part of the *cella* and 25 columns remain intact along with the drums of columns; the rest fell over the hill during a landslide. The stones bear reddish traces of fire damage where they were singed by flames.

The Western Zone

After retracing your steps to the entrance, cross the road to the **Tempio di Zeus Olimpico ❾** (the Temple of Olympian Zeus). Even at the peak of its golden age, the temple was unfinished. With the area of a football pitch, it was the largest Doric temple ever known. The U-shaped grooves on the stone blocks represent primitive pulley marks formed during construction. Today's fallen masonry is a challenge to the imagination: the best stone was plundered to build the port of Empédocle 9km (5½ miles) away. A frieze on the east side depicted the battle between Zeus (known also to the Romans as Jupiter or Jove, that is, Giove), and the Giants, matched by the War of Troy on the western side.

giants and by the columns of the peristyle. The telamons also had allegorical and aesthetic functions. They both broke up the uniformity of the peristyle and illustrated the war against Zeus; like Atlas, the defeated giants were compelled to carry the world on their shoulders.

A sandstone copy of a telamon lies on the ground, dreamily resting his head on his arms, and one of the originals is on display in the archaeological museum. On the temple, these male *giganti* (also known as atlantes, or Atlas figures) alternated with female caryatids and represented the three known racial types of the time: African, Asian and European.

West of the Temple of Zeus is the most confusing quarter, dotted with shrines dating from pre-Greek times. The Via Sacra leads to the **Tempio di Castore e Polluce** ❿ (Temple of Castor and Pollux, or the Dioscuri), spuriously named after the twin sons of Zeus. Although it has become the city symbol, the building is theatrical pastiche, erected in 1836 from the remains of several temples. Even so, it is a graceful and evocative reconstruc-

tion. Locally, the temple is known as *tre colonne*, since only three of the four columns are visible from the city. Despite its name, the temple was first dedicated to Persephone and Demeter, Chthonic (Underworld) deities, along with Dionysus.

This theory is supported by the temples in the surrounding area. Known as the **Sacelli ed Altare delle Divinità Ctonie** ⓫ (Sanctuary of the Chthonic Divinities), the quarter conceals sacrificial altars and ditches, a veritable shrine to fertility, immortality and eternal youth. Pale-coloured beasts were offered to the heavens but black animals were sacrificed to the gods of the Underworld. The altars took the form of flat, concentric circles or deep, well-shaped affairs. Now bounded by a gorge and an orange grove, this sanctuary of death was also the fount of life, with lush gardens and a lake full of exotic birds and fish.

Close to Piazzale dei Templi lies **Tomba di Terone** ⓬ (Theron's Tomb), a tribute to Agrigento's benevolent tyrant. This truncated tower in Doric-Ionic style is essentially

An exhibition of sculptures by Igor Mitoraj in the Valley of the Temples contrasted the contemporary with the classical in a dramatic setting.

BELOW: Temple of Hera.

Facade of San Nicola.

BELOW: Giardino di Kolymbetra.

a Roman funerary pyramid, more a celebration of conquest than glory to a local hero. Outside the ancient walls is the isolated **Tempio di Asclepio** (Temple of Asclepius), half-hidden in an almond grove. Dedicated to the god of healing, it lies between the River Akragas and a sacred spring.

From Piazzale dei Templi, a short drive along Via dei Templi leads to the **Villa Athena** with its restaurant (tel: 0922 596 288), the **museo archeologico** *(see below)*, the Hellenistic-Roman Quarter and a clutch of pagan shrines. En route are fortifications, a reminder that Agrigento was once enclosed by walls, towers and massive gates, of which the perimeter and craggy foundations remain. The sandy landscape is dotted with olives and pines. Subsidence has created strange slopes and whirling patterns on the soil.

San Nicola ⓮ (daily 9am–6pm) on Via Petrarca is a Romanesque church with 15th-century cloisters whose severe but grand facade is reminiscent of monuments in ancient Rome. This is not so far-fetched given that the church is built from Greek stone raided from the ruins and also purports to be a Roman temple dedicated to the sun god. A chapel contains the **Sarcophagus of Phaedra**, an exquisitely carved scene of Phaedra's grief at the loss of her lover and stepson Hippolytus.

Regional museum

Next door is the well-presented **Museo Archeologico Regionale** ⓯ (Sun–Sat 9am–7pm, Mon 9am–noon, combined ticket with the temples) incorporating a church, courtyard and temple foundations. The Graeco-Roman section is the centrepiece, along with a Bronze Age urn from a Sican tomb and a three-legged *Trinacria*, the ancient symbol of Sicily. Exhibits include a wealth of painted Attic vases dating from the 5th century BC, Greek lion's-head water spouts, a vibrant Roman mosaic of a gazelle, and a controversial *ephebe* (classical youth; *see "Safeguarding Sicilian treasures", page 122*). A poignant marble sarcophagus depicts the death of a child amidst weeping. The highlight is a telamon in all its massive glory accompanied by other powerful giant heads. Elsewhere are votive offerings and statues associated with orgiastic rites: phallic donkeys compete with a libidinous pygmy and a hermaphrodite.

The **Hellenistic-Roman Quarter** ⓰ (daily 9am–1hr before sunset) lies opposite, an ancient commercial and residential area laid out on a grid system. Whereas the Greeks created the grid system, the Romans overlaid it with a rational arrangement of public and private space. The well-preserved remains of aqueducts, terracotta and stone water channels are visible, as well as vestiges of shops, taverns and patrician villas. The frescoed villas are paved with patterned mosaics protected by glass enclosures.

On the far side of Strada Panoramica is a stretch of Greek walls and **San Biagio** ⓱, a Norman church perched on a rocky platform (currently closed

for restoration). It is carved into an ancient temple to Demeter and Persephone. Two circular altars lie between the church and another tribute to the goddess of fertility. At the foot of the cliff is the **Tempio Rupestre di Demetra** ⓲ (the Rock Sanctuary of Demeter), the oldest sanctuary in the valley, dating from the 7th century BC.

When visiting Sicily in 1885, Guy de Maupassant was lucky enough to see the temples without tourists or modern desecration. The writer was struck by their air of "magnificent desolation; dead, arid and yellowing on all sides". Yet with falcons hovering above, lizards scurrying at one's feet, the air heavy with the scent of blossoms, today's landscape throbs with life.

The **Giardino di Kolymbetra** ⓳ (daily 10am–6pm, tel: 335 129042) is the latest addition to the Valley of the Temples. This restored Greek garden, sandwiched between the Tempio di Castore e Polluce and the Tempio di Vulcano, began life as a vast pool, hence the name "*kolymbetra*" – Greek for pool. It was used for sacred rites and, conveniently, as a fish farm and irrigation system.

In the 3rd century BC the conquering Carthaginians buried it but created gardens instead, using sophisticated underground irrigation systems that still work perfectly. The Arabs cultivated sugar cane here, but today's gardens are an enchanting mix of orchards, citrus groves and evocative ruins.   ❏

EAT

Popular local dishes include *salsiccia al finocchio* (pasta and fennel), *coniglio in agrodolce* (sweet and sour rabbit) and *involtini di pesce spada* (stuffed swordfish). Combinations of shellfish, artichokes, pasta and pilchards are comon, as are sweet Arab staples such as *cassata* and *cannoli*.

RESTAURANTS, BARS AND CAFÉS

Agrigento

Bar la Promenade
Via Passeggiata Archeologica 6
Tel: 0922 24098
A café and *pasticceria* of note, especially if you like Sicilian specialities made with almonds: cakes, marzipan, *granita*, ice cream and *latte di mandorla* (a milky almond drink). Closed Tue.

Ambasciata di Sicilia
Via Giambertoni 2
Tel: 0922 20526 €€
A panoramic view not always matched by the cuisine but still reliable and value for money.

Concordia
Via Porcello 8
Tel: 0922 22668 €€
Good for grilled fish and seafood-based pasta dishes – try the spaghetti with prawns. Reasonably

priced fixed menus too. Outdoor seating in summer. Closed Sun in winter.

Da Giovanni
Piazzetta Vadalà 2
Tel: 0922 21110 €€
A small restaurant, but tempting for truly Sicilian dishes. Ask to be guided through the menu. Booking essential. Closed Sun and first 2 weeks Jan.

Kalos
Piazza San Calogero
Tel: 0922 26389
www.ristorantekalos.it €€€
Worth a visit for *involtini di pesce spada* (rolled and stuffed swordfish). Closed Sun.

La Corte degli Sfizzi
Via Atenea Cortile Contarini 4
Tel: 349 579 2922 €€
A trendy and fairly inexpensive restaurant/pizzeria. Several set menus

at differing prices. Pizza available at lunchtime. Closed Tue.

Le Caprice
Via Cavalieri Magazzeni
Tel: 0922 411 364 €€€
Sicilian specialities in a garden setting, and a great choice given the array of *antipasti* and shellfish; tasty swordfish, shrimps and mussels. Pizza at dinner only.

Leon D'Oro
Viale Emporium 102 (Marina di Agrigento)
Tel: 0922 414 400 €€
Handy for the Marina di Agrigento, this is an original seafood restaurant.

Per Bacco
Vicolo lo Presti
Tel: 0922 553 369 €€
A small fish trattoria favoured by the locals, but dinner only. Closed Mon.

Ruga Reali
Cortile Scribani 8
Tel: 0922 20370 €–€€
A friendly, simple place for Sicilian fare but no outdoor seating.

Trattoria dei Templi
Via Panoramica d. Templi 15
Tel: 0922 403 110 €€€
Reliable seafood but also traditional Sicilian meat dishes. Closed Sun in July and Aug.

Villa Athena
Via dei Templi 33
Tel: 0922 596 288
www.athenahotels.com €€€
Recently revamped, this lovely hotel-restaurant scores highly on atmosphere and views across the Valley of the Temples. Reservation advisable. No jeans or T-shirts.

• • • • • • • •

Prices for a three-course dinner per person and a half-bottle of house wine. €€€€ = over €70, €€€ = €35–70, €€ = €20–35, € = under €20.

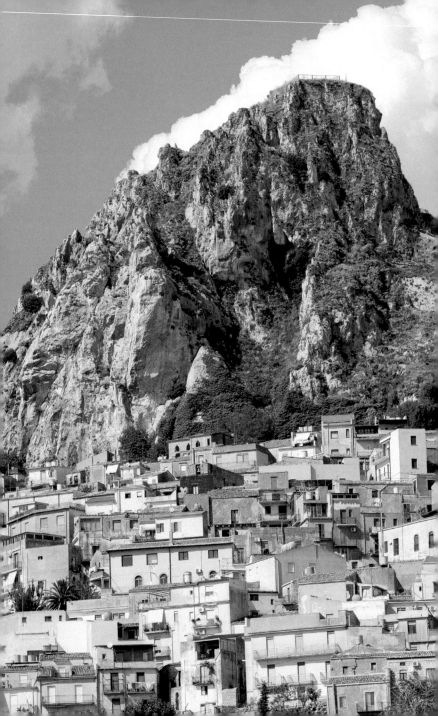

AGRIGENTO PROVINCE

This enigmatic province embraces everything from earthquake-struck towns to spectacular hilltop villages, from mineral spas and coastal forts to distant Moorish islands

People from Agrigento are a mysterious breed, often referred to as *né carne né pesce*, neither fish nor fowl. Yet this elusive province has produced exceptional Sicilians: Empedocles, the pre-Socratic philosopher; Pirandello, the playwright; and Sciascia, the political novelist. All were gifted mavericks who shared a bitter-sweet relationship with their homeland. Empedocles committed suicide on Etna. Pirandello was the master of split personalities. Sciascia called his land a "wicked stepmother" yet rarely left, except to visit Paris.

Outside the capital, Agrigento is barely touched by tourism. There are no obvious sights in this low-key province. Instead, there are myriad chance discoveries of a lesser order: distinctive hilltop towns; deserted classical sites; coastal fortresses; remnants of former feudal estates; Arab-Norman ports; prosperous vineyards.

But weighed against this are: shabby towns; suburban sprawl; neglected fields; and the scars left by disused sulphur mines. Agrigento's additional drawbacks are extreme poverty, the lingering grip of the Mafia, and a torpor conditioned by

centuries of failure. The province's insularity and lassitude make few concessions to visitors' demands for decent service, charming hotels and reliable roads.

That said, the roads are improving, as is the wine around Menfi, while the opening of the luxurious Verdura Golf and Spa Resort has brought a glimmer of hope to the region.

An eastern foray

The route into the hinterland east of Agrigento passes rugged hilltop towns

Main attractions
NARO
THE *LEOPARD* LITERARY TRAIL
ERACLEA MINOA
SCIACCA
CALTABELLOTTA
LINOSA

LEFT: Caltabellotta.
RIGHT: one of the giant heads made of lava stone near Castello Bentivegna.

Sicily's Carnivale at the beginning of Lent involves entire communities in parades and contests.

of Arab origin which were fortified during the Muslim conquest and later. Many of these were sulphur-mining centres until the early 20th century and, despite a slight agricultural revival or diversification into wine, have yet to recover from the collapse of the traditional industry.

Leaving **Agrigento ❶** in the direction of Caltanissetta, follow the SS122 through the rolling countryside to **Favara**, a former sulphur centre, with a dilapidated Chiaramonte castle (rebuilt in 1488 from an original 1275 castle), two 16th-century churches, the **Purgatorio** and the **Rosario**, and an elegantly Baroque main square.

From here, choose the hilly road east to the neighbouring medieval hilltop town of **Naro ❷**, an important market town. It is an appealing place, with battlement walls (*c.*1265) enclosing a late 13th-century Chiaramonte castle and some impressive Baroque mansions.

Palma di Montechiaro

Follow the SS410 south to the sea: the rewarding 17km (11-mile) drive lined with olive trees and vineyards leads to **Palma di Montechiaro ❸** with panoramic views over the coast. The town may strike a romantic chord with readers of Lampedusa's novel, *Il Gattopardo (The Leopard)*. It was established in 1637 by the Prince of Lampedusa, an ancestor of Giuseppe Tomasi di Lampedusa (1896–1957), who used much of the life in this town as his inspiration for the novel (his only one), which he wrote shortly before he died. The action takes place in Sicily in 1860, as the kingdom of Naples and Sicily is brought to an end by Garibaldi and his army invading Sicily in order to forge a united Italy *(for more on Lampedusa landmarks, see box opposite)*.

Today, however, the town of Palma di Montechiaro conjures up a catalogue of Sicilian ills: Mafia intervention, disturbing images of poverty,

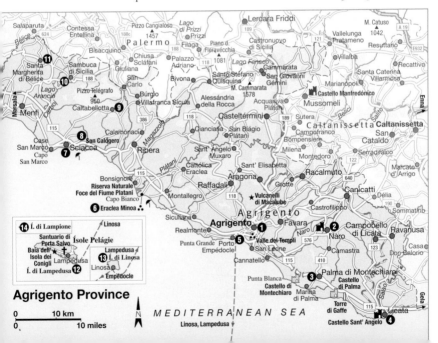

Agrigento Province

MEDITERRANEAN SEA

0   10 km
0   10 miles

Linosa, Lampedusa

unemployment, public indifference, despair and dogs. The once splendid late 17th-century **Palazzo Ducale** is crumbling, and the town's only dusty glory is the **Chiesa Madre**, built above imposing steps between 1666 and 1703, decaying under the weight of civic inertia. To qualify for funding, the church steps must be restored in the same stone as before. However, the original quarry is closed, so Sicilian bureaucracy decrees that renovation is impossible.

About 4km (2½ miles) south, the coastal road ends in the fishing port of **Marina di Palma**. From here, the SS115 leads back to Agrigento. However, castle aficionados can follow the same road east to see the remains of a string of fortifications along the coast, notably the striking **Castello di Palma** and, just east, **Torre di Gaffe**.

Further east lies downtrodden **Licata ❹**, a working port that witnessed the Allied invasion in 1943. Licata also has a 16th-century castello, layers of palazzi, the 17th-century convent of **San Francesco** that is now a school, and a 17th-century church dedicated to **San Domenico**.

The **Museo Archeologico** (closed for refurbishment) has prehistoric and Greek period relics.

The southwestern coast

Just outside Agrigento city, the hamlet of **Caos** on the Porto Empédocle road is where Luigi Pirandello, one of Italy's greatest and most wide-ranging writers, was born in 1867. The irony of the village name was not wasted on Pirandello, who called himself a "son of chaos" *(see box page 132)*.

The traditional farmhouse in which the "master of the absurd" was born is now a small but pleasing museum (daily 9am–1pm, 2–7pm; charge). In 1936, in accordance with his wishes, the playwright's ashes were buried in the countryside. Although this once idyllic spot now overlooks industrial sprawl, Pirandello, whose life was a lesson in defeat snatched from the jaws of victory, would have appreciated his posthumous fall from grace.

Just 7km (4½ miles) south of Agrigento is **San Leone**, the city's pleasant but unexceptional seaside resort, which was a humble fishing village

Family loyalty extends to the village as a whole, especially when villagers face outsiders. It's not unusual to hear people refer to themselves first as members of a village – Sciaccatani, Caltabellotesi – and only then as Sicilians.

On the trail of *The Leopard*

Giuseppe Tomasi di Lampedusa was a Palermitan prince born into a life of leisure in 1896, at his happiest ensconced in a café with a good book. Yet out of such glorious self-indulgence came *The Leopard*, an elegy to aristocratic Sicily, a complex novel covering immutability and nostalgia. Both a great aristocrat and discerning critic of his own class, he lost his first family palace in an Allied bombing raid in 1943.

In Palermo, follow in the prince's footsteps by passing **Palazzo Lanza Tomasi** (Via Butera 28), his last home, overlooking the sea. This was where the prince moved after losing his family home in the bombings, where he died in 1957, and where you can stay.

Cross lovely Piazza Marina towards Teatro Massimo, stopping en route at the glorious Baroque **Oratorio di Santa Cita**, beside the ruins of the prince's first palazzo. East of Teatro Massimo, call in at **Pasticceria Mazzara** (Via Generale Magliocco 19) to toast Lampedusa in the café where *The Leopard* was largely written.

Diehard *Leopard* fans can visit the prince's fictional summer palace, Donnafugata, inspired by his beloved ancestral palazzo in **Santa Margherita di Bélice**. Although ravaged by an earthquake in 1968, the palace shell has been restored. Even so, the family museum is overshadowed by the peaceful gardens and an overwhelming sense of pathos, typified by the melancholic cryptomeria trees which somehow survived the earthquake. The trail then takes in **Palma di Montechiaro**, the Lampedusas' feudal hilltop town, tarnished by urban sprawl yet redeemed by a *Leopard*-like twist – a taste of the almond cakes made by the local nuns – which sent the fictional prince into raptures. To appreciate the *Leopard* trail, book a tour through the Lampedusa Literary Park (tel: 091 625 4011, www.parcotomasi.it) or visit Lampedusa's palace in Palermo (groups only, or stay overnight, or book a cookery course, +39 333 316 5432, www.butera28.it).

After the Saracens invaded Sicily in the 9th century, Sciacca became the main port for the export of grain to North Africa, and the town's fishing industry thrived as well. In 1101 Count Roger bequeathed the town to his daughter, Juliet. She replaced the mosques with Christian churches and monasteries.

until the 1960s, and **Porto Empédocle ❺**, just west of San Leone, an unmitigated black spot, despite its illustrious past. The port authorities quarried the classical site for stone to build its harbour walls and, it would seem, in revenge the temple gods cursed it with ugliness. The benighted city can be avoided unless you are taking a ferry trip to the remote **Isole Pelágie** *(see page 135)*.

Fortunately, the SS115 soon passes through sparsely populated countryside leading to the province's most delightful, but isolated, classical site. En route are views of the coast, which borders a fertile valley and overlooks neat orange plantations and smoothly contoured fields.

Eraclea Minoa

The classical site of **Eraclea Minoa ❻** (daily 9am–1 hour before sunset; charge) squats on bleached soil alongside olive-covered slopes at the mouth of the River Platani. As one looks down from this idyllic headland, there is a view over the white cliffs of **Capo Bianco** emcompassing a crescent of golden sands and

pine groves. Eraclea was a satellite of Selinunte, but suffered a grim fate at the hands of the Carthaginians when it was depopulated and became a no-man's-land in Greek and Punic territorial disputes. The name Minoa suggests a Minoan settlement and evokes the legend of King Minos of Crete who pursued Daedalus from Crete to Sicily, but the connection is tenuous.

While the site is delightful and the atmosphere therapeutic, the excavations have been laborious and the results far from spectacular. So far, Eraclea has revealed substantial city walls, a Hellenistic theatre (4 BC), a necropolis, and ruined villas dating from Greek and Punic times. Concerts and productions of classical drama take place in July and August (tel: 0922 846 005).

Sciacca

Further along the coast is **Sciacca ❼**, a working fishing port and spa town with a population of 42,000, many of Arab descent. The town was evangelised by San Calógero and prospered in Arab times thanks to

BELOW: the coast at Eraclea Minoa.

Luigi Pirandello

The playwright and novelist, born in Caos in 1867, won the Nobel Prize for Literature in 1934, two years before his death. His pervasive influence on European drama challenged the conventions of the day in their naturalism, personal relationships, disillusionment and reality, and his play *Sei Personaggi in Cerca di Autore (Six Characters in Search of an Author)*, written in 1921, is still in constant repertory around the world. His writings anticipated the works of Brecht, Beckett and O'Neill. His novel *L'Esclusa (The Outcast)* broke all society's rules when published in 1901, as it concerned a woman's desire for independence in Sicily's patriarchal society.

its location, midway between Mazara and Agrigento. Its name derives from the Arabic *As-saqah*, meaning "cleft" – a reference to the caves of Mount Kronion, whose thermal springs were to make the area an important spa. In the 16th century Sciacca was torn apart by two warring families, the Norman Perollo and the Catalan Luna, and it suffered a gradual decline until the revival of the port and mineral spa, aided by an injection of Mafia funds and its close links with North Africa.

Sciacca lacks great architecture, but some exhilarating sea views and an engaging ensemble of tawny, weather-beaten buildings justify a visit.

Corso Vittorio Emanuele, the main street, has sumptuous palazzi from all periods, including **Palazzo Steripinto** (1501), with its crenellated facade of diamond-shaped design, a rusticated style borrowed from Neapolitan architecture.

The terrace of **Piazza Scandaliato** is the bustling Baroque centre of both the town and the Corso. Its scenic balcony is perfect for drinking in the views of the sea over an *aperitivo*. On summer evenings, the square usually belongs to Tunisian hawkers selling exotic clothes and local ceramics.

The **Duomo** (daily 8.30am–6pm) presents a confused image, with Arab-Norman apses buried in a Baroque facade. It was built in 1656, replacing a church erected in 1108. It has considerable charm, as well as statues by Antonino and Gian Domenico Gagini.

Set in the neighbouring Palazzo Scaglione, the **Museo Scaglione** (Wed and Fri 9am–1.30pm, 3–7pm) houses a quirky private collection of paintings, ceramics, sculpture and a much-admired 18th-century crucifix.

From Piazza Scandaliato, steps lead down to the port and numerous fish restaurants. After the slightly oppressive hinterland, visitors tend to appreciate this forthright, living town, noted for its sandy beaches, spa waters and seafood platters.

Sciacca's churches embrace all periods and styles. **San Calógero** and **San Domenico** are sober Baroque works, while the **Convento di San Francesco** combines clean lines with Moorish cloisters. The **Chiesa**

Ceramic shop in Sciacca.

BELOW LEFT: Sciacca city gate. **BELOW:** view over Sciacca waterfront.

Basilica Santa Maria del Soccorso in Sciacca.

BELOW: Filippo Bentivegna's heads carved from lava.

del Carmine is a Norman abbey with a Gothic rose window and half-hearted Baroque restoration. Facing is a sculpted medieval gate and the Gothic portal of **Santa Margherita**.

To the east is the ruined Romanesque **San Nicolò** church which contrasts with **Santa Maria della Giummare**, a Catalan Gothic church with crenellated Norman towers and a Baroque interior. Just within the walls is the Badia Grande, an impressive 14th-century abbey.

Set among almond and olive groves just 2km (1¼ miles) outside Sciacca, **Castello Bentivegna** (May–Sept 10am–noon, 4–8pm, Oct–Apr 9am–1pm, 3–5pm; closed Mon) is also called the "enchanted castle". It is a folly in stone created by a peasant sculptor, a forest of statues that is the work of one man. In 1946, after great personal tragedy, Filippo Bentivegna returned from the United States and bought a patch of land in his native town. Using the rocks at the foot of Monte Kronio as his material, he sculpted 3,000 primitive heads of devils, politicians and knights. Not content with his work above ground,

the sculptor set about carving heads from olive wood and creating frescoed caverns in the mountain. Bentivegna died in 1967.

Spa centres

Sciacca is also a noted spa centre, with thermal spas close to town. Known to the Romans as Thermae Selinuntinae, the **Terme**, the Sciacca thermal spa, is open from April to November. Used since prehistoric times and praised by Pliny, the spa's mud baths and volcanic vapours occupy a grand Art Nouveau establishment that proposes cures for rheumatic and respiratory conditions.

Just north is the **San Calógero** ❽ spa on Monte Kronio that harnesses the powers of a "mini" volcano, with bubbling hot springs and vapour-drenched grottoes used as saunas. The galleries, seats and water channels were hollowed out in ancient times by the Sicani or, according to the myth-makers, by Daedalus. The place takes its name from the patron saint of the harvest.

Outside town is the famous **Verdura Golf and Spa Resort** (*see page*

Leonardo Sciascia

Sciascia (1921–89), born at Racalmuto, remained emotionally tied to Sicily all his life and said he had never left the island for more than three months (then generally to Paris). He was an intellectual and one of the greatest Italian writers of the 20th century, and his novels were infused with Sicilian life that revolved around the sulphur mines and the farms. His most famous novels include *Il Giorno della Civetta* (*The Day of the Owl*, 1961) and *A Ciascuno il Suo* (*To Each his Own*,1966). In *The Moro Affair* he tackled the murky world of Italian politics in the 1970s. A Communist Party member of Palermo City Council, he later became a member of the European Parliament.

273), whose destination spa is helping to kickstart tourism in the province.

The rugged west

From Sciacca, a circular route and winding road leads 20km (12 miles) inland, up to the mysterious mountain village of **Caltabellotta** ❾, the highlight of this rural route, with its cluster of towers, churches, grey roofs and a population of 4,500. The commanding village is spectacular, whether seen through spring blossom or swathed in mist. On the highest level, below the hulk of the ruined castle, is the restored Norman **Chiesa Madre** with its original portal and pointed arches. On the level underneath is the lopsided **Piazza Umberto** and the handsome **Chiesa del Carmine,** which has also been restored recently. Below stretch shadowy mountain views from the spacious **Belvedere** and the white **Chiesa San Agostino**. The peace that brought the Sicilian Vespers to an end in 1302 was signed here. On the edge of the village lies the **Eremo di San Pellegrino**, an abandoned hermitage with stupendous views of a mountainside studded with necropoli. Legend has it that a dragon lived here which feasted on young maidens until it was killed by the saint.

Northwest of Caltabellotta, but linked by circuitous country roads, is **Sambuca di Sicilia** ❿, an Arab-Norman town with its old centre near Piazza Navarro showing its Islamic antecedents. There is also a popular lake and facilities for watersports and barbecues. Amateur archaeologists are drawn to the neighbouring Zona Archeologica di **Monte Adranone**, where the remains of a Greek colony have recently come to light, as well as huts and burial chambers from an Iron Age village.

Santa Margherita di Bélice

Further west still is **Santa Margherita di Bélice** ⓫, inextricably linked with *The Leopard (see box page 131).*

In the novel, the fictional town of Donnafugata includes existing and easily recognisable places, including the **Palazzo Filangieri Cutò**, which belonged to the family of Lampedusa's mother. According to the information contained in a letter he wrote to his friend Baron Enrico di Merlo Tagliavia, "The palace at Donnafugata is one and the same as the one at Santa Margherita, while for the town as a whole, the reference is to Palma Montechiaro" *(see margin right)*.

In recent times Santa Margherita has become better known as the epicentre of the earthquake zone. Between here and the coast lies **Menfi**, another earthquake-damaged town, and a centre for the province's winemaking.

Isole Pelágie

This remote, sun-baked archipelago of three islands lies amid strong currents off the North African coast, closer to Tunisia's Cap Bon than the Sicilian mainland. Although there are pockets of agriculture, the islands are unnaturally barren due to wanton deforestation, neglect, water shortages

The 17th-century Palazzo Filangieri Cutò in Santa Margherita di Bélice is where Lampedusa spent happy summers as a child. He writes: "Set in the middle of the town... it spread over a vast expanse and contained about a hundred rooms... including state rooms, living rooms, quarters for thirty guests... three great courtyards, stables and coach-houses, a theatre and church, a large and very lovely garden, and a big orchard." (Places of My Infancy, *Giuseppe Tomasi di Lampedusa*).

BELOW: local life, Caltabelotta.

Collapsed volcanic crater in the small island of Linosa.

and strong winds that have caused a virtual disappearance of the native olive groves and carob plantations. Fifty years ago, much of this lunar landscape was farmland bounded by dry-stone walls, but today the economy rests on sponge fishing, canning and tourism.

There are no outstanding cultural sites, but the translucent waters are as appealing as the local couscous. The rugged native character and cuisine are distinctly Tunisian, as are the Moorish *dammusi* houses.

Lampedusa and Linosa

Due to its location, **Lampedusa** ⑫ used to be known as "a gift from Africa to Europe" but is now dubbed "the backdoor into Italy". The normal population of Sicilians and weather-beaten Tunisian fishermen has been usurped by waves of refugees from North Africa. Since the Arab Spring revolutions in 2011, boatloads of illegal immigrants have overwhelmed the island, and crushed tourism for the immediate future.

Lampedusa port, with its ferry service to Porto Empédocle and

BELOW: swimming in a cove on Lampedusa.

Linosa, contains a rabbit warren of a kasbah that reeks of spices, sardines and anchovies. Indeed, the port is the best place for sampling pasta with sardines, sweet and sour rabbit or Sicilian candied fruit and spicy desserts.

Buses from the port are infrequent so, despite the rocky roads, bicycles and mopeds are a popular way of exploring the interior. At the centre of the island is **Santuario di Porto Salvo**, a church in a lush garden surrounded by grottoes once inhabited by Saracen pirates.

A boat trip is the best way of appreciating Lampedusa's secluded grottoes, craggy inlets and sheer limestone cliffs. The island of Conigli, just offshore, is a nature reserve with the **Baia dell' Isola dei Conigli** (Bay of the Island of Rabbits), the island's greatest attraction.

Linosa ⑬ (pop. 500) is the island closest to Sicily and can be reached on a day trip from Lampedusa, 42km (26 miles) to the north, as can uninhabited Lampione. Linosa, formed by the tips of three vast submerged volcanoes, is popular with scuba-divers and sunbathers.

There is little to do here except rest, roast, swim, hike along dusty paths through vineyards or spot *dammusi*, the pastel-coloured cube-like houses with white window frames. These traditional Arab houses date back to designs created by the first Tunisian settlers. The domed roofs are designed to keep the interior cool. Massimo Errera (tel: 0922 972 082) organises trips around the island, as well as days trekking and excursions to the craters.

About two hours by boat from Lampedusa, **Lampione** ⑭ is an uninhabited island, with a modest area of just 1.5 sq km (370 acres), scorched dry thanks to man's negligence. Its drama lies underwater: the translucent sea is unpolluted and rich in marine life, from sponge beds to basking sharks. Sicilian pleasures are notoriously double-edged. ❑

BEST RESTAURANTS, BARS AND CAFÉS

Prices for a three-course dinner per person and a half-bottle of house wine:
€ = under €20
€€ = €20–35
€€€ = €35–70
€€€€ = over €70

Apart from in the Caltabelotta hinterland, seafood tends to prevail. For gourmet Italian cuisine, consider the internationally minded Verdura Golf and Spa Resort (see page 273). However, La Madia, Sicily's star destination restaurant, is annoyingly located in the grim town of Licata.

(see page 273)

Caltabellotta
Trattoria La Ferla
Via Roma 29
Tel: 0925 951 444 €€
A lovely restaurant with authentic rural cuisine in a scenic mountain village. Closed Mon.

Sciacca
In Sciacca itself head for the fish restaurants in the lower town, near the port. Also try the *tabisca*, a traditional local pizza with onion and cheese.
Le Gourmet Verso
Via Monte Kronio 7, at San Calógero
Tel: 0925 26460 €€€
Classic Sicilian cooking. Locals come here for fish. Garden. Closed

Tue and Nov.
Hostaria del Vicolo
10 Vicolo Sammaritano
Tel: 0925 23071 €€
Unpretentious but serious about its pasta, seafood and wine. Closed Mon and Nov.
Miramare
Piazza Scandagliato 6
Tel: 0925 26050 €€
Fish dishes but also tasty pizza; fine sea views from the terrace.
La Scogliera
Via San Pietro 54, Siciliana Marina
Tel: 0922 817 532 €€–€€€
Offers only a fish menu from start to finish, but excellent.
Trattoria del Buongustaio
Via Maglienti 62
Tel: 0925 902 698 €–€€
Family-run restaurant in the historical centre of Sciacca. Regional cuisine based on seafood.

Licata
La Madia
Corso Filippo Re Capriata 22
Tel: 0922 771 443
www.ristorantelamadia.it €€€
Licata is an ugly town marooned between Ragusa and Agrigento but boasts the island's most celebrated restaurant. Chef Pino Cuttaia delights with his inventive (two-Michelin-starred) cuisine. Typical is his version of *arancino*

(a fried rice ball and classic Sicilian street snack) in a sauce of red mullet and wild fennel. Closed Sun pm and Tue.

Porto Palo di Menfi
Da Vittorio
Via Friuli Venezia Giulia
Tel: 092 578 381
www.davittorioristorante.com €€
Family-run restaurant on a sandy beach serving simple but fresh seafood.

Lampedusa
Al Gallo d'Oro
Via Ariosto
Tel: 0922 971 297 €€€
Friendly trattoria with excellent fish dishes, plus Arab-inspired options. Closed Nov–Easter.
Gemelli
Via Cala Pisana 2

Tel: 0922 970 699
milano@ristorantegemelli.it €€€
Close to the airport. Excellent dishes typical of the island, including dishes of Arab origin, are served under a delightful pergola. Dinner only. Open June–end Oct.
Grand Caffè Royal
Via Roma 59
Tel: 0922 970 354 €
Join the locals for home-made ice cream and *granita*.

Linosa
Anna
Via Vittorio Veneto 1
Tel: 0922 972 048
www.linosavacanze.it €€
Simple, inexpensive trattoria that also has rooms to rent. Good home cooking. Closed winter.

RIGHT: chefs at the Verdura Golf and Spa Resort.

FESTIVALS SACRED AND PROFANE

Christianity and paganism, classical myth and memory, folklore and food, magic and music all combine in Sicily's frequent and fervent celebrations

Many Sicilian festivals mark a historical event with an overlay of religious worship. Palermo's **Festa di Santa Rosalia** celebrates the saint reputedly saving the city from plague in 1624 with a mixture of prayer and wild festivities. Similarly, Catania's **Festa di Sant'Agata** combines prayers, and processions with pastries made to honour the patron saint.

Other Catholic *feste* have pagan elements lurking just beneath the surface. Thus **Carnevale** (literally "farewell to meat") marks the beginning of Lent and a period of abstinence, but is celebrated in many places with a licentious abandon that echoes the ancient Saturnalia.

Easter (*Pasqua*) is the dominant Christian festival, but is celebrated in a variety of forms: processions of floats and *tableaux vivants* or holy relics, re-enactments of the Passion by chosen citizens, respects paid to the *Addolorata* (Our Lady of the Sorrows).

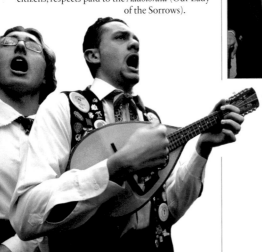

ABOVE: on Easter Sunday in Prizzi, the Dance of the Devils *(Abballu de li diavoli)* has devils in grotesque masks trying to prevent the Madonna meeting the resurrected Christ. It's a dramatic reworking of the Christian story, but also an unconscious echo of *Lupercalia*, a distinctly demonic pre-Christian festival.

LEFT: the Sagra del Mandorlo in Fiore, a celebration of spring with folk dancing and music, takes place every year in the Valley of the Temples in Agrigento.

ABOVE: celebrating the festival of Saint Agata, patron saint of Catania, who is believed to have saved the city from Mount Etna's lava.

ABOVE: a float featuring giant figures takes part in a carnival in Sciacca. Thousands of people follow the procession which ends with the burning of the characters.

SECULAR CELEBRATIONS

Not all Sicily's *feste* have a religious basis. Historical events are commemorated with equal gusto, including the Piazza Armerina's medieval pageant, the Palio dei Normanni, when the exploits of Roger II are recalled with flag-waving and jousting, Norman-style.

The first signs of spring are excuse enough for a festival in Agrigento, where, in February, the Sagra del Mandorlo in Fiore celebrates the almond blossom in the Valley of the Temples.

On the west coast, near Erice, San Vito lo Capo's September Couscous Festival is a multiethnic party where chefs from around the world compete to make the best couscous.

In the southeast, the most captivating autumn festivals are Módica's Chocobarocco chocolate extravaganza and the Ibla Buskers Festival, when Ragusa's atmospheric old town is taken over by jugglers, fire-eaters, magicians and mime artists.

ABOVE: fireworks in Trapani celebrate Easter.

RIGHT: in Enna on Good Friday, white-hooded members of the medieval fraternities hold a procession in total silence.

CALTANISSETTA PROVINCE

At the heart of Sicily's west, this dramatic, often wild, landscape is a beguiling place with its craggy scenery, traditional customs and Mafia lore

BELOW: Butera.

The province of Caltanissetta is a place of subtle moods rather than specific sights. Although from the hilltop villages there are spectacular views of mountain ridges and purple canyons, abandoned farms and ruined Norman castles, the province is sparsely populated and the visitor is often alone with this beguiling scenery.

"This is ancient Sicily, the land of *latifundia* (feudal estates), sulphur mines, hunger and insecurity," wrote the French writer Dominique Fernandez, relishing the feeling of its desolation and lawlessness.

Caltanissetta occupies a central position on a sulphur-bearing plain, its yellowish soil scarred with disused mines. Yet the province is far from uniform. There is a difference in character between the siege mentality of the bleak hilltop towns and the more accessible Greek flavour of Gela's coastal plains. This is a province that feels betrayed by recent history: just as the sulphur mines brought hardship and a high mortality rate to the

hinterland, so coastal industrialisation brought pollution but not prosperity, and mass emigration brought depopulation and despair. Although not the most poverty-stricken province, Caltanissetta is arguably the most aggrieved.

Provincial capital

Caltanissetta 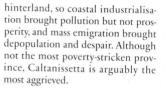, the provincial capital, is a harsh summation of the region's struggle for survival. Its name reflects its cosmopolitan past: Arab conquerors added the prefix *kalat* (Arab for castle) to the name *an-nisa*, meaning ladies. The first documented reference to the city is dated 1086 when Conte Ruggero (Roger the Norman) took the region under the jurisdiction of the Catholic Church, conquered the fort of Pietrarossa and established the abbey of Santo Spirito. As befits an ancient bastion on hilly ground, it is a closed city, its defences raised against outsiders.

Modern war damage means that medieval monuments are restricted to the outskirts, along with the original Greek settlements. Nonetheless, Caltanissetta is no mere market town but the agricultural heart of Sicily's interior, with grain and cotton long grown in the countryside. As the historical hub of Sicilian mining operations, the city fell into decline in the 1960s with the collapse of the sulphur industry. Potassium and magnesium mining have now supplanted sulphur and the city has achieved modest prosperity. Still, life here remains tough.

Mafia lore

As the headquarters of the criminal justice courts, Caltanissetta is entrusted with trying controversial Mafia cases. Ironically, the province is itself tainted by Mafia association, while local citizens have been reluctant to express the resurgence in civic values that characterises optimistic new Sicily.

In 1992, despite public dismay, the town was entrusted with the investigation into the murder of Judge Falcone, his wife and bodyguards *(see page 39)*. Much to the astonishment of American FBI agents cooperating on the case, Caltanissetta magistrates hoped to compete with the Mafia

The highlight of Easter Week in Caltanissetta is the Maundy Thursday procession of the Mysteries of the Passion, with sculptures borne by representatives of the ancient guilds. The mournful dirges of the cortège are a throwback to Arab and Greek cultures.

BELOW: Easter fireworks in Caltanissetta.

The sulphur mines

At the height of demand for sulphur in the 19th century, more than two-thirds of all of Sicily's production came from sulphur mines in the Caltanissetta region. But aggressively marketed production from the United States destroyed its competitiveness and by 1945 the industry had collapsed, causing widespread emigration. Today it is possible to visit a number of mines and see the long corridors where the dangerous extraction and processing were carried out. Many of the workers sent to the narrowest and deepest shafts were boys under 15. There are sites at Delia, Montedoro, Sommatino, Riesi and San Cataldo, but the region is putting its faith in the creation of new mining museums to attract more visitors.

A statue of Umberto I stands in front of the late Renaissance church of St Agatha, Caltanissetta.

without access to a computer. Despite its presumed probity, the city's magistrates court remains Sicily's most understaffed and overworked. Cynics may say that this is intentional, giving *mafiosi* suspects a head start.

City sights

Caltanissetta's heart, in so far as it has one, lies in Piazza Garibaldi. Here, the Baroque **Duomo** (1570–1622), flanked by bell towers, overlooks the ugly neo-Romanesque church of **San Sebastiano**, the Baroque Town Hall and a bronze statue of Neptune. The cathedral interior is an engaging explosion of kitsch, highlighted by sugary ceiling paintings by Wilhelm Borremans (1720) the Flemish painter. A triumphal angel and cherubs adorn a gaudy glass and gold coffin, a Sicilian disguise for a rotting corpse.

Behind the Town Hall, Via Palazzo Paterno leads to the crumbling **Palazzo Moncada**. This was the home of the Moncada dynasty, the feudal rulers of the region from 1406 onwards. The Baroque mansion is emblazoned with snarling lions posing as gargoyles.

Corso Umberto, the main street, is lined with dark buildings and scruffy bars where wizened men drink Amaro, a reminder that Caltanissetta is the main producer of this famous *digestivo*.

The **Museo Archeologico** (daily 9am–1pm, 3.30–7pm; charge), on Via Napoleone Colajanni, has prehistoric and Greek remains from local settlements, including rock tombs. Finest are the Attic vases, painted urns, and the earliest Bronze Age figures found in Sicily.

Around the capital

Fortunately, the disappointing provincial capital is a stone's throw from several significant medieval or prehistoric sites. **Santa Maria degli Angeli,** on the city's eastern outskirts, is a ruined Norman church

Caltanissetta Province

0   10 km

0   10 miles

with a richly carved Gothic porch. Almost next door is the stump of **Castello di Pietrarossa**, perched on a jagged spur, an Arab-Norman castle tossed into a pitiful heap by the 1567 earthquake. Further east, the **Abbazia di Santo Spirito**, established by King Roger I in 1153, is the region's finest Norman church. Commonly known as the Badia, this severe structure is reasonably well kept.

On the flanks of **Monte Sabbucina** lies a significant prehistoric necropolis, even if the best finds are now in Caltanissetta's Museo Archeologico. Take the SS122 road from Caltanissetta to Enna, leaving town through the barren Terra Pilata. The road crosses the Salso river at **Ponte Capodarso,** a delicate 16th-century Venetian bridge: 6km (4 miles) along the Enna road, a scenic route is marked to the archaeological park of **Sabbucina ❷** (9am–sunset). This Bronze Age settlement was later occupied by Hellenised Siculi (Sicel) tribes, who flourished here from the 6th to the 4th centuries BC. The Sicels lived within a square-towered fortress, parts of which survive.

The wild west

A sweeping circular route west passes a series of shabby but atmospheric hill towns. As for the fortresses, although feuding barons once inhabited these lofty strongholds, depopulation and desolation have turned many into virtual ghost towns. From such windswept eyries stretch views of ravines and deserted plains, sulphurous hills and abandoned mines.

Santa Caterina Villarmosa ❸, 20km (12 miles) north of Caltanissetta along the SS122 bis, is worth a cursory glance if you are interested in looking at lace and delicate embroidery, the town's main claim to fame.

Villalba ❹, about 35km (22 miles) west, just off the SS121, is a notoriously down-at-heel Mafia haunt, once held by Don Calógero Vizzini. Vizzini was the main Mafia boss from 1942 until his death in 1954, and as mayor he ran this scruffy town like a private fiefdom. His tombstone in Villalba cemetery laments the death of a gentleman and praises his Robin Hood status as a defender of the weak.

Even before the rise of the Mafia, Villalba was doomed to be milked

A local man, Pompeo Colajanni (1906–87) was one of Sicily's best-known partisans during World War II. A communist by conviction, he fought alongside the Allied invaders to overcome Fascist resistance. The partisan movement's role in Sicily is downplayed today because many of its participants were indiscriminate in their attacks on suspected Fascists.

BELOW: Castello di Pietrarossa.

Mussomeli, a former Mafia stronghold.

by absentee landlords whose revenues from the production of wine and grain here provided them with a noble lifestyle in Palermo.

The local **Regaleali wine estates**, produced by Count Tasca d'Almerita, are heirs to this feudal system, but the dynasty can also take credit for not sitting on its laurels. Regaleali wines regularly outshine ones produced by Donnafugata and other reputable estates. Wine-tasting sessions and traditional cookery courses are run on the estate (*see box below*).

More than most surrounding market towns, **Mussomeli ⑤**, 20km (12 miles) south of Villalba, has suffered from Mafia mythology and emigration. New York received some of Mussomeli's finest Mafia members in the 1960s.

Castello Manfredónico

Just east of town, on the Villalba road, stands **Castello Manfredónico**, named after Manfredi Chiaramonte, Frederick II's son, killed defending his kingdom against Charles of Anjou. Set on an impregnable crag, the lopsided castle blends into the rock. From the fortress are vertiginous views over the desolate valley below.

The country road zigzags south for 13km (8 miles) to **Sutera ⑥**, the first of several ragged towns set on rocky outcrops in old mining country around Caltanissetta. Beyond a series of acrobatic bends lies Sutera's shadow, **Bompensiere ⑦**. (From Sutera, follow the SS189 south for 4km/2½ miles before taking the rural road east towards Caltanissetta.) **Serradifalco ⑧**, 15km (9 miles) east, is another neglected hilltop town, linked across a ridge to Villalba. **San Cataldo ⑨**, nestling in wooded hills to the east, was once the administrative heart of a great agricultural estate, but is today noted for its crafts, especially terracotta pots and wrought ironwork. Nearby is the archaeological site of **Vassallaggi** (9am–1pm), where there are traces of a Greek settlement.

South to the coast

Sinuous upland roads link the craggy countryside with the Gela plains to the south. The higher peaks

Cooking and wine-tasting

Wine, not blood, runs through the patrician Lanza family veins. The **Regaleali estate** *(see above)* has belonged to the dynasty since 1800 and owns wineries here, as well as on Mózia, the Aeolian Islands and on the slopes of Mount Etna. Visitors are welcome at wine-tasting sessions over estate-produced nibbles (tel: 091 843 1605/0921 544 011, www.regaleali.it). However, for a full foodie experience, try the **Anna Tasca Lanza cookery school**, also run by the wine-producing dynasty (+338 152 3175, www.annatascalanza.com). Until her death in 2010, Contessa Anna Tasca Lanza was the doyenne of Sicilian cooking, and author of several Sicilian cookery books. Fabrizia, her daughter, now runs the school, introducing her

charges to chickpea fritters, unctious *cannoli* and marzipan sweets, often matched to estate wines.

The Anna Tasca Lanza cookery school may be the best known in Sicily, but there are many others, ranging from simple farmstay experiences to cooking with a chef in your villa. Now a culinary hotspot, the Módica area is an appealing place for taster sessions, naturally featuring the artisanal local chocolate. Courses need to be booked through upmarket tour operators, such as Love Sicily (tel: 0932 950 222, www. lovesicily.com). Simpler tasting experiences are available from the rural **Tenuta Stoccatello** in Menfi (tel: 0925 195 5499, www.tenutas toccatello.it) and **Tenuta Cefalà** (tel: 091 931545, www.tenutace fala.it) outside Palermo.

are covered in mountainous vegetation, but the wooded slopes soon give way to olives and almonds. The journey passes sleepy towns with populations reduced by emigration. They share a battered rural economy and dignified poverty. **Sommatino, Riesi** and **Niscemi** are typical of such spots, though the ruined castle at **Délia** ⑩ helps distinguish it from its neighbours.

From Caltanissetta, the SS626 bridges the rugged hinterland and the coastal plains towards Gela. **Mazzarino** ⑪ lies 10km (6 miles) east of the main thoroughfare, reached along the SS190. The town's modest reputation rests on Mafia lore and a ruined castle. Founded by the princes of Butera, the castle retains its original keep and some defensive walls.

Ragged palazzi and a couple of undervalued churches add to the atmosphere of gentle nostalgia. **Chiesa San Domenico** contains a touching *Madonna* by Paladino, while **Chiesa dei Carmelitani** houses an 18th-century marble tabernacle encrusted with ivory, ebony, coral and tortoiseshell.

Butera

Butera ⑫, a crumbling hill village perched on a chalky crest 18km (11 miles) south, is the most attractive in the province. The fief prospered under Spanish rule, held by the Branciforte family, the princes of Butera. Although currently closed, the battlemented 11th-century castle is fairly well preserved, with a powerful keep and mullioned windows. The **Chiesa Madre** has a Paladino Madonna and a Renaissance triptych. Nearby, the **Palazzo Comunale** (Town Hall) has an intricate 14th-century portal and panoramic views over the Gela plains to the coast.

Just east of Butera as the crow flies is **Lago di Disueri** ⑬, a dam with a late Bronze Age necropolis on its rocky shores.

Southeast of Butera, on the SS117 bis, the curious mound of **Il Castelluccio** ⑭ presents a dramatic break in the fertile Gela plains. This tumbledown castle keep, jutting out of fields of artichokes and wheat, was built by the warlike Frederick II. Nearby is a modern **war memorial**, a reminder that these fields witnessed the Allied

Don Genco Russo, based in Mussomeli, was a Mafia capo di tutti capi after the death of Calógero Vizzini.

BELOW: the keep at Butera.

The lure of quick commissions attracted the finest Greek literary and artistic talents to affluent Sicily. Among them was the founder of Greek tragic drama, the playwright Aeschylus, who died an extraordinary death at Gela in 456 BC. An eagle seized a tortoise and, looking down from a great height for a rock on which to drop and break it, mistook Aeschylus's bald pate for a polished stone. That was the end of the tragedian.

Below: beach at Falconara.

landing in Sicily in 1943. Il Castelluccio overlooks the fertile **Gela plain**, rich in grain, wine and olives as well as artichokes and oranges, lemons and cotton.

Gela ⓯, the gateway to this land of plenty, was an open invitation to the ancient Greeks, the first and most welcome wave of settlers. Devastation struck in 1943 when the Allies liberated Sicily and bombed Gela to smithereens. Unbridled industrialisation has been Gela's ultimate desecration, so only those with a passion for Greek archaeology will brave the polluted outskirts.

Gela's Greek tragedy

Gela was renowned for its entrepreneurial spirit, inspired military architecture and artistic excellence. It became a Doric colony in 688 BC, settled by Greeks from Rhodes and Crete. However, the indigenous Sicani tribe transmuted the superior Greek culture into a unique shape. Exquisite coins, terracotta figurines, sculpted walls, and flourishing agriculture remain a testament to these times. From here, Hellenistic influence spread to the rest of Sicily. Yet Gela was sacked by the Carthaginians in 405 BC, a year after Agrigento's fall, and was eventually razed by the tyrant of Agrigento in 282 BC, who deported the entire population. Since then, the ancient city has been a symbol of an almost Greek Sicilian tragedy.

There is nothing between Gela's glorious Greek heritage and today's grim sprawl. Still it is worth sifting through the industrial debris to reach the ancient city. The walls built by Timoleon, the good tyrant of Siracusa, are set amongst mimosa, eucalyptus and pines; just beyond the sand dunes are futuristic domes and glittering pipes of modern power generation.

The **Museo Archaeologico** (daily 9am–1.30pm, 2–7pm; charge), on Corso Vittorio Emanuele, is built alongside the ancient **Molino a Vento** acropolis, with its recently excavated remains of Hellenistic houses open to inspection. The museum itself displays painted Attic vases, coins, Ionic capitals and terracotta sarcophagi. Gela terracotta was

renowned throughout Magna Graecia, prized for its painted designs and the delicacy of the figurative work. The star piece is a noble terracotta horse's head from the 6th century BC, part of a temple pediment. **Parco della Rimembranza**, close by, is a park with a single Doric column, the remains of a temple to Athena.

Capo Soprano

Outside the city, the 5th-century BC walls and the site of **Capo Soprano** (9am–1 hour before sunset; charge) are Gela's chief glory. Situated at the western end of town, on Viale Indipendenza, these romantic walls were covered with sand dunes, preserved in their full height and glory, until 1948 when excavation was begun. Running parallel with the sea, the battlemented ramparts were rebuilt by Timoleon after the Carthaginians razed the city. The thick walls are topped with angle towers and sentry posts, with the remains of barracks inside the northern sections. The **Greek baths**, the only ones to have survived in Sicily, date from the 4th century BC.

From here, you can turn east to Ragusa and Siracusa. West of Gela, the sandy shore is littered with military pillboxes, relics of Gela's most recent defences and invasion.

Falconara

Falconara ⑯, to the west, is a small resort with two appealing beaches, **Manfria** and **Roccazzelle**. The stretches of golden sands beckon invitingly. **Castello di Falconara**, the local castle, is set in lush grounds overlooking the sea. Built in sandy-coloured stone, the feudal castle has crenellations and a 14th-century keep. This atmospheric spot is used by Palermitan aristocrats for their summer residences.

If the oil-laden winds are blowing the wrong way, take the SS117 bus north across the plains, passing eucalyptus and cork plantations en route to Piazza Armerina and Roman Sicily.

These are Virgil's celebrated **Campi Geloi**, the plains in which the poet Aeschylus supposedly met his death *(see margin left)*. Archaeologists are still searching for the great tragedian's tomb. ❏

EAT

Sicily's most depressing towns often have excellent cuisine. If you're marooned on the Gela riviera, at least sample macaroni with aubergines or *stigghuilata 'mpanata*, focaccia-style bread stuffed with vegetables, meat or fish – a meal naturally accompanied by aristocratic Regaleali wines.

BEST RESTAURANTS, BARS AND CAFÉS

Caltanissetta

L'Archetto
Via Palmieri 10
Tel: 0934 21031 €€
A friendly trattoria with fish specialities including a couscous paella, and pizza. Closed Tue.

Cortese
Viale Sicilia 166
Tel: 0934 591 686 €€
The pretty, flower-strewn restaurant offers traditional Sicilian specialities at moderate prices. Closed Mon and two weeks in Aug.

Delfino Bianco
Via Scovazzo Gaetano 19
Tel: 0934 25435 €€
Fresh, modern decor and a varied and inexpensive menu. Closed Sun.

Il Gattopardo
Via Pacini 20
Tel: 0934 598 384 €
Both restaurant and pizzeria. Dinner only. Closed Mon and one week Aug.

La Lanterna
Loc Milena, Via Penni
Tel: 0934 933 478 €€
A simple *trattoria-pizzeria*, it also makes a good spot

for an aperitif and a bit of people-watching.

Gela

Casanova
Via Venezia 89
Tel: 0933 918 580 €€€
Near the port, with cooking that is both traditional and adventurous. Booking essential. Closed Sun eve and Aug.

Centrale Totò
Via Generale Cascino 99
Tel: 0933 913 104 €€
Simple regional cuisine, but only useful if stuck in

grim Gela *(see margin tip above)*. Closed Sun.

Mazzarino

Alessi
Via Caltanissetta 20
Tel: 0934 381 549 €€
Restaurant and pizzeria.

Mussomeli

La Baracca
Via Dogliotti
Tel: 0934 952 190 €
Friendly café. Shut Fri.

• • • • • • • •
Prices for a three-course dinner per person and a half-bottle of house wine. €€€€ = over €70, €€€ = €35–70, €€ = €20–35, € = under €20.

ENNA PROVINCE

This elevated inland province possesses the island's greatest Roman villa and a succession of hill towns and strategic castles in its fertile landscape

The desolate, sun-parched centre of Sicily is the only province without an outlet to the sea. Yet there is much to proclaim, from the Roman villa at Piazza Armerina, one of the wonders of the ancient world, to a hinterland studded with hilltop towns and Norman castles. Around its historical sites is an agricultural province producing corn, olives, cheese, nuts and wine.

Enna ❶, known as Sicily's navel for its central position 942 metres (3,090ft) above the countryside, is sacred thanks to the cult of Demeter (the Olympian goddess of corn and sustainer of life) and the myth of Persephone (Demeter's daughter by Zeus, carried off by Hades to be queen of the Underworld). Despite Persephone's gift of spring, Enna often feels cloaked in winter, shrouded above the plains in mist or blown by wintry gusts. However in summer, while Sicily swelters, this elevated position offers locals a refuge from the heat.

City in the clouds

Enna's sights are fairly compact, but if the mist falls, expect to cling to the city walls between churches. Tradition has it that the restored **cathedral** (daily 9am–1pm, 3.30pm–7pm)

was begun by Eleanor of Aragon in 1307, but a fire in 1446 swept away most of the treasures. Nonetheless, the cathedral on **Via Roma** is a fascinating romp through Enna's mystical past. The elaborately carved white pulpit is encrusted with cherubs and rests on a Graeco-Roman base removed from a temple to Demeter, as does the marble stoup nearby. The quaint portico is matched by Gothic transepts and apses, while the wrought-iron sacristy gate once graced a Moorish harem in the **Castello di**

Main attractions
ENNA
CALASCIBETTA
SPERLINGA
NICOSIA
TROINA
PIAZZA ARMERINA
VILLA ROMANA DEL CASALE
VILLA DELLE MERAVIGLIE
AIDONE
MORGANTINA

LEFT: Calascibetta.
RIGHT: inside Enna Cathedral.

TIP

In Enna, go through **Stupor Mundi**, a local agency which is far more helpful than the tourist office, to book cosy B&Bs, reliable restaurants or to embark on themed excursions (Via Roma, tel: 0935 502 214, www.stupor mundiviaggi.com).

Lombardia. There are works attributed to Paladino and the beloved 15th-century statue of the *Madonna della Visitazione* (the city's patron saint), which is carried through the streets in procession on 2 July.

Enna's esoteric past would appear to make it susceptible to pagan magic. The black basalt base of the capitals incorporate sculptures of Hades and demonic symbols in an attempt to crush evil forces by fair means or foul. The adjoining **Museo Alessi** (currently closed) displays the contents of the cathedral's **treasury**, including the prized **Corona della Madonna** (Madonna's Crown), a sacred 17th-century enamelled diadem studded with precious stones.

Along bustling Via Roma lies a string of dignified mansions and churches, such as the Catalan-Gothic **Palazzo Pollicarini** and the Baroque **Chiesa San Benedetto**. Via Roma is pedestrianised for the evening *passeggiata* and contains a good *pasticceria* as well as cosy restaurants. At the bottom are sweeping views from the belvedere and **Torre di Federico II**, a tumbledown octagonal tower built by Frederick II. The tower is linked by secret passageways to **Castello di**

Lombardia (daily 8am–8pm) at the top of the hill, in Piazzale Lombardia. As one of Sicily's largest medieval castles, this imposing fortress began as a draughty Byzantine keep but acquired towers with each wave of invaders, from the Normans to the Swabians. A series of three courtyards leads to the majestic eyrie of **Torre Pisano**, the tallest of the castle's six surviving towers, and views over the entire island.

Just beyond the castle looms a massive boulder on the tip of the plateau, the **Rocca di Cerere**, also known as the Temple of Demeter. Legend has it that Demeter's daughter Persephone was abducted by Hades and swept off into **Lago di Pergusa**, gateway to the Underworld.

Castles and citadels

This circuitous route explores the castle-studded landscape north of Enna. Facing the city is **Calascibetta ❷**, a decrepit but atmospheric hill village built by the Arabs while besieging Enna in 951. Rust-coloured buildings cling to the slopes, and the **Chiesa Madre** is perched on top of a blustery cliff.

From here, the SS121 winds north to **Leonforte ❸**, a 17th-century Branciforte fiefdom best known for its colourful Good Friday procession and its **Granfonte**, a delightful fountain that is a testament to feudal largesse. Set on the edge of town, the graceful arched fountain fills troughs from 24 spouts.

Picturesque **Sperlinga ❹**, north of Leonforte, may well be Sicily's most intriguing castle (daily 9.30am–1pm, 4–6.30pm; charge), with battlemented Norman towers and bastions that reach to the bottom of the cliff. Above ground, the village is a string of modest cottages; below the castle, the rock is riddled with chambers, a secret underground city. The rocky slopes are pitted with caves, some of which have been inhabited since

Sicani times. The caves were occupied by Sperlinga's poorest peasants and their livestock until the 1980s (*for more about the castle see page 95*).

Nicosia ❺, 8km (5 miles) southeast of Sperlinga, is a charming medieval town set on four hills and ringed by rocky spurs. It has been a Greek city, Byzantine bishopric, Arab fort and Norman citadel. In the Middle Ages it was riven by religious rivalry between Roman Catholic newcomers from the north and the indigenous population who, in Byzantine tradition, followed the Greek Orthodox rite. After pitched battles, the matter was settled in favour of the natives.

The 14th-century **San Nicolò** triumphed as the city cathedral, with its 14th-century facade and lacy campanile. From the cathedral, which dominates the town, Salita Salamone climbs to **San Salvatore**, a Romanesque church that would look at home in Burgundy.

Piazza Garibaldi, the main square, is dotted with dingy bars and *circoli*, working men's clubs. Old men sit and chat in gallo-italico, a Lombard dialect stemming from northern settlers

Nicosia, isolated by the new motorway, typifies the time-warp towns of the interior, where, between 1950 and 1970, half the adult population emigrated and have never returned.

BELOW: view from Enna.

SHOP

For shopaholics, **Sicilia Fashion Village**, Agira's new mall and designer outlet village, has put the town on the map. If you're not passing through Agira, consider taking the free shuttle from Agrigento, Catania, Messina, Palermo, Siracusa or Trápani (tel: 0935 950 040, www. siciliafashionvillage.it).

and shared with Aidone, Piazza Armerina and Sperlinga. Leading off Piazza Garibaldi are myriad *vicoli*, crooked alleys climbing Nicosia's hills. From here, the steep **Via Salamone** winds above the cathedral, passing dilapidated palazzi and convents encrusted with garlands or gargoyles. At the top is **Santa Maria Maggiore**, a Norman church rebuilt in Baroque style which faces a montage of bells that fell when the campanile came down in the last earthquake, in 1978. From the terrace, the tumbledown castle is visible, overgrown with cacti and thistles on a rocky spur.

The SS120, a meandering mountain road, leads 20km (12 miles) northeast to **Cerami** ❻, a jagged village dominated by a ruined castle. The wooded countryside is interspersed with orchards and lolling cattle.

Just north of the SS120 is the scenic **Lago di Ancipa**, a lake set in a lush wilderness. East of Nicosia are windswept views across the bleak Nebrodi mountains.

Further along the SS120 lies **Troìna** ❼, at 1,120 metres (3,674ft) the loftiest town in Sicily, which occupies an Arab-Norman stronghold on a solitary ridge. This citadel has declined into an austere hill town with a nest of churches crammed into winding medieval alleys. Tall, draughty convents look out over scruffy terraces and the makeshift houses of returning emigrants.

The grand Norman churches include the **Chiesa Matrice**, with its hulking bell tower, nave, crypt, tower and solid external walls. Inside, the fusty church has been revamped in Baroque style, complete with flaking gold leaf and late Byzantine art. Outside, an arched walk slopes under the bell tower and returns to the atmospheric Norman stronghold. On the belvedere, Troìna's youth gather to enjoy rugged windswept views over the distant blue-grey hills.

On the last Sunday in May, devotees gather to celebrate the **festa di San Silvestro**, patron saint of the village, wreathed in laurel leaves with processions and banquets.

Agira

Agira ❽, a tortuous 30km (19 miles) south of Troìna, is set on a hill surmounted by a Saracen castle and adorned with several fine churches, even if the new designer shopping mall is more of a magnet to young Sicilians (*see margin left*). The slopes once housed a Siculi settlement but are now given over to olives, grapes and almonds. These hills saw heavy fighting during the Sicilian campaign in 1943, hence the Canadian war cemetery on the town outskirts.

The churches contain several fine works of art. **Santa Maria Maggiore**, in the shadow of the castle, boasts a 15th-century triptych and sculpted Norman capitals, while the church of **Santa Maria di Gesù** contains a painted crucifix by Fra' Umile da Petralia. The Gothic **San Salvatore**, laden down by a 16th-century facade, has a treasury containing a bejewelled medieval mitre.

BELOW: Nicosia.

Balcony over Sicily

Further east, past **Lago di Pozzillo**, an artificial lake, a minor road winds through orange and olive groves to **Centùripe ❾**. The name supposedly comes from the Latin for steep slopes, justifying the town's tag used by Garibaldi in 1862, *il balcone della Sicilia* (the balcony over Sicily), with its magnificent valley views to Catania and Etna. In the heart of town is a pink and white 17th-century **Duomo**, contrasting with the town's modern, ugly buildings. Classical statues, terracotta and vases are visible in the **Museo Archeologico** (Tue–Fri 8.30am–1pm, Sat–Sun also 3–7pm; closed Mon).

On the outskirts of Centùripe, classical finds have been made at **Castello di Corradino**, the site of a clifftop Roman mausoleum. At the foot of Monte Calvario are the ruins of a Greek villa and, in the Bagni Valley, the remains of Roman baths.

Echoes of ancient Rome

The territory south of Enna has its fair share of crumbling hill towns, but the countryside is also home to several Greek settlements and Roman outposts, notably the magnificent Roman villa at Piazza Armerina.

Southwest of Enna are a couple of isolated hill towns, notably **Pietraperzia ❿**, a market town stacked up on the slopes south of Caltanissetta, and **Barrafranca ⓫**, set on a spur in the **Monti Erei** (Erei mountains). These former feudal estates once provided a living for the landowning Barresi dynasty. Established by the Arabs, Barrafranca was conquered by the Normans before being swallowed up by the Barresi clan in 1330. The Baroque **Chiesa Madre**, with its campanile and arabesque dome, comes a poor second to sampling the local produce, including olives, almonds and grapes. Further east are Piazza Armerina and the Villa Romana at Casale, Sicily's greatest wonder of the Roman world.

Piazza Armerina

Piazza Armerina ⓬ is upstaged by the Roman villa but still has a faded elegance all of its own. The closure of the sulphur mines cast a pall over the town, but low-key tourism is slowly reviving the *centro storico*, helped by a dynamic tourist board and ongoing restoration projects.

Surrounded by farmland and trees, the ancient settlement was favoured by the Romans, the Byzantines and the Arabs, but truly flourished with the arrival of the Normans. This event is celebrated on 13 and 14 August each year with the **Palio dei Normanni**, a heartfelt medieval pageant featuring costumed riders, recalling the trouncing of the Arabs and the Normans' victorious entry into the city.

Even if the Normans made their mark on Piazza Armerina, the town is rich in late medieval and Baroque monuments which merge together seamlessly, largely thanks to the rust-coloured local stonework.

In town, a series of flights of steps and alleys leads to the Baroque **Duomo** (9am–noon, 1.20–5.20pm), crowning the terraced hill. Erected in

Drinks in this region are not for the weight-conscious.

BELOW: Piazza Armerina.

EAT

When in Piazza Armerina, call in to the **Enoteca** (Piazza Garibaldi 9) to sample good-value local wines or, if you're heading to the Villa Romana, to stock up on a picnic feast of tasty cheeses and cold cuts. .

1604 on the site of an earlier church, the cathedral balances a Baroque facade with theatrical staircases, accentuating the spacious belvedere. A Catalan-Gothic campanile (*c.*1490) with blind arcading remains from the original church and sets the tone for the bold interior.

Bordering the cathedral is **Palazzo Trigona**, a sober 18th-century counterpoint to the baroque flights of fancy. The palace is being turned into the city museum but can still be visited by appointment. For a taste of how the noble Trigona family now lives, stay in their delightful Villa Trigona outside town *(see page 274).*

The hilltop quarter radiates from Piazza Duomo and Piazza Garibaldi. In keeping with 13th-century urban design, this is in fishbone formation, with tiny alleys fanning out delicately along the contours of the slopes. The town clings to its traditional districts, with the lofty **Quartiere Monti** around the cathedral considered the noble district, and the former Moorish and Jewish sections below. A stroll down the steep **Via Monte**, the medieval main street, reveals an evocative

slice of history, passing palazzi dating from Norman and Aragonese times. From Via Monte the route leads past turreted mansions to Via Crocifisso, a turning on the right, and to the Gothic church of **San Martino.**

Once back at the cathedral, take Via Floresta beside Palazzo Trigona to the picturesque **Castello Aragonese**, the Aragonese castle. From here, Via Vittorio Emanuele II leads to Largo Capodarso and the **Convento dei Gesuiti**, a former Jesuit foundation which is now home to the **Biblioteca Comunale** (daily 8am–2pm), a remarkable public library encrusted in Baroque stuccowork.

Further north, the steep Via Castellina nudges the city walls and an old watchtower.

Just north of the compact hillside quarter is **Sant'Andrea**, a delightful Norman priory and the oldest church in town. The unadorned but delightful priory has a frescoed interior designed in a Coptic cross plan.

To visit the monuments, check opening times with the helpful **tourist office** (Via Generale Muscara; tel: 0935 680 201) as some churches, for instance, are only open for early morning Mass.

At night, moody lighting casts a soft glow over the *centro storico*, setting the scene for an inviting stroll from the cathedral square down the cobblestoned Via Monte, taking in **Piazza Garibaldi** and Largo Capodarso, ideally ending a rustic-style dinner in **da Toto** (Via Mazzini 29).

Villa Romana del Casale

Nestling among oak and hazel woods, the **Villa Romana del Casale** ⓭ (daily 8am–1 hour before sunset; charge; www.villaromanadelcasale.it) lies 5km (3 miles) southwest of Piazza Armerina at **Casale**. The excellent hunting in these forests was the bait that drew the villa's original Roman owners. It was occupied throughout the Arab period but destroyed by the Norman King

Below: an Easter procession in Pietraperzia.

William the Bad in 1160 and then covered by a landslide.

Now a Unesco World Heritage site, the Villa's fluid, impressionistic mosaics may have inspired the Normans in their designs for Palermo's Palazzo dei Normanni. In splendour, the only rivals are Hadrian's villa at Tivoli or Diocletian's palace at Split. But Sicily's mosaics better reflect the flux of Roman politics, with the emergence of separate Eastern and Western empires. One theory is that, after Diocletian realised that the Roman world was too vast to be ruled by one mind and retired to his villa in Split, so Maximian withdrew to contemplation here.

Whether hunting lodge or country mansion, the villa disappeared under the landslide for 700 years but, after a hoard of treasure was found in 1950, serious excavations were begun. Much remains to be unearthed in the hazelnut orchards, from the slave quarters to the water system. A shameful Sicilian muddle has delayed the full restoration of the mosaics, even if the site is due to be finished by the end of 2012, complete with roofing that reflects the original Roman design. Until then, a number of rooms may be closed.

The vaulting may be lost and the frescoes faded, but the villa's magic lies in the 40 rooms covered in Roman-African mosaics. Their vitality, expressive power and free-ranging content set them apart from models in Tunisia or Antioch. The stylisation of these mosaics is undercut by humour, realism, sensuality and subtlety. Above all, the mosaics' visual energy shines through.

Visitors inspect the mosaics of hunting scenes at the Villa Romana del Casale.

Exploring the site

The current path leads to a massive triumphal arch leading into an **atrium ⓐ**, surrounded by a portico of marble columns, then crashes down to earth in the male **latrines ⓑ** that were once lined with marble seats. Mosaics here

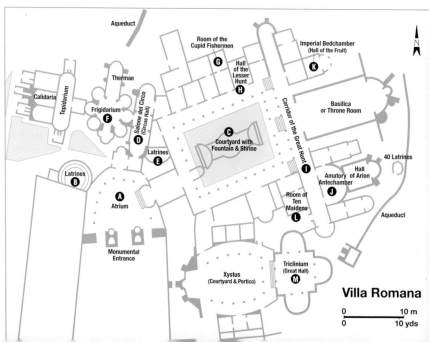

Villa Romana

Uncovered room in the Villa Romana del Casale, which has stunning Roman mosaics.

BELOW: ancient bikinis in the Room of Ten Maidens.

feature a bestiary of Persian ass, ram and pouncing leopard. The villa's centrepiece is the **courtyard** **C**, with peristyle, pond and statue. The mosaics depict whimsical animals' heads framed in wreaths, from a fierce bear and tiger to a horse with a stunted nose. The design has a symmetry, pairing domestic and wild or male and female animals; a fierce ram thus sits beside a gracious deer.

The **Salone del Circo** **D** (Circus Hall) illustrates chaotic races at the Circus Maximus. These are the most extensive of their kind so far uncovered anywhere. Nearby, outside the **Thermae**, the thermal baths complex, is the small **latrine** **E**, with bidets for women. In the octagonal **frigidarium** **F** (leading to the warm and hot rooms) are vestibules and plunge baths adorned with tritons, centaurs and marine monsters, while in the anointment room next door, a man is depicted being massaged and perfumed by his naked servant.

Off the courtyard the **Room of the Cupid Fishermen** **G** depicts a naked mermaid clasping a dolphin in the presence of fishermen exposing

their chests or bare buttocks. Nearby is the **Hall of the Lesser Hunt** **H**, with a frenetic deer hunt, the snaring of a wild boar, and a toast to a successful day's sport. To the Romans, hunting meant food, sport, sensuality, adventure and pleasure, preferably all at once.

Edging the courtyard is the **Corridor of the Great Hunt** **I**, the finest mosaics ever known, a gloriously animated work meant to be appreciated while walking. In this swirling mass of movement, chariots, lions, cheetahs, rhinos and huge swans merge in lovely autumnal colours. A mosaic sea separates Africa and Europe, echoing the division of the Roman Empire. Africa is personified by a tiger, elephant and a phoenix fleeing a burning house. The exotic, bare-breasted Queen of Sheba is being ogled by a tiger as well as by Romans.

Sport and erotica are often neatly entwined in the mosaics. The **amatory antechamber** **J**, part of the empress's suite, features Cupid fishermen netting a fine catch. The **Imperial bedchamber** **K** is decorated with figs, grapes and pomegranates,

A temple of paganism

Allll the scenes normally excluded from Christian art lie here, in the Villa Romana. This entrancing Roman site depicts a kaleidoscope of everyday life, highlighting intimate pleasures such as child's play and youthful dancing, hunting, feasting, massage and lovemaking. A timeless quality also infuses the mosaics' undisguised eroticism: the female nudes may have odd-shaped breasts but they dance in pagan abandon. The more accomplished male nudes are studies in virility. The Romans worshipped heroism and masculine valour, a vitality crushed by cool Christian art. In essence, this villa remains a temple of paganism and a celebration of everyday life that reverberates down the centuries.

snatching at Greek fertility symbols. The **Room of Ten Maidens**  presents prancing girl gymnasts in costumes that prove conclusively that the bikini was not invented by Coco Chanel in the 1950s.

Nearby, steps lead up to the **Triclinium**  (Great Hall), the villa's masterpiece, 12 metres (39ft) square and with deep apses, where the mosaic of the central pavement is a flowing mythological pageant based on the **10 Labours of Hercules**. It is a symphony of pathos and poetic vision worthy of Michelangelo: the gods are threatened by chaos and decay; tortured giants writhe in agony; and a mighty nude Hercules is glorified. Passion is present in Cerberus, the three-headed dog, and in the fierce Hydra, which has a woman's face but snake-encrusted hair.

Villa delle Maraviglie

When sated with Roman sights, consider picnicking in the surrounding pine and eucalyptus woods. Alternatively, visit an eclectic villa-museum overlooking the Villa Romana. **Villa delle Maraviglie**  (daily 9am–7pm,

until 5pm in winter; charge; tel: 0935 689 055) is owned by a baronial family who lived in the villa until recently. If you are lucky, you will be guided by Enzo Cammarata himself, both a classical scholar and Sicily's foremost authority on Greek and Roman coins. Even the grounds of this gracious 18th-century villa are dotted with classical statuary. But beyond the majolica collection, Hellenistic busts and Greek-inspired paintings, this is a fascinating portrait of how the Sicilian landowning aristocracy once lived. Now a Unesco Heritage site, the glorious Villa Romana was unearthed on the Cammarata family estate, a fact which the *Barone* notes ruefully.

Aidone

Aidone , 10km (6 miles) northeast of Piazza Armerina, represents a window on the Greek world. This warm, red-stone town boasts a ruined castle and a clutch of austere churches, including San Domenico, noted for its diamond-point facade. But the main attraction is the revamped **Museo Archeologico** (daily 8.30am–6.30pm;

> *Aphrodite is dead: the ideal goddess of beauty has been superseded by this plurality of particular girls, portrayed on a pavement where the feet of huntsmen can trample them.*
>
> Vincent Cronin
> on the "Bikini Girls"

BELOW: detail of a mosaic in the Hunting Corridor.

Venus of Morgantina.

charge), which contains one of the most magnificent Greek sculptures in Sicily *(see below)*. Set in a restored 17th-century Capuchin monastery in the upper part of the village, the museum also serves as an introduction to the rural site of Morgantina, perhaps the most legible site in antiquity.

Morgantina

Morgantina ⑯ (daily 9am–1 hour before sunset; charge; includes Museo Archeologico at Aidone), just 5km (3 miles) east, occupies a rural paradise worthy of Persephone, its slopes covered in calendula, pomegranate, pines and olives, and framed by grey-blue hills. Morgantina is divided into two sections by a deep valley, with Serra Orlando on the ridge to the west, and hilly Cittadella to the east. This huge ancient Siculi settlement was Hellenised in the 6th century BC and survived for 500 years, including under the Romans. Sometimes dubbed a Sicilian Pompeii, the site is not aesthetically beautiful like Piazza Armerina but is supremely clear, an exposition of a classical city in stone. The *polis* (Greek city) reveals a civic

and sacred centre bounded by commercial and residential quarters.

Cittadella, the hilly Bronze Age settlement, is pitted with chamber tombs. Visible Hellenistic sections include: the *macellum* (covered market), designed like a shopping mall; a schoolroom complete with benches; a gymnasium with an athletics track; the *bouleuterion* (Senate); a theatre, magistrates' chamber, granary and bakery. Several noble villas contain the earliest known mosaics in the Western Mediterranean, including a floor inscription saying welcome (*euexei*), which is now in the museum at Aidone. Theatrical steps lead to the *agora*, complete with aqueducts and fountain. Nearby stands a temple with a *bothros*, a round well-altar once used for sacrifices.

Morgantina is a reminder that Enna marked the crossroads of Trinacria, ancient Sicily's three provinces. According to one historian, Enna is the hub of a giant geomantic chart, lying on ley lines spanning the island. This network of sacred spots supposedly provides the key to the region's occult power. ❏

Venus returns to Sicily

A priceless Sicilian statue stolen by tomb-robbers and trafficked to the United States has finally found her way back to Sicily. The so-called *Venus of Morgantina*, a life-size Greek marble statue made in the 5th century BC, was stolen from a Greek sanctuary in Morgantina over 30 years ago. Now fully restored and complete with anti-seismic protection, the statue is the showpiece of the newly unveiled classical collection in Aidone. But the debate continues: the Venus/Aphrodite figure is more likely to be Demeter/Ceres, the goddess of the harvest and fertility, than the goddess of beauty, although some scholars still see her as Persephone, Demeter's abducted daughter, whisked to Hades by Pluto.

BEST RESTAURANTS, BARS AND CAFÉS

Prices for a three-course dinner per person and a half-bottle of house wine:
€ = under €20
€€ = €20–35
€€€ = €35–70
€€€€ = over €70

Enna has a reasonable selection of places to eat. The smaller towns all have trattorie, but the choice and quality are limited in Sicily's heartland.

Enna

Ariston
Via Roma 353
Tel: 0935 26038
www.aristonenna.com €€
A long-established restaurant serving regional dishes. Closed Sun and two weeks in Aug.

Centrale
Piazza VI Dicembre 9
Tel: 0935 500 963
www.ristorantecentrale.net €€
Another long-established restaurant, this one at the heart of the town. Good family fare, reasonably priced. Try the pasta and lamb when on menu. Benito Mussolini's signature is in the guestbook. Closed Sat lunch.

La Fontana
Via Volturno 6
Tel: 0935 25465 €
A simple, family-run trattoria.

Grotta Azzurra
Via Colaianni 1
Tel: 0935 24328 €
This lively restaurant has been serving up good-value, hearty meals for almost half a century. Closed Sat in winter. No credit cards.

Pasticceria Il Dolce
Piazza Sant' Agostino 40
Tel: 0935 24018 €
Said to have the finest *cannoli*, almond biscuits, ricotta-filled cakes and more. If you have a sweet tooth, this is an essential place to visit, especially at weekends.

San Gennaro
Via Belvedere Marconi 6
Tel: 0935 24067 €€
Family-run restaurant serving hearty soups, stuffed lamb, grilled vegetables. Outside tables with view. Closed Wed.

Tiffany
Via Roma 487
Tel: 0935 501 368 €€
Near the Duomo, specialises in fish (try the *pennette pasta* with artichoke hearts and prawns), but offers pizza and some meaty options too. Closed Thur.

Centuripe

Pasticceria Centrale
Piazza Sciacca 11
Tel: 0935 573 576 €
Pleasant café with excellent snacks and pastries.

Nicosia

Baglio San Pietro
Contrada San Pietro
Tel: 0935 640 529
www.bagliosanpietro.com €
A small farmhouse conversion with 10 guest rooms and pool. Simple, good-quality dishes. Closed Nov–Mar.

Pasticceria al Bocconcino
Via Roma 8
Tel: 0935 638 894 €
If you like almonds and hazelnuts, this is the place.

Vigneta
Contrada San Basile
Tel: 0935 646 074
vigneta@hotmail.com €
There is not a wide choice in this town, but Vigneta offers good Sicilian family cooking. Known for their vegetarian dishes and pizza too. Garden. Closed Tue.

Sperlinga

Bar Li Calzi
Via Roma 92 €
The most popular place in town.

Piazza Amerina

Al Fogher
Contrada Bellia
Tel: 0935 684 123
www.alfogher.net €€–€€€
Worth an excursion on the SS117, 3km (2 miles) north, for creative Sicilian cuisine in an elegant, family-run country restaurant with a summery garden terrace. Try the red mullet fillet in yellow pepper sauce with pistachio-sprinkled wild rice or the flan of Piacen-tino salami in Nero d'Avola sauce flavoured with cocoa. Tasting menu too. Closed Sun pm, and all day Mon.

Al Teatro
Via del Teatro 6
Tel: 0935 85662 €€
Delicious, crisp pizza. Closed Wed in winter.

Centrale da Totò
Via Mazzini 29
Tel: 0935 680 153 €
Very popular with locals. Serves moderately priced Italian dishes, as well as crispy pizzas. Closed Mon in winter.

Pasticceria Zingale
Via Generale Muscarà 8
Tel: 0935 686 111 €
A welcome stop, a *pasticceria* with wide variety of local specialities.

La Ruota
Contrada Paratore (near Villa Romana)
Tel: 0935 680 542
www.trattorialaruota.it €€
A good trattoria specialising in home-made pasta. Try the delicious maccheroni, fresh tomato pasta and *melanzane in agrodolce* (aubergines in sweet-sour vinaigrette). Book. Lunch only.

La Tavernetta
Via Cavour 40 (near the Duomo)
Tel: 0935 685 883 €€
This town trattoria in a steep lane serves very tasty pasta dishes. Fish specialities are also recommended. Closed Sun in winter.

RAGUSA PROVINCE

Currently Sicily's most flourishing region, Ragusa favours subtlety over drama. Rolling countryside framed by dry-stone walls gives way to classical sites by sandy beaches or cave settlements by Baroque towns

Main attractions

RAGUSA IBLA
TRENO DEL BAROCCO (BAROQUE TRAIN)
CHIARAMONTE GULFI
MONTI IBLEI (IBLEAN MOUNTAINS)
CASTELLO DI DONNAFUGATA
CAMARINA
MÓDICA
CAVA D'ISPICA
SCICLI
MONTALBANO TRAIL
MARINA DI RAGUSA (IN SUMMER)

Discreet wellbeing is the keynote to the region. Novelist Gesualdo Bufalino proudly described his province as "*un isola nell'isola*", an island within an island. Historically, this was home to a cave-dwelling population who for millennia felt more secure clustering in grottoes or ravines, a tradition that survived until recently, with caves around Ragusa, Módica and Scicli inhabited until the 1980s. It is perhaps not accidental that this earthy, community-minded province is an almost a crime-free haven, surviving beyond the Mafia's reptilian gaze. Here the typical conditions for Sicilian crime are absent.

Low-key tourism

Industry and tourism reached the province relatively late, with the result that Ragusa has not concreted over its coast but cultivated low-key tourism in the same way that it tends the land, selling itself as an off-the-beaten-track destination. Unlike much of Sicily, there is a civilised balance between ancient *cultura contadina* (peasant culture) and the creativity of the *borghesia*. Class distinctions aside, the Ragusani are deeply hospitable, more open than those in the mountainous interior.

The city of **Ragusa** was a Norman stronghold that became a fief of the Cabrera dynasty. However, the 1693 earthquake reduced most of Ragusa to rubble. The merchant class responded by building **Ragusa Alta** ❶ (sometimes called **Superiore**), the new city on the hill. But the aristocracy refused to desert their charred homes, and recreated **Ragusa Ibla** ❷ (Lower Ragusa) on the original valley site. The towns only merged in 1926, so now Ragusa is a hilltop town divided into two parts. While Ragusa

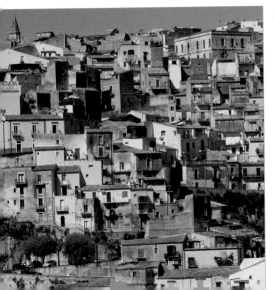

LEFT: Ragusa Ibla.

Ibla is an enchanting, timeless pocket of Sicily, Ragusa Alta is the business centre, riven by gorges, and redeemed only by several Baroque mansions and churches.

Ragusa Alta

In the upper town, **San Giovanni Battista** (daily 7am–12.30pm, 3pm–7pm) is the city's theatrical Baroque cathedral, with an ornate facade and soaring, pretty **campanile**.

Nearby, Baroque mansions have wrought-iron balconies featuring sculpted cornices. One such is **Palazzo Bertini** on Corso Italia, with its grotesque masks representing "the three powers": a peasant, a nobleman and a merchant – a fair introduction to Ragusa's class concerns.

On Corso Vittorio Veneto is the crumbling Baroque **Palazzo Zacco**: a gap-toothed monster sticks out his tongue, mocking the church of San Vito opposite. Just south is the gorge criss-crossed by three bridges, one of which was built by a friar who tired of the daily uphill trek to his parish. The **Museo Archeologico Ibleo** (daily 9am–1pm, 3.30–7.30pm; charge) at Ponte Nuovo, one of the bridges, is rich in finds from Camarina and Siculi necropoli, including prehistoric pottery and Greek vases. On the far side of the chasm lies densely packed Ragusa Ibla, now easily reached by shuttle bus along the scenic ring road, faced in subtle local stone.

Santa Maria delle Scale (daily 10am–1pm, 4–6pm;), framed by parched hills, represents the gateway to Ibla, joining the old to the new. This Gothic church was remodelled after the 1693 earthquake. A medieval portal remains, as does the Catalan-Gothic nave, complete with Renaissance ornamentation. From this balcony over old Ragusa, 250 steps lead down into Ibla, offering a commanding view over the blue-tinged cupola of the cathedral below.

Ragusa Ibla

In Ragusa Ibla, the Baroque city recreated on a medieval street plan, an old-world charm and intimacy prevails. Snapshot vistas of Ibla capture secret shrines, family crests and Baroque fountains. Shrines lurk in narrow alleys and on facades, representing

The provincial economy thrives on wine-growing, cattle-breeding and cheese-making as well as market gardening, hot-house flowers and genetically modified tomatoes. Although Ragusa hoped to grow rich on asphalt and oil, agriculture has brought more lasting prosperity.

BELOW: classic cars in Ragusa Ibla.

Taking the Baroque train

Known as the Treno del Barocco, this rail *tour de force* travels through southeastern Sicily en route to the region's best Baroque cities, churches and palaces – all in a day. Vintage trains, including steam trains and period carriages dating from the 1930s, follow a virtually disued rail route, delighting rail enthusiasts and fans of Baroque architecture. The train runs from Siracusa to Ragusa, or vice versa, stopping off in Noto, Scicli, Módica and Ragusa Ibla, the finest Baroque towns in southeastern Sicily. In every town, guides point out churches and palaces, balconies and staircases as you stroll around (tel: 0932 759 634; visits in Italian only; www.treno-barocco.blogspot.com)

EAT

Ragusa province is noted for its scented honey and robust cheeses, among the best in Sicily. Ricotta, mozzarella, provola and cacciocavallo are the main cheeses to sample, either in savoury or sweet dishes. Although caciocavallo has cow's milk as its base, goat's milk is added to give it a distinctive flavour. Its texture is smooth, with a sharp, smoky flavour.

a need for reassurance as well as an expression of faith and a superstitious belief in future miracles. Ibla is also oriel windows, tiny squares and showy staircases, tawny-coloured stone mansions and filigree balconies hung with washing, dark courtyards popular with ambling dogs, secret arches and yellowing palm trees.

Gentrification has reversed the neglect of Ibla in recent years. The crumbling mansions are being restored and cherished by young, middle-class couples returning to the old city. Easier access too has helped open Ibla up to citizens from the upper town without losing its sense of separateness or leisurely pace of life. Where once Ibla was deserted in the evening, its pedestrianised quarter is now the focus for Ragusa's low-key nightlife. Semi-hidden restaurants and bars have taken over historic palaces, with tasteful bohemian conversions coexisting with the clubby, patrician side of town.

Baroque drama

Palazzo Nicastro, the Baroque chancery erected in 1760, sits astride the winding staircase linking old and new Ragusa. To the left is **Santa Maria dell'Idria**, a Baroque church owned by the Cosentini, one of Ibla's leading families. Given the narrowness of the alley, it takes time to gain a perspective on the robust bell tower and majolica-encrusted dome. Crushed between the church steps and Corso Mazzini is **Palazzo Cosentini**, an ancestral home adjoining the family church of Santa Maria. The sculpted Baroque balconies are a mélange of fantastic bare-breasted sirens and monsters with flaring nostrils. Leering faces proffer scorpions or serpents instead of tongues, a warning not to gossip.

On Piazza della Repubblica, the next square down, stands the **Chiesa del Purgatorio**, a dramatic Baroque church surmounting an elegant staircase. The bell tower is built on Byzan-

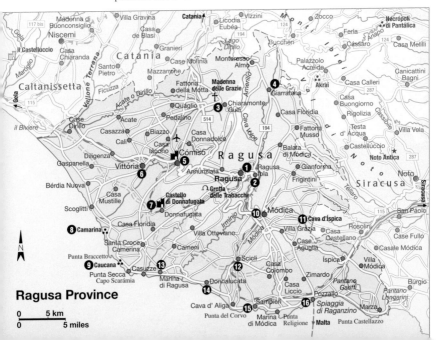

Ragusa Province

0   5 km

0   5 miles

tine city walls, visible from the steps of Salita dell'Orologio.

Piazza del Duomo

After the cosy claustrophobia so far, the spacious **Piazza del Duomo** below comes as a shock. The square is lined with palm trees, Baroque mansions and aristocratic clubs. The far end of the piazza is dominated by Rosario Gagliardi's cathedral dedicated to **San Giorgio** (Mon–Sat 10am–noon, 4–6pm), a masterpiece of Sicilian Baroque. As the city centrepiece, completed in 1775, this wedding-cake cathedral was patronised by the nobility (St George was considered the unofficial patron saint of the Sicilian aristocracy).

The sandstone church occupies a raised terrace and tricks one's eyes up from its convex centre, seemingly writhing with statues, in a crescendo to the balconied campanile, topped by a blue neoclassical dome that is a city landmark.

Its smaller imitator on the Corso is the church of **San Giuseppe** (Mon–Sat 10am–1pm, 4–6pm), which gains in subtlety what it lacks in theatrical-ity. The church facade is attributed to the school of Gagliardi.

Palazzo Arezzo

Adjoining Piazza Duomo is Baron Arezzo's arched **Palazzo Arezzo**, whose facade is adorned with sculpted hedgehogs, the family crest. The Arezzo dynasty still owns much of the province, from farmland to villas and a castle. Given their credo of enlightened paternalism, the family has endowed local hospitals, parks and churches. Ibla's nobles have always immortalised themselves in stone, linking grand Baroque mansions to a graceful family chapel or even a gentlemen's club.

Frieze in Ragusa Ibla.

Nearby is the **Circolo di Conversazione** (ring for admission), a literary salon founded by local noblemen. The *belle époque* interior contains an allegorical *trompe l'œil* ceiling and busts of Michelangelo, Galileo, Dante and Bellini, representing art, science, poetry and music. Nor is the art of aristocratic conversation dead in sleepy Ibla: here, men sit amongst frescoed nymphs while chatting over news or playing cards.

BELOW LEFT: Duomo San Giorgio. **BELOW:** Baroque decoration inside the cathedral.

TIP

Giardino Ibleo is the focal point of the Ibla Buskers' Festival each October, when performers from all around the world are offered free hospitality in return for entertainment.

The adjoining **Palazzo Donnafugata** was the nobles' private theatre, gallery and reading club until opened to a slightly wider membership. Sadly, the sculpted marble staircase, sumptuous salons and gallery adorned with old masters are only visible during private banquets, but you can visit the theatre (booking through the bar next door). Most symbolic is the heavily shuttered loggia on the *piano nobile*, a secret spot from which to view visitors.

Ancient Jewish ghetto

Behind the cathedral on Via Capitano Bocchieri is **Palazzo La Rocca**, an austere Baroque mansion transformed into the welcoming **provincial tourist office** (tel: 0932 675 111). The facade is enlivened by bizarre balconies depicting 18th-century aristocratic entertainment: a lute player and cherub blowing a hunting horn vie with gawky, naked lovers clinging to each other in gauche poses.

The alleys in the shadow of the cathedral are what Italians readily term *suggestivo* (atmospheric).

This, the heart of the ancient Jewish ghetto and artisan quarter, is slowly being restored and repopulated with younger residents and craft shops. In the square of Largo Camerina, however, a traditional cabinet-maker survives, creating tables from olive, carob, cherry, cyprus and orange wood. More typical of the reinvigorated quarter is Al Portale, a fashionable bar carved out of former stables, close to Portale San Giorgio, or L'Antica Drogheria, on Corso XXV Aprile, a superior delicatessen selling Iblean honey and herbs, cheeses, salami and biscuits.

Ibleo Park

The **Giardino Ibleo** (8am–8pm), created in the 19th century around the (closed) church of **San Giacomo,** is a charming landscaped park set on a spur at the eastern end of Ibla. In spring, the statues, palm trees and pool are complemented by daffodils, broom and irises. Around the grounds are three ruined churches, victims of the 1693 earthquake, and a popular café. The multicoloured majolica dome of **San Domenico**

BELOW: Ragusa Ibla from Largo Santa Maria.

overlooks Gothic **San Giacomo**, built on the site of a pagan temple, and the church of the **Cappuccini**, a Baroque monastic church. On the far side of the gardens on Via Normanni is the dilapidated 15th-century Gothic doorway to the church of **San Giorgio Vecchio**, with a relief depicting *St George and the Dragon*. Carved in soft local stone, this is all that remains of the original church destroyed in the earthquake that devastated Ragusa. From this uncharacteristically lush corner of old Ibla, both ancient locals and young lovers take time to look out over terraces and dry-stone walls to a valley encrusted with ancient Siculi tombs.

Yet, despite its noble veneer, parts of Ibla are still poor. Within view of the heart of town are outlying quarters riddled with blind alleys, abandoned hovels and rock dwellings, side by side with remains of medieval, Byzantine and even pre-Christian Ragusa. Set below the jagged landscape of modern Ragusa, the ancient Siculi tombs now tend to be used as storerooms, wine cellars or even garages. The valley floor is cut by a river that fed several mills until the 1980s; the scene is one of whitewashed cottages, steep steps, pots of geraniums, and peppers dried on walls Arab-style.

North of Ragusa

Chiaramonte Gulfi ❸ (population 8,300) was founded in the late 7th century as Gulfi but destroyed by the Angevins in 1299. It was then revived by Manfredi I, the Count of Módica, one of the Chiaramonte dynasty. The town flourished until overtaken by neighbouring Vittória which, as it grew in size, gained in prosperity and power. The citizens of Gulfi added Chiaramonte to their town's name in 1881 to honour its original benefactor.

The infamous 1693 earthquake destroyed much of Chiaramonte's

small-town splendour, but the c*entro storico* has been preserved. Although the **Arco dell'Annunziata** is the one remaining medieval gateway, other low-key attractions include several lofty churches and a cluster of endearing museums, including a costume museum, local history museum and, best of all, an olive oil museum. Today Chiaramonte Gulfi is famous among Sicilians for its superb olive oil, country food and hearty trattorie. A well-organised olive oil trail leads through the scenic **Monti Iblei**, with opportunities to stop for tastings at oil or wine estates or to sample rustic meals at farmstays.

At about 2km (1¼ miles) away in the countryside is the **Santuario dell Madonna delle Grazie**, restored in 1710, but more a place for picnics than religious devotion.

Giarratana ❹, sandwiched between the Iblean mountains and the plains, represents a rural Sicilian backwater, complete with ruined castle. After the 1693 earthquake the town was rebuilt on the sunnier adjoining hill, and produced a trio of impressive (but irregularly open)

Balcony detail in Ragusa Ibla.

BELOW: Giardino Ibleo.

Vittória was founded in 1607 by Vittoria Colonna, the daughter of a Spanish viceroy and wife of the count of Módica. Since aristocractic power in Parliament was closely linked to the size of the feudal estates, Vittória tried to make the town as populous as possible.

Baroque churches that survive today: the Chiesa Madre, Sant'Antonio and San Bartolomeo.

West of Ragusa

From Ragusa, the rural hinterland unfolds. On higher ground, olives, almonds and carobs abound but, in well-irrigated areas, greenhouse cultivation is gaining ground. Where there is enough water, on the coast or in river canyons, dwarf palms, holm-oaks, plane trees and Aleppo pines flourish. But on the plains, the view is of dust-coloured farmhouses, low dry-stone walls, endless fields, rugged limestone plains beaten to the colour of sandstone.

A dramatic descent from the Iblean hills leads across a vast plain to **Cómiso ❺** (population 28,000), an attractive Baroque town that had the misfortune to become a NATO military base in the 1980s. Peace protests were the price residents paid for housing the last cruise missiles located on European soil. As a bonus, 7,000 American soldiers subsidised the local economy until the final removal of the missiles in 1991.

BELOW: Fonte Diana, the Roman fountain in Cómiso.

Fortunately, Cómiso reopens as a low-cost airport in 2012.

Ruled by the Aragonese Naselli dynasty from the 15th to the 18th centuries, Cómiso still has a feudal castle. The restored 14th-century **Castello dei Naselli** retains its original Gothic portal and octagonal tower, converted from a Byzantine baptistery. Although shattered by the 1693 earthquake, fragments of classical Cómiso survive: Piazza di Municipio contains **Fonte Diana**, a Roman fountain whose waters once gushed into the Roman baths now under the municipal offices.

In Piazza delle Erbe there is **San Francesco**, with the fine Antonello Gagini marble **mausoleum** and, just off the piazza, is the **covered market** (1871). Adding to the Baroque scenery is the vast domed **Basilica dell'Annunziata** and the slim-domed **Santa Maria delle Grazie**, a monastic chapel which offers the town's most gruesome sight: mummified bodies of monks and benefactors stacked in frightening poses.

Vittória ❻, further west, is a wealthy wine-producing centre on the slopes of the Iblean hills. While perfectly safe for visitors, this neat city remains wealthy rather than healthy – as under the surface the Mafia maintains a toehold. Giuseppe Fava, a Sicilian journalist murdered by the Mafia, once dismissed Vittória as "a city built by those without the time, money, imagination or background to make anywhere better".

Even so, the elegant **Piazza del Pòpolo** contains the Baroque church of **Santa Maria delle Grazie** and the monumental **Teatro Comunale**, a fine example of neoclassical architecture.

On Piazza Libertà is the **Palazzo dei Principe** (Sat 6–8pm, Sun 10am–noon, 5.30–8.30pm). Amid the bland modernity are bourgeois mansions with grand courtyards. From the city gardens are views across the fertile valley to the sea, with flowers and peaches supplementing the traditional crops of olive oil and wine. The illustrious wine producer Florio has an important base here.

South of Ragusa

Castello di Donnafugata ❼ (Tue, Thur, Sun 9am–1pm, 3–4.30pm, Wed, Fri, Sat 9am–1pm; charge) lies 20km (12 miles) southwest of Ragusa. Set in a carob and palm plantation, this modern Moorish pastiche feels authentically Sicilian. The castle dates from 1648 but was redesigned as a full-blown Ottocento fantasy by Corrado Arezzo, the baron of Donnafugata, in the 19th century, and remained in the family until the 1970s. Arezzo, a campaigner for Sicilian independence, created Donnafugata as his whimsical refuge from revolutionary politics.

The exterior is a Venetian palace transplanted by magic carpet to *The Arabian Nights*. The crenellated facade, inspired by an austere Arab desert fort, is softened by an arcaded Moorish balcony. Below the arched windows opens an amazing loggia in Venetian-Gothic style. The finest rooms include a picture gallery, billiards room, winter garden and a salon for conversation. The frescoed music room illustrates the noble pastimes of painting, *bel canto* and piano recitals.

Charmingly faded, this palace of 122 rooms is quietly being restored. But for now, the floating drapes, tarnished gilt, inlaid tables and dusty chandeliers conspire to create an atmosphere straight out of *The Leopard*. Unsurprisingly, the castle is a sought-after film set.

During World War II, the Luftwaffe commandeered the castle but respected Donnafugata, so all the baron's quirky touches remain, from the cute well and the children's maze in the garden to the artificial grotto and glorious parkland.

The ancient Greek site of **Camarina**, the **Parco archeologico di Camarina ❽** (daily 9am–1.30pm), lies on the coast just 12km (7 miles) southwest of Donnafugata. Founded in 598 BC, two centuries after Siracusa (the ferocity of the local Siculi tribes was a deterrent to earlier settlement),

TIP

Around Vittória there are several wine trails, to put you on the right track for Cerasuolo di Vittoria and Nero d'Avola wines and producers. Although the trails aren't yet signposted, a wine route map can be picked up from the local tourist office.

BELOW: the Basilica dell'Annunziata, Cómiso.

The Castello di Donnafugata, a 19th-century palace built on the site of an Arab village, combines Venetian Gothic with Moorish whimsy.

Camarina is a sophisticated example of urban planning covering three hills at the mouth of the River Ippari. But it was attacked, sacked and rebuilt many times until finally the city of perfect parallel lines was destroyed by the Romans in AD 258. The first excavations of the site were begun in 1896; then, after a hiatus, excavations continued again in 1958 and are still in progress.

In the park are traces of the 6th-century BC walls that stretched 7km (4 miles) to encircle and protect a city that was divided into distinct public, civil, religious and residential areas.

Close to the **museum** (daily 9am–2pm, 3–7pm; charge) lie the foundations of a **tempio di Athena** (temple of Athena). The museum contains objects retrieved from shipwrecks on this shoreline, including sarcophagi and amphorae as well as a Greek bronze helmet (4th century BC) and 1,000 coins found in a treasure chest. Nearby, the **House of the Altar** has rooms radiating from the central courtyard with a battered mosaic floor. Other Hellenistic dwellings include a merchant's house, con-

BELOW: in Vittória's Piazza del Popolo.

firmed by the presence of scales and measuring devices.

On the headland just south of Camarina, at **Punta Secca**, is the Roman port of **Caucana** ❾. Now slowly being excavated, the port was partly preserved by sand, as at Gela (*see page 146*) further down the coast. The lush site is lovely but inscrutable, a puzzle compounded by the discovery of Hellenistic amphorae, Roman coins and Jewish candelabra. Amid the rubble, the clearest find is a Byzantine church with a colourful mosaic of a goat. It was in this port that the navy of Count Roger the Norman gathered in 1091 before the conquest of Malta.

To visit this **Parco Archeologico**, you have to book (daily 8am–7pm; tel: 0932 916 142).

Southeast to Módica

Beyond farmsteads and stone walls are two high road bridges that provide a sudden, terrifying glimpse of a grey-brown town in the deep valley below. **Módica** ❿, the former regional capital, is perched on a ridge spilling down into the valley.

Culinary renaissance

Sicily's culinary renaissance is in the southeast of the island, and the Val di Noto, centred on Ragusa and Módica. Sicily now has everything from Slow Food organic eateries and creative trattorie to country-style restaurants and Michelin-starred establishments that are setting the agenda for *la cucina siciliana*. Over half the new Italian entries to the 2011 Michelin guide were from Sicily, with Ragusa's Don Serafino and La Fenice both awarded Michelin stars. The region is noted for rustic cheeses and meats, so even the most celebrated chefs offer affectionate nods to the island's peasant traditions. For a memorable meal, choose Duomo in Ragusa or La Gazza Ladra in Módica (*see pages 174–5*).

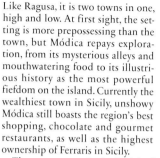

Like Ragusa, it is two towns in one, high and low. At first sight, the setting is more prepossessing than the town, but Módica repays exploration, from its mysterious alleys and mouthwatering food to its illustrious history as the most powerful fiefdom on the island. Currently the wealthiest town in Sicily, unshowy Módica still boasts the region's best shopping, chocolate and gourmet restaurants, as well as the highest ownership of Ferraris in Sicily.

The prosperous Arab citadel of Mudiqah became a fief of the Chiaramonte family in 1296 and merged into the county of Módica. After succumbing to Spanish influence, it passed from the Caprera viceroys to the Henriquez, Spanish absentee landlords. Around town are the family crests of the three dynasties: respectively mountains, a goat, and two castles. Módica's charm lies in the complexity of the multi-layered town, with its tiers of sumptuous churches and shabby palaces stacked up on the hill.

At the entrance to the town is the **Convento dei Padri Mercedari**, which houses the dull **Museo Civico** (9am–1pm) and the more interesting **Museo Ibleo delle Arti e Tradizioni popolari** (daily, summer 10am–1pm, 4.30–7.30pm, winter 10am–1pm, 3.30–6.30pm; charge), depicting local trades such as shoemaking and cart-making, along with farming and winemaking.

San Giorgio Cathedral

Above, perched precariously on the slope of the hill, looms the Baroque landmark of **San Giorgio** (daily 9am–1pm, 4–7pm). Set in Módica Alta (Upper Módica), against a backdrop of rocky terraces, the church makes a bold statement and surmounts a daunting Baroque flight of 250 steps. Climb the stairs only if you are feeling fit: there is little to see in the church behind its ornate facade. Not that Gagliardi's masterpiece disappoints: its exuberance and inventiveness encapsulate Sicilian Baroque. This frothy concoction of flowing lines and curvy ornament seems barely rooted to the spot. The vision is one of Rococo splendour, shadowy recesses and a soaring belfry silhouetted against the sky.

The writer Vincent Cronin summed up Módica's San Giorgio cathedral by saying: "After such a meandering introduction, which arouses our hopes to the highest pitch, all but the greatest building would appear to fail."

BELOW: Módica.

EAT

In Módica call in at the **Antica Dolceria Bonajuto** at 159 Corso Umberto 1 (www. bonajuto.it) to sample *'mpanatigghi*, a sweet biscuit made with meat and chocolate, or meat and carob. Signor Ruta is famous for his unusual chocolate combinations, including *testa di Moro*, fried pastry filled with chocolate custard.

BELOW: interior and exterior of San Pietro, Módica.

Corso Umberto I

After such spectacle, other churches play walk-on parts. However, on Corso Umberto I is the **Chiesa del Carmine**, with a marble group representing *The Annunciation*, attributed to Antonello Gagini. In the centre of town, where the Corso meets Via Marchesa Tedeschi, stands **San Domenico**, a church which was hit by two 17th-century earthquakes.

Just around the corner is the town hall, embracing the **Cripta del Convento di San Domenico** (key and guide from the tourist office on Via Grimaldi). The Dominicans used this mysterious medieval crypt as a burial chamber, but it was also a torture chamber linked to the Inquisition.

Still on the Corso, reached by a theatrical staircase along which tiers of the 12 apostles welcome visitors much like today's party greeters, is the great San Giorgio's nearest rival, the opulent church of **San Pietro** (built after 1693). Gagliardi may have designed this church, too.

Close to San Pietro is the ancient church of **San Niccolò Inferiore**, essentially a grotto displaying 11th-century frescoes. Also on the Corso are the 16th-century church of **Santa Maria del Soccorso**, the 18th-century **Teatro Garibaldi** and 18th-century **Palazzo Manenti** with its balcony and Baroque embellishments.

Museo Campailla (Mon–Fri 9am–noon) is the most bizarre minor museum in Sicily: an early syphilis clinic founded by Tommaso Campailla, a 17th-century doctor and philosopher, and used until the early 20th century. The cure, a refinement on an 8th-century Arab practice, involved placing patients in the hot mercury chambers, heated by hot coals to produce a sauna-like effect, and subjecting sufferers to vaporous infusions. The eerie original chambers are still visible, surreally interconnected with rooms where city council workers go about their normal business.

Nearby, back on Via Marchese Tedeschi, is the 15th-century church of **Santa Maria di Betlem**, which appears to be four tiny churches converted into one. In the right nave, a magnificent portal opens into the late Gothic-Renaissance **Cappella**

del Sacramento where a *Madonna and Child Enthroned* is painted on stone above the altar. The side chapel contains a **crib** (1882) adorned with terracotta figurines.

Caves and tombs

From Módica, it's a short drive south to Baroque Scicli and the coast, or southeast to the Ispica canyon and to Siracusa province. The **Cava d'Ispica** ⑪ (daily, 9am–1pm, Wed and Sat closes 6pm; charge) is an 11km (7-mile) limestone gorge, typical of local gorges but on a giant scale, where ghostly galleries and caves have been inhabited almost continuously since prehistoric times. There are prehistoric tombs and medieval cave dwellings. The southern end of the narrow valley is overlooked by the **castello**, a castle-like rock which acted as a four-storey dwelling.

The better tombs are in the northern end of the gorge, close to the entrance to the site. The honeycomb of galleries conceal native Siculi oven-shaped tombs, Greek necropoli and early Christian tombs. Highlights include the **Larderia**, the most complete set of early Christian catacombs in southeastern Sicily, and the **Grotta di Santa Maria**, a rock chapel with wall paintings that was inhabited until the 1950s. Sections of the site are often closed, but it's best to visit with a guide, in any case.

At the far end of the Cava d'Ispica gorge is the **Parco Archeologico della Forza** (daily 9am–1pm, Wed and Sat until 6pm), outside the small town of Ispica. The Parco too has its catacombs and traces of prehistoric settlements. Ispica was rebuilt after the great earthquake in a safer position. On Via XX Settembre is the Baroque church of **Santa Maria Maggiore**, while on the Corso, **Palazzo Bruno di Belmonte** (1906), now the town hall, is an Art Nouveau castle created by the great Ernesto Basile.

Scicli

Southwest of the canyons is **Scicli** ⑫, a gorgeous Baroque gem that is coming into its own as a film set, thanks to an enlightened mayor and the worldwide popularity of the *Montalbano* detective films *(see below)*.

San Giovanni in Scicli.

BELOW: Forza, an archaeological park outside Ispica.

The Montalbano Trail

Set in Sicily, Camillieri's *Montalbano* detective novels have become the best-read books to come out of Italy since *The Leopard*. Since the novels were turned into equally popular films, set in Ragusa Province, the Montalbano Trail has become a major attraction. Literary sleuths can now sit in Commissioner Montalbano's office in the Town Hall *(Comune)* in Scicli, which doubles as the likeable detective's office in the fictional town of Vigata. Scicli's churches and convoluted Baroque facades still feature in most episodes of the series, as does Montalbano's beachside home at Punta Secca (Marinella in the films). Visitors can also visit the Castello di Donnafugata, the fictional home of the book's Mafia boss.

*Stone monster on a
Scicli mansion facade.*

The Baroque centre is experiencing a revival, with an influx of young craftspeople and arty types as well as canny second-home-owners in search of a civilised but forgotten corner of Sicily. A sprinkling of boutique hotels and chic B&Bs now make Sicli a lovely touring base.

The road from Ispica reveals vistas of a grotto-encrusted hillside opening onto the restored remains of the church of **San Matteo**, part of a medieval settlement once on the slopes, now overlooking the Baroque heart of Scicli on the valley floor below. Scicli's fusty city churches and fantastic Baroque mansions seem out of place in this sleepy world. The ochre-coloured facades are decorated with sirens, monsters and fauns, part of the cavalcade of Christian and mythological creatures inspired by designs on Greek temples or Romanesque cathedrals.

Piazza Italia, the main square, opens with the Baroque 18th-century **Duomo**, the **Chiesa Sant'Ignazio.** Its gilded interior holds a painting of a historic battle for Scicli between the Turks and Christians in 1091, where

BELOW: view over Scicli.

the successful intercession of a bellicose Madonna supposedly brought victory, an event celebrated in Scicli's own festival in May.

The most theatrical part of town is around **Via Mormino Penna**, the best-preserved Baroque street. Here stands the elegant church of **San Giovanni**, with its concave-convex facade and dazzling exterior matched by an equally impressive interior: the exuberantly stuccoed surface has a gaudy emerald and turquoise Moorish design. The church was previously the preserve of cloistered nuns, who sat in balconied splendour to watch processions on feast days.

Just south, **Palazzo Beneventano** has beautiful balconies, with fantastic corbels representing mythical beasts, Moors and ghoulish human masks. Almost as splendid is nearby **Palazzo Fava**, representing a riot of galloping griffins and horses ridden by cherubs. Just east, at the foot of the rock, loom the majestic cupola and domed apses of **Santa Maria la Nuova**, signalling the start of Scicli's intriguing medieval quarter, dotted

with alleys and steps overflowing with pot plants.

An attractive path that winds up to the top, where the ruined castle and Chiesa San Matteo overlook the town, has won favour as a popular summer stroll. From here, secret passageways dating from the Saracen sieges reputedly lead out of town. The hill is pitted with former cavehomes that were inhabited until the 1980s but which now serve as wine cellars, garages and storerooms.

Beside the seaside

Ragusa province has some of Sicily's best beaches. Less than 10km (6 miles) from Scicli, the coastal landscape is wild and unspoilt (*see below*). Sandy beaches await around the archaeological site of **Camarina**, with a secluded rocky beach on **Punta Braccetto,** the headland beyond.

Heading eastwards, **Marina di Ragusa** ⑬, lined with inviting fish restaurants, contains the only managed beaches, equipped for windsurfing and various other watersports. In summer, this winter ghost town turns into a newly fashionable resort, popular with yachting types and families.

Just east is the wooded coastal reserve of **Fiume Irmínio**, with the broad sandy beaches of **Donnalucata** ⑭ beyond, a stretch of coast rapidly being swamped by greenhouses.

A 7km (4-mile) coastal drive leads east to the rocky headland of Punta del Corvo, and on to coastline that lies further south than Tunisia's northern coastline.

Sampieri ⑮ stands out for its self-consciously quaint atmosphere, a prettified fishing village popular with Ragusani out for a family romp in the sand dunes. Further along the coast, at the port of **Pozzallo** ⑯, the industrial complex is too close to the beach for comfort, although the beaches are perfectly acceptable further east, towards Siracusa province. Still, Pozzallo is a pleasant enough place to stay for a lunch of salted tuna or sardines, both caught and processed in the port.

From here, you can escape on a day trip to Malta by catamaran (Virtu Ferries; tel: 0932 954 062; www.virtuferries. com) or visit the Baroque masterpiece of Noto. ❏

TIP

Sicily can be combined with Malta on a two-island holiday using Virtu Ferries (www. virtuferries.com). Fast catamarans run between Valletta, the capital of Malta, and Pozzallo in Ragusa province (90 minutes) or on the longer (three-hour) sailing from Valletta to Catania.

BELOW: Marina di Ragusa.

The best beaches

Ragusa's coastal landscape spans sand dunes, marshes, rocky beaches, and shingle stretches dotted with heather. Given the unspoilt nature of the coastline, Ragusa province has some of Sicily's best beaches. From Scicli, the coast is under 10km (6 miles) away, whether at sandy Donnalucata, rocky Cava d'Aliga, or at the romantic fishing village of Sampieri, with its fetching sand dunes. Some of the finest shores stretch between Camarina and Marina di Ragusa: delightful sandy beaches await around the archaeological site of Camarina, with a secluded rocky beach on the Punta Braccetto headland beyond. Heading eastwards, Marina di Ragusa offers boating and windsurfing, as well as posing over a seafood lunch.

BEST RESTAURANTS, BARS AND CAFÉS

Restaurants

Prices for a three-course dinner per person and a half-bottle of house wine:
€ = under €20
€€ = €20–35
€€€ = €35–70
€€€€ = over €70

The region is currently a culinary hotspot, with some of the most varied and creative cooking in Sicily. Allow time to savour the flavours, especially in Ragusa, Módica and Chiaramonte.

Ragusa

Baglio la Pergola
Piazza Luigi Sturzo, Contrada Selvaggio
Tel: 0932 686 430
info@lapergolarg.it €€€

Popular, elegant spot for updated versions of local dishes. Fish too. Closed Tue and Aug.

Il Barocco
Via Orfanotrofio 29, Ibla
Tel: 0932 652 397
www.ilbarocco.it €–€€
Dependable pizzeria and restaurant. Closed Wed and two weeks in Aug.

Duomo
Via Capitano Boccheri 31, Ibla
Tel: 0932 651 265
www.ristoranteduomo.it €€€–€€€€
Elegant, close to the cathedral, and renowned for intense, elaborate reinterpretations of Sicilian cuisine, as Baroque as Ibla itself. Celebrated chef Ciccio Sultano wins awards for his inventive

cooking. Closed Mon lunch and Sun.

Locandina Don Serafino
Via Avvocato Ottaviano, Ibla
Tel: 0932 248 778
www.locandadonserafino.it €€€–€€€€
Burrowed into the basement of an atmospheric mansion, one of Sicily's most seductive restaurants boasts equally delectable cuisine, from the sea (seafood salad) to sophisticated interpretations of Sicilian street food (rice balls with saffron) or to Ragusan rabbit. The boutique hotel is equally lovely. Closed Tue.

Monna Lisa
Via Ettore Fieramosca
Tel: 0932 642 250 €€
Richly flavoured Sicilian dishes in large trattoria with a garden. Pizza in evenings. Closed Mon.

La Piazzetta
Piazza Duomo 14
Tel: 0932 686 131
www.lapiazzettaragusaibla.it €€
Genuine *cucina ragusana* so grilled vegetables, cheeses and an array of meats, but little fish.

U' Saracinu
Via Convento 9, Ibla
Tel: 0932 246 976 €€
Facing San Giorgio, a relaxed place serving rustic dishes in a vaulted cellar. Closed Sun.

Marina di Ragusa

Eremo della Giubiliana
Contrada Giubiliana
Tel: 0932 669 119
www.eremodellagiubiliana.it €€€
Set en route to the sea, this delightful former monastery is now a boutique hotel with a pool, a wine estate and an excellent restaurant serving unusual Sicilian dishes. Closed Jan–Feb.

Da Serafino
Longomare Doria
Tel: 0932 239 522
www.locandadonserafino.it €€
Run by the Don Serafino team *(see Ragusa)*, this is a more typical trattoria by the sea. Good fish and pizza. Closed Oct–Mar.

Trattoria Carmelo
Lungomare Doria
Tel: 0932 239 913 €€
Contemporary seafood restaurant overlooking the beach. Closed Mon.

Villa Fortugno
4km (2½ miles) along road to Marina di Ragusa
Tel: 0932 667 134
www.villafortugno.it €€€
Country cooking with Sicilian sausages, pork stews and fine desserts. Closed Mon.

Chiaramonte Gulfi

Antica Stazione
Contrada Santissimo
Tel: 0932 928 083 €

LEFT: elaborate dish at Eremo della Giubiliana.
RIGHT: Locanda Don Serafino.

Set in an old railway station, this easy-going trattoria and pizzeria (with summer terrace) is popular with the locals. Dishes use delicious Chiaramonte olive oil and Ragusan cheeses. Superb value.

Locanda Gulfi
Contrada Patria
Tel: 0932 928 081
www.gulfi.it €–€€
Simple fare from the Monte Iblei hills, including salami and cheeses, matched by wines produced on the noted Gulfi estate.

Majore
Via Martiri Ungherese 12
Tel: 0932 928 019
www.majore.it €€
Their motto here is *Qui si magnifica il porco* (here we glorify the pig). The kitchen is devoted to cooking pork. Very popular. Closed Mon and July.

Ristorante Valle di Chiaramonte
Contrada Piano Zocchi Pantanelli
Tel: 0932 926 079 €–€€
Unpretentious *agriturismo* (farmstay) serving farm fresh produce, from rustic vegetable *antipasti* to *salumeria* (charcuterie), cheeses and oil.

Módica

Antica Dolceria Bonajuto
Corso Umberto I 159
Tel: 0932 941 225
www.bonajuto.it €
A famous establishment. You can try *'mpanatigghi*, made with meat and chocolate, *testa di Moro*, fried pastry filled with chocolate custard, or *cannoli*, filled with sweet ricotta cheese.

Bonomo
Viale Medaglie d'Oro 3–5
Tel: 0932 941 520
www.pasticceriabonomo.it
The Pasticceria Bonomo delivers artisanal chocolate. Ask for the amazing *pasticcini ripieni con carne e cioccolato*, sweet pastries filled with chocolate and meat, not that you'd know.

Fattoria delle Torri
Vico Napolitano 14, Módica Alta
Tel: 0932 751 286 €€€
Tucked away in an alley, this charming trattoria serves wonderful traditional fare in a Baroque palatial setting. Dinner served under lemon trees in warm weather. Reservations essential.

La Gazza Ladra
Via Blandini 5, Módica Alta
Tel: 0932 755 655
www.ristorantelagazzaladra.it €€€
Michelin-starred spot run by renowned chef Accursio Craparo in the lovely boutique hotel of Palazzo Failla *(see page 275)*. The ambience is ultra-refined, while the cuisine has strongly Sicilian roots, with a *nouvelle* twist.

Locanda del Colonnello
Via Blandini 5, Módica Alta €€
La Gazza Ladra's chef has opened an inn celebrating *cucina povera*, rustic cuisine inspired by the simplest produce. Authentic dishes featuring local cheeses, cold cuts and pastries.

Taverna Nicastro
Via Sant'Antonio 28
Tel: 0932 945 884
www.tavernanicastro.it €–€€
Only open for dinner, this established spot specialises in robust flavours, including rabbit dishes.

Scicli

Osteria del Ponte
Via Aleardi 24
Tel: 0932 831 713 €–€€
Set in a striking mansion in the centre of town, the restaurant is a showcase of local cuisine.

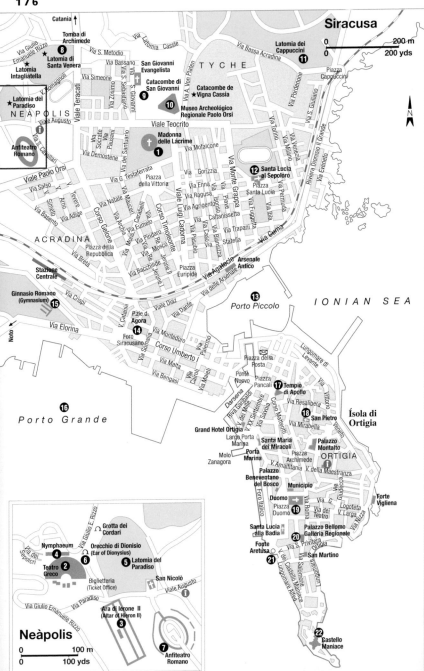

Siracusa

	200 m
0	
0	200 yds

Catania ↑

Tomba di Archimede **8**

Via Giulio Emanuele Rizzo

★ Latomia di Santa Venera 8

Via S. Metodio

Via Romagnoli

★ Latomia Intagliatella

Via Bassano

★ Latomia del Paradiso

Via S. Sebastiano

San Giovanni Evangelista

Via Simeone

NEÀPOLIS

Viale Teracati

Via Zosimo

Catacombe di San Giovanni **9**

Via S. Giovanni

Viale Augusto

Via S. Cagliari

Catacombe de **★ Vigna Cassia**

Museo Archeológico Regionale Paolo Orsi **10**

T Y C H E

Via Bassa Acradina

Latomia dei Cappuccini 11

Piazza Cappuccini

Via S. Giuliano

Via A. Von Platen

Viale Teocrito

Anfiteatro Romano

Madonna delle Lácrime **1**

Via Mofalcone

Via Demostene

Via G. Testaferrata

Via Santuario

Via Pausani

Via Sociale

Piazza della Vittoria

Via Gorizzia

Via Enna

Via Ragusa

Santa Lucia al Sepolcro **12**

Via Monte Grappa

Piazza Santa Lucia

Via Pordenone

Via Torino

Via Venezia

Via Milano

Rivera Dionisio Il Grande

Viale Paolo Orsi

Via Salso

Via Natale

Via Archia

Via Maurei

Viale Luigi Cadorna

Corso Timoleonte

Via Tagola

Via Plave

Via Caltanissetta

Via Trapani

Via Fuggetta

Via Ibla

Via Permuda

Via S. Giuliano

Via Evento

Via Arno

Via Tevere

Via Adige

Via Sineto

Via Basento

ACRADINA

Via Moria

Via Carabella

Via Eumelo

Via Pindaro

Via Mosco

Via Jerone Il

Via Bacchilde

Piazza della Repubblica

Via Breta

Piazza Euripide

Via Bianzizza

Via Casio

Via Pisubio

Via Statella

Via Cuma

Arsenale Antico

Via Agatocle

Via delle Arsenale

Stazione Centrale

Via Crispi

Ginnasio Romano (Gymnasium) 15

Via Catania

Viale Diaz

Viale Dante

13 Porto Piccolo

I O N I A N   S E A

Noto ←

Via Elorina

P.zle d. Agora **14**

Foro Siracusano

Via Somalia

Via Montedoro

Corso Umberto I

Via Palermo

Via Malta

Via Bengasi

Via Cairoli

Via Maltei

Piazza della Posta

Ponte Nuovo

Piazza Pancali

Tempio di Apollo **17**

Lungomare di Levante

Via Vittorio

16 Porto Grande

Darsena

Riva Garibaldi

Via dei Mille

V. XX Settembre

Corso Matteotti

Via Resalibera

Via Mirabella

San Pietro **18**

Palazzo Montalto

Ísola di Ortigia

Grand Hotel Ortigia

Largo Porta Marina

Porta Marina

Molo Zanagora

Santa Maria dei Miracoli

Piazza Archimede

ORTIGIA

V. Amalfitania

V. della Maestranza

Via Guidecca

Palazzo Benevantano del Bosco

Municipio

Foro Italico

Duomo

Piazza Duomo **19**

Via Roma

Via G.

Via del Teatro

Logoteta

V. Larga

Via Nizza

Forte Vigliena

Santa Lucia alla Badia

Palazzo Bellomo Galleria Regionale **18**

V. S. Privitera

20

San Martino

Ortigia

Via Salomone

Forte Aretusa 21

V. del Castello Malace

Lungomare Alfeo

Lungomare Maniace

Castello Maniace 22

Neàpolis

Via del Sepolcri

Via Giulio E. Rizzo

Grotta dei Cordari

Nymphaeum **4**

Teatro Greco **2**

Orecchio di Dionisio (Ear of Dionysius) **6**

Latomia del Paradiso 5

San Nicolò

Biglietteria (Ticket Office)

Via Paradiso

Via Giulio Emanuele Rizzo

Ara di Ierone II (Altar of Hieron II) **3**

Viale Augusto

Anfiteatro Romano 7

	100 m
0	
0	100 yds

SIRACUSA

Alluring, civilised and sleepy, Siracusa is less dynamic than Catania, less sultry than Palermo, yet somehow charmingly steals most visitors' hearts as the capital of sheer indulgence

Cicero called the island of Ortigia, part of the city of Siracusa today but separated from the mainland by a narrow channel, the loveliest city in the world, and, like Siracusa itself (Syracuse in English-speaking countries), Ortigia's name resounds in academic circles abroad. Siracusa is the summation of Sicilian splendour, with an emphasis on Greek heritage. It was this cultivated city that supposedly witnessed the birth of comedy in its Greek theatre and now boasts the only school of classical drama outside Athens.

Apart from tales of Artemis and Apollo, Siracusa gave the world architectural beauty with a Baroque heart: Ortigia has facades framed by wrought-iron balconies that are as free as billowing sails. In fact, as Sicily's greatest seafaring power, Siracusa indulged an affinity with the sea that still pervades city myths and art. The city's sensual sculpture of Venus emerging from the breeze-swept sea embodies this cult of water.

Perhaps daunted by such a glorious past, today's citizens have a reputation for being dreamers and underachievers, better at wallowing in the past than at preserving it for posterity. But the end result is a city of such languid charm that it feels pernickety to point out such failings. Arguably more beautiful than Ragusa, Siracusa offers the marine nonchalance Ragusa Ibla lacks, while urban regeneration in the island heart of Siracusa is making the city lovelier than ever (*see page 184*).

Classical glory

The city was founded in 733 BC, a year after Naxos, by Corinthian settlers who maintained links with Sparta. Although it was ruled by a succession of cruel but occasionally benevolent

Main attractions

NEÀPOLIS
TEATRO GRECO
CATACOMBE DI SAN GIOVANNI
MUSEO ARCHEOLOGICO
PORTO GRANDE boat trip
ORTIGIA
DUOMO
PALAZZO BELLOMO (GALLERIA REGIONALE)
FONTE ARETUSA
LUNGOMARE DI LEVANTE
CASTELLO MANIACE

RIGHT: marriage in Siracusa.

TIP

Although Ortigia would be a perfect spot for cycling, all the new bicycle ranks have been permanently vandalised, so visitors are restricted to lovely walks or to the tourist train which covers the city's main sites (picked up in Piazza Archimede, and operational until mid-October).

tyrants, Siracusa rose to become the supreme Mediterranean power of its age under Dionysius the Elder. The decisive battle was Siracusa's defeat of Athens in 415 BC at sea. During a despotic 38-year rule, however, Dionysius personified Sicilian tyranny *(see box below)*.

City sectors

Siracusa is a diffuse, segmented city whose ancient Greek divisions still resonate deeply with residents. **Ortigia**, the cultural island at the heart of the Greek city, remains true to its vocation: despite a grand Baroque and Catalan carapace, this beguiling backwater feels intimate, informal and quietly cultured. This is where the locals while away the long summer evenings.

By contrast, **Tyche**, the northern quarter on the mainland, can feel like the city of the dead: studded with ancient catacombs. Tyche lay beyond the bounds of Roman Syracuse and thus remains a testament to the impact of early Christianity. **Acradina**, bordering Ortigia, remains the commercial quarter,

complete with railway station, while **Neàpolis**, to the northwest, though no longer "new", still embodies the ancient Greeks' notion of public and sacred space, ranging from theatres to sanctuaries.

Both as a useful landmark and as an antidote to classical beauty, the ugly modern **Santuario della Madonna delle Lacrime** ❶ signals the way to the archaeological zones of Neàpolis and Tyche. Visible from most of the city with its statue of the Madonna on top, this popular pilgrimage centre (daily 7am–8pm; www.madonnadellelacrime.it) commemorates a modern miracle: in 1953 a statue of Mary reputedly cried for five days and the spot became a shrine in the shape of a giant teardrop.

To the west, Neàpolis, the ancient quarter, is synonymous with its sprawling archaeological park, **Parco Archeologico della Neàpolis** (Tue–Sun 9am–5pm, Sun 8am–1pm; charge), containing rough-hewn quarries, grandiose theatres and tombs. Although set among shady fir trees and olive groves, the site can be sweltering in summer. But it's easy

BELOW: Darsena, the docks at Siracusa.

The legacy of Dionysius

Dionysius was a megalomaniac, a military strategist, a monumental builder, an inspired engineer and an execrable tragedian. He presided over Siracusa's golden age, with the grandest public works in the Western world. After the sun set on ancient Greece, Siracusa became a Roman province and was supposedly evangelised by St Peter and St Paul on their way to Rome. It became the capital of Byzantium, albeit briefly, in the 7th century and produced several popes and patriarchs of Constantinople. After being sacked by the Arabs in AD 878 and the Normans in 1085, the city sank into oblivion but quietly prospered under Spanish rule.

enough to avoid the tawdry stalls selling painted papyrus scrolls and melt into the spacious Greek ruins.

Teatro Greco

In the park, a stroll to the **Teatro Greco ❷** passes the rubble of the **Ara di Ierone II** (Altar of Hieron II) **❸**, a sacrificial altar once decorated by imposing *telamones* (giants). Surrounded by trees, the vast open theatre seats 15,000 and is often called the masterpiece of ancient Greece.

This astonishing accomplishment dates from 474 BC, although much was altered in the 3rd century BC. Carved into the rock, the *cavea* (horseshoe of tiered seats) is divided into two by a *diazoma* (corridor), and vertically cut into nine blocks of seats bearing inscriptions to deities and dignitaries. A satisfying climb to the top provides striking views over modern Siracusa and the sea. On the terrace is a **nymphaeum ❹**, a complex of waterfall, springs and grotto that once contained statues and niches for votive offerings.

In the Roman era, the theatre became an amphitheatre, with water

dammed and diverted to flood the arena for mock naval battles or gladiatorial combat. But, among the Greeks, it was a stage that witnessed the first performances of all Aeschylus's tragedies. The theatrical tradition is maintained today, with the dramas of Sophocles and Euripides played on a stage once viewed by such notables as Plato and Archimedes.

Although partially closed, above the theatre, **Via dei Sepolcri** is a path of tombs, offering glimpses of tombs and carved niches at the upper level, while the lower level leads down to the *latomie*, giant quarries that were also used as prisons in classical times. A wooded path slopes behind the back of the Greek theatre to a secret rocky arch and the lush **Latomia del Paradiso ❺**. These ancient quarries were once vaulted but are now open to the sun, bursting with olive and citrus groves or overgrown with cacti and ferns.

Here, too, is the cavernous **Orecchio di Dionisio** (Ear of Dionysius) **❻**, man-made and in places 47 metres (154ft) high, with excellent acoustics. It was given its name by Caravaggio

The Ear of Dionysius, a man-made cave named by Caravaggio.

BELOW: Teatro Greco.

TIP

The Papyrus Museum may be closed, but Egyptian papermaking techniques linger on in Siracusa. Various studios throughout the city offer to reproduce anything in papyrus, from old masters on papyrus to holiday snapshots on parchment.

after its resemblance to an ear. The poetic painter fancied that this echoing, dank, weirdly shaped cave was used by Dionysius to eavesdrop on his prisoners.

The adjoining **Grotta dei Cordari** (currently closed) is scored with chisel marks, because it was here that rope makers (*cordari*) stretched out their damp strands and tested their ropes for stress. A tunnel links Latomia del Paradiso with **Latomia Intagliatella**, and a rocky arch leads on to **Latomia di Santa Venera,** lemon-scented quarries which are pitted with votive niches.

It is hard to imagine that these lush gardens were once torture chambers. After Siracusa's decisive victory over Athens, the prisoners of war were lowered by rope into these pits. There was no need to mount guard: keeping captives alive involved no more than lowering a slave's half-rations and a drop of water. After 10 gruelling weeks, the non-Athenians who had survived were hauled out and sold as slaves. Athenians were branded with the mark of the Siracusan horse and also sold as slaves.

Roman amphitheatre

A separate entrance (but the same ticket) leads to the **Anfiteatro Romano** ❼, the Roman amphitheatre ringed by trees. While this tumbledown affair is not comparable with, say, the amphitheatre in France, at Nîmes, the site has charm. A path lined with stone sarcophagi leads to the imposing theatre carved by master craftsmen. Below a parapet circling the arena is a corridor where both animals and gladiators made their entrances for the spectacles.

Between the Greek theatre and Roman amphitheatre is San Nicolò, a Romanesque church concealing a Roman cistern. A circuit along **Via Giulio Emanuele Rizzo** reveals a cross-section of the classical city, including an aqueduct and the tomb-studded Via dei Sepolcri.

Ancient tombs

Further uphill lie the **Necropoli delle Grotticelli,** a warren of Hellenistic and Byzantine tombs, including the supposed **Tomba di Archimede** (Tomb of Archimedes) ❽, framed by a dignified Roman portico. The

BELOW: Roman amphitheatre.

Romans insisted that Archimedes' death was accidental, despite his creation of diabolical death traps used against them during the city's siege. This quarter forms part of ancient Tyche, characterised by labyrinthine catacombs that often follow the course of Greek aqueducts.

The **Catacombe di San Giovanni** ❾ (San Giovanni Catacombs; daily, 9.30am–noon, 2.30–5pm; charge) provide entry to the persecuted world of the early Christians. Escorted by a friar, visitors view early Christian sarcophagi, a 4th-century drawing of St Peter and a mosaic depicting *Original Sin*. The galleries open into space-creating rotundas decorated with primitive frescoes and arcane symbols, including a mysterious fish-headed boat or dead dove bound by an alpha and omega. Could this be a secret Christian code? Or a pagan transmigration of souls? Academics disagree.

In the wild garden outside is the shell of **San Giovanni Evangelista**, with its rose window and sculpted door often masked by monastic underwear drying in the sun. This modest church was Siracusa's first cathedral and is dedicated to St Marcian, the city's earliest bishop. Crooked steps lead down to **Cripta di San Marziano** and more catacombs. Light filters in on faded frescoes of St Lucy, sculpted cornices and an altar supposedly used by St Paul. Amid Greek lettering and crosses are primitive depictions of a phoenix and a bull.

Museum of Archeology

Probably the finest archaeological collection in Sicily lies in Villa Landolina, fittingly built over a quarry and pagan necropolis, in the **Museo Archeologico Regionale Paolo Orsi** ❿ (Tue–Sat 9am–6pm, Sun 9am–1pm; charge; tel: 0931 464 022) on the neighbouring Viale Teocrito. The well-organised museum reveals a succession of superb collections, prehistoric and Greek, coming from

Siracusa and its colonies, including finds at Gela and Agrigento. In the prehistory section, the stars are reconstructed necropoli, earthenware pots from Pantalica, and depictions of Cyclopes and dwarf elephants.

In the classical sections, the tone is set by two strikingly different works: the "immodest modesty" of the headless **Venere Anadiomene** (known also as **Venus Landolina** because it was unearthed here where the villa stands) and an Archaic sculpture of a seated fertility goddess suckling her twins, found in Megara Hyblaea. Elsewhere, the collection bursts with beauty and horror: lion's-head gargoyles, Aztec-like masks, a *Winged Victory*, a terracotta frieze of grinning gorgons and a Medusa with her tongue lolling out. Away from the horrors, smoothly virile marble torsos of *kouroi* (heroic youths) await. Beauty, both pure and sensual, lingers in the Roman sarcophagus of a couple called Valerius and Adelphia and in fragments of friezes from Selinunte and Siracusa.

Off the adjoining Via Augusto Von Platen are the **Catacombe di Vigna Cassia**, catacombs with 3rd-century

Exhibition at the Museo Archeologico Regionale Paolo Orsi.

BELOW: giant statues of classic masks from Greek drama.

The Eureka Man

Archimedes was no mere theoreti-
cian but an intensely practical
inventor, master engineer and
scientist when Siracusa was the
most inventive place on earth

The image of Archimedes leaping from his bath with a cry of *Eureka!* (Greek for "I have found it") is, despite the efforts of generations of physics teachers, not based in fact. While testing a gold crown suspected of being a mere alloy, Archimedes realised that the mass of water displaced by an object reveals its volume, and the mass of the object divided by its volume gives its density. The crown was found to be a fake as its density was less than that of solid gold. This discovery became known as Archimedes' Principle: the principle of specific gravity and the basis of hydrostatics.

Born in 287 BC, Archimedes worked for Hieron, the tyrant of Siracusa. While watching the tyrant's marine engineers, he devised theories worth a *Eureka!* each. His greatest discoveries were the formulae for the areas and volumes of spheres, cylinders and other shapes, anticipating the theories of integration by 1,800 years.

Dionysius's think-tank devised the long-range catapult which saved Siracusa from the Carthaginian fleet. Archimedes built on this tradition with the Archimedean screw, still used for raising water, and with siege engines that did sterling service against the Romans. Polybius says the Romans "failed to reckon with the ability of Archimedes, nor did they foresee that, in some cases, the genius of one man is more effective than any number of hands."

Archimedes is often quoted as saying "Give me a place to stand and I will move the world," implying that he understood the principles of leverage. It is unproven that he anticipated the laser beam by arranging magnifying glasses to set fire to the Roman fleet at long range, but he did produce a hydraulic serpent contraption that enabled just one man to operate a ship's pumps.

He also played a part in the construction of Hieron's remarkable 4,000-ton ship. Enough timber to build 60 conventional ships was used for the hull. It had three decks, one of which had a mosaic floor depicting scenes from the *Iliad*. The upper deck had a gymnasium, a garden and a temple to Venus paved with agate. The state cabin had a marble bath and 10 horses in stalls. Yet this was no pleasure craft. It carried a long-range catapult fitted to the masts which swung out over an attacking vessel and disgorged a huge rock, supported by a "cannon" that fired giant arrows. It was then loaded with corn, jars of Sicilian salt fish and 500 tons of wool and despatched to Ptolemy in Egypt as a gift.

Keen to exploit Archimedes' genius, the Roman commander Marcellus wanted him taken alive when the Romans occupied Siracusa. But, as legend has it, a Roman soldier came across an old codger apparently doodling in sand. Archimedes was working on his latest brainwave, so protested sharply when the soldier unwittingly stepped on his drawing. The soldier drew his sword and casually killed one of the greatest men in the world. ❑

Left: gold coin featuring Archimedes.

tombs and frescoed chambers which lead on to **Latomia dei Cappuccini** , the most picturesque quarries, alongside a former Capuchin monastery. Set on the coast, these huge honeycombed pits are matched by sculptural vegetation, but currently they can only be viewed from Via Acradina above. From the adjoining Piazza Cappuccini are stirring views of the rocky shore.

Further south again, near the sports stadium, are a series of (closed) catacombs surrounding the church of **Santa Lucia al Sepolcro** (daily 11am–2pm, 5–7pm; closed on Monday; charge), a Byzantine church founded by San Zozimo, the first Greek bishop of Siracusa, and dedicated to St Lucy, the city's virginal patron saint who was martyred here. Next door, connected by an underground passage, is the octagonal **Cappella del Sepolcro**, which was constructed in 1630 as a saintly sepulchre.

Porto Piccolo to Porto Grande

On the banks of the **Porto Piccolo** , the small harbour, are the scant remains of the city's ancient arsenal. Nearby stands the Byzantine **bath-house**, where legend has it that Emperor Constans was assassinated with a soap dish in AD 668. On **Piazzale del Foro Siracusano**, just behind the port, is the original **Greek agora**  of Acradina. This was the commercial centre of the Greek city but sadly suffered bombing by both the Allies and the Luftwaffe in 1943. At its centre is a war memorial.

Further west lies the ruins of the **Ginnasio Romano** , the Roman gymnasium (daily 9am–1pm; closed public holidays), a 1st-century theatre and shrine occupying a picturesquely flooded spot. Although its origins are obscure, the shrine was conceivably dedicated to oriental deities. The raised portico is well preserved and shimmers obligingly.

Nearby, the **Porto Grande** , where Dionysius defeated the Athenian navy in 415 BC, has become a busy mercantile harbour and pleasure port, with a new yacht marina under construction (*see box page 184*).

Ortigia

A stroll across the main bridge, Ponte Nuovo, leads past bobbing boats and pastel-coloured palazzi the **Darsena**, the inner docks. This is the tiny but atmospheric island of Ortigia, jutting into the **Mare Ionio**, the Ionian Sea. Rivalled only by Ragusa as a centre of aimless wandering, this largely pedestrianised island is the place for leisurely lunches, summer promenades and dreamy ruminations amid crumbling history.

Graced with two natural harbours, fresh springs and the blessing of the Delphic oracle, this seductive island was dedicated to the huntress Artemis, with the chief temple known as "the couch of Artemis". In Christian times, the goddess fused with St Lucy, the city's patron saint, and her cult is still venerated in city festivals.

TIP

One excursion worth considering is a short cruise from Porto Grande around Ortigia, following the coastline and fascinating fortifications. Several boat companies on Porto Grande ply their wares but, as in classical times, remember that bargaining is a Sicilian art form.

BELOW: Siracusians.

SHOP

Traditional craft specialities include the brightly decorated wooden puppets *(pupi)* connected with both Siracusa and Palermo. On Ortigia, visit the **Bottega del Puparo** (Via della Giudecca 19; tel: 0931 465 540, www.pupari.com).

BELOW RIGHT: outside Siracusa's Duomo.

Heralding the entrance to Ortigia is the **Tempio di Apollo** (Temple of Apollo), sunken and dishevelled but still the oldest city temple in Sicily. This Doric temple was built in 565 BC and discovered by chance in 1862. It is dedicated to Apollo, whose name is legible on the steps of the base. The squat temple has accrued Byzantine and Norman remains, and is thought to have functioned as both a church and a mosque.

In the maze of streets behind the temple is **San Pietro** , supposedly founded by St Peter before being converted into a Byzantine basilica. The 8th-century apses and blind arcading are incorporated into a 15th-century shell. Just west, Via XX Settembre contains tracts of the massive Greek walls. Dionysius was an indefatigable builder, and the immense wall, 5km (3 miles) in length, was built in 20 days by 60,000 men on double time, and is still visible in other parts of the town.

Ortigia's centre

From the temple, it is a short stroll along Via Roma to Piazza Archimede, the grandiose centre of Ortigia. This Baroque stage set, adorned by a decorative fountain, is home to dignified mansions and open-air cafés. On the next square awaits the magnificent **Duomo** (daily 8am–noon, 4–7pm). This 5th-century temple to Athena was converted into a Christian cathedral in AD 640. Classical columns bulge through the external walls in Via Minerva, a sign that the temple has only been encased in a church since the 7th century. Before then, the temple was a beacon to sailors, with its ivory doors and a gold facade surmounted by the goddess Athena bearing a glinting bronze shield.

The exterior conjures up a unique spell: a rich Baroque facade (1754) with dramatic chiaroscuro effects, including an inside porch boasting twisted barley-stick columns. Yet the cool, striking interior betrays its Greek origins; the worn but lovely fluted Doric columns set into the outer walls belong to the Temple to Athena. Notwithstanding a Greek soul, the temple also glorifies later conquerors. A Greek baptismal font rests on Norman bronze lions; above

Ortigia's reawakening

After decades of neglect, Ortigia is slowly returning to its ancient splendour. The most charming part of Siracusa is already awash with waterfront bars and cosy restaurants, but now the locals are moving back, turning Baroque palaces into boutique hotels and upmarket B&Bs. Creeping gentrification is taking place everywhere, attracting a more enlightened generation, particularly young professionals in search of urban charm.

The transformation is far from complete. Despite EU funds earmarked for Ortigia's restoration, the city's bureaucratic lethargy and lobbying by vested interest groups mean that many projects remain stalled, including the marina at Porto Grande. But rather than grumbling, entrepreneurial citizens are exerting pressure for urban renewal, with the waterfront promenades a success story in the making. Even if parts of the Lungomare di Levante are still to be restored, this moody promenade makes a glorious seafront stroll in any season. The classic stroll leads to the newly restored Castello Maniace, now a museum and events centre, and winds its way round to Fonte Aretusa and the promenade of Lungomare di Ponente on the western side of Ortigia.

is a medieval wood-panelled ceiling; a Baroque choir and Byzantine apses strike newer notes; only the Arab presence is missing. The apses were slightly damaged in the 1991 earthquake, but the Greek sandstone fluted columns survived. In the side chapel, **Cappella del Crocifisso**, is a painting of *St Zosimus* by Antonello da Messina, and one of *St Marcian* attributed to the school of Antonello, also believed to have painted the 13 panels in the **Sagrestia** (Sacristy).

Virtually next door is the church of **Santa Lucia alla Badia**, which is now home to Caravaggio's masterpiece *The Burial of St Lucy* (1608). Also in Piazza del Duomo is the Palazzo Vermexio (1633), **the Municipio** (Town Hall), built on the ruins of a small Ionic temple possibly dedicated to Artemis.

Just a short distance away, on Via Capodieci, stands **Palazzo Bellomo** ⓴ the loveliest Catalan-Gothic mansion in Ortigia, and the city's compact art gallery, **Galleria Regionale** (Tue–Sat 9am–7pm, Sun 9am–1pm; charge).

Inside, an elegant courtyard leads to the intimate gallery housing Antonello da Messina's remarkable *Annunciation* (1474) and the grandiose **funerary monument** for Eleonora Branciforte d'Aragona by Giovan Battista Mazzolo. Other highlights include 14th- to 18th-century works, from Byzantine icons to Catalan and Spanish paintings, Renaissance tombs and important pieces in gold, silver, coral, ceramics and terracotta.

Fonte Aretusa

At the southern end of Via Capodieci is **Fonte Aretusa** ㉑, a freshwater spring that is the symbol of Siracusa. Legend has it that the nymph Arethusa, a follower of great Olympian deity Artemis (Diana), was loved and pursued by the river god Alpheius after she bathed in his waters in the Peloponnese.

As she fled from his embrace to Sicily, she prayed to Artemis for help and, on reaching Ortigia, was changed by Artemis into a spring called Arethusa (Aretusa). Alpheius, however, did not give up. He flowed below the sea and mingled his waters with hers. Whether this was rape or the uniting of lovers, Siracusani continue to disagree.

After a 17th-century earthquake, however, the spring is supposed to have mingled with sea water but, in reality, Ortigia has an abundance of fresh water coming from the Iblei mountains through a peculiar geological land fault. Many houses have serviceable wells.

In any case, ducks make the clumps of reedy papyrus plants in spring water a romantic love nest. At night, the fountain sees a parade of Siracusa's youth, accompanied by flirtation and the obligatory stop for a water-ice nearby. In 1798 Admiral Nelson's fleet drew water at the fountain before proceeding to Malta and then on to the battle of the Nile.

From Fonte Aretusa, the panoramic terraces of **Passeggio Adorno** lead

Temple of Apollo.

BELOW: strolling at Fonte Aretusa at night.

EAT

Some of Siracusa's most atmospheric restaurants are in the back streets of Ortigia. Specialities include seafood, especially swordfish and shrimps, stuffed artichokes and *stimpirata di coniglio*, a rabbit and vegetable flan.

back to the Porto Grande quays via the **Porta Marina** archway, one of the city gates created in the 15th-century Spanish fortifications. Known as the **Lungomare di Ponente,** this charming promenade makes a lovely stroll. The triumphal archway itself leads to the Catalan-Gothic Quarter, centred on **Santa Maria dei Miracoli.** Set off Via Savoia, this finely sculpted 15th-century church is a prelude to lunch at one of the seafood inns tucked into the side streets.

Lungomare di Levante

The other side of the island is skirted by **Lungomare di Levante,** the atmospheric eastern waterfront, easily approached via the Temple of Apollo. The waterfront borders the Arab Quarter, with its tortuous, narrow streets designed to create breezes and keep homes cool even in summer.

You can also get to the Lungomare from Piazza Archimede, along **Via della Maestranza** and the old guilds' quarter, graced with Spanish palaces that have been reborn as gracious B&Bs or bohemian bars. Amid the sombre courtyards and swirling

sculpture, local *pasticcerie* literally represent the icing on the cake. There is a vegetable and fish market on the Lungomare on weekday mornings.

On the southernmost tip of Ortigia, the fortified hulk of **Castello Maniace** ㉒ (daily 9am–1-.30pm) dominates the promontory and once served as protector of Siracusa's two shores. Constructed in 1239 by Frederick II, it takes its name from the Byzantine general Giorgio Maniace, who was in charge of the city's defences. Even if largely empty, the Swabian castle is a magnificent monument in terms of ambition and scale. By the northwest tower is the castle's secret freshwater supply, the Bagno della Regina, a chamber fed by a freshwater spring which was fundamental to the siting of the castle here.

Until 2001 the fortress was an army base, but is now open to the public, apart from one section that houses Italy's art police, responsible for recovering (or safeguarding) national treasures.

While the castle was a major military base, the troops stationed

BELOW: puppet workshop. **BELOW RIGHT:** Castello Maniace.

here played an important role in anti-Mafia campaigns in the 1990s. Temporary exhibitions and summer concerts are also staged here.

Great escapes

Close to the city are sandy beaches and two unique spots, a Greek castle and a dreamy riverscape of papyrus plantations. Alternatively, to sample Siracusa's funky urban beach, you can join the locals on the Ortigia pontoons built over the waterside at **Forte Vigliena** *(see page 196)*.

South of Siracusa, off the SS115 (the route to Noto and Módica), lie popular beaches at the small resorts of **Arenella**, **Ognina** and **Fontane Bianche**. Although Siracusa's beaches tend to be full of golden bodies rather than golden sands, a more atmospheric swimming spot is 20km (12 miles) north of Siracusa, past Augusta, at **Brùcoli**. It is a rocky beach set around a Spanish castle that enjoys views of Etna on clear days.

In ancient **Epipolae**, 8km (5 miles) northwest of Siracusa, is **Castello Eurialo** (daily 9am–4pm, Sun 9am–1pm); follow signs to Belvedere). The fort represented the fifth component of the Greek pentapolis and was the most magnificent of Greek military outposts. Designed by Dionysius, the castle protected Siracusa's most exposed flank, the conjunction of the northern and southern city walls.

Apart from amazingly solid masonry and moats hewn out of the rock, the castle had labyrinthine passageways and a keep surrounded by five towers. As a final security measure, the sole entrance was concealed by a patchwork of walls. When Dionysius was in residence, he would not allow his wives into his bed unless they were first searched. According to legend, his bed was surrounded by a moat, and his wives reached it across a little wooden drawbridge, which he then drew up.

Fonte Ciane

South of the city, after 5km (3 miles) is **Fonte Ciane** (Spring of Ciane), a picturesque spot close to the ruined Temple of Olympian Zeus. (Follow signs to Fonte Ciane.) Ciane is the mythical spring and pool dedicated to the water-nymph Ciane (Cyane), who dissolved into her own pool with grief as she wept, having failed to prevent the rape of Persephone by Hades who had risen from the Underworld through the pool.

Canoes, easily rented from the tiny riverside marina from March onwards, are a way to explore the relaxing rivers, framed by canopies of lush foliage. The bohemian boutique hotel of Caol Ishka *(see page 276)* is on the neighbouring Anapo river and can book trips for guests, as well as gourmet dinners.

The Ciane weaves through groves of papyrus with tendrils as delicate as cobwebs. The origins of this wild plant are obscure: it was either imported from Egypt or native to Siracusa. Either way, its habitat is endangered, but it flourishes in this idyllic backwater. ❏

TIP

For many visitors Siracusa is the place for market shopping. Best bets are the markets (daily except Sunday) on Ortigia, on the Lungomare close to the Tempio di Apollo, and the larger, rambling general market, La Fiera, on the outskirts, on Via Algeri. Coaches bring in the crowds from the surrounding towns and villages, so you will not be alone.

BELOW: swimming near Ortigia.

BEST RESTAURANTS, BARS AND CAFÉS

Prices for a three-
course dinner per
person and a half-
bottle of house wine:
€ = under €20
€€ = €20–35
€€€ = €35–70
€€€€ = over €70

Siracusa is benefiting
from the popularity of
the Val di Noto. Partly as
a result, the city restaurants and cafés tend to
be diverse and atmos-
pheric, especially on the
island of Ortigia.

Antico Caffè Minerva
Via Minerva 15
Tel: 0931 22606 **€**
One of the oldest in the
city. Enjoy their specialities in the tearooms or at
tables outside.

Archimede
Via Gemellaro 8 Ortigia
Tel: 0931 69701
www.trattoriaarchimede.it **€€€**
A reliable restaurant in
Siracusa with friendly
service; the menu is

interesting but seafood
predominates. There is
always an array of subtle
(and fishy) *antipasti*.
Pizza too. Closed Sun,
except Mar–Nov.

Cantinaccia
Via XX Settembre 13
Tel: 333 351 2113 **€€€**
Rustic cooking, good
pasta and meat dishes
served on a pretty
veranda facing sea and
garden. Closed Tue,
except in summer.

Castello Fiorentino
Via del Crocefisso 6
Tel: 0931 21097 **€**
The town's most popular
pizzeria can be chaotic
and you may have to
queue, but it's really
good value and the
superb pizzas are worth
the wait. Closed Mon.

Da Mariano
Vicolo Zuccala' 9
Tel: 0931 67444
www.osteriadamariano.it **€€–€€€**
Set in the heart of
Ortigia, this inn offers

typical Sicilian dishes,
both meat and fish.

Darsena da Iannuzzo
Riva Garibaldi 6, Ortigia
Tel: 0931 61522
www.ristorantedarsena.it **€€€**
Just across the bridge,
this bold, bright, popular
trattoria serves the
freshest fish and local
dishes. Closed Wed.

Don Camillo
Via Maestranza 46
Tel: 0931 67133
www.ristorantedoncamillo
siracusa.it **€€€**
Highly regarded. Exten-
sive wine cellars. Closed
two weeks July.

Don Carmelo
Via Claudio Maria Arezzo 7
Tel: 0931 483 633 **€€**
This popular Ortigia spot
serves pasta, pizza,
crepes and
Mediterranean-style cui-
sine.

Enoteca Solaria
Via Roma 86, Ortigia
Tel: 0931 463 0047
www.enotecasolaria.com **€**

Wine bar and shop where
food is served. A fine
place to try local wines.

La Foglia
Via Capodieci 29 Ortigia
(close to Fonte Aretusa)
Tel: 0931 66233
www.lafoglia.it **€€€**
Vegetarians welcomed.
Sicilian and fish dishes
also served. Owned by
an artist and reflected in
the profusion of paint-
ings and statuary, plus
the antique glasses. Try
the subtle seafood.
Closed Tue, except in
summer.

La Gazza Ladra
Via Cavour 8
Tel: 340 060 2428
www.gazzaladrasiracusa.com **€€**
This small, family-run
trattoria uses the fresh-
est of local ingredients in
their daily fish specials
and generous plates of
antipasti. Closed Mon.

Gran Caffè del Duomo
Piazza del Duomo 18
Tel: 0931 21544

www.grancaffedelduomo.com €
A typical *pasticceria* and bar. Try their ricotta filled pastries if you crave something sweet.

Medusa
Via Santa Teresa 21
Tel: 0931 61403 €€
A delicious blend of Sicilian and Tunisian dishes. Lots of fish. Closed Mon and two weeks in Aug.

Minerva
Piazza Duomo 20
Tel: 0931 69404 €€
Conveniently placed for lunch after a cathedral visit. Closed Mon.

Osteria da Mariano
Vicolo Zuccolà 9, Ortigia
Tel: 0931 67444
www.osteriadamariano.it €€
Set off Fonte Aretusa, this wholesome trattoria is far stronger on the meaty cuisine of the Iblei mountains. The menu

runs from ricotta sprinkled with pistachio nuts to meaty mains and the house dessert made of sesame biscuits and fortified wine. Closed Tue.

Il Podere
Traversa Torre Landolina 11
Tel: 0931 449 390 €–€€
Dinner in a charming *masseria* (country manor) with low-key Sicilian cuisine.

Porticciolo
Via Trento
Tel: 0931 61914 €€
Near the market. Offers delicious mixed-fish grills or fresh lobster. Closed Mon and 10 days in Nov.

Spiaggetta
Viale dei Lidi 473, Fontane Bianche
Tel: 0931 790 334 €€
Modern and welcoming with windows overlooking the picturesque

creek. Sicilian dishes, pizzeria. Closed Tue in winter.

Taverna Sveva
Piazza Federico di Svevia 1–2
Tel: 0931 24663 €€
Try the *gnocchi* with pistachio or the fish dishes, and sit outside in fine weather.

La Terrazza sul Mare
Grand Hotel Ortigia, Viale Mazzini 12
Tel: 0931 464 600 €€€
Traditional Sicilian cuisine done superbly well, especially the seafood. Elegant yet relaxing setting on the rooftop by the marina. A romantic place for dinner. Friendly yet highly professional.

Tinkitè
Via della Giudecca 63
www.tinkite.it €
Come for a bite for breakfast in this boho bar, and probably return for nibbles at cocktail

hour, when the locals mingle over *aperitivi*, or even pop in for tea in the afternoon. Open 10am–midnight, closed Wed.

Zafferano
Caol Ishka, Via Elorina 154
Tel: 0931 69057 €€–€€€
Set in a funky design hotel *(see page 276)* on the peaceful outskirts of Siracusa, this elegant contemporary restaurant reflects the creative setting. Expect charming service and a subtle mix of flavours, with Sicilian dishes infused with a touch of exoticism.

Zsa
Piazza Galermi 22,
Tel: 0931 464 280 €€
Siracusan specialities: grilled swordfish, seafood risotto, pasta (with pine nuts, sultanas and anchovies) and local. Closed Mon.

LEFT: Zafferano.
ABOVE: iced coffee Sicilian-style.

SIRACUSA PROVINCE

Outside the city, this southeastern province offers a cross-section of Sicily: Baroque, classical and prehistoric blended with a leisurely way of life

The Greeks colonised this area two centuries after settling the rest of eastern Sicily. Since then Siracusa has rested on its laurels, parading its Greek heart and Levantine soul with the effortless superiority of a born aristocrat.

The province has been shaped by the cataclysm of the 1693 earthquake. Although all Norman castles were razed to the ground, the region responded by building some of the greatest Baroque architecture in Sicily, notably in the newly restored town of Noto.

Farming country

The journey southwards from **Siracusa ❶** passes gentle farming country dotted with olive and almond groves, citrus orchards and low-slung farms. Just inland of the flat coastal strip and sandy beaches, the farmland is interspersed with rugged terrain spanning limestone escarpments and rocky gorges.

At **Cassibile**, south of Siracusa, surrounded by grand sweeps of land cultivating citrus, almonds and cereals, is the spot where, on 3 September 1943, US general Bedell Smith signed the Allied terms of surrender with the Italian general, Castellano.

From that day onwards Italy's army was no longer in World War II. The event is commemorated by a stone plaque on the SS115 route south.

Further south is the flourishing market town of **Avola**, whose prosperity stems from its role as Italy's almond capital. Avola is merely the prelude to the Baroque setting of Noto, stacked up on a hill. On Piazza Umberto I, in the heart of this hexagonally shaped town, is the **Chiesa Madre**, built after the 1693 earthquake.

Main attractions

SIRACUSA (SYRACUSE)
NOTO
PALAZZO NICOLACI DI
  VILLADORATA
ELORO
VENDICARI WETLANDS
MARZAMENI
CAPO PASSERO
NECRÓPOLI DI PANTÁLICA
AKRAI

LEFT: Cattedrale di San Niccolò.
RIGHT: street scene in Noto.

EAT

In Noto, **Caffè Sicilia** (Corso Vittorio Emanuele 12; tel: 0931 835 013) celebrates sweet Sicilian classics, including *cannoli* (pastries stuffed with sweet ricotta and candied fruit) and *cassata* (a ricotta, chocolate, candied fruit and marzipan treat), as well as recherché but less calorific concoctions, such as mulberry sorbet.

BELOW: Madonna and Child in Santa Chiara.

Noto

Then there is **Noto** ❷, the finest Baroque town in Sicily, one that is both blatantly theatrical and deeply rational. With justification, visitors praise its proportion, symmetry, spaciousness and innate sense of spectacle. Sicilians simply call it a garden of stone. For many years much of it lay crumbling and neglected, but with restoration in hand, this Unesco World Heritage site is rapidly returning to its former glory. Noto is now one of Sicily's most delightful towns, best seen in the late afternoon when the sun strikes the golden facades and the chic cafés confirm the impression of walking in a stage set.

After the original Noto, known now as **Noto Antica** ❸, was destroyed in the 1693 earthquake, it lay buried under rubble, abandoned ruins nestling in the foothills of the Iblei mountains, the phoenix that never rose from the ashes. It was a complex city full of classical foundations, Romanesque and Baroque churches, convents and mansions, a home over the centuries to Romans, Arabs and Normans as it grew into a flourishing medieval city. All this was obliterated in 1693.

Ten years later a new site on safer ground 10km (6 miles) away was selected by the inhabitants and, headed by Giuseppe Lanza (duke of Camastra) and Prince Giovanni Landolina, new Noto was planted on the flanks of a distant hill. The city was composed around three parallel axes running horizontally across the hillside, with straight streets and three squares to create interest, each enlivened by a scenic church as a backdrop. The whole design was clothed in warm, golden limestone, with monumental flights of steps to enchant with tricks of perspective. The project was entrusted to Gagliardi and Sinatra, gifted local architects closely associated with masterpieces in Ragusa province.

Despite the beauteous architecture, the glowing limestone buildings are inherently fragile and susceptible to erosion and pollution. The city faced its greatest crisis in 1996 when the cupola and roof of the Cathedral of San Niccolò collapsed after a heavy thunderstorm. Since then, civic pride and impressive restoration have brought Noto to life once more.

Corso Vittorio Emanuele

The monumental gateway **Porta Reale** (1838) at the end of the tree-lined public gardens leads to **Corso Vittorio Emanuele**, Noto's stately main thoroughfare. Broken by three equally monumental squares, this processional avenue is dotted along its length with inviting cafés and kiosks for ices and *granita*. To the left, the town slopes downwards; to the right, it rises graciously to meet **Noto Alta** (Upper Noto).

The first building on the right, on **Piazza dell'Immacolata**, gives a fine idea of what is to follow. At the top of a theatrical, grand flight of stairs (only for the fittest), the church of **San Francesco** (daily 9.30am–12.30pm, 4–7pm) looks like the backdrop for a film set. Built between 1704 and 1745 by Rosario Gagliardi and Vincenzo Sinatra, it has a pleasant facade and simple, stucco interior. The **Seminario**, once the Benedictine monastery of **San Salvatore** (1706), sits alongside the church, facing it across the steep incline of Via Zanardelli. It has a fine 18th-century facade attributed to Rosario Gagliardi. Also on this piazza is the richly decorated church of **Santa Chiara** (daily 9.30am–1pm, 3.30pm–7pm), containing Antonello Gagini's marble statue of the *Madonna and Child*.

The Corso sweeps onwards to **Piazza Municipio**, the second square, Noto's stage set. The golden grace of the buildings matches the majestic proportions of the design. On the square is the **Palazzo Ducezio**, (9am–1.30pm, 3–6pm; charge), the elegantly grand town hall designed by Vincenzo Sinatra in 1746. The *pièce de résistance* is the **Sala degli Specchi,** an oval, mirrored reception room designed in Louis XV style.

Opposite is the splendid towering **Cattedrale di San Niccolò** (entrance

An eyewitness recorded Noto Antica's 1693 quake as "so horrible that the soil undulated like the waves of a stormy sea, and the mountains danced as if drunk." More than 1,000 people died as the city collapsed in one terrible moment.

BELOW: Cattedrale di San Niccolò steps.

The gamble that failed

Economically, the province has fallen behind its more entrepreneurial neighbours, Catania and Ragusa. In the 1950s Siracusa short-sightedly allowed a sizeable stretch of the coastline to be taken over in the rush for petrochemical riches. It is now paying the price for this gain in the form of polluted beaches, poor additional industrial development and a lack of tourist facilities – just when the whole island is waking up to the fact that tourism is big business and, used properly, can enhance both local lifestyles and the environment. Most visitors, however, turn a blind eye to the faults and simply relish Siracusa's traditional sense of *discreto benessere*, discreet wellbeing.

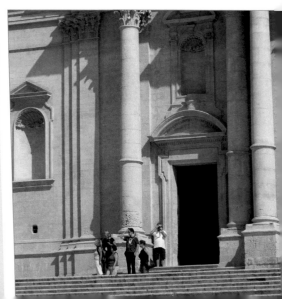

*Noto, although no longer in peril, requires constant upkeep. Despite its beauty and air of permanence, the golden tufa stone is fragile and soft; it was not designed to last through the ages like marble. Appreciate the city from a gorgeous bedroom in **Seven Rooms** in Palazzo Nicolaci (see page 276).*

on Via Cavour; daily 9.30am–1pm, 3.30–8pm; charge). The cathedral boasts a theatrical staircase, wide 18th-century facade, cupola and cool pastel interior, with the restoration story recounted in the adjoining museum.

Next to the cathedral is **Palazzo Landolina**, the Bishop's Palace that was once the home of one of Noto's benefactors.

The Corso progresses to **Piazza XVI Maggio**, graced by gardens of palms, monkey puzzle trees and a fountain of Hercules taken from Noto Antica. (The helpful tourist office is in this garden; tel: 0931 573 779.) Dominating the shady garden lies the well-restored church of **San Domenico**, a curvilinear Gagliardi masterpiece with a beautiful facade influenced by Roman and Spanish Baroque.

Facing it is the restored, ornately gilded 1850 **Teatro Vittorio Emanuele** and the **Collegio dei Gesuiti**, now a school. On the downwards slope, where Via Ruggero VII meets Via Ducezio, stands **Santa Maria del Carmine** (9.30am–1pm, 4–7pm), created by Gagliardi's assistant, Vincenzo Sinatra. Its concave doorway

is guarded by two *putti* (cherubs), the symbol of the Carmelite order.

Palazzo Nicolaci di Villadorata

Leading uphill from Piazza Municipio is Noto's pride and joy, the **Palazzo Nicolaci di Villadorata** (daily 10am–1.30pm, 3.30–6.30pm; charge). Set on Via Nicolaci and named after the noble Nicolaci dynasty, this Baroque jewel has finally been restored to its former glory.

Don Giacomo Nicolaci, a patron of the arts, donated part of his huge library to the town, but the palace itself now belongs to Noto citizens too. Around the windows are ornate balconies and friezes of mythical monsters, a snarling parade of griffins, sphinxes, sirens and cherubs. Arabesques climb the walls, clashing with crested cornices and billowing wrought-iron balconies. The sloped courtyard was designed for carriages and includes an access ramp so that the prince could ride directly into the *piano nobile*. The palatial interiors convey the opulence yet intimacy of aristocratic life in Noto, from

BELOW: Palazzo Ducezio.
BELOW RIGHT: church of San Francesco.

the frescoed ceilings to the antique ceramic floors and the views over Baroque Noto.

Palazzo Nicolaci plays a starring role in the city drama away from the Corso, but secondary characters should not be overlooked, especially in convents, churches and cafés. Around the corner, on Via Nicolaci, call into **Cantina Módica di San Giovanni** to see the private museum of Alessandro Módica while sampling Monti Iblei cheeses, salami and wine from this young baron's wine estate.

On Via Cavour, parallel to the Corso, is the church of **Monte-vergine** (1748–50) with its concave frontage, while Via Giovanni XXIII, behind San Niccolò, reveals ornate niches, sculpted cornices and bulging "goose-breast" balconies.

Paradoxically, the higher the level, the lower the class of the residents. Even so, the two-tiered city looks entirely homogeneous. The spacious lower town was originally only for the clergy and aristocracy. On the hill above the grandiose public face of Noto rises the *popolare* district, clustered around the hilly Piazza Mazzini, dominated by the **Crocifisso**, a domed church attributed to Gagliardi that has a portal flanked by Romanesque lions rescued from Noto Antica. Inside is a Francesco Laurana masterpiece, *Madonna della Neve* (Madonna of the Snow, 1471), a serene sculpture amid the frenzy of Baroque.

The massive building with an attractive facade stretching from Via Trigona to Piazza Mazzini is the former monastery, **Monastero di San Tommaso** (1720), now a prison.

The **Giardino Pubblico** at the eastern end of the Corso is a peaceful end to any visit to Noto.

The southern coast

Southeast of Noto are well-signposted sandy beaches that become busy only in July and August. Visitors in search of distinctiveness will prefer the Vendìcari sands and wetlands to the unassuming beach resorts of the **Lido di Noto** and **Lido d'Avola,** which essentially cater to Sicilian families.

Eloro ❹ is a classical site on the unpolluted stretch that leads south to Capo Pàssero. Now in ruins, the Siracusan city of Elorus (site currently closed, so check with Siracusa tourist office) was founded at the end of the 6th century BC. Well-preserved turreted walls survive, as do porticoes, a pair of gateways, the *agora* and a Sanctuary of Demeter. Just outside the site stands the **Colonna della Pizzuta**, a curious Hellenistic funerary column that looks like a chimney stack. In the neighbouring hamlet of **Caddeddi**, a villa from the same period has been unearthed, along with mosaics depicting hunting scenes.

Oasi Vendìcari

The 6km (4-mile) journey south to the deserted **Vendìcari wetlands ❺** (Riserva Naturale Oasi Faunistica di Vendìcari; tel: 0931 67450; www. oasivendicari.net) passes citrus and almond groves. The Vendìcari salt marshes appeal to both beach-lovers

Ceiling fresco at the Palazzo Nicolaci di Villadorata.

BELOW: Noto at night.

TIP

Siracusa boasts several
fine beaches in the
south of the province. In
Ortigia itself, visitors can
sunbathe or swim from
the new bathing
platform erected over
the sculpted rocks at
Forte Vigliena. South of
the city, off the SS115
to Noto, lie popular
sandy beaches at the
small resorts of
Arenella, Ognina and
Fontane Bianche.
However, discerning
locals prefer to travel
to the wilder shores of
the Vendìcari nature
reserve further south
(see page 195).

BELOW: Marzamemi
harbour.

and birdwatchers, as this haven for
flamingos, storks and egrets also
embraces a sweeping crescent of sand.
Invigorating walks and marked trails
run through the salt marshes, with
medieval water channels cut to reach
the saltpans. The site also includes
battered medieval fortifications, a
Swabian tower, Byzantine catacombs
and an abandoned 18th-century *tonnara*, one of the tuna fisheries that
made Sicily's fortune. Although
sun-worshippers will prefer summer,
birdwatchers and walkers should opt
for autumn and spring, when waders
and ducks share the waters with the
flamingos. (Bring a picnic as there are
virtually no facilities in the reserve.)

Marzamemi

Further down the coast lies **Marzamemi ⑥**, the most appealing fishing
village in the province. As a former
feudal domain, the village retains a
crumbling noble palace, adorned with
the Villadorata family crest. Despite
becoming a small-time summer
resort and summer marina, at heart
Marzamemi remains a working fishing village, complete with lobster pots

and the obligatory fishing nets drying
in the sun. *Cernia* (grouper), like *pesce
spada* (swordfish), is a prized Mediterranean fish, but mullet, mussels and
tuna are also on local menus.

In summer, Sicilians also flock to
Pachino ⑦ and the sandy beaches
around Capo Pàssero. The pillboxes
littering this stretch of coast are a
testament to troubled times. In July
1943 the Allied invasion of Sicily
took place on these shores. While
General Patton and the American
forces landed near Gela, General
Montgomery and the British 8th
Army landed between Pachino
and Pozzallo. Giuseppe Tornatore's
film *Malena* includes a dramatic re-
enactment of the landing on Pachino's beaches. Nowadays, Pachino is
a quiet tomato- and wine-producing
centre with a faded Baroque heart.

Beyond is **Capo Pàssero ⑧**, the
southernmost tip of the province,
and home to several low-key seaside resorts that were, until recently,
entirely dependent on tuna fishing.
Today, only one tuna fishery remains,
run by Don Bruno di Belmonte.
Energetic visitors can rent a boat to
row to Isola di Capo Pàssero and the
other island rocks here.

North of Siracusa

Swimming is not advisable on the
northern stretch of coast, in the **Golfo
di Augusta** between Siracusa and
Augusta, except at Brùcoli, just north
of Augusta, where the Golfo di Catania begins. As the coastline reputed
to have Europe's highest concentration of chemical effluents, this area is
an ecological disaster. Petrochemical
plants based around Augusta have
destroyed 48km (30 miles) of beach.
At night, however, this stretch has a
savage, futuristic beauty of its own,
with its glittering towers, gargantuan
oil tanks and livid smokestacks.

The classical sites of Thapsos on
Penisola Magnisi and neighbouring
Megara Hyblaea are too close for

comfort to the belching fumes. Acrid fumes threaten to engulf the important site of **Megara Hyblaea** , one of the earliest Greek cities in Sicily, founded in 728 BC. Cypresses shield it in poetic desolation, but industrial blight is tangible. A wall and a group of sarcophagi front the ramparts of a Hellenistic fortress. Beyond are the foundations of an Archaic city, as yet unexplored.

As a smaller mirror image of Siracusa, **Augusta** once had charm and prestige. However, while its islet setting, double harbour and faded Baroque centre remain, so does rampant industrialisation.

The ancient interior

The rocky, wild, sparsely populated hinterland is one of Siracusa's charms. The summer-parched slopes and odd mounds conceal several significant classical sites. The desolate countryside generates an austere appeal that is matched by the dusty Baroque country towns along the route. This is Sicily with its roots laid bare, a prehistoric and Siculi land that predates Siracusa city by centuries. The rocky tableland is home to **Pantálica**, the region's foremost prehistoric site. The drive to Pantálica skirts the bleached white or pale-green Iblean hills before reaching the lush **Anapo Valley**.

Dedicated hikers with a full day to spend in Pantálica will choose the northern entrance, reached through Palazzolo. However, for less walking, choose the southern route through **Sortino**, following signs for Pantálica Sud. This rural drive passes country villas, citrus groves and dry-stone walls.

Despite their importance, the **Necrópoli di Pantálica**  (daily 9am–sunset) are off the beaten track. However, Siracusani have long been drawn to the lush gorges, a verdant paradise remote from the barren image of the Iblean hills. Apart from the loveliness of this sprawling site, Pantálica offers a slice of Sicily's earliest history: this Siculi necropolis contains rock tombs dating from the 13th to the 8th century BC. As the largest Bronze and Iron Age cemetery in Sicily, it contains over 5,000 tombs carved into the sheer cliffs of a limestone plateau, not to mention cave dwellings. Although Pantálica's

Pachino, the site of the Allied invasion of Sicily in 1943.

BELOW: Capo Pàssero.

TIP

Take the revived **Baroque Train** (il Treno del Barocco) to explore southeastern Sicily's best Baroque towns, including Noto, Módica, Scicli and Siracusa. You need to book this full-day guided rail tour well in advance (see box page 164).

history is shrouded in mystery, tradition claims it as Hybla, the capital of the Siculi king who allowed Greek colonists to occupy Megara Hyblaea. Certainly, some of these gaping holes are 3,000 years old.

The tombs lie at the end of a gorge carved by the River Anapo and studded with citrus trees and wild flowers and prickly pears. In this secret garden lie tiered rows of tombs, a honeycomb-pitted surface of jagged rectangular openings cut into the pale rock. Mule tracks and marked paths follow the river towards a disused railway line, with easier paths marked "A", and more challenging ones marked "B". Walkers are rewarded with discreet picnic spots, as well as views of sheer rock faces and deep ravines. Apart from the tombs and dwellings, there remains a Byzantine rock chapel, and early Christian frescoes. In spring this sacred chasm is a beauty spot bursting with snapdragons, asphodel and daisies.

A country drive leads southwest to **Palazzolo Acrèide** ⓫, a sleepy Norman town surprised to discover that outsiders should stray so far. The Baroque centre displays several theatrical set-pieces, whose charms are only slightly diminished by the air of abandon. The town's rough-hewn charms are apparent in Palazzo Zocco on Via Umberto, with its chaotic Baroque ornamentation, and the early Baroque **Chiesa Annunziata**, with a portal guarded by Spanish barley-shape columns. However, many rewards are low-key: the occasional gargoyle, carved doorpost or billowing balcony. Palazzolo Acrèide is also known for its traditional carnival and its marvellous feast day that celebrates San Sebastiano. The pork sausages from **Casa della Salsiccia** (Via Roma 183; tel: 0931 882 410; closed Wed pm) are much favoured too.

Akrai

A signposted road for **Teatro Greco** leads to the Classical city of **Akrai** ⓬, a Greek site set on high, windy moorland. The attractive walled park (daily, summer 9am–1 hour before sunset, winter 9am–2pm; charge) encloses quarries and temples founded in 644 BC by Siracusa, and a Greek theatre (3rd century BC), but then also used by the Romans) built on a grand scale.

The confusing site contains stone carvings, votive niches, a necropolis, catacombs and the remains of a Temple to Aphrodite. The most impressive views are of the deep quarries framed by dry-stone walls, firs, bay trees and wild olives. The lovely site suffers from poor management, with temples and sculptures arbitrarily locked. Across the hillside are the Santoni (Holy Ones), a series of 12 crudely carved sculptures made in honour of the goddess Cybele, the Magna Mater whose esoteric cult originated in Asia. These precious finds lie a few fields away, and a visit there requires a custodian's presence.

Leading out of town, the **Strada Panoramica** circling Akrai lives up to its name, offering fabulous views across the Greek settlements towards Ragusa province. ❏

BELOW: Pantálica.

BEST RESTAURANTS, BARS AND CAFÉS

Prices for a three-course dinner per person and a half-bottle of house wine:
€ = under €20
€€ = €20–35
€€€ = €35–70
€€€€ = over €70

Augusta

Donna Ina
Loc. Faro Santa Croce Est
4km (2½ miles) out of town
Tel: 0931 983 422 €€
Seasonal seafood specialities prepared with care. Closed Mon, unless it is a public holiday.

Avola

Finocchiaro
Piazza Umberto I, 1
Tel: 0931 831 062 €
Renowned café with *cannoli*, fruit flans and nougat made with local almonds.

Rustico
Via Santa Lucia 52
Tel: 0931 831 084 €€
Ignore the setting – this simple spot serves excellent dishes inexpensively. Delicious *spaghetti alle vongole*, grilled swordfish and Nero d'Avola wine. Pizza too.

Noto

Al Terrazzo
Via Baccarini 4
Tel: 0931 839 710
www.ristorantealterrazzonoto.it €
Worth visiting to try the delightful table of *antipasti*. Pizza too.

Il Barocco
Ronco Sgadari 8
Tel: 0931 835 999 €€
An atmospheric courtyard setting and tasty dishes – pasta, pizza, grilled meat and fish.

Caffè Sicilia
Corso Vittorio Emanuele 125
Tel: 0931 835 013
caffe.sicilia@tin.it €
One of Sicily's most celebrated *pasticcerie*, with home-made pastries, *granite* and ice creams. Good selection of wines and jams to take away.

Carmine
Via Ducezio 9
Tel: 0931 838 705
www.trattoriadelcarmine.it €
Home cooking and local dishes, including rabbit. Closed Mon.

Costanzo
Via Spaventa 7
Tel: 0931 835 243 €
Try the *granite* with a brioche, as locals often do.

Giglio
Piazza Municipio
Tel: 0931 838 640
www.ristoranteilgiglio.eu €€
Typical trattoria with excellent pasta dishes. Choose the ravioli.

Modica di San Giovanni
Palazzo Modica, Via Nicolaci
Tel: 345 369 3045 €
Owned by Alessandro Modica, whose ancestral palazzo this is, this delightful wine bar serves award-winning

wines produced by the family estate matched by unfussy dishes, including cheeses and salami from the Monti Iblei and fish from the *tonnara* in Marzamemi. All this in an atmospheric palace.

Ristorante Baglieri
Contrada Falconara,
Lido di Noto
Tel: 0931 812 571 €€
Family recipes are used in the making of pasta dishes and desserts.

Sapori della Val di Noto
Ronco Bernardi Leanti 9
Tel: 0931 839 322 €€
Rigorously local, with seasonal produce from the Val di Noto.

Trattoria Ducezio
Via Ducezio 51
Tel: 347 858 7319 €€
Simple trattoria with good service, robust flavours and portions to match.

Marzamemi

Adelfio
Via Marzamemi 7
Tel: 0931 841 307
www.adelfionline.com €€–€€€
Deservedly popular traditional seafood restau-

rant: tuna roes, smoked swordfish, fresh fish baked in salt.

Portopalo di Capo Passero

Da Maurizio
Via Taglimento 22
Tel: 0931 842 644 €€
The best of Sicilian cooking served on terraces, weather permitting. Fish arrive direct from the fishermen. Evening pizzeria. Closed Tue and Nov.

Rosolini

Locanda del Borgo
Via Controscieri 11
Tel: 0931 850 514 €€–€€€
A frescoed affair in which a talented, cosmopolitan chef focuses on local produce.

Vendicari

Il Roveto
Contrada da Roveto
Tel: 0931 66024
www.roveto.it €€
This restored farmhouse is a charming place to stay. It also has a small restaurant with good family cooking using produce from the farm.

RIGHT: marzipan is sculpted to resemble real fruit.

THE ART OF PUPPETRY AND PAINTED CARTS

Flamboyant manifestations of the nation's folklore, puppets and carts portray Sicily's history in brash primary colours

The travelling puppet show has provided entertainment in Sicily for centuries, telling tales of saints, bandits or heroes, but most commonly the Paladins, the knights of Charlemagne's court, and their battles against the Saracens.

The Christians traditionally strut on the left of the stage, the turbaned, baggy-trousered Saracens on the right. The audience knows all the characters – the knights Orlando and Rinaldo, the beautiful Angelica and the wicked traitor Gano di Magonza – and identifies with them as characters in a familiar soap opera.

The great writer Carlo Levi said of the tradition: "The Paladins are actual idols, we delight in their victories and cry at their deaths." Not so long ago, watching a puppet show was an evening ritual for many Sicilians. Now it is more of a beloved folk memory, even if the tradition is still kept alive in Palermo, Catania and Siracusa. Puppetry was even added to the Unesco World Heritage List as a recognition of its unique place in Sicilian life.

ABOVE: a puppet show at the Teatro dei Pupi, Siracusa; metal wires move the hands and a thicker bar turns their heads.

LEFT: old puppets at the Puppet Workshop and Museum in Syracusa.

EXHILARATING POTTERY

Traditional Sicilian ceramics display the same vivacity and vibrant use of colour as the island's puppets and carts. Even if pottery is far more usual, some of the greatest Sicilian palaces will have decorations, even floor tiles, made by Caltagirone crafsmen.

Thanks to the inexhaustible deposits of clay surrounding the town, Caltagirone had a reputation for pottery even before the Arabs introduced local craftsmen to the glazed polychromatic colours – particularly blues, greens and yellows – that have become typical of Sicilian ceramics.

As well as functional items such as vases, bowls and jugs, Caltagirone craftsmen also produce decorative tiles, medallions and figurines in the same lively colours.

Santo Stéfano di Camastra is the second great ceramics centre on the island. On the Messina–Palermo road, the small town seems overwhelmed with its pottery: tiers of dishes, tureens and bowls line both sides of the road. The traditional style here has a rustic look and feel, often featuring fish designs. The other local speciality is tiles decorated with smiling suns and saints.

(See pages 282 and 285 for more on puppetry; and page 285 for pottery and the best places to buy it.)

ABOVE: the artists who decorate these traditional painted carts raid motifs from their multiracial heritage: Arab adornment and arabesques; chivalric legends and Biblical epics; the Crusades and the Napoleonic wars.

ABOVE RIGHT: Santo Stefano ceramics

ABOVE: ceramics maker in Santo Stefano.

RIGHT: painted clown pottery figure from Sciacca.

CATANIA

As Sicily's second city, Catania is a slow burn, both a bold Baroque affair bustling with commerce and the natural springboard to Mount Etna

Catania is a city of contradictions: brash, belligerent and beleagured yet also vibrant, cultured and resilient. It is a commercial success as well as a showcase of Sicilian Baroque. But the city has an edginess, not least because its 340,000 people live permanently in the southern shadow of Mount Etna, a volcano that can seem menacing, glowing red in the night sky. The approach to Catania along the *circonvallazione* (ring road) reveals the extent of nature's wrath. Etna's recent volcanic flows are visible between the grim tenements or piled like black slag heaps by the roadside.

In keeping with its volcanic temperament, Catania celebrates a vibrant arts scene, offering *bel canto* opera in the homeland of Bellini, as well as classical music, live jazz and blues. The city also boasts the best nightlife in Sicily, with a profusion of cool galleries, bars, restaurants and clubs tucked away in the historic centre. As an energetic university city, Catania offers events ranging from pop-rock spectaculars to open-air summer festivals. The venues vary from converted refineries to cosy clubs in the city centre.

City sights

Visually, Catania seems the most homogeneous Sicilian city. From 1730 it was stamped with the vision of one man, Giovan Battista Vaccarini, an architect from Palermo influenced by grand Roman Baroque. His work has a sculptural quality allied to a native vigour. Billowing balconies, sweeping S-curves and a taste for chiaroscuro are intermixed. Until your eyes adjust, the dark colour of the volcanic stone can seem oppressive, but the chromatic effects are skilful.

LEFT: locals doing a deal near Catania's fish market.

Piazza del Duomo ❶ is the Baroque centrepiece, a dignified composition on a grand scale. The buildings in the square make use of flat facades, restrained decoration, elegant windows and huge pilasters. At the centre is the city's famous symbol, Vaccarini's delightful **Fontana dell'Elefante**, a black lava-stone elephant supporting a towering Egyptian obelisk taken from the Roman circus.

The **Duomo ❷** (daily 8am–noon, 3–6pm, museum 9am–2pm), the cathedral dedicated to Sant'Agata, was begun by Count Roger in 1092 and rebuilt by Vaccarini after the 1693 earthquake. It is a magnificently confused summation of Catanese history: Roman theatres were raided for granite columns to adorn the lugubrious Baroque facade, and the interior conceals vaulted subterranean Roman baths and a Romanesque basilica under the nave.

Roman and Byzantine columns line the transepts. St Agata's chapel, a gaudy shrine of multicoloured marble, is where St Agatha's relics are displayed on feast days. At other times, the locals content themselves with pistachio pastries inspired by the patron saint's breasts, available from Savia (*see page 209*).

The tombs of the 14th-century Spanish rulers of Sicily are sited in the nave, including the graceful tomb of Costanza d'Aragona, wife of King Federico III, and the Roman sarcophagus containing the ashes of other Aragonese royals. The tomb of Catania's famous composer, Vincenzo Bellini (1801–35), is here, too.

Across Via Vittorio Emanuelle II is the church of **Sant' Agata** with its grand dome, and on the piazza itself are the **Municipio** (1741) with its decorated windows, and **Porta Uzeda**, an archway (1696). This leads into a small, popular park where pensioners while away time and also to **Porto Vecchio**, Catania's port. On weekdays a colourful fish market fills the neighbourhood streets.

In Via Museo Biscari is **Palazzo Biscari ❸**, the most accomplished Baroque mansion in Catania, still partly owned by the Moncada family, the Biscari descendants, who have even turned their private theatre into a restaurant.

The Baroque mansion of Palazzo Biscari.

BELOW LEFT: fish market.
BELOW: couple in a Catania street.

TIP

The opera season at **Teatro Bellini** runs from October to May, with tickets for all operas, concerts or ballets highly sought after, especially operas composed by Bellini himself.

Via Dusmet offers the best view of the facade, with its frolicking cherubs, caryatids and grinning monsters. Ideally attend a concert in the *salone della musica*, a Rococo wonder, with a grand staircase, minstrels' gallery and allegorical ceiling. Otherwise, book a palatial tour (tel: 095 715 2508) and visit their fashion museum (closed Mon; tel: 095 250 3188).

As for dinner, **La Fiaschetteria** is the palace's seafood restaurant (tel: 095 093 2761), while **I Quattro Venti**, the former theatre, is an atmospheric place for dinner jazz and blues (tel: 095 327 477). You can even stay in this Baroque masterpiece (tel: 095 321 818).

Ancient remains

The city's ancient remains are unlike the spacious marble theatres or golden sandstone temples found elsewhere. Instead Catania offers cramped, low-lying monuments in sombre black lava stone. If you traipse down unpromising alleys, the rewards are worthwhile. While most classical remains enjoy splendid isolation, Catania's are fully integrated in the urban fabric, generally in dilapidated parts of town, where every second turning reveals the odd Roman column, tomb or hypocaust (underfloor heating, Roman-style).

A good example is the **Teatro Romano** ❹ (daily 9am–1pm, 3–6pm; charge), with its entrance at 266 Via Vittorio Emanuele. The theatre was built on the site of a Greek theatre, but has Roman underground passages and *cavea* as well as some of the *scena* and orchestra. The original marble facing was plundered by the Normans to embellish the cathedral. Next door is the semicircular **Odeon**, used for oratory and rehearsals. The building materials were chosen for their contrasts: volcanic stone, red brickwork and marble facing.

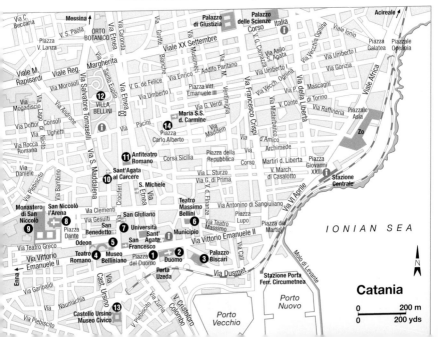

Catania

0   200 m
0   200 yds

Tributes to Bellini

On Piazza San Francesco is the well-restored Baroque church of **San Francesco** (daily 9am–12.30pm, 4–7.30pm) and the **Museo Belliniano** ❺ (daily 9am–1pm), with a shabby Baroque facade concealing a museum of musical memorabilia and original scores of the composer's work.

The father of *bel canto*, Bellini is buried in the cathedral, but he is also commemorated in the richly decorated **Teatro Bellini** ❻, which opened in 1890 with Bellini's opera *Norma*.

Via Crociferi

Beyond the arch of **San Benedetto** (1777) leading off Piazza San Francesco is **Via Crociferi**, Catania's most charming street, with its succession of monumental 18th-century Baroque churches, convents and noble palazzi. Excavations have brought to light signs of a Roman city beneath the street. North along the street stands Vaccarini's church of **San Giuliano** ❼ (1739–51), distinguished by a graceful loggia and elliptical interior.

From here, Via Clementi leads to Piazza Dante, with the monumental church and Benedictine monastery of **San Niccolò l'Arena** ❽ (daily 9am–1pm). It resembles a grim religious factory rather than a church complex. As the largest church in Sicily, this 16th-century work was conceived on a colossal scale but never completed because its sheer size would be unable to withstand an earthquake. It has an eerie, amputated look, with truncated stumps of columns framing the door like elephant tusks. Inside is a Hollywoodesque folly, Sicily's first classical staircase. After a long period of closure, the church is being restored, especially the vast cupola, 62 metres (203ft) high.

The adjoining **Monastero di San Niccolò** ❾ (Mon, Wed–Fri 9am–5pm, Tue, Sat–Sun 9am–noon; guided visits of monastery and library, tel: 095 710 2767; www.officineculturali. net) was the Benedictine monastery and now houses Catania University's Faculties of Arts and Philosophy. The original monastery was almost totally destroyed in the 1693 earthquake, then rebuilt on an even grander scale after 1703. Long-term archaeological excavations are under way in the

Inside Chiesa San Benedetto in Via Crociferi.

BELOW: Teatro Romano.

Catania's new face

While Catania's architecture is less ebullient than that of Noto or Siracusa, this is still trail-blazing Baroque, a city with spacious streets and sinuous churches. However, as Sicily's commercial powerhouse, modern Catania stands accused of selling its soul to property speculation and neglecting its Baroque heritage. Until recently, the city centre was undervalued and dilapidated, the province of students and the poor, at least after nightfall. But a new city dynamism has seen the cathedral restored, Baroque palaces cleaned and the restoration of churches and classical sites under way. With art galleries and cool cafés increasingly sited in restored palaces, the future is looking promising.

Castello Ursino, a Swabian castle, is now an art museum and exhibition space.

BELOW RIGHT: police in Villa Bellini.

entrance courtyard, but beyond lie the charming former cloisters, complete with a battered garden and a curiously decorated folly.

North along Via Crociferi is the church of **Sant'Agata al Carcere** ❿ (St Agatha in Prison; open mornings only). According to legend, and supported by graffiti on these Roman walls, it was here that St Agatha was imprisoned before her martyrdom. Although the site was converted into a fortified church in the 12th century, the 3rd-century crypt remains. More impressive is the Romanesque portal, moved from the cathedral after the 1693 earthquake. Sculpted with griffins and glowering beasts, the door conjures up suitable horrors of the church's original function as a prison.

Further on, adjoining Via Etnea lies the **Anfiteatro Romano** ⓫ (daily 9am–1pm, 3–6pm), the battered remains of the largest amphitheatre in Sicily, dating back to the 2nd or 3rd century AD and able to seat 16,000 spectators. This is where St Agatha supposedly met her fate and where earthquake ruins were dumped in 1693. Ancient necropoli stretch

north and east of this site and are visible in many spots, including below the Rinascente store in Via Etnea.

Via Etnea

The grandiose **Via Etnea**, the main city thoroughfare, runs parallel to Via Crociferi and climaxes in a stunning view of Mount Etna. Busy throughout the day, the street is particularly popular at night when the Catanesi indulge in the evening *passeggiata*, parading past chic shops selling fashion, jewellery, shoes, fruit sorbets and nougat ice cream.

The most elegant, richer, section of the street lies between Piazza Duomo and **Villa Bellini** ⓬, not a palazzo but public gardens. This delightful and well-kept public park represents a retreat from Catania's constant bustle. One part is named *labirinto* after the maze of paths, all leading to aviaries and an oriental bandstand. Between the fig trees and palms are snowcapped or smouldering views of Etna.

To the south of Via Etnea, on Piazza Federico di Svevia, is **Castello Ursino** ⓭, a restored Swabian castle

A sharp citizenry

The people of Catania, the *Catanesi*, have long had a reputation for being sharp operators with a flair for commerce. This entrepreneurial spirit is traced back to the citizens' Greek ancestry, presenting a counterpoint to the more indolent, aristocratic "Arab" temperament prevalent in Palermo. This ancient Siculi settlement was colonised by settlers from Naxos in 729 BC and, by 415 BC had become a significant Athenian base. As an ally of Athens, Catania incurred the wrath of Siracusa and after Dionysius conquered the city in 403 BC, the *Catanesi* were sold into slavery. By contrast, after the Roman conquest in 263 BC, the new regime ushered in a degree of prosperity.

In modern times, the city has produced many of the island's best engineers and entrepreneurs – as well as many of the Mafia's most active leaders. By the 1960s Catania won plaudits for being commercially vibrant, the Milan of the South. But several decades later the corruption in both Milan and Catania gave the praise a hollow echo. Since then, the city administration is no longer so compromised and Catania, if not quite enjoying a resurgence, is at least demonstrating resilience and dynamism, especially with regard to its nightlife.

built on a steep bastion. It commands a view of what was once the harbour: the moat was filled in by the lava flow of 1669, which also left the castle marooned inland, and deposited a large lump of lava outside the walls. Now an art museum and exhibition space, it was the Aragonese seat of government in the 13th century and became a palace under the Spanish viceroys. The courtyard displays a cavalcade of Sicilian history, featuring fine Hellenistic and Roman sculpture. The **Museo Civico** (daily 9am–7pm) on the upper floors contains a wide-ranging art gallery.

Fish market

South of the Duomo, sandwiched between the cathedral quarter and the port, is **La Pescheria**, the noisy morning fish market (Mon–Sat). On slabs of marble lie sea bream and swordfish, mussels and sea urchins, squirming eels and lobsters. The area is centred on **Porta Uzeda**, the monumental Baroque city gate connecting the port with the public city. Beyond the adjoining park of Villa Pacini, the colourful portside area encircling Via Dusmet is given over to fishermen and traders.

Not far away is **Zo** (tel: 095 533 871, www.zoculture.it), a futuristic cultural centre housed in an ex-sulphur refinery. As well as hosting concerts, events and exhibitions, the centre is home to a small cinema museum (Wed, Fri and Sun 9am–12.30pm, Tue and Thur 9am–5.30pm; charge) and a museum dedicated to the Allied invasion of Sicily in 1943 (Wed and Fri–Sun 9am–12.30pm, Tue and Thur 9am–12.30pm, 3–5pm; charge).

A visit to the scruffy but appealing **Fera o Luni** market (daily except Sun) on **Piazza Carlo Alberto** ⓮ creates an appetite for Catania's varied cuisine, including *pasta alla Norma* (made with aubergine/eggplant), named after Bellini's opera. Framed by two churches and hemmed in by backstreets, the rectangular square is a sea of bright awnings; below lie displays of lemons, garlic and herbs, with clothes, household goods and leatherware on the far side. The Sunday antiques market here sells everything from junk to Sicilian ceramics and country-style furniture. ❑

DRINK

Find refreshment in summer at *chioschi* (kiosks), which serve fruit syrups drunk with *seltz* (soda water) and sometimes salt. The usual one is *seltz e limone con/senza sale*, a soda water and crushed lemon concoction with or without salt.

BELOW: Catania's fish market.

BEST RESTAURANTS, BARS AND CAFÉS

Restaurants

Prices for a three-course dinner per person and a half-bottle of house wine:
€ = under €20
€€ = €20–35
€€€ = €35–70
€€€€ = over €70

Catania is renowned for its excellent and diverse restaurants. They display eastern Sicilian seasonal dishes, such as *pasta con il cavolfiore e la ricotta* (pasta with cauliflower and ricotta) and *agnello alla menta* (lamb with bacon, mint and garlic). The city has good café life, and pastry shops and street food aplenty.

Ai Vecchi Criteri
Contrada Rosella 4
Tel: 095 968 151
www.aivecchicriteri.it €
Gentrified-rustic farm-stay with a reliable restaurant serving local produce, especially meat.

Al Gabbiano
Via Giordano Bruno 128
Tel: 095 537 842 €€€
Respected trattoria serving traditional Sicilian fare. Closed Sun and Aug.

Antica Marina
Via Pardo 29
Tel: 095 348 197 €€€
In the middle of the fish market, so the fish couldn't be fresher. Fish *antipasti*, pasta dishes with fish sauces and grilled fish. Closed Wed.

La Cantinaccia
Via Calatafimi 1/a
Tel: 095 537 291 €€
This upmarket but intimate restaurant is designed in rustic style. The cuisine is international and Sicilian with pizza served in the evening. Closed Mon and Aug.

Cantine del Cugno
Loc. Mezzano, Via Museo Biscari 8
Tel: 095 715 8710 €€
In the stables of 16th-century Palazzo Biscari, this *ristorante-enoteca* has a wide selection of top wines (not only Sicilian), wine-tasting and a Mediterranean menu. Closed Sun, Mon lunch and two weeks Aug.

Da Rinaldo
Via Simili 59
Tel: 095 532 312 €
Inexpensive trattoria with a wide selection of Sicilian dishes, not simply dishes from this province. Closed Aug.

La Fiaschetteria
Via Museo Biscari 8
Tel: 095 0932 761
www.fiaschetteriabiscari.it €€€
Set in the wonderful Palazzo Biscari, this elegant restaurant serves fish that comes straight from the nearby fish market.

La Marchesana
Via Mazza 4
Tel: 095 315 171
.lamarchesana.com €€
The menu is particularly strong on fish at this small restaurant, and the friendly owners offer a warm welcome. Eat outside in fine weather, or inside in the elegant vaulted dining room.

La Paglia
Via Pardo 23
Tel: 095 346 838 €€
Well placed right by the fish market, this simple trattoria serves the freshest of seafood. Try the spaghetti with clams. Closed Sun.

Sicilia in Bocca
Via Dusmet 35
Tel: 095 250 0208 €€€
A restaurant with a pleasant terrace set in the sea wall. For a cheaper option, go for the pizza. Closed Mon.

La Siciliana
Viale Marco Polo 52
Tel: 095 376 400
www.lasiciliana.it €€€
Sicilian cooking at its best in a charming garden setting. One of Catania's most renowned restaurants, so it is expensive. Specialities include roast lamb, seafood, imaginative vegetable dishes and good red Cerasuolo wine. Closed Sun evening and Mon. Booking essential.

I Tre Bicchieri
Via San Giuseppe al Duomo 31

Tel: 095 715 3540
www.osteriatrebicchieri.it €€€
Smart, modern establishment praised for its presentation and varied Mediterranean cooking. Known for both meat and fish dishes. Wine bar. Closed Sun and Aug.

Cafés, street food and pastry shops

Dolci di Nonna Vincenza
Palazzo Biscari, Piazza San Placido 7
Tel: 0957 151 844
www.dolcinonnavincenza.it
Set in the Baroque heart of town, the pastry shop produces suitably Baroque *dolci* (sweets and pastries). Try those made in honour of St Agatha, such as the *olivette di sant'Agata* using lemons and almonds.

Friggitoria Stella
Mercato La Pescheria, Via Ventimiglia 66
Tel: 095 535 5002 €
Set in the fish market, this is a great place for street food, including *sfinciuni*, Sicilian pizza with tuma cheese and anchovies.

Menza
Viale Mario Rapisardi 143
Tel: 095 350 606
www.menza.it €€
A typical Sicilian *rosticceria* (takeaway roast meats) and street snacks: try the *arancini* (savoury filled rice balls)

or the sweet *crespelle* (pancakes) with honey. Closed Mon.

Mercati Generali
Strada Statale (SS) 417 Caltagirone to Gela
Tel: 095 571 458
www.mercatigenerali.org €
Set in the southern suburbs, this cult multitasking bar, club and music venue occupies an old winery, with the warehouse home to summer partying in the courtyard (May–Oct). Food is incidental as top DJs appear here, as do big-name pop and rock acts.

Pasticceria Savia
Via Etnea 302
Tel: 095 325 667 €
A historic *pasticceria* that's a favourite with the locals – try the

ricotta-and-pistachio-stuffed *cannoli* or the *minnuzze di Sant'Agata*, shaped in honour of the patron saint's breasts: very Sicilian. Closed Mon.

I Perivancu
Via Bellini 18, Viagrande
Tel: 095 789 4698
www.perivancu.it
Produce from Monti Iblei around Ragusa: cheeses, charcuterie, dried mushrooms, *dolci* (pastries and biscuits), artisanal dried pasta and regional wines.

Spinella
Via Etnea 300
Tel: 095 327 247
www.pasticceriaspinella.it €
Catanese street food makes a tasty snack, especially the *arancini* (rice balls).

LEFT: café at Piazza del Duomo, Catania.
ABOVE: local dishes.

MOUNT ETNA AND CATANIA PROVINCE

Although the province embraces a popular coastline crowded with lidos, beaches and quaint fishing villages, at its heart is the glowering volcanic hinterland of Mount Etna

Sicilians are always concerned that one day there may be a "big one", an earthquake or eruption that will reverberate down the centuries. Until then, however, they are happy to live the good life, enjoying the wines and crops that thrive in the volcanic soil. More than 20 percent of all Sicilians live on the flanks of the volcano. Farmers are enticed there by the fertile soil, while wealthy city residents have constructed villas on the mountain's slopes for the views, cooler summer climate and opportunity for skiing in the winter.

Coastal Catania, however, turns away from the volcanic hinterland with atavistic spirit and peasant culture. This is commercial Sicily, profiting from its ancient entrepreneurial roots established when it was a Greek trading colony. From Catania the economic ripples reach the rest of the province, as do the effects of a healthy public administration allied to the native entrepreneurial spirit. Catania University's noted Engineering Faculty provides the impetus for Italy's microelectronics and telecommunications industries. To dub it Silicon Valley, as the locals sometimes do, is a wishful overstatement, but tourism is thriving, thanks to the increasing popularity of Etna's natural wonderland.

South of Catania

The southwest is dominated by the Piana di Catania, a dullish plain that comes a poor second to Mount Etna's attractions north of **Catania** ❶. The plain was reputedly the abode of the mythological race of man-eating giants, the Laestrygonians, who appear in Homer's *Odyssey*, but is now home to little more

LEFT: the Scalazza, a dramatic staircase in the heart of Caltagirone.

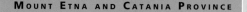

than giant citrus groves. **Militello in Val di Catania** is underwhelming despite its medieval quarter, ruined castle and Baroque churches.

By contrast, the hilly southern interior has considerable charm, especially Caltagirone, Sicily's ceramics capital.

Grammichele ❷, approached via the SS417 from Catania, is a bizarre Baroque town, a champion of bold town planning after the 1693 earthquake. Within a hexagonal design, roads radiate from the central square like the spokes of a wheel. The Chiesa Madre and town hall epitomise the city's rigorously Baroque image and clean geometric design. However, the clinical effect is mocked by the down-at-heel population.

Caltagirone

Further along the SS417, spread over three hills, **Caltagirone ❸** is charming. Its name derives from the Arabic words for castle and cave, but the town was previously settled by the Greeks. Like Acireale and Noto, hilly Caltagirone feels like a bold Baroque theatre, with spacious squares, majestic mansions and monumental churches, often enlivened by ceramic decorative touches *(see page 285)*.

The upper town is surprisingly grand, with imposing public buildings clustered around the **Duomo.** The cathedral contains a *Madonna and Child* attributed to the school of Antonello Gagini (1594).

Close by is the **Corte Capitaniale**, a dignified mansion decorated by school of Gagini sculptures and, beyond, the **Scalazza**, a staircase of 142 steps leading up to the church of **Santa Maria del Monte**. This stunning staircase links the old and new districts. Each lava-stone step is decorated with majolica tiles depicting mythological scenes. On 24–5 July, the feast of **San Giacomo** is celebrated with "the tapestry of fire", featuring a costumed procession and carpet of light. Illuminating the staircase are 5,000 tiny oil lamps, covered by delicate paper cylinders called *coppi*.

On the other side of the long piazza, on Via Roma below the cathedral, the **Museo Civico** (Tue–Sat, Sun 9.30am–1.30pm, 4–7pm; closed

Plate-maker in Caltagirone, where ceramics have been produced for centuries.

Below: cathedral interior and town hall clock, Caltagirone.

Dome of Caltagirone Cathedral.

Mon; charge) was once a fearsome Bourbon prison and still retains its barbaric, spike-studded metal doors. The museum contains Greek and Roman finds and prized Renaissance ceramics. Off Via Roma is **San Francesco d'Assisi**, a Gothic church remodelled in Baroque style after yet another earthquake.

Signs of Caltagirone's thriving ceramics trade abound; workshops display decorative majolica vases, tiles and objets d'art; ceramics adorn city niches, window-ledges, balconies and bandstands. Ceramic flowers even grace the **Ponte San Francesco** (1626–66), the bridge close to San Francesco church. The **Giardino Pubblico**, the municipal gardens below Piazza Umberto, were modelled on English public gardens and boast balustraded terraces, a charming ceramic-decorated bandstand and a belvedere (1792). Predictably, the gardens are home to the **Museo Regionale della Cerámica** (daily 9am–6.30pm; charge), which showcases Sicilian pottery from prehistoric times to the present day, proof that terracotta and glazed ceramics have been produced in Caltagirone since time immemorial.

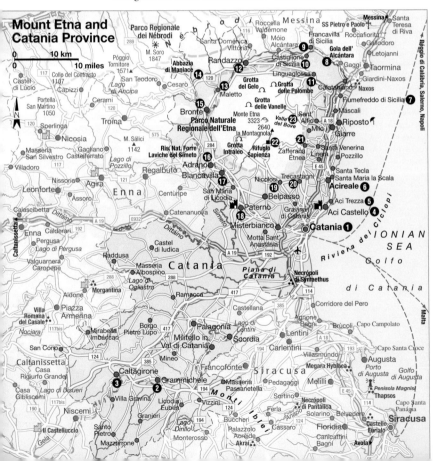

The Coast of Cyclops

Heading north from **Catania** is a welcome release: sea breezes sweep away images of Catania's scruffy outskirts. The province hugs the Ionian coast towards the hillside resort of Taormina, and the Coast of Cyclops, named after the Homeric myth, presents a spectacular seascape. The **Faraglioni dei Ciclopi** (Cyclops) are jagged lumps jutting out of the sea just off the coast at Aci Trezza. Legend has it that these basalt rocks were flung at the fleeing Odysseus by the enraged, blinded Cyclops Polyphemus. The scenic rocks are now used as an oceanography station by Catania University.

In summer, the seafood restaurants are full and flotillas of fishing craft double up as pleasure boats. But essentially the character of the local fishing villages remains unchanged: the daily markets display catches of anchovies and sardines.

Aci Castello ❹, on the Riviera dei Ciclopi near Catania, is memorable for its dramatic castle perched on a rocky crag overlooking the sea. The crenellated Norman **fortress**, built on a site used for defensive purposes since Byzantine times, is well preserved despite frequent eruptions and a fierce attack by the Aragonese. A charming garden of local plants has been created on the roof terrace. From the castle, which houses the **Museo Civico** (daily 9am–1pm, 3–5pm) containing trophies found at sea, locals potter on the rocks or wander down to the fish restaurants along the gnarled coast.

Aci Trezza ❺, a fishing village hoping to become a resort, is celebrated for its connection with Catania-born novelist and dramatist Giovanni Verga (1840–1922). His finest works reflect life at the poorer social levels and his novel, *I Malavoglia* (translated as *Under the Medlar Tree*, 1881), was inspired by this seafaring community. The novel depicts the benighted lives of a fishing family, a theme echoed by Visconti's film, *La Terra Trema (The Earth Quakes)* which was shot nearby. Verga was only too aware of the precarious nature of the fishermen's existence: "Property at sea is writ on water."

The dramatic staircase leading up to Santa Maria del Monte in Caltagirone.

BELOW: rocky beach at Aci Castello.

A decorative tile on the Ponte San Francesco.

BELOW: market stalls and cathedral detail, Acireale.

Close to the harbour is the **Casa del Nespolo** (daily 9.30am–12.30pm, 4–6pm; charge), a tiny fishing museum linked to Verga's novel.

Acireale

Acireale ❻ is the most important of the seven Etna towns with the prefix Aci. Legend has it that Aci (Acis) became the lover of sea-nymph Galatea, and when he was killed by a jealous rival she turned him into a river here. (The river, of course, vanished in an earthquake.)

The town is proud of its appellation *Reale* (royal) and stands aloof, both from the over-commercialised resorts and the rural hinterland. As Akis, it was a Greek settlement that fared badly in the face of eruptions and earthquakes. However, thanks to the continuing ravages of Etna and the talent of local craftsmen, today's town is predominantly Baroque. Compared with most coastal resorts, Acireale is a proper town, admired for its carnival, quality of life, spas and sweet pastries.

The **Duomo** occupies centre stage, its 17th-century grandeur somewhat marred by the addition of a pseudo-Gothic facade. In compensation, the grand Baroque portal is adorned with statues of the *Annunciation* and saints, while the vaulted interior displays *trompe l'œil* decoration and bold stuccowork. The inlaid marble floor contains an appealing 1848 Meridian Line.

The **Palazzo Comunale** represents the first flowering of Catanese Baroque with its elegant, graceful facade and delicate wrought-iron balconies. On the same square, set among the city cafés and grand churches, stands the restored white Baroque vision of **Santi Pietro e Paolo.** In Piazza Vigo further down is the **Basilica di San Sebastiano**, an exuberant Baroque feast, with the facade a riot of cherubs.

In the compact historic centre, the grandiose Baroque buildings are gathered around Piazza Duomo, presenting a contrast between the spacious public squares and the secretive side of town beyond. Yet even the dark alleys yield rewards in the form of pastry shops such as **Castorino** on Corso Savoia, famed for its ice cream,

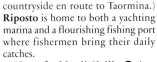

cassata and *pasta reale* – decorated marzipan confections. The city is even credited with inventing sorbets, aided by a profitable monopoly on snow held by the local archbishop until modern times.

Acireale is surrounded by citrus groves, a source of wealth that continues to sustain the local landowning class. From the public gardens stretches a fine view over the Coast of Cyclops, with the rocky shore riven by coves.

At the south entrance to the town, the **Terme di Santa Vénera**, a spa, exploits the healing properties of Etna's radioactive waters. Hot sulphurous lava mud baths (20°C/68°F) have been considered beneficial here for rheumatism and skin conditions since Roman times.

Just below Acireale is the quaint fishing hamlet of **Santa Maria la Scala**, with its lava-stone shore, beached boats, watchtower and simple inns. (The road, the SS114, follows the coast, and is slow-going, passing through Santa Tecla, Pozzillo and Riposto, compared with the A18 *autostrada*, which cuts through the countryside en route to Taormina.) **Riposto** is home to both a yachting marina and a flourishing fishing port where fishermen bring their daily catches.

Fiumefreddo di Sicilia ❼, just north, is named after a cooling river that flows through thick clumps of papyrus. This feudal town functions both as a calming interlude before the volcanic hinterland and as the springboard to chic Taormina *(see page 229)*. Fiumefreddo has a tumbledown Phoenician tower and two castellated mansions. **Castello degli Schiavi**, the stranger of the two villas, has sculpted stone slaves leaning over an 18th-century parapet. Apart from coastal views and clean beaches, the area also draws families to the **Etnaland theme park** *(see box below)*.

Mount Etna

Etna is the dramatic volcano where the heart of Catania province should be. The volcano munches Messina and the countryside too, with new lava mouths opening all the time. Locals joke that not even the Mafia can close Etna's myriad mouths. Mongibello or

Acireale boasts the best carnival in Sicily, borne out by the illuminations, the inventiveness of the decorated floats and the enthusiasm of the crowds. Stalls sell masks, puppets, feathered costumes, nougat, nuts and mushroom pastries.

BELOW LEFT:
Acireale Cathedral.

Volcanic family fun

Families keen to explore Etna can do so the exciting way *(see page 222)* or the easy way. The **Circumetnea train** (tel: 095 541 250; www.circumetnea.it), in existence since 1894, is the single-track rail route around Etna, a leisurely 110km (68-mile) journey from Catania, taking in Adrano, Bronte and Randazzo, returning to the coast at Giarre-Riposto, convenient for Taormina. Depending on the timetable and the sections open, you can stop off at a couple of stations en route before carrying on your journey.

Younger children will probably prefer **Etnavventura**, one of Sicily's best adventure playgrounds (Contrada Serra la Nave, Ragalno, mid-June–mid-Sept; tel: +333 151 5904; www.etnavventura.it). Set on the southern flanks of Mount Etna, it is close to the Rifugio Sapienza cable car, so it works well in tandem. You can even call ahead to request a picnic of local cheeses and ham. Instead, at Fiumefreddo, **Etnaland** (end June–early Sept; www.etnaland.eu) is Sicily's first theme park, complete with miniature volcanoes and simulated eruptions, as well as less obviously Etna-related attractions such as the Dinosaur Park and Crocodile Rapids. *For more information see page 49.*

The Wrath of Mount Etna

Etna's smouldering or snow-capped cone will already be a familiar, perversely friendly presence – to the Sicilians it represents an uneasy, distinctly double-edged relationship

Leonardo Sciascia, the Sicilian writer, called Etna "a huge house-cat that purrs quietly and awakens every so often". However, when Etna calls in her dues, the cat spits fire. And when Sicily's famous volcano erupts, the results are always unpredictable. As local resident Giovanni Giuffrida says: "Lava is like a mole; it takes cover, burrows and reappears where you are not ready to catch it." In terms of duration, an eruption can last 10 minutes or – like the outburst of 1614 – 10 years.

Over centuries, the Catania coastline has receded or advanced in response to Etna's major lava flows. Even the 1908 earthquake, which razed Messina and claimed over 60,000 victims, did not change the coastline. But lava flows from Etna have often redrawn the map, most recently in 1978–9 when lava spilled into the sea, and reached the chapel doors at Fornazzo, a village on the coast. A miraculous intervention was claimed after the molten lava was halted by a statue of the Madonna.

Historically, two of the most catastrophic eruptions occurred in 1381 and 1669, with lava flows that engulfed Catania and destroyed Nicolosi. In modern times, significant eruptions demolished the villages of Gerro and Mascali in the 1920s. Randazzo was narrowly spared by an eruption in 1981, which reached the town walls and destroyed surrounding vineyards. Closer to the volcanic heart, the 1983 eruption destroyed most of Refugio Sapienza and neighbouring property, lifts and roads.

During the 1992 eruption, the Americans were called in to save the resort of Zafferana Etnea, on Etna's eastern slopes. A US Navy and Marine task force, armed with the world's largest helicopters, made daring forays to the mouth of the crater, dropping blocks of concrete into the seething river of lava, and managed to stem the flow.

The last decade or so has seen a flurry of seismic activity, with the southeastern crater responsible for virtually all recent eruptions. In the year 2000 the southeastern crater split into two, with fireballs and eruptive matter tossed into the air to a height of 600 metres (2,000ft).

Intense eruptions have continued sporadically ever since, especially in 2011 and 2012, with spewing of lava and loud detonations heard in villages and towns all around Etna.

Every few years, Etna's glittering red cone is visible from Catania during the day, while tourists as far away as Taormina can see nightly firebombs shooting out from a secondary cone.

Given that major eruptions occur, on average, every 300 years, and that the last catastrophic volcano and earthquake were in 1669 and 1693 respectively, simple calculations suggest that doomsday could be nigh. Not that Sicilians who choose to live on the slopes of an active volcano see it like that, of course. ❑

LEFT: eruption of Mount Etna, February 2012.

Muncibeddu, the Sicilian name for Mount Etna, comes from the Latin and Arabic words for mountain (mons and gibel). It is one of the most active volcanoes in the world.

The sense of appeasing the mountain gods still survives in **Zafferana Etnea**, a hiking village and ski resort that found itself in the path of the 1992 volcanic eruption. Before abandoning his farmhouse to the volcano, Giuseppe Fichera left bread, cheese and wine to satisfy "the tired and hungry mountain". Even gods of destruction need food and rest.

The circular journey around the volcano is a game of light and shade. From the Ionian coast to the fertile Etna foothills is a feast of glistening citrus and olive groves, orchards and nut plantations. But clinging to Etna's flanks are dark volcanic villages and ruined Norman castles. It is a strange trail from green slopes to the moonscape above. From Taormina, a scenic railway runs to Randazzo, travelling along the valley floor, crossing a bridge made of lava blocks and even disappearing inside a lava cutting. But to appreciate Etna's grandeur, drive around the base or follow a similar route on the Circumetnea railway *(see box page 215)*.

Around the volcano

The best drive is the circular tour of Etna, around the **Parco Naturale Regionale dell'Etna**. Leave the coast at Fiumefreddo di Sicilia for a foray into the Alcántara Valley, starting with the **Gola dell'Alcántara ❽**.

This delightful gorge was discovered in the 1950s when a Taormina film director was so enchanted with the prospect of a secret gorge that he had a tortuous path built down to the river. He was the first of many to capture Alcántara on film. Seen from above, the view is of wooded crags descending to a weirdly pitted river canyon. The bed is rocky, the remains of a prehistoric lava flow that created the peninsula of Capo Schiso. The canyon was created not by erosion but by the splintering collision of volcanic magma and the cooling water of the river. The impact threw up lavic prisms in monstrous shapes: these warped black basalt boulders resemble a cross-section of a fossil.

Sicily's wines are intriguing. Reds include the fruity Nero d'Avola and the two Nerellos, Mascalese and Cappuccio, which together go into one of Sicily's most complex wines, Etna Rosso. The most surprising white variety is the aromatic Carricante, with its intense minerality.

BELOW: farmer, Castiglione di Sicilia.

Some place names are symbolic: Linguaglossa is a corruption of "lingua grossa", referring to the fat tongue of lava that engulfed the village. The native Siculi worshipped Etna long before the arrival of the Greeks. Adranus, their god of fire, was believed to inhabit the volcano's turbulent depths.

BELOW: Castiglione di Sicilia nestles below the mountains.

Now the centre of a well-organised nature reserve, Alcántara, with its botanical walk, permanent farmers' market and the gorge itself, makes for one of the most popular day trips from Taormina. The gorge can be explored in several ways, but especially by wading. A waterfall with a sheer drop is a barrier to further exploration of the gorge for anyone not wearing a wetsuit and on a canyoning trip. A lift leads down to the grey-green river and the so-called beach where, in summer, low water levels mean you can either paddle in the chilly waters or, more adventurously, hire waders and explore further. Beyond are fast-flowing currents in ever-narrowing tracts, deceptive rapids that can only be explored on a guided body-canyoning adventure, one only open to those over 16. The popularity of the gorge means it's best avoided on Sundays in August.

Francavilla di Sicilia ➒, just west along the SS185, is set in a fertile valley of citrus plantations and prickly pears. Founded by King Roger, Francavilla prospered under Spanish rule. Roger's **ruined castle** occupies a

lone mound in the valley and once guarded the route to Randazzo. The other Norman relic is the hermitage of **La Badiazza**, perched atop a rocky platform and victim of the 1693 earthquake. The **Chiesa Madre** has a Gagini *Madonna*, matched by the sculpted Gagini fountain in Piazza San Paolo. The **Matrice Vecchia** has a Renaissance door with a vine-leaf motif. The finest sight is the **Convento dei Cappuccini**, a 16th-century monastery on a lovely hillock, protected by Spanish sentry boxes and marble parapets. Inside is a profusion of *intarsia* work and carving, created by 17th-century monks.

Castiglione di Sicilia

Castiglione di Sicilia ➓, set on Etna's northern flank just south of Francavilla, is one of the most atmospheric Etna villages and is also a burgeoning wine-producing centre. Perched on a crag, this ancient bastion possesses Greek ramparts but is better known as a Norman fiefdom. Narrow medieval alleys wind to the crumbling lava-stone church of **San Pietro** and the grander **Santa Maria**

della Catena. The **Norman castle** dominates the valley, with its jagged lookout tower, walls and roofs, and is destined to become a wine museum and wine-tasting centre. This rocky citadel compels respect, as do the ominous views of rubble and debris trailing from Etna's summit.

Linguaglossa ⓫, 18km (11 miles) southeast of Castiglione, is a popular stop on the scenic Circumetnea rail route and doubles as a simple ski resort at 550 metres (1,800ft). It also makes a workaday hiking base, with treks leading through pine forests to **Grotta del Gelo**, a lava-stone cave with weird light effects, and up Etna itself. In town, the Baroque **Chiesa Madre** pays tribute to the forests, with 18th-century choir stalls and a coffered ceiling, while the village's lava-stone pavements attest to its proximity to Etna.

Randazzo

West of Castiglione, **Randazzo** ⓬ is the most atmospheric and coherent medieval town on the northern slopes of Etna, and the one closest to the volcano craters. Much of

the town is built using blocks cut from the dried lava streams. Originally settled by Greeks fleeing from Naxos, it reached its apogee under the Normans. During Swabian rule, Randazzo was a summer court and retreat from the heat of Messina. It remains a self-contained market town with crenellated churches and sturdy 14th-century walls.

For a town in the jaws of Etna, Randazzo has survived magnificently. The 1981 eruption threatened to engulf the walls and blocked surrounding vineyards, roads and railway lines, leaving a lava flow visible today. But nature is not to blame for damage to the medieval core: Allied bombing in 1943 destroyed the enemies' last stronghold in Sicily, including the fortress and finest palazzi.

Until the 16th century, competition for supremacy within the walls was fuelled by the presence of three rival communities talking different dialects. Each parish church took its turn as cathedral for a three-year term: the Latins were centred on the church of **Santa Maria**, the Greeks at San Niccolò and the Lombards at San

EAT

Wealthy families in this province often have kid instead of lamb as an Easter treat. *Capretto con stracciatella* is a slow stew made in an earthenware pot on the stove with the kid, onions, water and seasoning. After an hour, five eggs and grated pecorino cheese are beaten together and poured over the kid, which continues cooking.

BELOW: clock tower and view of Randazzo.

As duke of Bronte, the British sea hero Admiral Lord Nelson never visited his vast Sicilian estate, despite wistful dreams of retiring here with paramour Emma Hamilton. The closest he got was in Emma's nickname for him, "My Lord Thunder" – a reference to Brontes, the mythical giant who forged thunderbolts for Jupiter.

Martino. The churches were fiercely battlemented and ostentatious. Ultimately, the Catholics triumphed and the church of Santa Maria on Piazza Basilica is now the cathedral. Built between 1217 and 1239, it is a much-remodelled grey lava-stone church in Norman-Swabian design, with Norman apses and walls and side portals in Catalan-Gothic style. Its odd interior contrasts Satanic-looking black columns and altar with a pure Gagini font.

Porta San Martino, one of two surviving city gates, marks the entrance to the walled medieval town. The elegant Piazza San Martino is the heart of the damaged Lombard Quarter, set against the city walls. Appropriately, **Chiesa San Martino** has a 13th-century banded lava and limestone Lombard bell tower matched by an early Baroque facade in grey and white stone. Virtually next door is the **Castello-Carcere**, a medieval castle and Bourbon prison, now the **Museo Archeologico Paolo Vagliasindi** (daily, summer 9am–7.30pm, winter 10am–1pm; charge), an archeological museum. Beside the lava-stone win-

dows is an inscription to Philip II and bullet holes that attest to the military skirmishes in August 1943. A puppet museum, **Museo dei Pupi Siciliani** (same hours), is here too.

Via Umberto contains symbols of Randazzo's past role as a royal city, including the **Palazzo Reale,** the severe Swabian summer palace. Via Umberto ends in spacious **Piazza Municipio,** a bustling square dominated by **Palazzo Comunale,** the well-restored town hall. But leave the crowds by turning down the arcaded **Via degli Archi** to Piazza San Niccolò and the Greek Quarter, and the impressive Greek **San Niccolò**, with its original 14th-century apses, huge Baroque lava-stone facade and tapering campanile. Inside the church are several Gagini sculptures, including, appropriately, a St Nicholas.

The Admiral's estate

Between Randazzo and Bronte extends a wooded, volcanic landscape south to **Maletto** ⑬, noted for its wine and strawberries. Maletto marks the highest point on the Circumetnea railway line (1,200 metres/ 4,000ft) and offers views of recent lava flows. From Maletto, take a right fork to Admiral Nelson's castle at Maniace or continue south to Bronte. Following signs to Castello di Nelson leads to the **Abbazia di Maniace** ⑭ (daily 9am–1pm, 2.30–5pm; charge), one and the same. Set in a wooded hollow, the fortified abbey was founded by Count Roger, with the chapel commemorating a Saracen defeat in 1040. With Norman help, the Byzantine commander Maniakes routed the Arabs and regained Sicily for Constantinople. But the estate is better known as the fiefdom of Admiral Horatio Nelson, duke of Bronte.

The title and estates were presented to Nelson by Ferdinand IV in gratitude for the Admiral's part in crushing the 1799 rebellion in Naples. Nelson's descendant, Vis-

Below: countryside around Maletto.

count Bridport, only relinquished his Sicilian seat in 1981, when the 12,500-hectare (30,000-acre) estate was broken up and the orchards, nut plantations and dairy farms sold. Nevertheless, Nelson memorabilia remains, from paintings of sea battles to the Admiral's port decanter.

Inside the castle compound, the best part of the Benedictine abbey owes nothing to Nelson. The late Norman chapel has an original wooden ceiling, doorway and statuary. The original castle is unrecognisable, thanks to the 1693 earthquake and heavy anglicisation. It resembles a gracious Wiltshire manor from outside, an image confirmed by the genteel English cemetery. Even the gardens are home to neat hedges, as well as cypresses and palms.

Between Maletto and Bronte are subtle shifts in scenery. Walnut and chestnut groves on the higher hills are dotted with jagged volcanic clumps, including the lava flow of 1823. Around Bronte, the slopes are covered with small nut trees, a reminder that 80 percent of Italy's pistachio crop comes from these well-tended terraces.

Bronte

Bronte 🅕, at 760 metres (2,500ft) and with a population of 20,000, was founded in 1520 by Charles V and is an ill-planned town sandwiched between two lava flows on the western slopes of Mount Etna. Legend says it was founded by the Cyclops Brontes, son of Uranus, who was known as The Thunderer and whose forge was in a cavern beneath the mountain. Devastated three times by eruptions, Bronte hangs on as the administrative and agricultural centre of the region.

Pistachio nuts are exported worldwide from here, and each year a pistachio festival takes place on the first 10 days of October. Bronte is resolutely shabby, its dingy charm residing in the neglected late Renaissance churches with crenellated towers. The church of **l'Annunciata** (1535) has a polychrome marble group attributed to Antonello Gagini that, local lore says, has miraculous powers and on many occasions has been able to stem the flow of molten lava.

South of Bronte, the pistachio plantations cede to scruffy, cacti-

DRINK

One of Sicily's greatest successes is the creation of *granita* (water ices) made from fresh fruit and served in a tall glass accompanied by a brioche – a delightful mixture, especially on a hot day. Flavours change with the season. Watermelon *granita* is a summer favourite, and so are peach, apricot and grape.

BELOW: the steep slopes of Bronte.

In response to the often posed question of why people choose to live by an active volcano, a Catanese vulcanologist, Romolo Romano, muses: "It's the same reason people live in places like the San Andreas Fault: they are beautiful spots, so beautiful that you sometimes forget how dangerous they are."

strewn slopes, with lumps of lava interspersed with white lava-coated trees. The makeshift mood reflects a region devastated by the 1985 eruption: everything built in haste but, given Etna's whims, with no time to repent at leisure.

The fertile foothills

Adrano 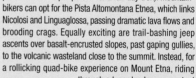, set on Etna's southwestern slopes, is a shabby market town with mythical roots. On the outskirts are the remains of a grander past: the Greek city of Adranon was founded here by Dionysius I in the 4th century BC. In antiquity, the city was celebrated for its sanctuary to Adranus, the Sicel god of fire. Still today, during the bizarre August festival, a child dressed as an angel "flies" along a cord linking the old city powers: the castle, town hall and a statue of the god of fire himself. So far, Adranus has kept his city safe from fiery Etna.

Its battered charm lies in the busy **Piazza Umberto**. Like Randazzo, wizened old men gather in the clubs clustered around the main square. Here, too, is the austere **Norman castle** (Tue–Sat 9am–1pm, 3–6pm,

Sun 9am–1pm; charge), sitting on its squat Saracen base. This powerful bastion was rebuilt by Roger I in the 11th century and remodelled by the Aragonese. The interior, once a Bourbon prison, houses an **archaeological museum** with minor Greek sculptures. On the floor above is Queen Adelaide's chapel, a mysterious room decorated with purplish lava-stone capitals by Roger's third wife.

Beside the castle, the **Chiesa Madre** is a Norman church disfigured by clumsy restoration in 1811. The heavy basalt columns conceivably came from the Greek Temple to Adranon that once occupied the site. Plutarch records a dramatic eve-of-battle appeal to the gods: in response, a bronze statue of Adranus suddenly quivered into life. A final twinge of nostalgia for ancient Adranon is evoked by the **Greek city walls**, lying at the end of Via Buglio.

Biancavilla , built on a basalt escarpment 5km (3 miles) south of Adrano, was founded by Albanian refugees in 1480. The sole Albanian link is the *Madonna of the Alms*, an icon brought over by the first refu-

---

Exploring Mount Etna

An exciting volcano has become yet more exhilarating with the creation of new adventures, from hiking and mountain-biking to quad-biking, skiing and helicopter tours. To explore the craters and summit of Mount Etna, the largest volcano in Europe, always trust the local guides. Memorable hikes start from the foothills or closer to the summit, such as Bocca Nuova and Cratere del Piano, along the western flank of Etna. The intrepid can hike to the underground lava caves of Grotta del Gelo and Grotta del Lampone, but winter hiking in high areas is not possible due to snow and bad visibility.

Local guides in Linguaglossa include **Etna Trekking** (tel: 335 130 9474, www.etnatrekking.com) and **Guide Etna Nord** (tel: 095 777 4502, www.guidetnanord.com;

prices from €70 per person for a full-day trek). Mountain-bikers can opt for the Pista Altomontana Etnea, which links Nicolosi and Linguaglossa, passing dramatic lava flows and brooding crags. Equally exciting are trail-bashing jeep ascents over basalt-encrusted slopes, past gaping gullies, to the volcanic wasteland close to the summit. Instead, for a rollicking quad-bike experience on Mount Etna, riding through a lunar landscape, contact **Etna Quad Adventure** (tel: 339 587 5145, www.etnaquad.it).

Etna also has two ski resorts, the larger Rifugio Sapienza and the smaller, prettier Piano Provenzana. You can ski down the northern flank through beech and birch, or indulge in off-piste snowboarding over lava bumps on the treeless upper slopes (www.parcoetna.ct.it).

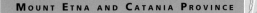

gees and visible in the comically grandiose Chiesa Madre.

If Biancavilla is best known for its prickly pears, **Paternò ⑱**, halfway between Biancavilla and Catania, is famous for its oranges, Sicily's juiciest. Set on a hilly volcanic site, the scruffy Baroque town has a striking Norman **castle** (Mon–Fri 8.30am–11am) founded in 1073 by Count Roger. The severity of the 14th-century lava-stone keep is echoed by the Great Hall and frescoed chapel. Frederick II died here while journeying to his favourite fortress of Enna.

Nearby is the **Chiesa Madre**, a Norman church with a Gothic facelift containing a majestic 17th-century wooden Crucifix, and the ruined Gothic church of **San Francesco**. In World War II, the German forces used this hill as an observation post and drew heavy Allied fire, leading to the death of 4,000 people. Known as **Rocca Normanna**, the castle quarter now enjoys happier associations: in summer, visitors can attend concerts, sample the stuffed aubergines, or simply drool over terraces glistening with orange groves.

Gateway to Etna

Nicolosi ⑲, northeast of Paternò, is both a charmless ski resort and the southern gateway to Etna's terraced wine and walking country, covered in oak, pine and chestnut trees. Lying east of the wooded Monti Rossi twin craters, the town has been reborn after repeated eruptions. Today it marks the start of bracing treks to Rifugio Sapienza *(see page 224)* and affords a fine view of Etna's active central crater and numerous secondary ones.

Just east, along the road to **Trecastagni ⑳**, the lava beds of 1886 and 1910 are visible. Once a medieval fiefdom, Trecastagni is noted for the **Chiesa Madre**, a Renaissance church attributed to Antonello Gagini, and for the Lombard-Romanesque **Sant'Antonio di Padova**, with its 17th-century lava-stone cloisters. Also take the time to appreciate traditional Etna craftsmanship: the local workshops are dedicated to Sicilian carts, wrought ironwork and colourful ceramics, as well as Etna carvings in lava stone or gnarled olive wood. Nor are Trecastagni's almond biscuits, sorbets and red wines to be sniffed at.

The Norman castle in Adrano was built of black volcanic rock by Roger I. Once a Bourbon prison, it now houses a museum of Greek and Bronze Age artefacts.

BELOW: in Adrano.

TIP

Below the murmuring summit of Etna is a vast depression, an area created by violent eruptions. Between Monte Rinatu (1,569 metres/5,147ft) and La Montagnola (2,640 metres/8,660ft), the Valle del Bove has deep lava walls that can reach 1,000 metres (3,280ft). A desolate, unreal silence fills the valley. One way to see this extraordinary phenomenon on foot is to start at Zafferana Etnea and follow the paths.

BELOW: hikers climbing Mount Etna.

From here head for Acireale and follow *autostrade* signs to return to Fiumefreddo the quick way.

Ascending the volcano

Circling the volcano is intriguing and safe, but an ascent requires caution. Depending on the season and Etna's mood, the menu may include a mere mass of clinker, a spent cone, a smoking cone, or even a seething lava front. When it works, it is wonderful, with sulphurous vapours, heat coursing through the soles of your shoes, and sightings of spitting fireballs.

An organised group trip is the sensible, relatively inexpensive way of experiencing Etna, but for sheer extravagant adventure, a private guide is recommended. Without a guide, suitably clad explorers can clamber about at their own risk up to a certain altitude, currently 3,000 metres (9,850ft), 323 metres (1,060ft) short of Etna's great height. Even so, it is essential to get advice on routes from local guides, unless you are taking the simplest option of the cable-car ticket that also includes a guided drive and walk to the summit.

At the cable-car summit, just outside the bar, suitable footwear and warm clothing can be hired, if needed. From here, reinforced minibuses ferry passengers to the different departure points, according to the chosen route and the level of volcanic activity.

Once driving in the volcanic foothills or national park, follow signs for **Etna Sud**, the main southern access point, reached via **Zafferana Etnea** ㉑. Set on Etna's eastern slopes, this unprepossessing mountain resort hit the national headlines in 1992 when Etna threatened to engulf the village. The resort had barely recovered from the 1984 earthquake, when the Baroque Chiesa Madre became the focus of fervent prayers as the local vineyards and citrus groves were swallowed up. The path of this eruption has now been landscaped into a strange garden memorial, signposted *Colata Lavica 1992* (Lava Flow 1992). Since Zafferana is only 500 metres (1,650ft) from the crater on Monte Serra Calvarina, landslides and eruptive activity are still common.

From here, a road leads to the **Rifugio Sapienza** base camp and an ascent of Etna. As one climbs the scenic **Casa Cantoniera** road, citrus groves and wooded slopes give way to a wasteland of lava flows, bare slabs of brown rubble half-covered by snow. Even in deepest winter, snow is unevenly distributed because of heat generated by the volcano.

Rifugio Sapienza

The base camp of **Rifugio Sapienza** ㉒, situated at 1,800 metres (5,900ft), includes a refuge run by the Italian Alpine Club. Like much on Mount Etna, the centre lives dangerously, and was rebuilt after an eruption in 1983, an event depicted in lurid technicolor inside. Before taking the cable car to the top, glance at the spent cone just in front of the refuge.

A winter **cable car** trip may be made in the company of skiers comparing eyewitness accounts of Etna's most recent devastation. En route are grim views of a burnt-out cable car destroyed in the 1983 eruption, along with the wreckage of a ski lift and the original mountain refuge, buried by lava in 1971. At the summit, most visitors set off by minibus, leaving the less adventurous simply to admire the snowcapped views, best in the morning or at sunset, before sloping off to the mountain bar.

Torre del Filósofo, Empedocles' so-called observation post, wrecked in a past eruption, currently marks the highest point one can go with a guide, close to the southeast crater. Empedocles did not live to tell the tale: the Greek philosopher allegedly leapt into the main crater in 433 BC trying to prove that the gases would support his body weight. The charitable interpretation is that it was also a quest for divine consciousness in death. But, as his sandal was found on the edge, perhaps he merely slipped.

The view from the top will depend on volcanic activity and the prevailing winds: it is vital to avoid the gases and burning volcanic matter emitted from active craters. Blue smoke indicates the presence of magma, while a corona, a halo of sulphurous vapour, is a rare event. At most, you may see an active crater belching out sulphurous fumes or exploding *bombe*, molten "bombs", or the bottom of the misty cone bubbling with incandescent lava. In periods of intense seismic activity, the volcano spits out molten rock or fireballs, a dramatic sight, especially at night.

On the summit, many guides entertain visitors with a demonstration of the forging of black Etna ashtrays from molten lava. In exceptional circumstances, you might be taken to see a lava front some distance away from the volcano. Usually bathed in mist and emitting a stench of sulphur, the lava front sounds like the clinking of china cups or the hissing of some chained animal.

The descent of Etna may not be an anticlimax if you can visit a lava front with a guide. **Valle del Bove ㉓**, best seen from **Milo**, was the most dramatic of recent lava fronts, hence its eerie, barren surface, devoid of vegetation: Etna at its most primeval. ❑

Fertile ground around Mount Etna.

BELOW: tourist bus on the volcano.

BEST RESTAURANTS, BARS AND CAFÉS

Prices for a three-course dinner per person and a half-bottle of house wine:
€ = under €20
€€ = €20–35
€€€ = €35–70
€€€€ = over €70

Taormina, in neighbouring Messina province, tends to be the magnet for foodies. Even so, the Catania coast and the fertile slopes of Mount Etna have underrated restaurants which come into their own during Etna's autumn foodie festivals dedicated to wine, honey and pistachios.

Caltagirone

I Marchesi di Santa Barbara
Via San Bonaventura 22
Tel: 0933 22406
www.imarchesidisantabarbara.it
€€
In a noble old palazzo in the upper town, this popular restaurant serves meat and fish mains, as well as pizza. Closed Mon.

La Scala
Scala Santa Maria del Monte 8
Tel: 0933 57781 €€
Alongside the staircase, two rooms in a 17th-century palazzo, with a charming courtyard and garden for summer. Traditional Sicilian cooking. Closed Wed.

Aci Castello

Alioto
Via Mollica 24
Tel: 095 494 444 €€€
On a terrace by the sea, a popular but expensive fish restaurant. Enjoy the pasta with lobster. Closed Tue.

Barbarossa
Strada Provinciale, the SS114 road to Aci Castello
Tel: 095 295 539 €€€
Range of seafood as well as stuffed pancakes and a good list of notable wines.

Aci Trezza

Galatea
Via Livorno 146a
Tel: 095 711 6902 €€€
Elegant restaurant with a sea view. Wide selection of fish and desserts. Closed Mon.

I Malavoglia
Lungomare dei Ciclopi 167
Tel: 095 711 6556 €€
Typical seafront trattoria where fish is naturally the mainstay of the menu. But at good prices. Closed Tue and 23 Dec–23 Jan.

La Cambusa del Capitano
Via Marina 65
Tel: 095 276 298 €€
A simple place on the banks of the sea serving only local produce and fish. Welcoming and easy-going. Closed Wed.

Acireale

La Grotta
Via Scalo Grande 46, Loc. Santa Maria alla Scala
Tel: 095 764 8153 €€
A casual, popular place with simple food that, due to demand, extends tables along the water's edge in the summer. Closed Tue and three weeks in Oct.

Nino Castorina
Corso Savoia 109 (closed Mon) and Corso Umberto

63 (closed Tue) €
Not restaurants, but
Nino Castorino is the
place for ice cream,
marzipan and pastries.

Panoramico
Viale Ionico 12, Litoranea
Tel: 095 885 291 €€€
A panoramic restaurant
with a pizzeria and a
piano bar. Good sea-
food. Closed Mon.

On Mount Etna

At Rifugio Sapienza
there are mediocre res-
taurants and snack
bars. The best of a poor
choice is La Cantoniera,
but you would be
advised to bring a picnic
or eat elsewhere, either
in one of the neighbour-
ing towns on the slopes
of the volcano, or in
Taormina.

Nicolosi

Corsaro
Piazza Cantoniera,

Etna Sud
Tel: 095 914 122
www.hotelcorsaro.it €€
A busy, small hotel (17
rooms) that is a popular,
inexpensive base for
young people exploring
Etna. The restaurant
offers substantial
meals.

Grotta del Gallo
Via Madonna delle Grazie
40
Tel: 095 911 301 €€
In a panoramic location,
the villa has a garden
and fine views of both
volcano and sea. Farm-
house and classic cook-
ing. Closed Thur.

Nero di Cenere
Via Garibaldi 64
Tel: 095 791 8513 €€
A well-regarded wine bar
and restaurant, with an
extensive list of regional
wines and a menu of
light pasta and vegetari-
an dishes. Terrace.
Closed Mon.

Trecastagni

Al Mulino
Via Mulino al Vento 48
Tel: 095 780 6634
www.alnuovomulino.it €€
Set in a grand villa over-
looking an old windmill.
Specialities include
pasta with mushrooms
and sausage with herbs.
Closed Mon.

Villa Taverna
Corso Colombo 42
Tel: 095 780 6458 €€
This is 17km (11 miles)
from Catania but popu-
lar with the Catanese
because it is atmos-
pheric and looks like a
film set, and good food
is served. Family-run
and welcoming. Book.

Zafferana Etnea

Parco dei Principi
Via delle Ginestre 1
Tel: 095 708 2335
www.ristoranteparcodeiprincipe.
it €€€
Elegant 18th-century
villa serving interesting
local cuisine, with Etna
produce. Closed Tue.

Randazzo

Parco Statella
Via Montelaguardia
Tel: 095 924 036
www.parcostatella.com €€
Between Randazzo and
Linguaglossa, this
charming trattoria, set
in a historic villa, has
wild mushrooms as a
speciality. Closed Wed;
open weekends only
Oct–May.

San Giorgio e Il Drago
Piazza San Giorgio 28
Tel: 095 923 972 €€
This attractive restau-
rant near Santa Maria
offers meaty mains.
Good value. Closed Tue.

Veneziano
Via Nazionale 120, Contrada Arena
Tel: 0957 991 353
www.ristoranteveneziano.it €€
A restaurant with pre-
tensions but tasty
regional dishes 1km (²⁄₃
mile) out of Randazzo.
Mushrooms from the
slopes of Etna are a
speciality. Closed Mon.

LEFT: trattorie offer classic Sicilian cooking.
ABOVE: traditional Sicilian sweets are part of a typical menu.

TAORMINA

As Sicily's foremost resort, Taormina has a languorous reputation, seductive hotels and a *dolce vita* image it proudly strives to maintain

Taormina is Sicily's most dramatic resort, a stirring place celebrated by poets from classical times onwards. Goethe waxed lyrical about the majestic setting: "Straight ahead one sees the long ridge of Etna, to the left the coastline as far as Catania or even Siracusa, and the whole panorama is capped by the huge, fuming, fiery mountain, the look of which, tempered by distance and atmosphere, is, however, more friendly than forbidding." D.H. Lawrence was equally enamoured, calling Taormina "the dawn-coast of Europe".

The Sicilian St Tropez

Today this elemental site has been domesticated into a safe, sophisticated, un-Sicilian pocket. A century of tourism has toned down the subversive native spirit, effaced poverty and displaced undesirables. French visitors liken Taormina to a Sicilian St Tropez, stylish but unreal. Still, after Sicily's chaotic major cities, or the wariness of some of the islands' remote mountain villages, who wants reality? May, September and October are the loveliest months in Taormina, when the city enjoys a semblance of solitude combined with the pleasures of a mild climate.

The terraced town was once a wintering place for frustrated northerners and gay exiles. Today, this safe haven appeals to romantic couples, sedate shoppers and the cultured middle classes. As a resort, Cefalù, near Palermo, is Taormina's only serious rival. But Taormina scores in terms of sophisticated hotels, sheer professionalism and an enlightened, if rampantly commercial, approach to tourism.

Local gossip has it that the town is uncontaminated by corruption

Main attractions

CORSO UMBERTO
NAUMACHIE
TEATRO GRECO (GREEK THEATRE)
PIAZZA IX APRILE
CATTEDRALE
GIARDINO PUBBLICO
CASTELMOLA
ISOLA BELLA
MAZZARÒ
LUXURIOUS HOTELS
CHIC SHOPPING

LEFT: strolling on Piazza IX Aprile.
RIGHT: view from the Teatro Greco.

*One of the top places for granita (water ices) on the island is **Bam Bar** (55 Via di San Giovanni, off Corso Umberto). The Sicilians eat granita at any time of day, including coffee granita and a brioche for breakfast.*

because even the Mafia likes a crime-free holiday haunt. Yet despite designer glamour and hordes of blasé cruise-liner passengers, the site's majesty is not manufactured. Nor is the heady decadence and timeless charm.

Taormina started as a Siculi settlement at the foot of Monte Tauro. It was an outpost of Naxos *(see page 248)* until the Greeks fled the first colony for Taoromenion in 403 BC. Under the Romans, the city acquired a garrison and the new name of Tauromenium. The town also prospered in medieval times and became the capital of Byzantine Sicily in the 9th century. It was the last Byzantine stronghold to fall to the Arabs, destroyed in 902. But it was rebuilt almost immediately, and captured in 1078 by the Norman Count Roger d'Altavilla, under whom it enjoyed a long period of prosperity. Aristocratic leanings later drew Taormina into the Aragonese camp and support for the Spanish, with the Catalan legacy reflected in the town's array of richly decorated palazzi.

The main entrance to the town is the medieval gate of **Porta Messina** ❶, close to the bus terminus on Via Pirandello where the cable car *(funivia)* takes you down to the resort beaches of **Mazzarò** on the coast below. Outside the gate is the tiny church of **San Pancrazio**, built over a temple to Isis.

Corso Umberto

Corso Umberto, the pedestrianised main street, leads through the town, from Porta Messina to Porta Catania, revealing 15th-century palazzi converted into craft shops, boutiques and bars. On display are piles of candied fruit, marzipan animals and fresh kumquats. These jostle for attention with majolica tiles, traditional puppets, cut-glass chandeliers and reproductions of classical statuary.

Just off the Corso lies the **Naumachie** ❷, a hybrid construction

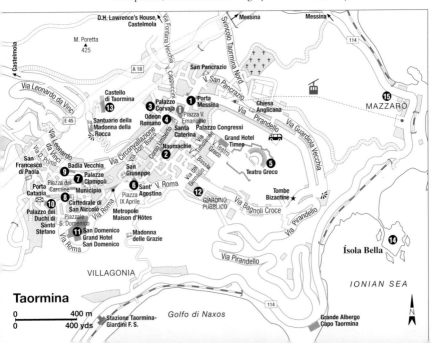

Taormina

second only to the Greek theatre in importance. Originally a vaulted cistern connected to the city baths, it evolved into a Hellenic nymphaeum and Roman gymnasium. The atmospheric arched buttress walls remain, propping up the Corso. For lunch, the restaurant terraces of the adjoining Via Naumachia beckon.

On **Piazza Vittorio Emanuele II**, the main square, is **Palazzo Corvaja** ❸, a historic mansion where the Sicilian Parliament met in 1411. Now a tourist office for Taormina and the Alcántara Gorge, this eclectic building incorporates a crenellated Saracenic tower, a secluded courtyard, sculpted parapet, and Catalan-Gothic decorative details around the doorway and windows. It also contains the small **Museo Siciliano di Arte e Tradizioni Popolari** (Tue–Sun 9am–1pm, 4–8pm; charge) with local puppets, carts, Christmas cribs and ceramics.

Next to the palazzo is the charming church of **Santa Caterina d'Alessandria**, constructed in the 17th century on part of the remains of the **Odeon Romano** ❹, or Teatrino Romano, a Roman concert auditorium partly hidden by the church.

Teatro Greco

Now we come to Taormina's *raison d'être* on Via Teatro Greco (just follow the crowds). This is the majestic **Teatro Greco** ❺ (daily 9am–one hour before sunset; charge). It is a setting that is pure drama, with the *cavea* (horseshoe of tiered seats) hewn out of the hillside.

In Greek theatres, sea and sky were the natural backdrop; the Romans preferred proscenium arches. Where the Greeks worshipped nature, the Romans tried to improve on it. The Hellenistic theatre was built under Hieron in the 3rd century BC and enlarged by the Romans in AD 2. Like Tindari's Greek theatre, Taormina's was turned into an arena for gladiatorial combat. Roman theatrical conventions caused the view to be obscured by arches. By adding a double portico and colonnades behind the stage, they showed insensitivity to the natural setting.

Romantics side with the Olympian gods in seeing Roman grandiosity as

TIP

Getting around by car is not advisable, as the resort is virtually pedestrianised. If booked in a hotel, you are allowed to arrive by car and park there. Otherwise head for the multi-storey car park below Porta Catania and take the lift up to town. The cable car *(funivia)* links Mazzarò and Taormina's Porta Messina entrance.

BELOW: Teatro Greco.

Get your portrait drawn on Piazza IX Aprile.

no match for the timeless character of Greek art. However, Roman erudition is evidenced in the well-preserved *scena* (the construction behind the stage that served as a backdrop and also storage area). But in the 19th century, the granite columns and Corinthian capitals were wrongly repositioned on the site. Still, Greek purists are delighted to see the Roman *scena* crumble, the better to appreciate the Greek atmosphere.

Not that the cats sunning themselves on the ruins distinguish between Greek marble and pinkish Roman brickwork. In high season, the theatre is best explored early in the morning or near closing time, to avoid the crowds. Views from the terraces above the *cavea* and *parascenia* (wings) reveal a perfect fusion of the elements. The writer Vincent Cronin likened the theatre to a seagull suspended between sky and sea. The scene is shrouded in mystery by a smouldering volcano or snowcapped peak. Citrus groves carpet the slopes, while the cliff face is a tangle of cacti and orchids. Make sure to climb to the very top for views of the craggy

BELOW: the *passeggiata* on Piazza IX Aprile.

coastline, bay and the romantic islet of Isola Bella.

The theatre is still used today, not just for performances of classical plays, as at Siracusa, but also as the venue for an international arts festival, Taormina Arte, which presents drama, cinema, ballet and music from June to August (tickets and information from the tourist office in Palazzo Corvaja, Piazza Santa Caterina; www. taormina-arte.com).

Piazza IX Aprile

Halfway down the Corso, **Piazza IX Aprile ❻** offers glittering views of Etna and close-ups of preening poseurs at classic cafés such as Wunderbar. **Sant'Agostino**, the forbidding 15th-century church on the square, has been converted into a cosy library and art gallery, confirmed by the cluster of caricaturists and street artists sketching outside. The other church feels more like a social than a spiritual centre: **San Giuseppe**'s Rococo interior overflows after a Sunday service; after much handshaking, the congregation spills into the cafés.

The Corso continues beyond the Porta di Mezzo, a clock tower marking the city's medieval quarter. Steps lead to the Catalan-Gothic **Palazzo Ciampoli ⑦**, now Hotel Palazzo Vecchio. After admiring its Aragonese battlemented facade and mullioned windows, call in for a sweet Sicilian pastry at Bar Saint Honoré before climbing Via Venezia, a charming alley by the Corso, or strolling further to the cathedral.

Piazza del Duomo

Piazza del Duomo is a central meeting place. At sunset, or at the first sign of spring sun, children fetch their footballs, the *jeunesse dorée* pose, and Taormina's perma-tanned lounge lizards, not a dying breed, search for foreign prey. Matrons still swan around in weighty furs: in Taormina, the fur-coat parade lasts until March.

The Duomo itself, the **Cattedrale di San Niccolò ⑧** (daily 8am–noon, 3.30–6.30pm) draws crowds to its winter cycle of classical concerts. The crenellated stone facade has a severity that survived Renaissance remodelling but is softened by the Baroque fountain on the square, which sports sea horses, cherubs and a podgy female centaur. This weird mythological creature is the city symbol, confirmed by a stone centaur unearthed on the Greek site.

Opposite the fountain, steps lead to Piazza del Carmine and the **Badia Vecchia ⑨**, a battlemented 15th-century abbey (Mon–Sat 9am–1pm, 3–7pm). Although over-restored, the abbey still has Trecento flourishes, Gothic arched windows, fretwork and friezes. Set on a lower level, **Palazzo dei Duchi di Santo Stefano ⑩** is a gracious ducal palace and Taormina's loveliest medieval building. Highlights are the Norman-Gothic windows, delicate lava-stone cornices and the lacy frieze of *intarsia* work (decorative wood inlay), a Saracenic legacy.

From here, Via del Ghetto winds down to **San Domenico ⑪**, a 15th-century monastery converted into a gorgeous de luxe hotel. During World War II, it was Marshal Kesselring's headquarters and suffered bomb damage, although the cells and cloisters were spared. The Corso

TIP

The Corso is dotted with travel agencies offering adventurous day trips to Mount Etna, to the Aeolian Islands or to the Alcántara Gorge. For a complete list, or for advice on tackling Mount Etna, visit the helpful tourist office in Palazzo Corvaja.

BELOW: San Domenico Palace.

Chic living

As Sicily's glitziest resort, Taormina is sophisticated fun, so join the chic set over cocktails at San Domenico or Gran Timeo *(see page 278)*. But even the poseurs are really here for the artful simplicity of balconies bedecked with bougainvillea and secret gardens adorned with lemon trees.

At night, the Catalan-Gothic facades are illuminated, and the squares seem tinged pink in the moonlight. From the belvedere, Etna's fiery cone glitters before dissolving into the sea, stars and smoky peaks.

Solitary walkers climb Salita Ibrahim to the Carmine, a tranquil monastic spot, while dreamers take Via Caruso to the Badia Vecchia and bay views.

Castelmola is dramatically perched on a limestone peak.

ends at **Porta Catania**, the archway that matches the Porta Messina entrance gate.

English connection

It is a short stroll to the **Giardino Pubblico** , a lush park on Via Roma bequeathed to the town by an eccentric Englishwoman in the 1920s. Florence Trevelyan adorned her hanging gardens with pagoda-style follies and observation towers for bird-spotting (she was a keen amateur ornithologist). The tiered gardens are linked by mosaic paths and wind past tropical plants, from spiky cacti and lilies to dull English hedges.

St George's Anglican Church also dates from Trevelyan's time. Her contemporary D.H. Lawrence lived for a few years in a villa in Via Fontana Vecchia, part of which has been renamed Via David Herbert Lawrence. When King George V visited, Lawrence was the only British resident to ignore him. Undeterred, the king called on the writer and helped water his garden. In Taormina, the sickly Lawrence chose to live a solitary life, writing of sensuality. His former home is still a private house, marked by a plaque: "D.H. Lawrence, English author, lived here 1920–23."

On the north side of town, perched on **Monte Táuro**, is a tumbledown medieval **Castello** . It can be reached by a half-hour ascent up a steep, winding path that passes by the clifftop **Santuario della Madonna della Rocca**. It is a strenuous climb, which should not be attempted in high summer, but the panoramas from the top are worth the effort.

Castelmola

Via Leonardo da Vinci climbs circuitously from Taormina to **Castelmola** above, a hamlet perched on a limestone peak (there is a bus service from Piazza San Pancrazio). From this natural balcony over the sea, there is a sense of what Taormina used to be. Out of season it is home to craftsmen and part-time potters, but in summer becomes a boisterous evening outing, with trinket shops and bars lining the alleys below the ruined castle. The best known is **Bar Turrisi** (tel: 0942 28181), a bizarre place decorated in honour of Priapus, and strewn with phallic symbols. Here, the eccentric owner plies fun-loving visitors with his sweet "aphrodisiac" almond wine.

Dipping and diving

Below Taormina, sheer cliffs drop to the tempting islet of **Isola Bella** , which is now a marine reserve and a good base for diving and snorkelling (*see box page 113*).

From Via Pirandello, the cable car links the city to the pebbled beach at **Mazzarò** . Nearby are entrances to underwater caverns, where scuba-divers spot shrimps, red starfish, perch, scorpion fish and sea urchins. If you prefer your fish on a plate, leave the sea for the grey and pink cliffs above Taormina. For details of beaches close to Taormina, see Giardini-Naxos (*see page 248*). ❑

Gay Taormina

From the *belle époque* to Edwardian times, Taormina was, along with Capri, the quintessential homosexual haunt and still relishes its (undeserved) racy reputation

When Harold Acton pronounced Sicily "a polite synonym for Sodom", he was really referring to Taormina. The town was founded during a period of Greek decadence and has always lived down to its debauched reputation. In this, it has been helped by its theatrical foreign residents.

The gay resort was first publicised by a trio of Germans: a poet, a painter and a photographer. Goethe pronounced Taormina a "patch of paradise on earth" in 1787. Otto Geleng, a landscape artist, settled there nearly a century later. The Prussian's paintings of the scenery drew gasps when they were exhibited in Paris salons. Although married to a Sicilian, he was a firm believer in the dictum of girls for procreation, boys for pleasure. His younger friend, Wilhelm von Gloeden, arrived in 1880 and stayed until his death 50 years later. The exiled blond baron photographed nude Sicilian shepherd boys whose beauty elevated them to the status of Greek gods. His lithe peasants, draped in panther skins or photographed against sunsets, soon entranced jaded Berliner high society.

Oscar Wilde often helped in the compositions, crowning the boy models with laurels or posing with pan pipes. Von Gloeden swooned over Wilde, declaring the poet "beautiful as a Greek god". Wilde returned the compliment, at least artistically, but preferred his "marvellous boys" as companions.

A later voluptuary with showbiz connections was the Bavarian Gayelord Hauser, the Hollywood dietician to the stars. In the 1940s, such luminaries as Gloria Vanderbilt, Marlene Dietrich, Rita Hayworth and Joan Crawford danced until dawn at his parties.

But while most of Taormina's male population ogled the screen goddesses, Hauser was more enamoured of the local gods.

Truman Capote and Tennessee Williams were regular guests at the wild parties at Villa Hauser. Both worked in Taormina before alcohol and drugs wreaked havoc with their writing. Capote accused Williams of "hiring boys for the afternoon", but both were often picked up drunk in bars on the Corso. Drunk or sober, Williams singularly failed to live up to his "lone wolf" reputation in Taormina. Somerset Maugham was a familiar figure on the Taormina scene, indulging in "the Disneyland of sin". Inspired by gossip about gay Taormina, the poet Jean Cocteau also came to see "the boys with almond eyes".

All this was seemingly at odds with Taormina's air of twee Edwardian gentility, not to mention the mores of the English expatriate community. Douglas Sladen's book on *fin de siècle* Sicily confessed: "Nobody goes about naked, as might be imagined from the photographs." Thus reassured or disappointed, the British turned Taormina into a cosy hillside resort. Still today, Taormina remains Sicily's most gay-friendly resort, beloved as much for its aesthetic allure as for its low-key scene. ❏

RIGHT: a shepherd boy poses for von Gloeden.

BEST RESTAURANTS, BARS AND CAFÉS

Prices for a three-course dinner per person and a half-bottle of house wine:
€ = under €20
€€ = €20–35
€€€ = €35–70
€€€€ = over €70

Taormina

Sophisticated Taormina runs from regional to international in style, with an array of gastronomic hotspots. The better restaurants tend to be off Corso Umberto, which is dominated by bland or overpriced places. In general, dining in Taormina is more elegant and select than eating out in Mazzarò or Castelmola. The same is true of the bars, with the most sophisticated piano bars in the top hotels, the Grand Timeo, the San Domenico and the Metropole. The hilltop village of Castelmola offers budget alternatives to dining in Taormina itself, while at the foot of the cliffs, reached by cable car, the coastal area of Mazzarò has lively and good-value seafood trattorie.

'A Zammara
Via Fratelli Bandiera 15
Tel: 0942 24408
www.zammara.it €€€
Pleasant garden setting for traditional Sicilian dishes and variations based on fresh, seasonal produce. Closed end Jan.

Al Duomo
Vico Ebrei 11
Tel: 0942 625 656
www.ristorantealduomo.it €€
A reliable haunt, from the lively rustic-chic interior to the terrace overlooking Piazza Duomo. Expect good service, hearty seafood cuisine and a special *tortino di cioccolato* dessert. Closed Wed.

Al Giardino
Via Bagnoli Croci 84
Tel: 0942 23453
www.algiardino.net €€
Another friendly, family-run restaurant specialising in traditional Sicilian food, with a seasonal menu. Closed Tue.

L'Arco dei Cappuccini
Via Cappuccini, 1
Near Porta Messina
Tel: 0942 24893 €€€
A busy, welcoming place where the smart set gather. Excellent Sicilian cooking with an emphasis on fresh fish as well as meat. Good Sicilian wines and liqueurs. Book. Closed Wed.

Baronessa
Corso Umberto I, 148
Tel: 0942 620 163
www.ristorantebaronessa.it €€€
Grand, frescoed palazzo owned by Baronessa Calanna; panoramic terrace and Sicilian dishes.

La Botte
Piazza Santa Domenica 4
Tel: 0942 24198
www.labotte1972.it €€
Simple trattoria with large terrace. Easy-going, casual and welcoming with traditional Sicilian cooking. Closed Wed.

La Capinera
Via Nazionale 177
Tel: 0942 626 247 €€–€€€
This Michelin-starred haunt favours local, seasonal produce from all over Sicily. From the home-made breads to the fish dishes, this is an excellent choice.

Casa Niclodi
Salita Humboldt 2
Tel: 0942 620 037
www.casaniclodi.net €–€€
Seafood rules, as well as typical Sicilian dishes and reliable pizzas.

La Giara
Vico la Floresta 1
Tel: 0942 23360
www.lagiara-taormina.com €€€€
Respected restaurant and piano bar. Elegant dining, on roof or terraces with traditional menu and service. Dress smart. Book. Closed Mon and Nov, Feb, Mar.

Da Lorenzo
Via Roma 12
Tel: 0942 23480 €€€€
Overpriced but a glorious setting. Closed Wed and mid-Dec–mid-Jan.

Da Nino
Via Luigi Pirandello 37
Tel: 0942 21265 €€
An excellent, un-touristy restaurant serving Sicilian specialities; try the *gnocchi*. Fairly priced.

Don Camillo
Via C. Ottaviano 2
Tel: 0942 23198
www.trattoriadoncamillo.com €€
Unpretentious and straightforward ingredients, but a huge choice of vegetable and seafood starters.

Gambero Rosso
Via Naumachia 11
Tel: 0942 24863 €€
Busy, family-run and welcoming, with good Sicilian cuisine. Closed Thur.

Grand Hotel Timeo Restaurant
Via Teatro Greco 40
Tel: 0942 627 0200
www.grandhoteltimeo.com €€€€
Dreamy fine dining framed by a timeless panorama in which Etna and Capo Taormina are the stars. With both a Sicilian chef and an internationally renowned Northerner, the accomplished cooking mixes island recipes (for pasta or desserts) and gourmet classics (risotto). Personable staff; fine regional wines explained by a superb sommelier.

Granduca
Corso Umberto I, 170
Tel: 0942 24983
www.granducataormina.com €€€
This chic, old-fashioned and rather grand restaurant offers lovely views over the bay. The price covers the view as much as the food. Closed Tue.

Grotta Azzurra
Via Bagnoli Croci 2
Tel: 0942 24163
www.ristorantegrottazzurra

taormina.com €–€€
Typical seafood and
shellfish, as well as classic Italian fare.

Licchio's
Via Patricio 10
Tel: 0942 625 327 €€€
Charming garden setting
by Porta Messina. Both
popular and fashionable.
Excellent fresh fish,
including fish carpaccio.
Pasta dishes include lin-
guine with sea urchins.
Closed Thur.

Mamma Rosa
Via Naumachia 10
Tel: 0942 24361
www.mammarosataormina.com
€€€
With tables lining the
lively alley in the summer
months, this busy spot
serves up crispy pizzas,
cooked in a wood-fired
oven, as well as standard
Italian fare. Closed Tue in
winter.

Morgana Bar
Scesa Morgana
Tel: 0942 620 056 €–€€
This time-warp late-night
cocktail bar, decorated in
1960s Surrealist style,
has a tiny dance floor
and decent cocktails.

Principedi Cerami
Piazza San Domenico 5
Tel: 0942 613 111 €€€€
Newly awarded a Miche-
lin star, this elegant
gourmet restaurant is in
the gorgeous San
Domenico Hotel, former-
ly a monastery. Dine on
the terrace in summer.
(Closed Nov–Mar).

Siciliana
Salita Ospedale 9
Tel: 0942 24780 €€€

Surprisingly good value
for Taormina, this trattoria has its own little terrace. Try the smoked
swordfish. Closed Wed.

Terrazza Angelo
Corso Umberto I, 38
Tel: 0942 24411
www.terrazzaangelotaormina.
com €€
In the historic centre,
with a panoramic terrace
offering regional cuisine
and pizzas.

Tiramisu
Via Cappuccini 1
Tel: 0942 24803
www.ristorantetiramisutaormina.
com €
Seafood, typical Sicilian
cuisine and pizzas.

Vecchia Taormina
Vico Ebrei 3
Tel: 0942 625 589 €
An excellent pizzeria in
the heart of town, with a
wood-burning oven and
courtyard seating. Closed
Wed and lunch July–Aug.

Wunderbar
Piazza IX Aprile €
Here, on the town's main
piazza, the view really is
wunderbar. All the stars
have sipped cocktails in
this unpretentious bar;
the potent house cock-
tail, the Liz, is named
after Elizabeth Taylor.

Castelmola
In season, this tiny village
above Taormina repre-
sents a boisterous alter-
native to the town – and
the steep climb is one
way of working up an
appetite. Expect inexpen-
sive bars and *paninote-
che* (sandwich places).

Ciccino's
Piazza Duomo 3
Tel: 0942 28081 €€
A rustic pizzeria near the
cathedral, excellent for
thin pizza cooked in a
wood-fired oven.

Il Maniero
Via Salita Castello
Tel: 0942 28180 €€€
Great sea views from this
restaurant in a tower that
was once part of a castle.
Book. Closed Wed.

Giardini-Naxos
Although this resort
comes under the prov-
ince of Messina, it is only
5km (3 miles) from
Taormina.

Caffè Cavallaro
Via Umberto I, 65
Tel: 0942 51259 €
Café serving delicious
pastries such as *sfoglie
alla ricotta*, traditional
Sicilian almond confec-
tions and *cassatelle* (ice-
cream cakes).

Sea Sound
Via Jannuzzo 37
Tel: 0942 54330 €€€
Fish a speciality, served
on a garden terrace

overlooking the sea.
Simple menu, large por-
tions. Open May–Oct.

Mazzarò
La Conchiglia
Piazzale Funivia (near the
cable car)
Tel: 0942 24739 €€
Serves very good pizza
at weekends in low sea-
son and all week in sum-
mer. Closed Tue and 20
days in Oct or Nov. **Da
Giovanni**
Via Nazionale 115
Tel: 0942 23531 €€
Classic water's-edge res-
taurant with traditional
sea fare. Closed Mon
and Jan–Feb.

Delfino
Via Nazionale
Tel: 0942 23004 €€
Serves traditional dishes
from the Messina region
on a pretty terrace with
bay views. Summer only.

Il Gabbiano
Via Nazionale 115
Tel: 0942 625 128
www.ilgabbianoristorante.it €€€
Locals go for the *risotto
alla marinara* (seafood
risotto). Closed Tue.

MESSINA PROVINCE

Where Sicily meets Italy, the province offers popular coastal resorts, a seemingly remote, mountainous hinterland waiting to be explored – and seaways to the Aeolian Islands

The province of Messina's slogan is *Monte e Mare*, mountains and seas. Certainly, the province delivers rugged mountain ranges and contrasting coastlines. The Tyrrhenian coast, the northern coastline leading to Palermo, is one of rocky inlets, saltwater lakes, sand dunes and dry gravelbeds; citrus groves are fringed by myrtle, broom and prickly pear. The Ionian coast is a gentler but equally exotic coastline as far south as Taormina, with sandy shores and resorts. Both coasts offer classical sites, stumpy castles, seafood dishes and an enticing hinterland.

Messina, the city

Messina ❶, settled by the Greeks in 730 BC, was a thriving seafaring

Messina Province

0   10 km
0   10 miles

N

T Y R R H E N I A N

S E A

Acq

Marina di
Caronía

Castèl   Canneto   113
Finale   di Tusa   Caronía
❶⑧   Santo Stefano
Halaesa   Motta   di Camastra
Tusa   d'Affermo   Reitano
Pettineo   Sto Stefano

Casa   Portella
Tiberio   San Mauro   dell' Obolo
Castelverde   ❶⑦   Mistretta   1503

117
Castèl   Colle del
di Lucio   Contrasto
Palermo   M 107

Geraci Siculo   Portella
Pizzo Catarineci   M. Sambughetti   San Marino
▲ 1660   1558   1050

Petralia   Gangi   Pancallo   En
Soprana   120

power, but one beset by calamities in modern times. The 1908 earthquake killed 84,000 people in 30 seconds, while in 1943 the wartime port represented the Germans' last stand: the city was devastated and 5,000 people died during Allied bombing. As a result Messina, completely overshadowed by neighbouring Taormina, is designed on a modern grid system and intersected by wide boulevards. Although not instantly appealing, the bustling port, sunken treasures and lively bars make Messina an engaging stop before catching a ferry or touring the coast. The city is poised to learn whether the building of a suspension bridge over the Straits will ever be resumed *(see box page 241)*.

The protectress of the port is the *Madonna*, the tall statue surmounting the ancient harbour walls of the 16th-century fort, **Forte San Salvatore**, which protects the inner harbour. Curved around the sickle-shaped harbour is the neglected **Cittadella**, the

16th-century Spanish bastions and the naval base. The harbour welcomes grey NATO warships docked in deep water and long-prowed *feluccas* in pursuit of swordfish. Ever-present are the coastguard boats, scouring the Straits for illegal immigrants and drug smugglers. Despite the bustle, the overwhelming feeling is of space and sweeping views.

Just above the port, the **Cattedrale** (Mon–Sat 7.15am–7.30pm, Sun until 1.30pm) symbolises the city's survivor mentality: this Norman cathedral has witnessed medieval fires, earthquakes and wartime American firebombing (1943). It is set on a lower level than the surrounding streets that were redeveloped after the 1908 earthquake, when the cathedral was shattered, its 26 granite columns reduced to rubble and its ceiling collapsed. The sculpted main portal and part of the Gothic facade are original, while the harmonious interior features a painted wooden ceiling, 14th-century

The Orion Fountain and Torre dell'Orologio in Piazza del Duomo, Messina.

FAR LEFT: fountain detail.

TIP

Messina's port is linked to Villa San Giovanni in Calabria by a continuous service of passenger, car and cargo ferries run by various lines. With so many ferries, you can just turn up and buy a ticket. Instead, Milazzo is the Sicilian link to the Aeolian Islands. For ferries and hydrofoils contact: **Siremar** (www.siremar.it; see page 263).

mosaics in the semicircular apses, glittering Renaissance altars and a Gagini statue of *St John the Baptist*.

An amusing curiosity is the free-standing **campanile** outside, which houses the world's largest astronomical clock; at midday, folkloristic mechanical figures, including a flapping cockerel, ring the bells to the roar of a flag-waving lion. There is even Jesus coming out of a tomb and the Madonna presenting a letter to the burghers of Messina to sounds of Schubert's *Ave Maria*. The **Tesorio** (Treasury; daily 9am–1.30pm; charge) displays silverware, reliquaries and a 14th-century *Madonna* surrounded by saints and archangels. The **Orion Fountain** (1547) in Piazza del Duomo is a surviving Renaissance masterpiece. It is a tribute to Orion, a mythical city founder, and also a celebration of the first aqueduct to supply the city with water. Human figures represent the rivers Tiber, Nile, Ebro and Camaro.

Piazza Antonello, just north, houses a cluster of Art Nouveau buildings leading to the vaulted Vittorio Emanuele gallery. In a neighbouring square is the small **Chiesa Annunziata dei Catalani** (Mon–Sat 8–11am), a sunken Arab-Norman church with Byzantine echoes. Built over a temple to Neptune, this eclectic church has Norman arches, blind arcading, 13th-century portals and honeycomb apses. The mellow stonework is often festooned with flowers: as Messina University chapel, it is much in demand for academic weddings.

Due to the earthquakes and war damage, the city churches are a wayward mixture of restoration and invention. However, **Santa Maria degli Alemanni**, a few blocks south of the cathedral, is an authentic roof-less Gothic ruin, founded by the Order of Teutonic Knights.

Messina's magpie approach to architecture is illustrated by the neoclassical Town Hall, mock-Renaissance Chamber of Commerce, Fascistic Tribunal and Art Deco Prefecture. Contemporary churches can be Rhenish, Bavarian, Spanish or, like San Giuliano, a Byzantine pastiche. Even genuine relics are given a contemporary twist by an incongruous setting: San Francesco, a Gothic fortress of a church, overlooks a frothy ice-cream parlour.

In Piazza Unità is Montorsoli's **Fountain of Neptune**, but the original Renaissance sculpture lies in the **Museo Regionale** (Mon–Tue and Thur–Sat 9am–1.30pm, and 4–6.30pm in summer, 3–5.30pm in winter, Sun 9am–1pm; charge), on Via della Libertà. The museum mostly displays art salvaged from the 1908 earthquake, including works by Caravaggio and Antonello da Messina (1430–78), Sicily's master painter and southern Italy's greatest Renaissance artist. His moving polyptych of the *Madonna with Saints Gregory and Benedict* blends Flemish technique with Italian delicacy and a Sicilian sense of light. The best-preserved panel is the *Madonna and Child*.

Writer Rodolfo de Mattei likened the city to "a sailing ship, low in the

BELOW: Messina's Fountain of Neptune.

water, ready for a night cruise". Indeed, mercantile Messina looks romantic at night, its lights glittering along the harbour front. Summer strollers take a *passeggiata* from the seafront to the lively *cafés* on Piazza Cairoli. After dinner, under-age lovers enjoy the scenic drive up Viale Umberto to the botanical gardens.

Lido di Mortelle

In summer, city life shifts to **Lido di Mortelle**, a youthful resort 10km (6 miles) north of Messina. En route, the coastal road passes the **Ganzirri lake**, once famed for its mussel beds, now a popular place for dinner in summer, and the lighthouse of **Torre del Faro** on Capo Pelaro, guarding the **Stretto di Messina**, the narrow Straits of Messina separating Sicily from Italy's toe. This peninsula was once graced by a temple of Neptune whose columns ended up, shattered, in Messina Cathedral. Today's view is sadly marred by gigantic pylons and power cables that supply Sicily with electricity.

Over-popular Lido di Mortelle, just around the cape, offers sandy beaches and fish restaurants. As a result, the air is heavy with a peculiar combination of petrol fumes and grilled swordfish.

The Tyrrhenian coast

To get from Messina to Milazzo 41km (26 miles) away – where ferries sail to Strómboli and Lípari – either take the fast route on the *autostrada* A20, or, for the best scenery, follow the SS113, the old Roman road. The first stretch climbs the **Monti Peloritani**, winding past pine groves, broom, oleanders and geraniums. But even from the motorway are dazzling glimpses of azure inlets through the pines. On the way out of town are views of three ruined forts and apricot-coloured churches in the hills.

Tunnels thread through pine and olive groves to **Milazzo ❷**. The vision of this verdant peninsula is slightly marred by the presence of an oil refinery. Compensations lie in the welcoming breezes and dramatic castle, with views of the jagged green spit stretching towards the Aeolian Islands (*see page 251*). While waiting for a ferry, be tempted to sample the local swordfish or *bottarga* (tuna roe).

The SS113 allows panoramic views of pine forests and the Straits, particularly from Portella San Rizzo, which hugs the crest of the Peloritani range. The coastline from Messina to Palermo has been heavily fortified since Aragonese times. The headlands are still dotted with Spanish defensive towers fully exploited by the French. The Napoleonic forces boasted of being able to transmit a message to Naples in under two hours by lighting a string of fires in the coastal towers.

BELOW LEFT:
Messina Cathedral.

The bridge over the Straits

The dream of building a bridge across the 3km (2-mile) Messina Straits separating Calabria from Sicily is currently just a pipe-dream. The Messina bridge, which would be the longest in the world, was the pet project of Silvio Berlusconi, but is currently on hold. While bridge supporters see it as a boost to the Sicilian economy, ferryboat operators, seismologists and environmentalists have long been against it, as are cynics who say the funds would only be siphoned off by the Mafia on both sides of the bridge. What's more, given the undeveloped nature of Sicily and the South, controversy rages over the wisdom of investing so much public money in a single engineering feat, with its six traffic lanes and two railway lines, when the money could be better spent on basic Sicilian infrastructure, especially roads and railways. Even on technical grounds, the project is fraught with doubts: the bridge will span a busy shipping lane and must also withstand high winds and earthquakes. Construction began in 2010, but is currently stalled while Mario Monti's technocratic government reassesses the scheme. It looks as if the Messina bridge, the final step in the unification of Italy, is still some way off.

TIP

In Milazzo, a stroll along the Al Faro promontory from the lighthouse to Capo di Milazzo leads through lush vegetation to the cape. For the energetic, a climb to the heights of Monte Trinità provides a view towards the Aeolian Islands.

Head for the walled city, passing the Baroque palaces that adorn the lower town, particularly along Via Umberto I. Here too, the **Duomo Nuovo**, the new cathedral, is memorable for its Renaissance paintings in the apse. **Salita San Francesco**, a steep stairway, climbs through the Spanish Quarter to the impressive medieval citadel, its flanks encrusted with churches. The 17th-century **San Salvatore** belonged to a Benedictine abbey whereas **San Rocco** represents an older, fortified church. **San Francesco di Paola** is a frescoed 15th-century shell with a Baroque facelift.

Facing the castle is the **Chiesa del Rosario**, once a seat of the Spanish Inquisition. This Dominican church is studded with stuccowork, an oddly fluffy vision for the rigorous interrogators.

The **Castello** (guided tours summer 11.30am, 4–6pm, winter 9.30–11.30am, 2.30–3.30pm; charge), perched beside a rocky precipice, occupies the site of the Greek acropolis. Erected between 1237 and 1240 and originally Arab-Norman, the citadel later fell into Hohenstaufen,

Aragonese and Spanish hands. The castle's finest hour was in July 1860, when its seizure by Garibaldi's forces spelt the rout of the Royalists and the Republican conquest of Sicily. The surviving fortress is of 13th-century Hohenstaufen dynastic design with Aragonese walls. A Gothic gateway leads to the keep and parliamentary Great Hall. Also within the castle walls is the Baroque **Duomo Vecchio**, and the ruins of the 14th-century Palazzo dei Giurati.

Boat trips to the **Baia del Tono** ❸ visit reefs, coves and grottoes, including favoured swimming spots such as the Baia San Antonio or Baia la Renella. Near the Baia del Tono is **Grotta di Polifemo**, Polyphemus' cave, where Odysseus blinded the Cyclops. The 7km (4-mile) boat trip around the peninsula from **Al Faro** (the lighthouse) to Baia del Tono affords views of Sicily's two active volcanoes, Etna and Strómboli.

Inland excursions

If the hinterland beckons, then **Santa Lucia del Mela** ❹, 20km (12 miles) inland from Milazzo along a winding rural road, is a Saracen village with a Norman castle once on the Lombard silk route. The Norman cathedral contains a Gothic portal and an Antonello Gagini statuette of St Lucy.

Back on the SS113, take the turning south for another foray into the hinterland. **Castroreale** ❺, a shabby upland village, was founded by the Siculi in the 8th century BC. Although the settlement flourished as a medieval barony, a ruined tower is all that remains of Frederick II's summer home.

The fertile coastal plain around Castoreale abounds in vineyards, olive plantations and orange groves, while the neighbouring coastal town of Castroreale Terme appeals to thermal spa enthusiasts. An inland road from **Castoreale Terme** leads to the archaeological site of **Longane** ❻

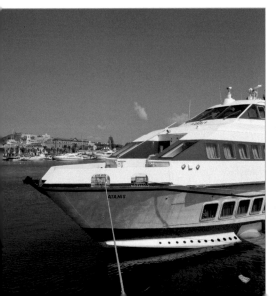

BELOW: Milazzo.

(9am–one hour before sunset), near **Rodi**. Set on the edge of the Peloritani mountains, this megalithic and Sikel settlement was razed by Messina in the 5th century BC. The remains of a turreted fort are visible, and there are Bronze Age cavity tombs in the nearby necropolis. From Rodi, join the SS185 as if returning to the coast.

Just before Castroreale Terme lies the Roman site of **San Biagio ⑦**, a Roman villa built in the 1st century (daily 9am–one hour before sunset; charge). The baths feature a black and white mosaic of fishermen and dancing dolphins.

The SS113 takes you westwards to **Oliveri ⑧** and a chance to exchange churches for seafood and excellent beaches. Between here and Cefalù is arguably the cleanest stretch of coastline on the island. Oliveri itself is a standard Sicilian resort with a Norman-Arab feudal castle and sandy beaches. On the seafront is a converted *tonnara*, the traditional tuna fishery, a reminder of life before tourism.

Oliveri is on the **Golfo di Patti**, a wilder spot than the Gulf of Milazzo, stretching west to the rocky ridges of Capo Calavà. Its bays are framed by the moody Nebrodi mountains. The coastal road crosses *fiumare*, wide, dry torrent-beds, and overlooks World War II pillbox defences.

Tindari

Dominating the Capo Tindari headland is **Tindari ⑨**, formerly Tyndaris, one of the last Greek colonies established in Sicily, founded by Dionysius in 396 BC. Pliny records that in AD 70 much of the city slipped into the sea. Despite subsidence and earthquake, the Graeco-Roman city prospered until razed by the Arabs in 836.

The **Santuario della Madonna Nera** (summer 6.45am–12.30pm, 2.30–8pm, winter 6.45am–12.45pm, 2.30–7pm) stands on the site of an ancient acropolis. The glittering sanctuary is revered all over southern Italy as a shrine to a black-faced Byzantine icon with miraculous powers. The seated 16th-century *Madonna Nera* bears the motto: *Nigra sum, sed hermosa* (I am black, but beautiful). Among other miracles, she is credited with causing the sea to withdraw to provide a magic mattress of sand to cushion a child's fall over the cliff.

The **archaeological park** (daily 9am–two hours before sunset; charge) is pleasingly wild. Italian visitors, of course, are more impressed by the sacred *Black Madonna* housed in the church bordering the park. The Greek city covers a Bronze Age site and has left its mark in impressive **boundary walls** (3rd century BC) and assorted public buildings. The **Graeco-Roman theatre** cannot compare with Taormina's but enjoys a superb natural setting overhanging the bay. Classical drama, concerts and opera are now performed here in summer. A wide thoroughfare, one of three original *decumani*, links the theatre to the vaulted **basilica**. This Augustan basilica was once a grand entrance to the *agora*, a ceremonial space for meetings and festivals.

Celebrating the Black Madonna, the Santuario della Madonna Nera is a contemporary effusion of kitsch beloved by Sicilians who make pilgrimages throughout the year, particularly on the Madonna's feast day, 8 September. The A20 autostrada exit is just 8km (5 miles) away, and Messina only 65km (40 miles).

BELOW: Santuario della Madonna Nera.

Sailors entering the Straits of Messina were wary of the twin demons of Scylla, a female six-headed sea monster, and Charybdis, a whirlpool. In reality, these were clashing currents meeting in the Straits. Although the sea's flow was diverted after the 1908 earthquake, strange counter-currents still exist, colourfully known as "bastardi".

BELOW: Santo Stéfano di Camastra ceramics.

Nearby are the remains of Roman baths, villas, workshops and taverns. One villa is adorned with geometrical mosaics, while the thermal baths enclose mosaics of dolphins, bulls, warriors and the *Trinacria*, the symbol of Sicily. The on-site **antiquarium** displays sculptures, ceramics, a tragic mask and a bust of Augustus.

Below Cape Tindari is the **Oliveri lagoon**, one of Sicily's loveliest natural havens. Migratory birds, including grebes, coots and egrets, are drawn to the pale-green saltwater pools and wide beaches of translucent grey pebbles. The lagoon's sands are a sublime spot for a picnic of fresh bread and local *caciocavallo* cheese.

Patti ⑩, set on a low hill facing the sea, was damaged in the 1978 earthquake but the medieval quarter, linking Via Ceraolo and the cathedral, has a quiet charm and several art-filled churches. The remodelled **cathedral** is home to remarkable treasures: a subtle *Madonna* by Antonello da Saliba and the Renaissance **sarcophagus** of Queen Adelasia, Roger I's wife, complete with the original Norman effigy.

Sadly, this historic hill town is ringed by a jagged necklace of new development. Even so, Patti has recently unearthed its greatest attraction, a **Roman villa** (daily 9am– one hour before sunset; charge) at **Marina di Patti**. This sumptuous late Imperial villa was destroyed by an earthquake in AD 4 but restored and then occupied until Byzantine times. After centuries of oblivion, it was rediscovered during the construction of the motorway in 1973. The gracious rooms lead off a porticoed peristyle, looking incongruous beside the motorway flyover. The mosaics display geometric, animal, figurative and floral motifs, often of African inspiration. But Patti suffers from wilful neglect.

After a surfeit of art and architecture, picnic among the poppies, as the Roman aristocracy did, or retreat to the beaches of Marina di Patti.

Forays inland

On the road from Patti to Capo d'Orlando are a cluster of resorts fighting a battle against coastal ribbon development and Mafia influ-

ence, currently losing the former but winning the latter. On the Capo's promontory, reached by a hard climb, are the remains of a medieval castle and the sanctuary of **Santa Maria di Capo d'Orlando**, erected in 1598.

From the sandy resort of **Gioiosa Marea ⓫**, walk up to the ghost town of **Gioiosa Vecchia**, abandoned after an 18th-century landslide. Brolo, just west, has a crenellated Saracen tower and crumbling city walls, but Sicilians come here for the fish soups, squid dishes and salami from the hills behind **Brolo**.

A rural foray inland visits Raccuja, Tortorici and Castell'Umberto, a case of the journey being more pleasurable than the destination. Citrus groves give way to pine forests and steep ridges, with stunning views from the hilltop villages to the Aeolian Islands. A tortuous inland road leads from Brolo to **Raccuja**. In winter, continue south along the SS116 to the ski resort of Floresta. Heading back to the coast from **Floresta**, turn off left to visit a couple of villages before returning to Capo d'Orlando. **Tortorici ⓬** is traditionally associated with the Mafia, but has several fine churches and school of Gagini sculptures.

About 10km (6 miles) north along switchback roads is **Castell'Umberto ⓭**, a former feudal domain with a long Dominican tradition. Constant landslides persuaded the citizens to abandon the *centro storico*, even if it still has a whimsical charm, with its ruined castle and vine-hung churches.

Capo d'Orlando and west

Capo d'Orlando ⓮ is a windswept headland subject to sudden storms. Set on the edge of a fertile plain, this sprawling resort offers a sandy beach strewn with whale-shaped boulders, or a climb to the ruined medieval castle and church perched on the cape.

Sant'Agata di Militello ⓯, the first significant resort west of Capo

d'Orlando, is known for its promenades, popular pebbled beach and seafood, with the local castle turned into a restaurant.

Pottery fans can follow the SS113 west to **Santo Stéfano di Camastra ⓰**, one of Sicily's main ceramics centres *(see page 201)*. Lining the roadside, the piles of pottery make purchase a mere formality.

From here, the enchanting SS117 road leads 16km (10 miles) inland across the Nebrodi range to **Mistretta ⓱**, a rust-coloured town commanding a ridge. With its ruined feudal castle, sculpted **Chiesa Madre** (1630), red-tiled houses and cobbled streets, the town has a faded charm.

Castel di Tusa ⓲, which borders Palermo Province, is noted for its ruined castle, rocky beach and eclectic avant-garde hotel, the Atelier sul Mare (tel: 0921 334 295; www.atelier sulmare.it).

Inland is the pretty town of **Tusa**, and access to the Greek site of **Halaesa** (9am–one hour before sunset), a city founded in 5 BC. Remains include the *agora*, boundary walls, theatre and temple.

The Trinacria, *the symbol of Sicily, represents the three capes of the island (which was once called* Trinacria*). The Medusa denotes the protection of Athena, Sicily's patron goddess.*

BELOW: reception at Atelier sul Mare, Castel di Tusa.

TIP

The **Festa dei Giudei** is a unique annual Easter event at San Fratello. Men and women dress up as *Giudei* (Jews) in bright red jackets and hose, covered with Arab ornament. They carry trumpets and wear grotesque masks. This is by no means anti-Semitic. It is assumed the tradition started in order to poke fun at the Jewish role in the Catholic ritual of the Easter Passion, but now it is just an occasion for making merry.

Monti Nebrodi

A rural drive through the wooded hinterland of the **Nebrodi** mountains takes you into remote, rugged hill-walking country. For an adventurous trail, try the circuit around the **Parco Regionale dei Nebrodi**, starting anywhere between Patti and Sant'Agata di Militello, where road signs indicate the Parco and San Fratello.

San Fratello ⑲, 18km (11 miles) from the coast, is one of the most evocative Nebrodi villages and is particularly colourful during its famous demonic Easter festival, the Feast of the Jews, **Festa dei Giudei**, a shrieking costumed chase. It is not so much anti-Semitic as Sicilian, hence a sacrifice of subtlety to spectacle (*see margin left*). This scenic mountain village has a Norman church and a 15th-century Franciscan monastery. Horse-breeding has always played a big part in community life here, and each September Arab horses are put through their paces in the village.

Further along, the SS289 snakes through rugged terrain to **Cesarò ⑳**, where on 15 August they, too, celebrate horses in the Palio dei Nebrodi.

This village of shepherds also has a ruined castle, destroyed during a battle between feuding dynasties in 1334.

From **Portella Fèmmina Morta ㉑**, before Cesarò, hikers can reach the lofty **Monte Soro**, the highest point in the Nebrodi at 1,847 metres (6,060ft), or adventure-seekers can opt for an off-road tour. Here, too, is the **Lago Biviere di Cesarò**, an ancient lake that turns bright pink with algae in the hotter months, and a spot popular with migratory storks and the marsh turtle.

At **Cesarò** an appealing detour of 20km (12 miles) along the SS120 leads to **Troìna ㉒**, at 1,120 metres (3,675ft) the highest town in Sicily. This panorama of hills and valleys was once enjoyed by prehistoric man. Still visible are the remains of ancient Greek walls, while the **Chiesa Madre** has a fine 16th-century campanile and medieval *Madonna and Child*.

To complete the Nebrodi circuit, from Cesarò the SS120 leads to **Abbazia di Maniace**, Admiral Nelson's home (*see page 220*) and on to Randazzo (*see page 219*), where the Sunday morning market displays Nebrodi crafts; then to **Floresta**, and after some breathtaking bends, back down to **Patti** and the coast. The complete circuit is about 230km (143 miles).

Messina's Ionian coast

This narrow coastal strip is characterised by a contrast between the barren slopes of the Monti Peloritani (highest point 1,374 metres/4,500ft) facing the shore and the wooded slopes facing inland. As you travel south, there are architectural contrasts between the Baroque or modern coastal towns and the medieval settlements in the hilly hinterland.

From Messina, the motorway hugs the shore south for 52km (32 miles) from the narrow Straits of Messina to **Taormina ㉓** (*see page 229*), hemmed in by mountains.

Exploring Monti Nebrodi

The rounded silhouettes of the Nebrodi offer vistas of rocky outcrops or rolling hills covered in oak and beech woods or rough pasture. Compared with the Madonie range, the Nebrodi mountains are less accessible: exploration is necessarily slow, since the lack of east–west roads frequently means retracing one's steps to the coast. Before **Cesarò**, as you climb the range, Portella Fèmmina Morta offers a detour on foot or with an off-road vehicle to **Monte Soro**, the highest point in the Nebrodi at 1,847 metres (6,060ft), with fabulous views, a lake, thick woods and wildlife that includes falcons, eagles, herons, or even wild cats and wolves. Near fresh water, look out for wild fowl, the Sicilian marsh tit, and the wonderfully named *Tachybaptus ruficolis*. The name means "fast-bathing red stomach", an apt description of the little grebe. As a base, the most typical Nebrodi village is arguably the strange **San Fratello** (Parco dei Nebrodi, www.parcodeinebrodi.it).

If travelling on the A18 motorway, at **Santa Teresa di Riva** leave the coastal crowds for mountain air and curious hamlets. Despite the proximity of Taormina, this is timeless Sicily, as remote as anywhere on the island. The scenery is stark: skeletal peaks and brooding ravines; mountains gouged by winter torrents and scorched brown in summer. Such fierceness is softened by sweet-scented scrub and the curves of Moorish monasteries.

Sávoca

Just inland is the battered mountain village of **Sávoca ㉔**, best known for its macabre mummies, embalmed in a crypt by local monks, and for its associations with *The Godfather (see box page 248)*.

The catacombs of the **Cappuccini monastery** (variable, tel: 349 425 4398; donation) contain 32 ghoulish mummified corpses dating from the 17th century. At a time when corpses were thrown into the communal ditch, genteel mummification was a tradition among noble families. The bodies were drained, sprinkled with salt and left to dry for a year before being washed in vinegar, aired and then dressed in their original clothes. These gruesome, wizened faces and shrunken puppet-like forms are mummified abbots, lawyers, noblemen and priests. Now run by a religious association, this spartan former monastery accepts guests in its unghoulish rooms.

After this macabre scene, leave the monastery for the evocative medieval village, a former Saracen stronghold. Sávoca's name derives from *sambuca*, not the famed Italian liqueur, but the elder trees that still perfume the hills. A paved path climbs cacti-dotted terraces and olive groves to the village, a scene embracing churches overgrown with prickly pear, a tumbledown dovecote, and terraces slipping into the sea. The church of San Niccolò lost its choir in a landslide but kept its dignity, while the **Chiesa Madre** retains the charm that caught Coppola's eye for *The Godfather.* This solitary church, on a narrow ridge overlooking the sea, was renovated with film money. The scruffy Bar Vitelli, immortalised in Michael Corleone's wedding banquet, comfortably hosts

Robert de Niro, who starred in The Godfather II, *said of Sicilians: "Ultimately, everyone else is a foreigner. Suspicion runs high. And although they are very cordial to you as a tourist, you are still aware of this. Sicilians have a way of watching without watching; they'll scrutinise you thoroughly and you won't even know it."*

BELOW: Sávoca.

Tourist signs.

BELOW: Giardini-Naxos.

peasants and *borghesi*, united in their thirst for a cool *granita di limone* (lemon sorbet).

Casalvécchio Sículo, charmingly set above Sávoca, is livelier but less complex, with a gilded parish church and windswept views over terraces. On the outskirts of the village, take the first turning left, a steep road signposted to **SS Pietro e Paolo d'Agro** ㉕, a monastic church down in the Val d'Agro. Despite its desolate location on the bank of the dry Agro river, this is the most significant Arab-Norman church in eastern Sicily. The twin-domed exterior is reminiscent of a Turkish mosque. A banded facade combines red brick, black lava, cool limestone and grey granite. Restored in 1171, the church is a synthesis of Byzantine and Norman styles. Moorish roundness and decorative flourishes compete with Norman verticality and austerity.

Giardini-Naxos

Before ascending to Taormina, consider neighbouring **Giardini-Naxos** ㉖, Sicily's first Greek colony. It was founded (as Naxos) on an ancient lava flow by Euboeans in 735 BC and became a springboard for colonisation of Catania and the east coast. But after supporting Athens against Siracusa, the colony was destroyed by Dionysius in 403 BC.

The archaeological site (daily 9am–one hour before sunset; charge) occupies the promontory of **Capo Schiso** (follow signs for *scavi*, excavations). A stretch of Greek lava-stone city walls remains, but the elusive **Temple of Aphrodite** is still being excavated, as are some villas. The small museum displays Greek, Roman and Byzantine finds, including a head of Silenus, god of fertility and wine.

Lemon groves are giving way to ribbon development, for Giardini-Naxos is Sicily's fastest-growing beach resort, as is neighbouring **Letojanni** ㉗. Still, for the young crowd there are compensations: cheap and cheerful trattorie, wide beaches fringed by volcanic rocks and a riotous nightlife that Silenus might have enjoyed. Moreover, unlike Catania province, this stretch of coast offers sandy, rocky or pebbled shores, with an abundance of free and private beaches. ❑

The Godfather's Sicily

The Godfather is still big business in Sicily. After Mount Etna, it remains the most popular excursion from Taormina. The typical tour whisks visitors to **Sávoca**, where *The Godfather* was filmed. Francis Ford Coppola found his perfect setting in its dusty piazza, the windswept church, the shots of Etna smouldering in the distance and the shimmer of the Ionian Sea. Follow in Al Pacino's footsteps by stopping for a lemon *granita* in the battered Vitelli bar. Then admire Santa Lucia, where the wedding scene between Apollonia and Michael was shot. The tour continues to **Forza d'Agro**, one of the loveliest medieval villages in Sicily, with panoramic views. (Book through Taormina agencies, such as Sicily Life, www.sicilylife.com.)

BEST RESTAURANTS, BARS AND CAFÉS

Prices for a three-course dinner per person and a half-bottle of house wine:
€ = under €20
€€ = €20–35
€€€ = €35–70
€€€€ = over €70

Messina

Al Padrino
Via Santa Cecilia 54
Tel: 090 292 1000 €€
This inexpensive trattoria is a good place to sample regional specialities; try the house dish, *melanzane al Padrino* (aubergine stuffed with pasta and ricotta). Closed Sat dinner and Sun.

Da Bacco
Via Cernaia 15
Tel: 090 771 420 €€
Hostaria with good range of seafood. Closed Sun.

Davai
Via XXVII Luglio 36
Tel: 090 293 4865 €€€
Welcoming restaurant based on the old Teatro Savoia serving *cucina messinese*, the best of Messina-style dishes. Closed Mon.

Le Due Sorelle
Piazza Municipio 4
Tel: 090 44720 €€
A long-established but modernised trattoria. Good wines and simple cooking. Book. Closed Sat lunch and Sun.

Gambero Rosso
Via Consolare Pompea
Tel: 090 393 873
www.ilgamberorossomessina.it
€€
Good, inexpensive. Fish, mostly. Closed Tue.

Osteria del Campanile
Via Loggia dei Mercanti 7
Tel: 090 711 418
www.osteriadelcampanile.com €€
Behind the Duomo, this simple restaurant has a good range of pasta dishes, as well as crispy pizzas. Closed Sun except summer.

Shawarma
Via MGiurba 8
Tel: 090 712 213 €
A welcome break from Italian cuisine, this restaurant serves up North African specialities such as tagines and couscous. Closed Mon.

Trattoria del Popolo
Piazza del Popolo 30
Tel: 090 671 148 €€
An appealing restaurant with outdoor tables and seafood specialities such as squid in breadcrumbs. Closed Sun.

Capri Leone, Messina

Antica Filanda
Contrada Raviola
Tel: 0941 919 704
www.anticafilanda.net €€
Overlooking the Aeolian Islands, this restaurant focuses on produce and dishes from the Nebrodi mountains. Expect black Nebrodi pork, Montalbano provola cheese, ricotta and Nebrodi goats' cheeses. Closed Mon and mid Jan to mid-Feb.

Milazzo

Al Castello
Via Federico di Svevia 20
Tel: 090 928 2175 €€€
A charming place to be in summer when tables are outside, lit by the floodlights on the walls of the Castello. Sicilian cooking. Closed Tue.

Al Pescatore
Via Marina Garibaldi 176
Tel: 090 928 6595 €€
Popular trattoria known for its seafood served at reasonable prices. Decorated to match its passion for fish. Closed Thur.

Covo del Pirata
Via San Francesco 2
Tel: 090 928 4437
www.ilcovodelpirata.it €€€
Cucina messinese served in rooms decorated with a marine theme. Closed Wed.

La Casalinga
Via D'Amico 13
Tel: 090 922 2697 €€
A fish specialist; the house dish is spaghetti with crab sauce. Closed Sun dinner Oct–June.

Piccolo Casale
Via Riccardo d'Amico 12
Tel: 090 922 4479
www.piccolocasale.it €€€
Discreet trattoria, elegant and with flowery terrace. A favourite with locals. Dinner only. Closed Jan and Aug.

Letojanni

Da Nino
Via Rizzo 29
Tel: 0942 36147
www.danino.it €€€
Warm and welcoming hotel/restaurant in a charming location. Lots of fresh fish dishes.

Peppe
Via Vittorio Emanuele 346
Tel: 094 236 159
www.hoteldapeppe.it €€
Old-style trattoria, part of 45-room hotel. Simple fare. Sicilian dishes. Closed Nov–Feb.

RIGHT: Sicilians have a sweet tooth.

THE AEOLIAN ISLANDS

Although two of the Isole Eolie still have active
volcanoes, the archipelago is characterised by a
sleepy charm and elemental landscape

Palermo

The setting is beguiling. Arching
out from the north coast of Sicily
lies an underwater volcanic ridge
200km (125 miles) long, from which
rise the rocky islands of the Aeolian
chain. But it is the exotic atmosphere
and elemental majesty that make the
Aeolians (Isole Eolie) unique.

Lípari is the largest island and
the gateway to the archipelago,
while Panarea is the most polished,
Salina the dreamiest, Vulcano the
most smouldering, and Filicudi
and Alicudi the least developed. For
adventure-lovers, the Aeolian Islands
are arguably the most dramatic in
Sicily, and the most brazenly beautiful, shaped by volcanic eruption and
wind erosion.

Even by Sicilian standards, the Aeolians have seen cavalcades of settlers on
their shores. Seven of the islands are
inhabited today, as they have been since
before the Bronze Age. The remains of
Iron Age villages and Roman sites vie
for attention, along with the Greek
graves within the Spanish walls of an
ancient citadel. And that's just Lípari,
the largest island.

There is also a lyrical quality to the
Aeolian Islands, with their clashing
colours, mysterious light and mythical resonance, especially on Salina. It

is this light, this wind that gives the
sense of what the islands felt like in
Homer's day.

Lípari

Home to just over 11,000 of the total
Aeolian population, Lípari is the
lively hub of the archipelago, and
the most interesting in terms of history and culture. Part of the appeal
of Lípari is also its blinding bright-
ness, contrasting white pumice, black
obsidian and the glittering sea, with
the seabed scoured white by pumice.

Main attractions

PARCO ARCHEOLOGICO DIANA (LÍPARI)
MUSEO ARCHEOLOGICO EOLIANO
  (LÍPARI)
SAN CALÓGERO (LÍPARI)
SANTA MARINA DI SALINA (SALINA)
POLLARA (SALINA)
GRAN CRATERE (VULCANO)
FANGHI, PORTO DI LEVANTE (MUD
  BATHS, VULCANO)
YACHTING VILLAGES (PANAREA)
CALCARA BEACH (PANAREA)
STROMBOLICCHIO (STRÓMBOLI)
GROTTA DEL BUE MARINO (FILICUDI)

LEFT: view from Vulcano.
RIGHT: bar in Lípari town.

As the boat approaches, the crowded roofs of **Lípari town**  come into view, dominated by a citadel, the Castello, set on a small hill, with the massive Spanish bastion enclosing the cathedral and the 17th-century bishop's palace. Hydrofoils dock at **Marina Corta** on the southern side of the citadel, ferries on the north side at **Marina Lunga**. The two are linked by the main shopping street, Corso Vittorio Emanuele. The main sights are all within a short stroll of the harbour within the **Castello** walls. These include the cathedral, museums and an archaeological park.

From the Castello you can look down on the whole town, a cool vantage point among the pines. This also provides the best views of the main classical sites, the **Parco Archeologico Diana** and the **necropolis**, both to the west of Corso Vittorio. The excavations of the earliest stronghold unpeel the historical layers, illustrating the settlement on

Fisherman in Lípari.

Lípari, beginning 2,000 years before the Romans.

The citadel is also home to a heavily remodelled Norman cathedral and the superb **Museo Archeologico Eoliano** (daily 9am–1pm, 3–6pm; closed Sun afternoon; charge), containing one of the finest Neolithic collections in Europe. This sprawling museum spans prehistoric and Roman times, with displays of prehistoric funerary urns, obsidian blades, Neolithic pottery, Roman amphorae and Greek masks. This is in addition to the re-creation of a Bronze Age burial ground and a big section on marine archaeology, complete with displays of wrecks.

If you are reeling from the Castello, retreat to the maze of backstreets off **Via Garibaldi**. Ringing the landward side of the Castello, these picturesque alleys will clear your mind and prepare you for your first taste of the Aeolians. Barbecued fish or pasta with tomatoes and capers will help.

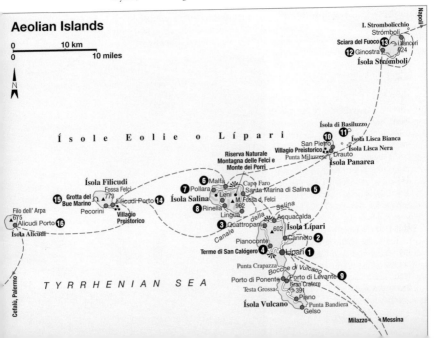

Aeolian Islands

Canneto

A reliable road rings Lípari, linking the eight main villages, and a taxi tour provides a sensible introduction to the island. **Canneto ❷**, 4km (2½ miles) north of Lípari town, has a long pebble and black sand beach and bustling bars and trattorie. About 1km (1,100 yards) further you can take a winding path down to **Spiaggia della Papesca**, a sandy beach whitened by pumice dust. It is this dust that turns the sea an extraordinary turquoise all along to **Porticello**, about 2km (1¼ miles) to the north. Pumice is still quarried here, and turned into building blocks, cosmetics and fertiliser, but you can pick up small pumice stones all along the beaches.

Continuing the circuit of the island for 2km (1¼ miles) or so, you come to the northernmost village, **Acquacalda**, on the slopes of **Monte Chirica**, at 602 metres (1,806ft) Lípari's tallest mountain, with pebbled beach views of Salina across the narrow straits. From Acquacalda the road winds up past the **Puntazze** rocks, overlooking Strómboli and Alicudi, and continues through green countryside for 5km

(3 miles) to **Quattropani ❸**, the site of a pretty church. Another 6km (4 miles) on, past several small hamlets, is **Pianoconte**, home to Lípari's largest vineyards. Just outside the village, down a narrow road towards the coast, are the thermal baths of **San Calógero ❹**, where you can explore the ancient site and splash yourself with the hot therapeutic waters that come out of the ground in a domed chamber dating from the Mycenaean period.

Back on the main road, the circular route winds back down another 4km (2½ miles) to Lípari town, passing **Quattrocchi** where the belvedere provides a resting place and views across to Vulcano.

Salina

Beguiling Salina represents the changing face of the islands. As with Panarea, the mellow island now welcomes a few hedonistic retreats. But Salina's boutique hotels are often surpassed by its boutique wine estates. Yet the verdant island also feels the most timeless, with quiet beaches matched by volcanic peaks thickly wooded with conifer, sweet chestnut and oak.

> ### DRINK
> No visit to Salina is complete without sampling the fine, honey-coloured Malvasia wine that leaves a slightly sulphurous aftertaste.

The Aeolians today

The mineral-rich volcanic rocks of the Aeolians provided the basis of their early wealth: obsidian, a black, glass-like rock used to make cutting tools, was mined in Lípari and traded all over the Mediterranean more than 5,000 years ago, and pumice works survive on the island. But the overall decline of mining still led to a mass exodus, from a population of over 20,000 in 1911 to around 12,600 today. Many resettled in Australia in the 1950s, and you will hear returned émigrés talking with a Queensland twang. There is even a Miss Eolie competition in Sydney.

Today, tourism has turned around the fortunes of the Aeolians, though not without an eco dimension. Amid fears for the future of the islands, a tourism tax is now levied, but it is still tokenistic and serves to safeguard the

future of these volcanic specks. Strict environmental controls, the designation of nature reserves and the relative remoteness of the islands ensure that even in high summer you can find an empty beach. Only Lípari has not been declared a nature reserve.

The islands have prospered, with volcano tourism taking off on Vulcano and Strómboli, cultural tourism boosting Lípari, wine tourism raising the spirits on Salina, and elite tourism transforming Panarea into an Italian St Tropez. Much tourism is sustainable or an extension of the traditional way of life, from the growing of capers to fishing, winemaking and walking holidays. Helped by the lack of decent roads, visitors happily don hiking boots or take to boat trips round the islands.

Lípari harbour.

Boats arrive at **Santa Marina di Salina** ❺, halfway along the island's east coast. The pretty village is an Aeolian blend of simplicity and sophistication, with chic shops and hearty inns that take in the comings and goings on the quayside. About 2km (1¼ miles) along the rocky palm-lined coast lies **Lingua**, its tiny lighthouse marking the southern tip of the island, and behind it a lagoon previously used for salt extraction, which gave the island its name.

The main town of **Malfa** ❻ is 7km (4½ miles) from Santa Marina, its small harbour backed by a steep jumble of picturesque old boatsheds and crumbling fishermen's houses. Everywhere are signs advertising Malvasia, a sweet golden dessert wine made from sun-dried grapes. Also sample the distinctive wines produced by Carlo Hauner's boutique estate or treat yourself to lunch at the chic Capofaro (*see page 281*). It will probably feature capers, which grow here in abundance. Lunch is best followed by a fig *granita*, a Sicilian take on a sorbet.

From Malfa, the road winds steeply for about 6km (4 miles) to the small

BELOW: street scene, Lípari.

village of **Pollara** ❼, perched on one side of a half-submerged crater. For ever associated with *Il Postino*, which was filmed here, the delectable fishing village boasts two beautiful beaches, reached by a small path 20 minutes' walk from the bus stop by the church. To the right is a tiny beach ringed with boathouses carved into the cliff. To the left the path leads down to a black sandy beach backed by huge white cliffs. In the summer canoes and pedaloes can be hired for exploring the dozens of coves and inlets.

Behind the church is the path up to **Monte Fossa delle Felci**, the highest point on the islands at 962 metres (3,156ft). The ascent is shaded by mixed woodland, and well signposted, culminating in a rocky scramble and fabulous views. Depending on the route you take, the walk is between four and six hours. The steep path down to Santa Marina is very slippery and has to be taken slowly.

From Val di Chiesa, the road descends steeply through the hamlet of **Leni** and twists 3km (2 miles) down to **Rinella** ❽, a pretty fishing port where most of the ferries and hydrofoils make a second stop.

Vulcano

Vulcano is the smelliest island. It is enough to dock at the small port to be overwhelmed by sulphurous odours and steaming fumaroles, a reminder of the looming presence of the menacing volcano. Known as **Gran Cratere**, the great volcano on the island of Vulcano rises behind its smaller cousin, **Monte Vulcanello** (123 metres/404ft), perched on the north of the island, which erupted from the sea in 183 BC. As the ferry arrives in **Porto di Levante** ❾ you can smell the sulphur fumes, and the lime-green, yellow and red rocks add to the extraordinary experience. Porto di Levante's **beach** is popular despite the smell, and immediately to the south of it, behind a huge multicoloured rock, are the famous therapeutic mud baths (*fanghi*). After a bath you can wash off in the thermally heated sea, taking care to test the water, as some areas are scaldingly hot. Fumaroles (fissures of escaping volcanic gases) cause the sea to bubble.

Ten minutes' walk across the island's isthmus is the beautiful curve of black sand at **Porto di Ponente**, on the western coast, dotted with bobbing boats. Sunset illuminates the jagged forms of the Pietralunga and Pietra Menalda rocks off the coast. Just north, the road leads to Monte Vulcanello and, about 2km (¼ miles) away on the northeastern edge of the island, to the **Valle dei Mostri** (Valley of the Monsters), a bizarre collection of sculptures created by lava eruptions in 1888 and erosion since; they are particularly evocative in the evening, when shadows create the impression of wild beasts.

Despite concerns that the influx of visitors is destroying the island's fragile habitat, any visit to Vulcano would be incomplete without a study of the volcano itself. Environmental-ists suggest a boat tour of the island is sufficient, but you can still climb to the active Gran Cratere (*see below*).

Panarea

Northeast of Lípari is Panarea, Sicily's prettiest and most fashionable island. Here poseurs can preen on yachts, retreat to bougainvillea-clad villas or take helicopter tours of the islands. Decidedly chic compared with its countrified neighbours, Panarea's tiny harbour fills up with a flotilla of yachts when it welcomes the summer smart set. The three villages of **Ditella**, **San Pietro and Drauto** form a huddle of pretty cottages and tiny lanes along the eastern coast. The ferries dock at **San Pietro** ⓿.

From Drauto it is an easy stroll to the sandy beach at **Punta Milazzese**, a beautiful rocky headland with the remains of a *villagio preistorico* (prehistoric village). The finds are displayed in the museum in Lípari. A path from Drauto also leads up to the highest point on Panarea, **Timpone del Corvo** (382 metres/1,254ft), with a wonderful view of Strómboli and its smoking volcano.

TIP

A trip around Vulcano by boat views the island at its dramatic best, and the passage through the narrow Bocche di Vulcano channel that separates Vulcano from Lípari is exhilarating. Fishermen will offer a trip in summer.

BELOW: walkers on the volcano on the island of Vulcano.

Exploring Gran Cratere

On Vulcano, visitors have to weigh up a passion to explore the volcano against the disapproval from environmentalists. Climbing the Gran Cratere is the goal. Although only 391 metres (1,125ft) high, the ascent takes an hour and, though it's hot and exposed, can be undertaken by anyone reasonably fit. The smell of sulphur intensifies as the path zigzags up the slope, over black sand and crusty volcanic rock, passing deep furrows hewn by previous eruptions. At the top you are greeted by an otherworldly scene of the massive bowl of the crater, hissing and steaming and encrusted with yellow and red crystals. (Take water and wear stout shoes.)

TIP

The ascent to Strómboli's summit and its four active craters is officially forbidden without a guide, but you can book to join a group at a number of agencies in the village. You should not attempt the climb if it is raining or there is heavy cloud on the summit. You will need to allow seven hours, and time your start to allow you to get down before dark.

Just past the headland is the tiny bay of **Cala Junco**, with excellent swimming. By boat it is also possible to see the caves and other tiny coves along the cliffs.

A steep signposted path leads from Cala Junco up into the high western side of the island, and back down to San Pietro, a fairly stiff but enjoyable three-hour walk. To the north of Ditella is **Calcara beach**, where a fumarole emits jets of gas and steam from fissures in the rock, coating the surface with yellow, white and green minerals and causing patches of sea to be decidedly warm.

From San Pietro you can get a boat trip out to **Basiluzzo** ⓫, now uninhabited, though a Roman jetty lies submerged and scraps of mosaic can be seen on its rocky heights, and to the tiny islets of **Datillo**, **Bottaro** and **Lisca Bianca**, where the swimming is superb.

Strómboli

Even those who have never heard of the Aeolian Islands have heard of Strómboli. The climb to its crater, blasting red-hot rock into the sky,

is an unforgettable reminder of the power below the earth's crust. **Strómboli town** is a lively spot, where you can relax while planning your 924-metre (3,000ft) ascent. Ascents are now only permitted when accompanied by a volcanologist guide. If that sounds too daunting, then retreat to the long, flat beaches, black sand to the north of the jetty, stone and shingly sand to the south.

Strómboli and Vulcano are still active volcanoes, though the last major eruptions – as opposed to continuous emissions of steam or smoke – were in the 1880s. Even so, a minor eruption on Strómboli in 2007 proved unsettling and provoked a rethink about the advisability of exploring independently.

Tiny **Ginostra** ⓬ on the southwest side of the island is accessible only by sea.

Boat trips are also possible to **Strombolicchio**, a tiny island of dramatic coloured craggy rock topped with a lighthouse, and round to the base of **Sciara del Fuoco** ⓭, the fiery slope where lava from the craters flows down to the sea. This is particularly exciting at night, when the booming explosions are matched by sightings of the glowing lava, lit up against the dark sky.

Filicudi

Deeply undeveloped, Filicudi is popular with families, divers and anyone in search of simplicity. Four hours by ferry westwards from Lípari, or an hour on the speeding hydrofoil, Filicudi's smooth whale-humped shape lies quietly in the clear water. The locals used to earn their living by diving for coral, but since coral is now protected, sponges are collected instead.

Filicudi Porto ⓮ is the gateway to an island of rugged beauty, explored along criss-crossing paths. A boat trip reveals the sheer northern side, the **Grotta del Bue Marino** ⓯, a cave where Mediterranean monk seals

BELOW: beach on Panarea.

used to live, and **La Canna**, a natural obelisk towering 70 metres (230ft) out of the sea.

Given the shrinking population, down to around 300, many houses are ruined tangles enveloped by giant *fichi d'India* (prickly pear cactus). On **Capo Graziano**, the tail of the island, further along from the port, are the remains of the oldest settlement on the Aeolians, a Bronze Age village dating from the 18th century BC. Also on this southern coast is the seaside village of **Pecorini**, linked to the port by the only road on the island. It is a good place to hire a boat for a tour of the island.

Alicudi

At the western end of the chain is the least visited island of the Isole Eolie, **Alicudi**, a near-perfect green cone, scattered with pink-and-white homes and terraced fields right up to its peak at **Filo dell'Arpa** (675 metres/2,025ft); here are the remains of the old settlements, secure from maurauding pirates, carpeted with gorse and heather. All the 200 or so residents live on the eastern side of

the island, around the port, **Alicudi Porto** . (This population shrinks to around 30 out of season.) The western side of the island, too steep for houses, is a nature reserve, the **Riserva Naturale**.

For the energetic visitor it is possible to circumnavigate the whole island on foot, but the 7km (4 miles) entails a scramble and two short swims around impassably steep sections. Allow six or seven hours and take water and a picnic. A boat trip round to see the twisted colourful strata and black lava flows offers a less strenuous option. There are two small shops and a hotel (summer only). Otherwise, this is Sicilian life as it was for centuries.

The tiny 17th-century church of **San Bartolo** perches high above the sea, looking down the steep slopes of **Scorbio** to the small plain of **Bassina** round the coast to the east. The lapping of the water on the rocky beaches and the sound of birdsong in the olive groves are the only sounds to be heard. Alicudi remains more interested in catching lobsters than tourists. ❑

Panarea cat.

BELOW: waiting to board the ferry at Lípari.

Island transport

While Lípari and Salina have a passable road network, on the other islands it is negligible. Alicudi has no driveable roads and donkeys carry their burdens up ancient stepped paths. As space is limited and the islands small, visitors should leave their cars on the mainland. Both these islands have reasonable bus services (for timetables, visit the port tourist offices). But beware of missing the last bus back, as taxis are virtually non-existent. Many fans of the islands hire scooters to get around. Regular ferries and hydrofoils run to the Aeolians from Milazzo, near Messina *(see page 264)*; while hydrofoils are faster, the ferry is cheaper and provides better views of each island as you pass by.

BEST RESTAURANTS, BARS AND CAFÉS

Dining on the Aeolians varies greatly from one island to another, with chic, sophisticated dining available on Panarea and far simpler fare on Filicudi. Salina covers both ends of the spectrum. Many restaurants close out of season, so check beforehand.

Lípari

E Pulera
Via Isabella Conti
Tel: 090 981 1158
www.pulera.it €€€€
Attractive setting with traditional local cuisine. Dinner only. Booking recommended. Open Apr–Oct.

Filippino
Piazza Municipio
Tel: 0909 811 002
www.filippino.it €€€€
A local favourite, pricey but good. Delicacies include fish risotto and complicated main courses. Garden. Book. Closed Mon in winter and 10 Nov–26 Dec.

Kasbah
Via Maurolico 25
Tel: 090 981 1075 €€€
Popular restaurant with a pleasant garden setting. Known for its creative fish dishes. Closed Mon and Oct–Mar.

La Nassa
Via Franza 36
Tel: 090 981 1319
www.lanassavacanze.it €€
Typical Aeolian cooking in welcoming surroundings. Open Mar–Nov.

Subba
Corso Vittorio Emanuele 92
Tel: 0761 353 859 €€
The island's most historic café, with shady terrace, is also a restaurant, serving up pizzas with a huge range of toppings.

Salina

Capofaro
Via Faro 3
Tel: 091 984 4330
www.capofaro.it
Romantic, Michelin-starred restaurant popular with the chic set. Fine dining but in a relaxed yet elegant setting. Based on seafood (Sicilian tradition) and a fine wine list. Closed Mon and May, also from mid Oct to mid-Apr.

Da Franco
Via Belvedere 8, Santa Marina di Salina
Tel: 090 984 3287 €€
Great views of sea and Lípari from a veranda. Simple local cooking with the emphasis on local produce. Closed Dec.

Il Delfino
Piazza Marina Garibaldi 5, Lingua
Tel: 090 984 3024
www.ildelfinosalina.it €€
Trattoria with good seafood at low prices.

Nni Lausta
Via Risorgimento 188, Santa Marina Salina
Tel: 090 984 3486
www.isolasalina.com €€€
Eccentric establishment. The owner says: "This is what I am cooking" – so stay or go. It's worth staying. Open Apr–Oct.

Porto Bello
Via Bianchi 1, Santa Marina Salina
Tel: 0909 984 3125 €€
Three simple terraces with good home cooking based on traditional Aeolian dishes. Closed Wed in low season and Dec–Feb.

Vulcano

Da Vincenzino
Loc. Porto Levante 25
Tel: 090 985 2016 €
Simple and inexpensive. Open Mar–Oct.

Maniaci
Gelso
Tel: 368 668 555 €€
You are offered only what the chef feels like cook-

ing that day. But it is good. Open Easter–end Oct.

Maria Tindara
Via Provinciale 38
Tel: 090 985 3004 €€
Home-made pasta with special sauces. Excellent meats and fresh fish. Popular, inexpensive. Open Mar–Oct.

Panarea

Cincotta
Via San Pietro
Tel: 090 983 014
www.hotelcincotta.it €€€€
Smart hotel with smart restaurant, where people dress down expensively and eat costly fish. Open Apr–Oct.

Hycesia
Via San Pietro
Tel: 090 983 041
www.hycesia.it €€€
Named after the old word for Panarea, this chic spot near the port

offers sophisticated, inventive cuisine, but still based on the catch of the day. Popular with the smart set. Great wine list. Closed in May and Nov to Mar.

Paolino
Via Ditella
Tel: 090 983 008 €€
Fresh fish at its best, as the place is owned by a fisherman. Open Apr–Dec.

La Sirena
Via Drauto 4
Tel: 0909 83012
www.hotelsirena-panarea.it €€
Simple but pleasing food with daily specials worth consideration. Open Easter–Oct.

Strómboli

Barbablù
Via Vittorio Emanuele 17
Tel: 090 986 118
www.barbablu.it €€€
Restaurant set in a hotel

garden. The food is cooked by the owner, who imaginatively combines Sicilian and Neapolitan recipes. Closed Nov–Feb.

Da Zurro
Via Picone 18, Scari
Tel: 090 986 283 €€€
Considered modestly better than rival places. Fish, of course. Open Easter–Oct.

Punta Lena
Via Marina, Ficogrande
Tel: 090 986 204 €€€
With a view over the tiny island of Strombolicchio, a charming fish restaurant. Open Apr–Oct.

Filicudi

La Canna
Via Rosa 43
Tel: 090 988 9956
www.lacannahotel.it €€
The pleasing restaurant is in a small hotel (14 rooms) with panoramic views and good food. Closed Nov.

La Sirena
Pecorini Mare
Tel: 090 988 9997
www.pensionelasirena.it €€
Charming trattoria with guest rooms. Dinner served on a terrace with a fine v iew. Closed 15 Dec–15 Jan and two weeks in Nov.

Alicudi

Ericusa
Via Regina Elena
Tel: 090 988 9902
www.alicudihotel.it €€
This is the only place to stay on the island, and it has a reasonable trattoria. Closed Oct–May.

Prices for a three-course dinner per person and a half-bottle of house wine:
€ = under €20
€€ = €20–35
€€€ = €35–70
€€€€ = over €70

LEFT: Lípari restaurant. **ABOVE:** dishes at Nni Lausta.

INSIGHT GUIDES **TRAVEL TIPS**
SICILY

T RANSPORT

GETTING THERE AND GETTING AROUND

GETTING THERE

By Air

Sicily currently has three international airports, but is soon to welcome its fourth: Cómiso, formerly an American base. **Palermo** (Falcone-Borsellini), **Catania** (Fontanarossa) and **Trápani** (Birgi) have all expanded in response to the budget flights phenomenon. The new airport, **Cómiso**, close to Ragusa, should be opening in 2012, which will help boost Ragusa's already thriving tourist industry.

Travellers for Messina use the **Reggio di Calabria airport** on the Italian mainland, just across the Straits of Messina. The bridge over the Straits project, potentially linking Messina and Calabria, is currently stalled, but would transform the tourism scene if it were to come to pass.

Lampedusa and **Pantelleria**, two of the small islands with their own airports, are linked by services from Palermo or Trápani, but tourism to the former has stalled due to the influx of refugees from North Africa.

Scheduled flights for Alitalia, the national airline, and other major international airlines are usually routed, with transfers,

through Milan, Rome or Naples. The major airlines include British Airways, Lufthansa, Air Malta, Meridiana, KLM and Air France. A number of low-cost airlines like Windjet, Blu Express, Ryanair and EasyJet also run regular services into Sicily.

Palermo

All major airlines use Palermo's Falcone-Borsellino airport, 30km (19 miles) from the city at **Punta Raisi**.

Bus services run every 30 mins, linking the airport with **Stazione Centrale** and with the general bus terminal at **Piazza Ruggero Settimo** (Teatro Politeama Garibaldi). Timetables vary according to the season and are displayed at both the airport and the station. The first journey to the airport departs at 5am, and

BETWEEN AIRPORTS

Should you need to transfer between different Sicilian airports, this can be done by pre-booked minibus. A taxi ride between Palermo and Catania airports costs well over €50, while a pre-booked airport shuttle minibus service charges €30 (tel: 091 685 9723 or mail@airporteasy shuttle.it).

the last leaves at 10.45pm. From the airport, the first bus is at 7.30am, and the last leaves at around midnight. The journey takes about an hour. The last bus usually waits for the final flight of the day. Bus ticket: €5.60.

The airport is also linked by the **Trinacria Express train** every 30 mins to and from Stazione Centrale, 4.30am to 8pm. Allow an hour for the journey. Fare: €5.50.

A taxi will charge about €50 for the trip. A pre-booked **airport shuttle minibus service** charges €30 for 2 passengers, and €5 for each additional passenger, plus €8 if it is between 10pm and 6am. Baggage is free. It must be pre-booked. Tel: 091 685 9723 or mail@airporteasyshuttle.it.

Flight information: tel: 091 702 0111 – or call toll-free 800 541 880, a line which occasionally functions. See also the Palermo airport website: www.gesap.it.

Catania

All flights arrive and depart from Catania's airport, **Fontanarossa**, just 5km (3 miles) south of the city. There is an Alibus service into town, 5am to midnight, departing every 20 mins for **Stazione Centrale** (railway station). Tickets can be bought from tobacconists. A metered taxi costs about €25.

Fontanarossa airport enquiries: www.aeroporto.catania.it.

Trápani

Trápani (Birgi) airport (www.aero
portoTrápani.com) is about 15km
(9 miles) from Trápani, reached on
an AST shuttle bus (€2.20), with
connections to Palermo (www.inter-
bus.it, tel: 091 616 7919), as well
as to Catania, Agrigento and
Marsala (check shuttle timetables at www.Trápaniwelcome.it).

Messina

Air travellers coming to or passing
through Messina usually use the
Reggio di Calabria airport on
mainland Italy or arrive via Catania
or Palermo. A hydrofoil shuttle
service links Messina and Villa
San Giovanni, a short distance
away from Reggio di Calabria's airport. Hotels and travel agents usually arrange a taxi or coach link.
   Airport information, Reggio di
Calabria, tel: 0965 642 681: www.
aeroportodellostretto.it.

By Sea

If you wish to avoid air travel, a
long car drive or, indeed, the train
journey through Italy, ferries
(traghetti) are an excellent alternative. They link Sicily with
Naples, **Genova** (Genoa),
Salerno and **Civitavecchia** in
Italy, with **Cagliari** in Sardinia,
and with **Ustica** and the **Isole
Eolie** (Aeolian Islands). There is
also a link with **Tunis**, Tunisia, and
Malta. Hydrofoils (aliscafi) also
link Sicily to its smaller islands.
Sicily can be combined with Malta
on a two-island holiday using Virtu
Ferries (www.virtuferries.com).
   You can now book all ferries
(traghetti) and hydrofoils (aliscafi)
to and from Sicily, including all
the islands (Aeolian, Egadi,
Pelagie, Ustica e Pantelleria)
through www.traghettilines.it. Ferry
companies in Sicilian waters
include: Siremar, Ustica Lines,
Tirrenia, and GNV; and those linking Sicily and the Italian mainland: Tirrenia, Grandi Navi Veloci,
Grimaldi Lines and Virtuferries.
Timetables still need to be
checked on the individual ferry
websites.

ABOVE: cruise liners off the coast of Lípari, one of the Aeolian Islands.

   Ferry prices tend to be low.
Remember that sailing schedules
are prone to change, and the
small islands are often cut off
during bad weather.

Palermo

Palermo's port is central, on Via
Francesco Crispi. Cruise ships,
ferries and hydrofoils embark and
disembark passengers on one of
the busy quays of the Stazione
Marittima. Taxis are on hand to
greet arrivals.
   Ferries link Palermo with
Cagliari in Sardinia, with Naples,
Genova (Genoa) and Civitavec-
chia on the Italian mainland, with
Ustica and the Isole Eolie (Aeolian
Islands) and with Tunis, Tunisia.
All travel agents and hotels can
arrange ticketing. Sailing sched-
ules are prone to change.
   Cagliari Weekly. Tirrenia: tel:
081 017 1998 or 892 123 (in
Italy only). www.tirrenia.it
   Civitavecchia Tue and Thur
8pm, Sun 6.30pm. SNAV: tel: 091
631 7900. www.snav.it
   Genoa Mon–Sat 10pm.
Grandi Navi Veloci: tel: 899 199
069. www.gnv.it
   Naples Daily 8pm. SNAV: tel:
091 631 7900. www.snav.it. Also
daily 8.15pm. Tirrenia: tel: 081
017 1998 or 892 123 (in Italy
only). www.tirrenia.it
   Tunis (Tunisia) Twice weekly.
Grimaldi: tel: 091 587 404. www.
grimaldi-ferries.com

   Ustica and Isole Eolie Daily
8am. Also daily June–Sept only by
aliscafo (hydrofoil) 8.15am and
5.30pm. Siremar: tel: 091 582
403. www.siremar.it

Messina

All ferries and the train link to
mainland Italy go through the
Porto. The quay is on Via Rizzo.

By Rail

The Italian mainland is linked to
Sicily by train, with Milan, Rome
and Naples the best connecting
stations to the south. Unfortunately, the great improvements in
the Italian rail system do not
extend to Sicily, and the overnight
sleeper service from Sicily to
northern Italy is being cancelled.
   Always book a seat for long-
distance travel. Credit-card booking can be made online (www.
trenitalia.com), or go through any local
travel agent – easier than the endless queues at railway stations.
   There is a daily rapido service
between Rome and Palermo, Catania and Siracusa.
   The crossing from Villa San
Giovanni to Messina is an experience in itself: the train carriages
are literally (and time-
consumingly) shunted into the
ferry, and then shunted off again
at Messina. If you arrive on an
overnight train, your first view of
Sicily from the ship's deck may be

of early morning sunlight on the sea and the mountains.

Palermo

The main station is **Stazione Centrale**. Toll-free information tel: 892 021. All principal destinations are linked to Palermo with daily services to and from Rome, Naples, Florence and Genoa.

By Coach

Palermo

Autolinee (coaches) run by various companies leave **Piazza Ruggero Settimo** daily. There are services not only to Sicily's main towns but also to Bologna, Florence, Parma, Modena, Rome and Siena. Timetables change, summer and winter, and coaches may not run on public holidays.

GETTING TO THE ISLANDS

Aeolian Islands

Ferries and hydrofoils run frequently from Milazzo (near Messina), which is reached by train from Messina and Palermo, and by bus from Messina and Catania airport.

In the summer, there are up to 11 hydrofoils a day to **Lípari** and **Vulcano**, and 6 a day to **Salina**. There are direct ferries to the islands several times a week, but all can best be reached through Lípari. The ferry takes about 2 hours to Lípari and the hydrofoil about 45 minutes.

Ferry details: Daily. Siremar: tel: 892 123 in Italy, +39 081 017 1998 from mobile phones or from abroad. Call centre open daily, 9am–8pm. www.siremar.it

Egadi Islands, Pantelleria

Ferries and hydrofoils from Trápani run several times a day to **Favignana**, **Lévanzo** and **Marét-**timo. The ferry trip to Favignana takes 45 minutes; the daily ferry to **Pantelleria** takes 6 hours.

Ferry details: Siremar: tel: 892 123 in Italy, +39 081 017 1998 from mobile phones or from abroad. www.siremar.it

Ustica

In summer both ferries and hydrofoils run daily between Palermo and Ustica. In the low season, there are ferries only. The operator is Siremar *(see above)*.

Pelagie Islands

By Air

Flights to these islands via Trápani Birgi. Information, tel: 0923 842 502.
Lampedusa. Daily flights, to and from Palermo, Milan and Rome. Information, AirOne, tel: 199 207 080; www.flyairone.it
Pantelleria. Daily flights to and from Trápani. Information, Meridiana, tel: 0923 911 398; www.meridiana.it

By Sea

Summer hydrofoils or overnight ferries (cabin advised) run from Porto Empédocle to Lampedusa, stopping at Linosa on the way. The operator is Siremar *(see above).*

GETTING AROUND

By Car

A car in Sicily is a great help for exploring, even though the island is well served by coaches and the many excellent tour agencies arrange visits to distant sites. In cities like Palermo or Siracusa where the traffic is so hectic and the sights so close to each other, it is easier to use public transport or taxis.

If you intend bringing your car to Sicily, the fastest crossing from the mainland is the 20-minute shuttle ferry service to and from Messina to Villa San Giovanni, in Calabria.

You will need a current driving licence (with an Italian translation unless it is the standard EU licence) and valid insurance. You must carry your driving licence, car registration and insurance documents with you at all times when driving.

Fuel and *autostrada* tolls can be paid with cash or credit card. The *Autostrada del Sole* south of Salerno leading to the Reggio di Calabria crossing point is free.
Car hire: Major hire companies include: Avis, Europcar, Hertz and Sixt. You'll find offices in the main airports, but it's usually cheaper to book ahead through major travel websites or specialists such as www.auto-europe.co.uk.

By Taxi

In cities, taxis are best telephoned or found at taxi ranks. Licensed taxis are white, with a Taxi sign on the roof, and have a meter which should be turned on at the start of a journey.
Palermo: To phone for a taxi: Autoradio Taxi, tel: 091 513 311, 091 513 198.
Radio Taxi: tel: 091 225455.
Catania: Radio Taxi, tel: 095 333 216 or 095 330 966.

By Rail

Catania

Catania is well linked with other major cities. Trains depart and arrive at Stazione Centrale, Piazza Papa Giovanni XXIII.

The narrow-gauge train, **Ferrovia Circumetnea**, that calls at all villages around Mount Etna on a circular route *(see page 215)* leaves from Corso delle Provincie.

Messina

Messina is well linked to both Palermo and Catania, and all trains to Italy pass through its port in order to cross the Straits of Messina by ferry. Trains depart and arrive at Stazione Centrale, Piazza Repubblica; the boat trains at neighbouring Stazione Marittima.

Ragusa

Ragusa Province runs a delightful Baroque Train service (**Il Treno Barocco**) that links the main baroque cities in the Val di Noto (advance booking necessary through Módica railway station).

By Coach

Fast buses link Sicily's main towns and offer relatively speedy access to the interior and the south. Generally speaking, coaches are more reliable and quicker than trains, but they cost more. The Palermo–Messina train route is improving, but the Catania–Palermo route takes twice as long by train as it does by coach.

The following lists the key routes on the island and the coach/bus company which runs them.

From Palermo

SAIS, Via Balsamo 16.
Tel: 091 616 6028/617 1141.
Buses go to Rome, Caltanissetta, Catania, Caltagirone, Enna, Piazza Armerina, Sciacca, Messina, Cefalù.
Cuffaro, Via P. Balsamo 13.
Tel: 091 616 1510.
Buses go to Agrigento.
Interbus, Via P. Balsamo 26.

BELOW: mopeds in Noto.

BUS AND TRAIN TICKETS

On trains, buses and the metro, tickets must be validated in the yellow franking machines at the entrance to each platform and on every bus or tram. Tickets are valid for 75 minutes, including changes of bus routes and metro lines. Anyone caught without a validated ticket can be fined up to €50 on the spot.

Bus tickets (€1) are sold from bars, tobacconists, and from machines at bus terminals and metro stations.

Railway stations have ticket desks and automated machines.

Tel: 091 616 7919.
Buses go to Catania and Siracusa.
Segesta, Via P. Balsamo 26.
Tel: 091 616 7919.
Buses go to Rome and Trápani.
Salemi, Via Rosario Gregorio.
Tel: 0923 981 120.
Buses go to Castelvetrano (near Selinunte), Marsala and Mazara del Vallo.

From Trápani

City buses and those for the rest of Trápani Province leave from Piazza Umberto.
AST, Piazza Malta.
Tel: 0923 23222.
For Palermo and Agrigento, buses start from Piazza Garibaldi.

From Agrigento

City buses leave from outside the station in Piazza Marconi. The main bus station for the rest of Sicily is in Piazza Roselli, near the Post Office. Main bus companies:
SAIS, Via Ragazzi del 99, 12.
Tel: 0922 595 933.
S. Lumia, Via F. Crispi 87.
Tel: 0922 20414.

From Enna

SAIS, Viale Diaz.
Tel: 0935 500 902.
Buses leave from Piazza Scelfo in the lower town and connect with Piazza Armerina, Catania, Palermo and Caltagirone.

From Ragusa

All buses stop outside the railway station. Destinations include Catania, Messina, Siracusa, Caltagirone and Piazza Armerina.

From Siracusa

AST, Tel: 0931 462 711.
Buses go to Lentini, Catania, Cómiso, Ispica, Módica, Noto, Pachino and Ragusa.
Interbus, Tel: 0931 66710.
Destinations include Catania, Noto, Pachino, Palermo and Taormina.

From Catania

The bus terminal is in front of the central station.
AST, Via Sturzo 220.
Tel: 095 746 1096.
Buses connect with Acireale, Etna Rifugio Sapienza and Caltagirone.
SAIS, Via d'Amico 181.
Tel: 095 536 168.
Buses go to Messina, Taormina, Enna, Agrigento, Caltanissetta, Palermo, Nicosia, Siracusa, Noto and Pachino.

From Messina

Giuntabus
Via Terranova 8, Milazzo.
Tel: 090 673 782.
SAIS
Piazza della Repubblica 6.
Tel: 090 771 914.
Buses connect with Taormina, Catania and Palermo.

TRANSPORT

ACCOMMODATION

ACTIVITIES

A – Z

LANGUAGE

ACCOMMODATION

WHERE TO STAY

Choosing a Hotel

Outside the main resorts, hotel standards may not be as consistent as in northern or central Italy. But standards are rising dramatically, and charm, personality and warmth often outweigh any failings. At the top end, especially in Taormina, and in boutique hotels all over the island, Sicily can compete with the best. There is also a swathe of special hotels in and around Siracusa, Ragusa, Módica, Scicli and Palermo.

It may prove harder to find luxurious or boutique beds in the interior, with the notable exception of Ragusa Province. Book ahead for hotels in popular resorts such as Taormina, Cefalù and Siracusa, especially in summer. The same applies to hotels on the Aeolian and Egadi Islands. Expect to find considerable differences in quality between hotels of the same grade in "touristy" and "un-touristy" towns. The gulf between urban and rural Sicily also means that in the mountainous hinterland, advise the hotel if you expect to check in late at night.

Price differentials prevail between high and low season, with many resorts open only in the high season (Easter to October). Some resort hotels insist on half or full board. Conversely, in the low season, you can risk asking

for a *sconto* (discount) because it is *bassa stagione* (low season). Stipulate if you want single beds or a double bed *(letto matrimoniale)*. Also, if arriving by car, ensure the hotel has overnight garaging.

Hotel Categories

Hotels are classified according to a star-rating system: 5-star are de luxe; 4-star are first class; 3-star are comfortable; 1–2-star are basic. However, except at the top end, only use this as a guideline as, particularly with the advent of boutique hotels, villa hotels and wine resorts, many of these classifications are outdated or irrelevant.

Although hotels are rapidly improving, generally avoid 1- and 2-star hotels in favour of a city bed and breakfast or an *agriturismo* (farmstay) in the countryside *(see below)*. For comparable rates, you are likely to have a friendlier, far more authentic experience than if staying in a basic hotel.

Boutique Hotels

By definition, boutique hotels are hard to define and reflect the personality of the owners. The charming ones used to be confined to Taormina but are now found all over Sicily, especially in and around Ragusa and Siracusa, and on the Aeolian Islands. Some

of the most memorable Aeolian Island hideaways include Capofaro on Salina and Hotel Raya on Panarea. Near Ragusa, Relais Parco Cavalonga is special, as is Villa Trigona outside Piazza Armerina, run by enthusiastic local aristocrats. In Siracusa, consider the funky Caol Ishka.

Bed and Breakfast

This is now a popular option in Sicily, especially in the historic centres of Palermo, Siracusa, Ragusa and Enna. Whether staying in a simple private house or a palatial apartment, you can usually be assured of a friendly Sicilian welcome. Prices reflect the huge differences in style and sophistication.

Wine Resorts

These are the latest wonderful addition to the accommodation scene, which are somewhere between a boutique hotel and a farmstay, but with wine-tasting and even cookery on offer *(see pages 45 and 286)*.

Rural farmstays (Agriturismi)

In theory, *agriturismi* are working farms serving locally produced cuisine, but some might be rural estates, country houses or rural apartments rather than farms per se. At best, these holidays offer direct contact with Sicilians and a traditional way of life. As with villas (see below), the farmstays could be masserie or bagli (grand Sicilian farmhouses). Views might take in a nature reserve, medieval hamlet, or even the beach. Some are honey-hued hideaways in the interior – possibly with a pool. Rental can be for a couple of nights or for far longer, with a farmstead apartment used as a family-style self-catering holiday. Popular destinations often insist on a week's rental in summer.

It helps to know some basic Italian when staying at some of these places, although all are welcoming. Farmstays in the Madonie, Palermo Province and the Val di Noto tend to be memorable.

Farmstays can be booked through tourist offices or on the internet, with the most comprehensive website: www.agriturismo-sicilia.com. For peace of mind, book a lovely farmstay through a specialist operator such as the UK-based **Sunvil** (+44) 020 8758 4747, www.sunvil.co.uk). They hand-pick the best options outside Catania, Siracusa, Ragusa, Enna, Palermo, Trápani and Agrigento, or Lípari in the Aeolian Islands. A typical example is the family-run Fattoria Mosé near Agrigento, which serves an organic breakfast of figs, fresh ricotta and fresh eggs.

Villa Rentals

Sicilian villas were a word-of-mouth business a decade ago – when there were few good villas with pools around. It's now big business thanks to foreign villa-owners and design-conscious locals – as well as reputable villa specialists abroad.

At the top end, villas can be straight out of The Leopard, with private chefs and infinity pools. The "villas" can also be masserie or bagli (grand Sicilian farmhouses) or even castles, Saracen strongholds, olive farms, or a designer-chic Moorish villa on the volcanic Aeolian Islands.

Villas are a popular alternative to hotels in Cefalù, Taormina, on the islands, and in the more salubrious coastal and mountain resorts. As an independent traveller, it is difficult to book villas on the spot since most are reserved in advance or have tie-ins with foreign agents. As a result, they tend to be booked through tour operators. The best is the UK-based **Think Sicily** (www.thinksicily.com, tel: +44 (0)20 7377 8518), which handles international requests.

Camping

There are around 100 official campsites in Sicily, the majority on the coast (www.camping.it). The sites are ranked from 1- to 4-star according to the facilities, ranging from basic to luxurious. In the summer, sites may be full – or closed if trade is slack. Camping rough is frowned upon.

Youth Hostels

Youth hostels in Sicily tend to close out of the summer season, so generally you would do better to stay in an inexpensive bed and breakfast or an agriturismo. Nevertheless, there are backpackers' hostels in the main towns. In Siracusa, **Lol Hostel** (Tel: 0931 465 088, www.lolhostel.com) is reliable and pleasant. In Palermo try **Casa Marconi** (Tel: 091 657 0611, www.casamarconi.it).

ACCOMMODATION LISTINGS

PALERMO

Palermo

Expect a concentration of hotels at the southern ends of Via Roma and Via Maqueda, between the station and Corso Vittorio

PRICE CATEGORIES

For a double room in high season:
€ = under €100
€€ = €100–180
€€€ = €180–250
€€€€ = €250–400
€€€€€ = over €400

Emanuele. The modern Viale della Libertà quarter, within walking distance of the historic centre, offers safety, convenience and fashionable neighbourhood bars but can lack old-world charm. For that, seek out Palermo's special B&Bs, including ones set in aristocratic palaces.
Villa Igiea Hilton
Salita Belmonte 43
Tel: 091 631 2111
www.villaigiea.hilton.com
Set out of town, in

Acquasanta, on cliffs above the bay, this is Palermo's prestigious landmark hotel. Once a villa built by the Florio dynasty, it has been restored to its Art Nouveau splendour. Enjoy the palm-fringed views over the Gulf of Palermo. A highlight is the Donna Franca Florio gourmet restaurant. **€€€€€**
Grand Hotel Piazza Borsa
Via dei Cartari
Tel: 091 320 075

www.piazzaborsa.it
The sober, atmospheric hotel combines a former monastery, church and cloisters as well as several ancient palazzi, including the former

stock exchange. Highlights include a spa, distinctively designed bedrooms, a bar in the cloisters, a winter garden and a gourmet restaurant in an Art Nouveau setting. **€€€€–€€€€€**

Centrale Palace
Corso Vittorio Emanuele 327
Tel: 091 336 666
www.centralepalacehotel.it
A luxururious, well-restored hotel, Centrale Palace exudes a charm lacking in many other Palermo hotels. Its location, close to the Quattro Canti crossroads, is central. Breakfast is served on the terrace with panoramic view over the old town roofs. **€€€€**

Excelsior Hilton
Via Marchese Ugo 3
Tel: 091 790 9001
www.excelsiorpalermo.it
Refurbished in elegant 19th-century style, this established hotel overlooks a park in the chic, new part of Palermo, but is still within reasonable distance of the historic centre. Rooms vary considerably, so you may wish to view before booking. Friendly staff. **€€€€**

Grand Hotel et des Palmes
Via Roma 398
Tel: 091 602 8111
www.grandhoteldespalmes.com
This splendidly faded landmark is in a good (if busy) location for exploring both the historic centre and the elegant new Palermo. *Belle époque* flourishes remain, as do the Art Nouveau lobby and intriguing Mafia and musical associations. Wagner completed *Parsifal* here in 1882. **€€€€**

Grand Hotel Federico II
Via Principe di Granatelli 60
Tel: 091 749 5052

www.grandhotelfedericoii.it
Converted into an efficient luxury hotel, its ambience reflects earlier epoques. Roof terrace. **€€€€**

Astoria Palace
Via Montepellegrino 62
Tel: 091 628 1111
www.ghshotels.it
Set slightly out of the main centre, in the shadow of Monte Pellegrino, this is a large, modern, highly efficient business-orientated hotel with a good restaurant. 320 rooms, 14 suites. Due to its size, it is popular for conferences. Garage. **€€€**

Hotel Garibaldi al Politeama
Via Emerico Amari 146
Tel: 091 601 7111
www.ghshotels.it
Its central location, close to the Politeama theatre, within walking distance of the major attractions, makes this a convenient spot. Friendly staff, contemporary bathrooms, spacious suites and garaging organised nearby make this a sensible, central choice. **€€€**

Massimo Plaza
Via Maqueda 437
Tel: 091 325 657
www.massimoplazahotel.com
Pleasing boutique hotel in a restored building close to Teatro Massimo, so a good choice for opera buffs. Comfortable, good service. **€€€**

Hotel Palazzo Sitano
Via Vittorio Emanuele 114
Tel: 091 611 9880
www.falkensteiner.com
Central, sought-after hotel, converted from a princely 18th-century palace. **€€€**

Hotel Porta Felice
Via Butera 45
Tel: 091 617 5678

www.portafelice.it
Set in the historic heart near the port, but convenient for the sights, this 18th-century palace is also convenient for the semi-restored Foro Italico seafront. **€€€**

Principe di Villafranca
Via G.Turrisi Colonna 4
Tel: 091 611 8523
www.principedivillafranca.it
Away from the centre, this distinctly sober hotel mixes contemporary art and Sicilian antiques. Restaurant has impeccable style. Garage. **€€€**

Allakala B&B
Corso Vittorio Emanuele 71
Tel: 091 743 4763
www.allakala.it
A stylish, friendly B&B with five individually designed rooms, all with views of the port. **€€**

BB22
Largo Cavalieri di Malta 22
Tel: 091 611 1610
www.bb22.it
With an excellent location, tucked behind San Domenico, this boutique B&B has relaxing decor and excellent service. **€€**

Conte Federico
Via dei Biscottari 4
Tel: 091 651 1881
www.contefederico.com
Run by a Palermitan count and his opera-singing Austrian wife, this palace in the heart of town offers an intriguing insight into Sicilian life. The apartments, all with private bathrooms, lead off the 17th-century courtyard. **€€**

Butera 28
Via Butera 28
Tel: 333 316 5432
www.butera28.it
B&B in the noble palace that belonged to Tomasi di Lampedusa, now owned by his heirs. Historic district by the port. **€**

Orientale
Via Maqueda 26
Tel: 091 616 5727
www.albergoorientale.191.it
Budget option. Only half the rooms are en suite, but there's a marble courtyard and plenty of atmosphere. **€**

Mondello

For families with young children or couples combining the beach with summer nightlife, Mondello makes a better summer base than Palermo. Fashionable Palermo society moves to the resort, so book early. The best hotels have private beaches.

Mondello Palace
Viale Principe di Scalea
Tel: 091 450 001
www.mondellopalacehotel.it
Modern, luxurious seafront hotel with private beach, pool, restaurant and bar. **€€€**

Splendid La Torre
Via Piano Gallo 11
Tel: 091 450 222
www.latorre.com
Modern hotel on the rocky point of the bay at the quieter end of Mondello Lido. Own beach, pool and tennis courts, and sea or garden views from the rooms. **€€**

Villa Esperia
Via Margherita di Savoia 53
Tel: 091 684 0717
www.hotelvillaesperia.it
An elegant hotel, recently refurbished, on the beach. **€€**

PRICE CATEGORIES

For a double room in high season:
€ = under €100
€€ = €100–180
€€€ = €180–250
€€€€ = €250–400
€€€€€ = over €400

PALERMO PROVINCE

Castelbuono

Relais Santa Anastasia
Contrada Santa Anastasia
Tel: 0921 672 233
www.santa-anastasia-relais.it
Luxury in a converted grand house in the liveliest town in the Madonie mountains. Pool. €€€€

Baita del Faggio
Acque del Faggio
Tel: 0921 662 194
www.baitadelfaggio.it
Popular resort hotel. €€€

Piano Torre Park
Piano Torre, near Piano Zucchi
Tel: 0921 662 671
www.pianotorreparkhotel.com
At the heart of the reserve with 27 charming rooms, pool and an excellent restaurant. €€

Cefalù

An easy-going, relaxing resort, Cefalù is popular with families, middle-aged culture-vultures and groups. The beaches are more accessible here than at Taormina.

Gli Alberi del Paradiso
Via dei Mulini 18
Tel: 0921 423 900
www.alberidelparadiso.it
Typical beach hotel with pools, tennis, restaurant. €€€€

Baia del Capitano
Contrada Mazzaforno
Tel: 0921 420 005
www.baiadelcapitano.it
About 5km (3 miles) west of Cefalù. Modern but set in an olive grove. Pool, tennis and nearby beach. €€€€

Carlton Riviera
Loc. Capo Plaia
Tel: 0921 420 200
www.carltonhotelriviera.it
Modern hotel on the cliffs about 5km (3 miles) west of Cefalù. Tennis, pool. Open Apr–1 Oct. €€€

BELOW: Excelsior Hilton Palermo.

Kalura
Via Vincenzo Cavallaro 13, Caldura
Tel: 0921 421 354
www.hotel-kalura.com
3km (2 miles) east of Cefalù. Slightly worn, but most rooms have a sea view. Beach. €€€

Monreale

Carrubella Park
Via Umberto 233
Tel: 091 640 2187
www.carrubellaparkhotel.com
About 1km (⅔ mile) outside Monreale, with wonderful views across Conca d'Oro. €€

Piana degli Albanesi

Masseria Rossella
Contrada Piana degli Albanesi
Tel: 091 846 0012
www.masseria-rossella.com
Reached along the SP 5, this country estate has converted the granary and stables into charming rural apartments. Pool; homely restaurant; cookery courses. €€.

Ustica

Between June and September, hotels fill up fast, but there are many opportunities to rent rooms: call in at Bar Centrale in Piazza Umberto.

Punta Spalmatore
Loc. Spalmatore
Tel: 091 844 9388
www.villaggiospalmatore.it
Holiday village with bungalows and rooms. Open June–Sept. €€–€€€

Clelia
Via Sindaco 29
Tel: 091 844 9039
www.hotelclelia.it
Small inn set on the main square, with a reliable restaurant. €€

Pelagie Islands

Residence la Posta
Via Alfieri, Linosa
Tel: 320 601 0556
ww.linosaresidencelaposta.it
Attractive, air-conditioned and in the heart of the village. €€

Medusa
Piazza Medusa 3, Lampedusa
Tel: 0922 970 126
www.medusahotels.it
20 modern rooms in Moorish style. €€€€

TRÁPANI PROVINCE

Trápani

Baia dei Mulini
Lungomare Dante Alighieri, San Cusumano
Tel: 0923 584 111
www.abitaliahotels.com
On waterfront towards Erice, comfortable with restaurant, bar, tennis, pool and beach. €€€

Crystal
Piazza Umberto 1
Tel: 0923 20000
www.nh-hotels.com
Central, modern hotel with 68 rooms, good restaurant. €€€

Moderno
Via Tenente Genovese 20
Tel: 0923 21247
www.hotelmoderno.Trápani.it
Centrally located, with 13 rooms. €€

Vittória
Via Francesco Crispi 4
Tel: 0923 873 044

TRANSPORT

ACCOMMODATION

ACTIVITIES

A – Z

LANGUAGE

www.hotelVittóriaTrápani.it
Central hotel with 65 rooms, some with sea view. Comfortable. Mostly business clientele. €€

Castellammare del Golfo

Both a charming fishing port and a small resort, Castellammare del Golfo suits both families and independent travellers who want to be close to Palermo yet based in a quieter location. It also appeals to those wishing to swim in clean waters near the nature reserve of Lo Zíngaro.

Punta Nord Est
Viale Leonardo da Vinci 67
Tel: 0924 30511
www.puntanordest.com
A holiday hotel with a private beach. €€

Al Madarig
Piazza Petrolo 7
Tel: 0924 33533
www.almadarig.com
Pleasant, modern, reasonably priced hotel with 33 rooms overlooking the port. €

Erice

Erice is an ideal base and an extremely attractive village. In summer its hilltop position makes it far more comfortable than Trápani. However, in high season it can be crowded and accommodation is in great demand, so early booking recommended.

Elimo
Via Vittorio Emanuele 75
Tel: 0923 869 377
www.hotelelimo.it
A small hotel in the old town with pleasant restaurant and views from rooms and roof terrace. €€

Moderno
Via Vittorio Emanuele 67
Tel: 0923 869 300
www.hotelmodernoerice.it
In the old town. Renovated, intimate, with a roof terrace and a good restaurant known for its fish couscous. €€

La Pineta
Viale Nunzio Nasi
Tel: 0923 860 127
www.lapinetadierice.com
A cluster of bungalows set among pine trees. Pleasant service. Good restaurant.€€

Ermione
Via Pineta Comunale 43
Tel: 0923 869 138
www.ermionehotel.it
Set in a pine grove just outside the walls, it looks unattractive but has large rooms, great views, a pool and an average restaurant.

Marinella

Marinella di Selinunte has a number of standard beach hotels on its seafront.

Paradise Beach
Contrada Belice di Mare
Tel: 0924 46333
Set beside the sea 6km (4 miles) from Marinella centre. An impressive hotel-club with sports facilities, a pool and tennis courts, 250 rooms. Closed Nov–Feb. €€€

Alceste
Via Alceste 23
Tel: 0924 46184
www.hotelalceste.it
1km (²⁄₃ mile) away from town, close to the sea. 26 simple but comfortable rooms. Terrace, garden and solarium. Closed 16 Nov–14 Dec; 16 Jan–14 Feb. €€

Lido Azzurro
Via Marco Polo 98
Tel: 0924 46256
Email: lazzurro@freemail.it

Small, friendly 2-star villa in the centre but close to beach. Some rooms with sea views. Restaurant. €

Marsala

New Hotel Palace
Longomare Mediterraneo 57
Tel: 0923 719 492
www.newhotelpalace.com
Charming 5-star hotel with sea-view rooms, pool and restaurant. €€€

Delfino Beach
Lungomare Mediterraneo 672
Tel: 0923 751 076
www.delfinobeach.com
Some 4km (2½ miles) south of the centre, with 91 rooms, conference facilities, pool, tennis, restaurant. €€

Villa Favorita
Via Favorita 27
Tel: 0923 989 100
www.villafavorita.com
A 19th-century villa set in an extensive garden with great views. Comfortable, with large rooms. €€

Garden
Via Gambini 36
Tel: 0923 982 320
Basic budget accommodation near the railway station. €

Mazara del Vallo

Giardino di Costanza
Via Salemi Km 7
Tel: 0923 675 000
www.giardinodicostanza.it
Situated only 7km (4½ miles) from the historic town of Salemi, this luxurious Kempinski resort has a pool, tennis courts, golf course, a fine restaurant and suites with Jacuzzis. Guests praise its winning combination of Italian style and German efficiency. €€€€€

Mahara Hotel
Lungomare San Vito 3
Tel: 0923 673 800
www.maharahotel.it
The best, good-value 4-star hotel on the seafront occupies a historic Marsala wine warehouse founded by the Englishman John Hopps. Rooms offer views of the internal gardens and pool or the seafront; spa, restaurant and bar. Ten minutes' walk to the old town; shuttle to the best beach; organised day trips to the Egadi islands. €€€

Hopps
Via G. Hopps 29
Tel: 0923 946 133
www.hoppshotel.it
Waterfront hotel with restaurant, garden, covered pool; private beach reached by shuttle bus. €€

San Vito Lo Capo

Complemented by Scopello (see below), San Vito Lo Capo is a scenic, low-key resort near Castellammare and popular with families and nature-lovers. Prices are dramatically higher in July and August, but there is also plenty of bed and breakfast (and apartment) accommodation, especially around Scopello.

Capo San Vito
Via San Vito 1
Tel: 0923 972 122
www.caposanvito.it
4-star hotel with 35 rooms, 10km (6 miles) south of Capo San Vito but on the beach. Private lido for guests; gardens and tennis courts. €€€

Egitarso
Via Lungomare 54
Tel: 0923 972 111

TRANSPORT

www.hotelegitarso.it
Basic hotel, with 42 rooms, but on the seafront. **€€**

Riva del Sole
Via Generale Arimondi 11
Tel: 0923 972 629
www.hotelrivadelsole.it
2-star hotel with only 9 rooms and run by a friendly and helpful family. Excellent restaurant with gastronomic aspirations. Open Apr–Sept. **€€**

Vecchio Mulino
Via Mulino 49
Tel: 0923 972 518

www.hotelvecchiomulino.com
Small hotel with panoramic terrace views and a good restaurant. Bicycle service. **€€**

Villaggio Cala Mancina
Via Eboli 29
Tel: 0923 621 611
www.calamancina.it
On the beach, with pool. 60 rooms. Family hotel. **€€**

Scopello

Casale Corcella
Contrada Scardina
Tel: 368 365 4482

www.casalecorcella.com
Five pleasant rooms close to both Scopello and the Tonnara, the scenic tunnery, and just 2km (1¼ miles) from the Riserva dello Zíngaro, Sicily's finest nature reserve. **€**

Giardino del Re
Baglio Isonzo 2
Tel: 091 549 338 &
340 550 2032
www.verasicilia.it
Private apartment in the village; it opens onto a garden once owned by Ferdinand IV. Even if this

bed and breakfast is in Scopello itself, nature is all around. **€**

La Vera Sicilia
Tel: 091 549 338 and 340 550 2032
www.verasicilia.it
A Sicilian-German couple own apartments in and around Scopello, so check the website to see which appeal. The cosy Giardino del Re apartment *(above)* is one of the best. The apartments are only ten minutes' walk to the sea. **€**

ACCOMMODATION

EGADI ISLANDS

Favignana

In July and August accommodation is hard to find on Favignana, so booking is essential. However, the ferries tend to be met by locals offering rooms.

BELOW: Levanzo.

Approdo di Ulisse
Cala Grande
Tel: 0923 925 000
www.aurumhotels.it
Comfortable resort hotel. 131 rooms. Beach, pool, tennis courts. Open Easter–Oct. **€€€**

Egadi
Via Cristoforo Colombo 17
Tel: 0923 921 232
www.albergoegadi.it
Stylish hotel with 9 rooms and the island's most highly regarded restaurant. Open Mar–Oct. **€€€**

Aegusa
Via Garibaldi 11
Tel: 0923 922 430
www.aegusahotel.it
Simple conversion of a palazzo at the centre of the island. Dining in the garden. Closed Jan–Feb. **€€**

Levanzo

Paradiso
Via Lungomare 8
Tel: 0923 924 080
www.albergoparadisolevanzo.it
Small hotel with 15 rooms. Simple restaurant on terrace overlooking sea. **€**

Pensione dei Fenici
Via Calvario 18
Tel: 0923 924 083
Family run *pensione* with 10 pleasant rooms and a terrace restaurant. **€**

Pantelleria

Club Village Punta Fram
at Punta Fram
Tel: 0923 918 075
www.aurumhotels.it
On the western coast. Pool, tennis courts, restaurant. **€€**

Cossyra
At Mursia
Tel: 0923 911 154
www.mursiahotel.it
On the northwest coast of the island, about 3km

PRICE CATEGORIES

For a double room in high season:
€ = under €100
€€ = €100–180
€€€ = €180–250
€€€€ = €250–400
€€€€€ = over €400

ACTIVITIES

A – Z

LANGUAGE

(2 miles) from Pantelleria port, in a spot famous for its sunsets. Pleasant grounds with pool, tennis courts, dive school and a private beach. All rooms have a terrace – those in the "Comfort" category offer sea views. €€

Miryam
Corso Umberto 1
Tel: 0923 911 374
www.miryamhotel.it
Traditional, comfortable hotel. €€
Mursia
At Mursia
Tel: 0923 911 217
www.mursiahotel.it

Modern, seafront hotel, not far from the airport. On its own beach with pools and tennis courts. Under the same ownership as Cossyra. €€
Papuscia
At Tracino
Contrada Sopra Portella 28
Tel: 0923 915 463

www.papuscia.it
Small, family-run *albergo* with only 11 spacious and simple rooms, in a typical *dammusi* (low building made of volcanic stone) setting; lots of lava. Tranquil location outside Tracino. (Dinner only, but delicious.) €€

AGRIGENTO CITY AND PROVINCE

ABOVE: bedroom view at Villa Athena.

Agrigento

Unlike the rest of the province, the city is well provided with good-quality hotels, especially Villa Athena and Baglio della Luna, both convenient for the Valley of the Temples.
Villa Athena
Via Passeggiata Archeologica 33
Tel: 0922 596 288
www.athenahotels.com
Newly renovated and effortlessly appealing, this 18th-century villa, a luxury boutique hotel, lies in an attractive garden overlooking the Tempio della Concordia. Come for the romantic views alone, even if only for lunch or dinner. €€€€

Baglio della Luna
Via Amabile Guastella 9
Tel: 0922 511 061
www.bagliodellaluna.com
Set in the countryside, this beguiling boutique hotel offers charming courtyards, a Mediterranean garden and the remains of an old watchtower. It also boasts a noted gastronomic restaurant. €€€
Colleverde Park
Passeggiata Archeologica
Tel: 0922 29555
www.topsicilia.it
Further up the slope from Villa Athena, at the start of Strada Panoramica. 48 rooms. Lovely temple views and a reasonable restaurant. €€
Atenea 191
Villa Atenea 191

Tel: 0922 595 594
www.atenea191.com
On Agrigento's main street, this appealing bed and breakfast has large rooms with sea views. There's a roof terrace too. No credit cards. €
Camere a Sud
Via Ficani 6
Tel: 349 638 4424
www.camereasud.it
A lovely boutique B&B off Via Atenea, with just three stylish rooms. Breakfast is served on the roof terrace in summer. No credit cards. €
Letto e Latte
Via Cannatello 101
Tel: 0922 651 945
www.lettolatte.it
This attractive, family-run bed and breakfast has just six rooms with private bathroom and balconies with temple views. Great value. No credit cards. €
Tre Torri
Viale Cannatello 7
Tel: 0922 606 733
www.hoteltretorri.eu
Large 3-star hotel just east of the temples. Restaurant, bar, indoor and outdoor swimming pools, sauna. €€

Licata

This historic but down-at-heel town is a

possible overnight stop if Agrigento hotels are full.
Baia d'Oro
Loc. Mallarella
Tel: 0922 774 666
www.baiadoro.info
Basic, but blessed with views and a beach. €
Piccadilly
Via Panoramica
Tel: 0922 893 626
Basic budget option. €

Palma di Montechiaro

Mandranova Hotel
Loc. Palma di Montechiaro
Tel: 393 986 2169
Reached along the SS115, this old farmhouse and former station is set among palm

PRICE CATEGORIES

For a double room in high season:
€ = under €100
€€ = €100–180
€€€ = €180–250
€€€€ = €250–400
€€€€€ = over €400

trees and African-style vegetation. Inside, the mood is Mediterranean. Romantic candelit restaurant. €€

Porto Empédocle

Not recommended as a base, but the town makes a sensible overnight stop if you are catching a ferry to the Pelagie Islands.

Dei Pini
On SS115, Loc. Vincenzella
Tel: 0922 634 844
Email: hdeipini@virgilio.it
Renovated, with garden and beach. €€

Sciacca

While distinctly scruffy, this spa resort town has undoubtedly benefited from the creation of the luxury Verdura resort.

Verdura Golf and Spa Resort
Contrada Verdura
Tel: 0925 998 180
www.verduraresort.it
This luxurious new golf and spa resort has put Sciacca on the map, even if the coast is somewhat underwhelming. The 5-star resort itself is luxurious, with high design standards, all the mod cons you'd

expect, fine dining, superb golf (an 18-hole and a 9-hole course), as well as a top spa. €€€€€

Hotel delle Terme
Via delle Nuove Terme
Tel: 0925 23133
Email: info@termehotel.com
72 rooms, covered and outdoor pools and reserved beach, with a thermal treatment centre and spa. €

CALTANISSETTA PROVINCE

The province has limited accommodation and, while the hinterland is

lovely, Caltanissetta itself is quite dull, while Gela is depressing.

Those who wish to stay in the mountains would do better going to Enna.

Caltanissetta

San Michele
Via Fasci Siciliani
Tel: 0934 553 750
www.hotelsanmichelesicilia.it
Stylish hotel close to the town centre, with swimming pool and good views from the garden over the valley. Some rooms have views over the hills. Restaurant. €€€

Butera

Stella del Mediterraneo
SS115, Loc. Falconara
Tel: 0934 349 004
www.stelladelmediterraneo.it
Comfortable. €

BELOW: church in Caltanissetta.

ENNA PROVINCE

Enna

Enna itself has few hotels, but compensates for this with good B&Bs. Because of Enna's altitude, take warmer clothes and expect to find views from your hotel window swathed in mist.

Bristol
Piazza Ghisleri 13
Tel: 0935 24415
www.hotelbristolenna.it
Rooms at this central hotel are simple and

comfortable, if a little bland. €€

Grand Albergo Sicilia
Piazza Colaianni 7
Tel: 0935 500 850
www.hotelsiciliaenna.it
Although underwhelming, this is a central, comfortable and friendly 3-star hotel. €€

Nicosia

This un-touristy inland town is a refreshing base for exploring Enna's hilly interior.

Baglio San Pietro
Contrada San Pietro
Tel: 0935 640 529
www.bagliosanpietro.com
Charming converted farmhouse with garden, swimming pool and 10 rooms. Closed Mar. Restaurant serves own produce. €

Vineta
Contrada San Basile
Tel: 0935 646 074
7km (4 miles) north of Nicosia, this is a modern, comfortable hotel. €

Piazza Armerina

This friendly, appealing town makes a good stop for visitors wishing to see its famous Villa Romana, the Roman villa. The town itself is mistakenly overlooked, but its palaces and churches are fascinating. The tourist office is also very helpful.

Suite d'Autore
Piazza Duomo
Tel: 0935 66853
www.suitedautore.it

Conceived as an art and design gallery, this bohemian boutique hotel goes down well with artists and urban couples. The provocative, art-studded rooms have quirky titles such as "lightness" or "magic and irony". Suites overlook the cathedral (clanging bells on Sunday), with rooms overlooking the hills. Take breakfast in the arty rooftop bar overlooking the rugged hills and city rooftops. **€€–€€€**

Villa Trigona
Contrada Bauccio
Tel: 0935 681 896
www.villatrigona.it

Set just outside town,

ABOVE: at the Eremo della Giubiliana.

the noble Trigona family's baronial country villa is now an engaging B&B. The highlights include old-world charm, highly individual rooms and even a private chapel, respecting old Sicilian traditions among the nobility. It is essential to try the wonderful dinner, which uses local dishes (good-value, all-inclusive price for dinner of around €30). A pool is planned. **€€–€€€**

Park Hotel Paradiso
Contrada Ramalda
Tel: 0935 680 841
www.parkhotelparadiso.it

Friendly owners and convenient for the Villa Romana. Pool, tennis courts. **€€**

Ostello del Borgo
Largo San Giovanni 6
Tel: 0935 687 019
www.ostellodelborgo.it

Inexpensive bed and breakfast accommodation in an old convent in the centre of Piazza

Armerina. Simple, dormitory-style rooms, formerly the nuns' quarters. There are more comfortable private rooms upstairs. Closed Dec–Feb. **€**

Troìna

Quiet town; good alternative to Nicosia.

Costellazioni
Contrada San Michele
Tel: 0935 653 966
Pool, riding, squash. **€€**

RAGUSA PROVINCE

This delightful province is currently the most sought-after region of the island, along with the rest of southeast Sicily. Ideally avoid the unappealing upper town, Ragusa Alta, in favour of a charming bed and breakfast in the lower town of Ragusa Ibla. Alternatively, stay in the countryside nearby, such as in the friendly yet stylish Artemisia Resort. Alternatively, head to the neighbouring hills of Chiaramonte Gulfi, where you'll receive a warm welcome.

Ragusa

Ragusa Ibla (the medieval "lower" town) makes a lovely base: choose a small hotel or B&B. Ragusa Alta (the Baroque and modern "upper" town) is only a fallback option, given its characterless business hotels. Parking can be tricky (though hotels can usually help out) and the town's sign-posting and one-way system confusing.

Eremo della Giubiliana
Contrada Giubiliana (Km 7,5)
Tel: 0932 669 119
www.eremodellagiubiliana.it

Outside Ragusa, near chic Marina di Ragusa, this fortified 15th-century hermitage, converted into one of Sicily's most delightful hotels, is both charming and austere. Pool, garden, reserved beach. **€€€€**

Locanda Don Serafino
Via XI Febbraio 15
Tel: 0932 222 0065
www.locandadonserafino.it

A boutique hotel in Ragusa Ibla with 10 beautifully decorated rooms and a noted restaurant. **€€€**

Artemisia Resort
Via E. Caruso 13
Tel: 0932 642 575

www.artemisiaresort.com

Set on the outskirts of Ragusa, but in the countryside, this lovely rural boutique hotel is much loved by its gracious owners, who also own a renowned pastry shop *(pasticceria)*, hence the delicious Módica-style cakes and pastries for breakfast. Pool with massage jets. Outside barbecue. Perfect for exploring the Montalbano detective trail (ask for the map), and a short hop to the beach and good walks. €€–€€€

Palazzo Castro al Duomo
Piazza del Duomo 2
Tel: 0932 621 887
www.palazzocastro.it
This atmospheric place is conveniently set on the cathedral square, and boasts a tranquil garden too. €

Risveglio Ibleo
Largo Camerina 3
Tel: 0932 247 811
www.risveglioibleo.com
Stylish self-catering suites in a lovely townhouse in Ragusa Ibla. Excellent breakfasts too. €

Chiaramonte Gulfi

This is a lesser-known Sicilian gem, with a cluster of offbeat museums and churches, plus very genuine, special (and good-value) restaurants and some of the best olive oil in Sicily.

Antica Stazione
Via Madonna Santissimo Rosario
Tel: 0932 928 083
www.anticastazione.com
Set in the Monte Iblei, in the Ragusa highlands, this exceptionally friendly, family-run hotel was once a railway station. Although convenient for Ragusa, Chiaramonte and local walks, the hotel feels peacefully aloof, set among dry-stone walls and carob trees. Warm service and utter professionalism are comple-

mented by quiet rooms, a highly popular restaurant (using local oils, cheeses and meat) and low prices. €

Valle di Chiaramonte
Contrada Pantanelli
Tel: 0932 926 079
www.valledichiaramonte.it
This friendly *agriturismo* (farmstay) comprises clusters of rustic self-catering apartments (though the owners will happily clean). Part of the delight of staying here is the chance to enjoy the farm-grown produce, from deliciously aromatic olive oil to salami, cooked meats, fresh cheeses, mature Ragusano DOP cheese, and red wines such as Nero d'Avola and Cerasuola di Vittória. €

Donnafugata

Donnafugata Golf Resort and Spa
Tel: 0932 914 200
www.donnafugatagolfresort.it
www.nh-hotels.com
The 5-star resort, close to Donnafugata Castle and 17km (11 miles) from Cómiso airport. Designed in peaceful earth tones, the resort has a swimming pool, an award-winning day spa, two championship courses and a golf academy complete with 70 driving tees. €€€–€€€€

Relais Parco Cavalonga
SP 80 Km
Tel: 0932 619 605
www.parcocavalonga.it
This chic retreat comprises a stylish contemporary hotel and country cottages, set near Donnafugata Castle, 10km (6 miles) from the sea,

but also close to Baroque Ragusa and the Nero d'Avola wine route. €€

Módica

Módica is the region's wealthiest provincial town but has kept its charm, and a number of special boutique hotels and upmarket B&Bs are adding to its appeal, the Palazzo Failla among them.

Palazzo Failla
Via Blandini 5
Tel: 0932 755 655
www.palazzofailla.it
Set in Módica Alta, this beguiling boutique hotel is suffused with Sicilian charm, left much as it was when the owners lived there – but made contemporary by the addition of a Michelin-starred restaurant, La Gazza Laddra. €€€–€€€€

Balarte Hotel
Contrada da Scorrione
Tel: 0932 779 014
www.balarte.it
Set in an old *masseria* (farmhouse) outside town, this arty hotel is as appealing as the delicious local food served for breakfast, including crepes made with carob flour and stuffed with ricotta and chocolate. €€–€€€

Ferro Hotel
Via Stazione SN 970
Tel: 0932 941 043
www.ferrohotel.it
This quirky station hotel is at the very end of the Módica station platform, even if trains are rare so sleep is guaranteed. The whole hotel evokes the train theme, including the restaurant, Binario 4 (Platform 4). €–€€

Il Cavaliere
Corso Umberto I, 259
Tel: 0932 947 219
www.palazzoilcavaliere.it
A lovely B&B with friendly owners in an elegant palazzo, with tastefully furnished rooms and a breakfast room with a frescoed ceiling. €

Pozzallo

Villa Ada
Corso Vittorio Veneto 3
Tel: 0932 954 022
www.hotelvillaada.it
Functional hotel used by ferry port passengers but perfect for an overnight stay before taking the ferry to Malta. €€

Scicli

Scicli is one of the rising stars in Ragusa Province, an enchanting Baroque town with a number of charming boutique hotels, perfect for the Montalbano detective trail tour *(see page 171).*

Palazzo Hedone
Via Loreto 51
Tel: 0932 841 187
www.palazzohedone.it
Run by two French designers, this lavender-tinged boutique hotel is studded with French antiques. A charming and restful retreat (complete with pool with sliding roof) in a gorgeous Baroque town. €€–€€€

PRICE CATEGORIES

For a double room in high season:
€ = under €100
€€ = €100–180
€€€ = €180–250
€€€€ = €250–400
€€€€€ = over €400

SIRACUSA CITY AND PROVINCE

Siracusa

Compared with much of Sicily, hotels here tend to be both highly professional and attuned to foreign tastes. Resist the bland hotels in the newer part of town, which are not convenient for the archaeological sites or the island of Ortigia. Instead choose a special haven in Ortigia or close by.

Grand Hotel Ortigia
Via Mazzini 12
Tel: 0931 464 600
www.grandhotelortigia.it
This appealing, well-renovated, well-run Art Nouveau hotel overlooks Porto Grande and the projected new yacht marina. Bedrooms are faintly nautical. The roof garden has an excellent classic Sicilian restaurant and enjoys panoramic views. Spa and small archaeological museum. €€€€

Caol Ishka
Via Elorina, Contrada Pantanelli
Tel: 0931 69057
www.caolishka.com
Set 2km (1¼ miles) outside Siracusa, on the banks of the Anapo river, but with views of Ortigia, this arty boutique hotel is run by a Sicilian-Irish couple, hence the Gaelic name. Both a peaceful haven from the city and a sophisticated urban retreat, Caol Ishka offers a pool, stylish bar, small library, friendly service and, above all, a noted gastronomic restaurant where creative cuisine is blended with subtle Sicilian flavours. €€–€€€€

Gutowski
Lungomare Vittorini 26
Tel: 0931 465 861
www.guthotel.it
Small but comfortable. 13 rooms plus small sunny terrace with panoramic views. €€

Palazzo del Sale
Via Santa Teresa 25, Ortigia
Tel: 0931 65958
www.palazzodelsale.it
Set in a former salt workshop, this quirky but upmarket B&B is decorated in warm colours, and is convenient for exploring the most atmospheric part of Siracusa: the island of Ortigia. €€

B & B Dolce Casa
Loc. Fontane Bianche Via Lido Sacramento 4
Tel: 0931 721 135
www.bbdolcecasa.it
With its tranquil garden and old-world charm, this noted villa B&B makes a charming base from which to enjoy the countryside, the beach and the historical sights. The villa is only 10 minutes from one of Siracusa's best beaches, Fontane Bianche. The other draw is the food, with tasty home-made pastries produced for breakfast. €–€€

Domus Mariae
Via Vittoria Veneto 76
Tel: 0931 24854
www.sistemia.it/domusmariae
A restored ancient building in the historic centre, this small hotel with 13 rooms is run by Ursuline nuns, who offer a warm welcome. €–€€

Augusta

This is an emergency overnight stop for those catching an early ferry the next day. In the vicinity there is the touristy resort village of Brucoli.

Villa dei Cesari
Loc. Monte Tauro
Tel: 0931 983 311
www.hotelvilladeicesari.com
24 rooms, garden, private beach. Simple but comfortable. €€

Noto

Restoration is progressing well, but the town is already looking lovely once more. Noto is a great base from which to explore southeastern Sicily, as it's covenient for both the rugged interior and the beach. Book rooms ahead in summer.

Seven Rooms Villadorata
Via Nicolaci 18
Tel: 338 509 5643
www.7roomsvilladorata.it
In the grandiose, Baroque Palazzo Nicolaci, this upmarket B&B respects the 18th-century spirit of the palace and princely former owners. The seven frescoed bedrooms overlook the magnificent cathedral, and from the top terrace stretch views of the Vendìcari nature reserve. €€€

La Fontanella
Via Rosalino Pilo 3
Tel: 0931 894 724
www.albergolafontanella.it
Central, tasteful, attractive 3-star hotel. €€

Centro Storico
Corso Vittorio Emanuele 64
Tel: 0931 573 967
www.centro-storico.com
A quaint B&B in the centre of historic Noto, with en suite rooms. Closed

Feb and Nov. No credit cards. €

Outside Noto

La Moresca Maison de Charme
Via Danolo 63, Marina di Ragusa
www.lamorescahotel.it
Set in Noto's upmarket beach resort, this is a stylish Art Nouveau villa dotted with design pieces. €€€

Villa Favorita
Contrada Falconara
Tel: 0931 820 219
www.villafavoritanoto.it
Country retreat with pool south of Noto. Charming rooms and service. €€€

Terre di Vendicari
Contrada Vaddeddi
Tel: 346 359 3845
www.terredivendicari.it
Not far from Noto, this friendly, well-run old farmhouse serves lovely organic breakfasts in a setting surrounded by lemon, almond, carob and olive trees. €€

Villa Mediterranea
Viale Lido, at Lido di Noto
Tel: 0931 812 330
www.villamediterranea.it
Small, unassuming villa across the road from the beach. €€

Borgo Alveria
Contrada Noto Antica
Tel: 0931 810 003
www.borgoalveria.com
Formerly a religious order, it is now a charm-

ing *agriturismo*, even if the bedrooms are very simple. It is reached via the SP 64. €

Portopalo di Capo Passero

Jonic
Viale Vittorio Emanuele 19
Tel: 0931 842 723
www.jonichotel.com
Small and inexpensive seafront hotel in the southernmost resort on the island. €

Solarino

Zaiera Resort
Contrada Zaiera, Solarino
Tel: 0931 922 674
www.zaieraresort.com
Set in an olive grove 15km (9 miles) from Siracusa, the stylish, rural resort also overlooks Mount Etna. The appealing spot has individualistic rooms, a spa, swimming pool and good sports facilities.
€–€€

ABOVE: room at Caol Ishka near Siracusa.

CATANIA CITY AND PROVINCE

Catania

Many of the hotels in Catania are geared to business travellers and so can seem somewhat charmless, if efficient, although B&Bs are springing up to offer an appealing urban alternative.

Excelsior
Piazza G. Verga 39
Tel: 095 747 6111
www.hotelexcelsiorcatania.com
Contemporary elegance (but lack of character), compensated for by its professionalism and the reputable La Zagare restaurant. €€€–€€€€

Una Hotel Palace
Via Etnea 218
Tel: 095 250 5111
www.unahotels.it
Luxurious, recently refurbished and situated on the main shopping street. €€€–€€€€

Donna Carmela
Contrada Grotte 5, Carruba di Riposto
Tel: 095 809 383
www.donnacarmela.com
Charming villa hotel where the owners cultivate flowers for sale. Good restaurant with a

menu based on local specialities from the Catania area. €€–€€€
Bellini
Piazza Trento 13
Tel: 095 316 933
www.nh-hotels.com
Recently modernised hotel in city centre. 130 rooms. €€
Etnea 316
Via Etnea 316
Tel: 0952 503 076
www.hoteletnea316.it
Refurbished B&B that offers a lovely home-from-home, with spacious, beautifully decorated rooms and a welcoming atmosphere. €
Nettuno
Viale Ruggero di Lauria 121
Tel: 095 712 2006
www.hotel-nettuno.it
With pool and restaurant. €€
Palazzo Biscari B&B
Via Museo Biscari 16
Tel: 095 321 818
Two small apartments in the noble Palazzo Biscari, Catania's grandest aristocratic palace, still owned by the family. A tour of the palace is automatically included. There is a

good restaurant within another part of the vast palace. €
La Vecchia Palma
Via Etnea 668
Tel: 095 432 025
www.lavecchiapalma.com
Charming Art Nouveau villa in the centre with 12 rooms. €

Aci Castello

President Park
Via Vampolieri 49
Tel: 095 711 6111
www.presidentparkhotel.com
Modern, on a small hill with garden, covered pool and private beach. 96 rooms. Good restaurant. €€

Aci Trezza

Faraglioni
Lungomare dei Ciclopi 115
Tel: 095 093 0464
www.grandhotelfaraglioni.com
Set in a fishing village with its own private lido and a good regional restaurant. €€

Acireale

Santa Tecla Palace
Via Balestrate 100 at

Santa Tecla
Tel: 095 763 4015
www.hotelsantatecla.it
Holiday hotel in excellent, panoramic location 3km (2 miles) from Acireale. Garden, swimming pool, restaurant.
€€€

Orizzonte Acireale
Via C. Colombo
Tel: 095 886 006
www.hotelorizzonte.it
Large comfortable hotel, 125 rooms, with swimming pool and panoramic terrace view.
€€

PRICE CATEGORIES

For a double room in high season:
€ = under €100
€€ = €100–180
€€€ = €180–250
€€€€ = €250–400
€€€€€ = over €400

TRANSPORT

ACCOMMODATION

ACTIVITIES

A – Z

LANGUAGE

Caltagirone

Villa San Mauro
Via Porto Salvo 14
Tel: 0933 26500
www.nh-hotels.com
Good base in the hills with a swimming pool. Rather corporate decor, but rooms are comfortable, with balconies overlooking Caltagirone. €€
La Pilozza Infiorata
Via Santissimo Salvatore 97
Tel: 0933 22162
www.lapilozzainfiorata.com
Stylish, Art Nouveaustyle bed and breakfast in the historic centre, with a comfortable, tastefully decorated rooms and a terrace. €
Tre Metri Sopra il Cielo
Via Bongiovanni 72
Tel: 0933 193 5106
www.bbtremetrisopurailcielo.it

A small but friendly B&B overlooking the Santa Maria del Monte steps, with just two rooms (one en suite) and a lovely breakfast terrace with stunning views. €

Cannizzaro

Baia Verde
Via Angelo Musco 8
Tel: 095 491 522
www.baiaverde.it
Right on the water's edge, with modern rooms and good services. €€
Sheraton Catania
Via A da Messina, 6km (4 miles) from Catania
Tel: 095 711 4111
www.sheratoncatania.com
Comfortable hotel with a pool, suites, and renowned restaurant, Il Timo. €€

Linguaglossa

On the northern slopes of Mount Etna, so it tends to be fully booked during the ski season.
Happy Day
Via Mareneve 9
Tel: 095 643 484
Basic hotel. Open in winter only. €

Nicolosi

If you plan to stay during the winter, book early, especially if it is predicted to be snowy. There are mountain walks from Nicolosi, organised by the local tourist office, year-round.
Biancaneve
Via Etnea 163
Tel: 095 911 176
www.hotelbiancaneve.com

Family-friendly hotel open all year, with pool, spa and view of Mount Etna. €€
Gemmellaro
Via Etnea 160
Tel: 095 911 060
www.hotelgemmellaro.it
Quiet, modern and popular. €

Zafferana Etnea

On southern slopes of Etna. Good skiing base.
Airone
Via Cassone 67
Tel: 095 708 1819
www.hotel-airone.it
Views reaching coast. 60 rooms, garden. €€€
Primavera dell'Etna
Via Cassone 86
Tel: 095 708 2348
www.hotel-primavera.it
With 55 rooms, terrace with panoramic views. €

TAORMINA

The Taormina hotel listing also covers accommodation in Mazzarò beach below the resort and in Castelmola, which looms over the resort. Unlike almost anywhere else in Sicily, Taormina has several destination hotels, notably Grand Timeo, now run with supreme professionalism by the Orient Express group, and the de luxe beach hotel Villa Sant'Andrea. These are matched by the mystique and fine dining at San Domenico. During the peak season (Apr–Oct) and around Christmas, many hotels insist on half-board. Some have beach concessions on the coast, below the town, and can provide transfers.

Grand Hotel Timeo
Via Teatro Greco 59
Tel: 0942 627 0200
www.grandhoteltimeo.com
Set beside the Teatro Greco, Taormina's (and Sicily's) grandest hotel is back to its original splendour. Newly renovated, airy, sophisticated suites (often with "his and her" bathrooms) overlook terraced gardens and the sea. Panoramic views from the terrace; superb restaurant *(see page 236)*; shuttle to private beach at sister hotel. Wonderfully engaging staff, excellent female sommelier and the best service in Sicily. €€€€€
San Domenico Palace
Piazza San Domenico 5
Tel: 0942 613 111
www.amthotels.it

For romantic history-lovers, the former Dominican monastery feels like a living museum and a private world, with several cloisters, gorgeous gardens and more public rooms than any other hotel. The top suite has a Jacuzzi on the terrace. Discuss the rooms before booking, because while some are grand, others are smaller, though arguably more atmospheric. Magnificent views, especially from the terrace towards Etna and the sea. Superb restaurant *(see page 237)* won a Michelin star in 2011. €€€€€
San Pietro
Via Pirandello 50
Tel: 0942 620 711
www.grandhotelsanpietro.net

Charming luxury hotel with superb views, comfort, terraces, pool and delightful garden. €€€€€
Miramare
Via Guardiola Vecchia 27
Tel: 0942 23401
www.miramaretaormina.it
Elegant building with 68 rooms, pool, parking, tennis, gardens and views. Closed mid-Nov–mid-Dec. €€€€
Villa Diodoro
Via Bagnoli Croci 75
Tel: 0942 23312

www.gaishotels.com
Favoured because both its pool and restaurant have wonderful panoramic views of Mount Etna and the coastline. Shuttle to sister hotel on the beach. A few minutes' stroll into the centre. **€€€€**

Villa Taormina
Via Fazzello 49
Tel: 0942 620 072
www.hotelvillataormina.com
A charming boutique hotel, with rooms full of antiques, a lovely terrace, parking and a shuttle service to the beach. **€€€€**

Isabella
Corso Umberto 58
Tel: 0942 23153
www.gaishotels.com
Small but charming hotel in the centre of the pedestrianised Corso. **€€€**

Villa Belvedere
Via Bagnoli Croce 79
Tel: 0942 23791
www.villabelvedere.it
Comfortable, with covered pool, garden and parking. 47 rooms. Open Mar–Nov. **€€€**

Villa Paradiso
Via Roma 2
Tel: 0942 23921
www.hotelvillaparadisotaormina.com
Family hotel. All rooms with fine views and a private beach. **€€€**

Victoria
Corso Umberto 81
Tel: 0942 23372
www.albergovictoria.it
On the pedestrianised Corso in the centre of town. Simple but charming rooms. Roof terrace breakfasts. **€€**

Villa Fiorita
Via Pirandello 39
Tel: 0942 24122
www.villafioritahotel.com
On the hillside edging the town. 25 pleasant

rooms, many with wonderful views. Garden. **€€**

Villa Greta
Via Leonardo da Vinci 46
Tel: 0942 28286
www.villagreta.it
A small, family-run hotel which is surprisingly affordable, considering most rooms come with a balcony and incredible views. It's a 15-minute walk from Taormina on the Castelmola road. **€€**

Villa Schuler
Piazzetta Bastione 16
Tel: 0942 23481
www.hotelvillaschuler.com
Lots of charm. Comfortable with beach concession arrangements. Closed Dec–Feb. **€€**

La Campanella
Via Circonvallazione 3
Tel: 0942 23381
Pleasant, but hillside location not suitable for the disabled. **€**

Palazzo Vecchio
Salita Ciampoli 9
Tel: 0942 23033
Charming and quaint medieval mansion in the town centre. Sea views. Closed Nov–Feb. **€**

Mazzarò

Mazzarò is the beach resort below Taormina. A cable car connects the two. Mazzarò's popularity is confirmed by a variety of lively restaurants and clubs which tend to be less expensive than those in Taormina.

Villa Sant'Andrea
Via Nazionale 137
Tel: 0942 627 1200
www.hotelvillasantandrea.com
Originally an English-owned villa, the sister hotel to Grand Timeo lacks the grandeur of its older sister but makes up for it in the relaxing setting, majestic ter-

ABOVE: gardens at the San Domenico Palace, Taormina.

race, gourmet restaurant, spa, covered pool and private beach. Great for families. **€€€€–€€€€€**

Mazzarò Sea Palace
Via Nazionale 147
Tel: 0942 612 111
www.mazzaroseapalace.it
Luxurious holiday hotel over the small bay. Open Apr–Oct. **€€€€**

Capotaormina
Via Nazionale 105
Tel: 0942 572 111
www.atahotels.it
Sleek hotel perched above the beautiful bay of Mazzarò. Saltwater pool built into the cliff. All rooms have private terraces. Private beach. **€€€€**

Castelmola

Villa Sonia
Via Porta Mola 9, 5km (3 miles) outside Taormina
Tel: 0942 28082
www.hotelvillasonia.com
Popular villa-hotel on the steep hill between Taormina and Castelmola. Swimming pool, garden and view of

Mount Etna. Regular buses down to Taormina or up to Castelmola. Closed Nov–end Feb. **€€€**

Sant'Alessio Siculo

NH Capo dei Greci
Sant'Alessio Siculo SS114, Km 38
Tel: 0913 864 661
www.nh-hoteles.com
This new spa resort overlooks Taormina Bay, affording spectacular panoramic views of the striking landscape. The pool is an architectural marvel, reached by lifts carved into the side of a mountain. There are four international restaurants, three cafés, a spa, fitness centre and tennis court.

PRICE CATEGORIES

For a double room in high season:
€ = under €100
€€ = €100–180
€€€ = €180–250
€€€€ = €250–400
€€€€€ = over €400

MESSINA PROVINCE

Messina

Messina is a place for a brief stay before heading off to the islands or to Taormina.

Grand Hotel Liberty
Via I Settembre 15
Tel: 090 640 9436
www.nh-hotels.it
An Art Nouveau-style business hotel opposite the station. €€€

Royal Palace
Via Tommaso Cannizzaro 224
Tel: 090 6503
www.nh-hotels.com
A comfortable but unremarkable hotel in the heart of the commercial district. €€€

Capo d'Orlando

Il Mulino
Via Andrea Doria 46
Tel: 0941 902 431
www.hotelilmulino.it
Pleasant place with views; dine in on Sicilian dishes. €€

La Tartaruga
Via Consolare Antica 70, at Lido San Gregorio
Tel: 0941 955 012
www.hoteltartaruga.it
Comfortable, with private beach and highly regarded Tartaruga restaurant known for delicious Messina specialities. €

Giardini-Naxos

A pleasant mass-market resort close to Taormina; popular with families on a budget.

Hellenia Yachting
Via Jannuzzo 41
Tel: 0942 51737
www.hotel-hellenia.it
Large hotel with private sandy beach and with pool and restaurant. €€€

Naxos Beach
Via Recanati 26
Tel: 0942 6611
www.atahotels.it
Resort hotel with 189 rooms, four swimming pools, beach, sports facilities, entertainment. €€€

Arathena Rocks
Via Calcide Eubea 55
Tel: 0942 51349
Set on the rocks a little out of town (free bus available). Very tranquil. Garden, pool, tennis. Rooms are sea-facing or air-conditioned. Closed Nov–Easter. €€

Letojanni

Olimpo
Loc. Poggio Mastropietro
Tel: 0942 6400
Great views. 323 rooms, garden, pool. Not suitable for disabled or older

guests due to its position. €€€€

San Pietro
Via L. Rizzo
Tel: 0942 36081
Comfortable and with private beach. Open Easter–end Oct. €€

Milazzo

This is the port for the Aeolian Islands connections. Milazzo is not particularly panoramic, but it is convenient for an overnight stop if you plan to cross to the islands.

Petit
Via dei Mille 37
Tel: 090 928 6784
www.petithotel.it
Small, friendly, attractive

hotel opposite the harbour, with an eco-friendly outlook. Good restaurant using seasonal, organic ingredients. €€€

Riviera Lido
Via Panoramica
Tel: 0909 283 457
www.hotelrivieralido.it
Garden, private beach, parking. Some rooms offer a sea view. €€€

BELOW: Giardini-Naxos.

AEOLIAN ISLANDS (ISOLE EOLIE)

The Aeolian Islands have a number of inns (*locande*) where you should expect to take full board – this is the custom here. The islanders are keen to let rooms to tourists and will greet each ferry.

Alicudi

Ericusa
Via Regina Elena
Tel: 090 988 9902
www.alicudihotel.it
Basic but fine accommodation on water's edge. 21 rooms. Half- or

full board only during peak season. Closed Oct–May. €

Filicudi

La Canna
Contrada Rosa 43
Tel: 090 9889 956

www.lacannahotel.it
Located above the harbour, the best position in Filicudi, with fine views. The rooms are cosy and stylish, all overlooking the sea. Closed mid-Nov–Dec. €€

Phenicusa
Via Porto
Tel: 0909 889 9946
www.hotelphenicusa.com
The 34 rooms are a bit run-down, but those facing the sea have a superb view. Open May–end Sept. €

Lípari

Gattopardo Park
Viale Diana
Tel: 0909 811 035
www.gattopardoparkhotel.it
Near the centre of Lípari, an 18th-century villa and bungalows. Open Mar–Oct. €€€

Giardino sul Mare
Via Maddalena 65
Tel: 0909 811 004
www.giardinosulmare.it
On the sea and not far from the centre of Lípari. With swimming pool and direct access to sea. €€€

Villa Meligunis
Via Marte 7
Tel: 090 981 2426
www.villameligunis.it
Villa near the sea and the centre of Lípari. Panoramic terrace. €€€

Carasco
Porto delle Genti
Tel: 0909 811 605
www.carasco.it
Popular hotel with its own private rocky beach and excellent views. Open Easter–end Oct. €€

Oriente
Via Marconi 35
Tel: 0909 811 493
www.hotelorientelipari.it
Lots of character, and a garden setting. €€

Hotel Rocce Azzurre
Via Maddalena 69

Tel: 090 981 3248
www.hotelrocceazzurre.it
Newly refurbished rooms, located at the water's edge. €€

Diana Brown
Vico Himera 3
Tel: 090 981 2584
www.dianabrown.it
Run by a friendly couple, this B&B has 7 rooms with self-catering facilities and a roof terrace. €

Panarea

Cincotta
Via San Pietro
Tel: 0909 83014
www.hotelcincotta.it
On the water's edge, with fine terraces and pool. €€€€

Hycesia
Via San Pietro
Tel: 0909 83041
www.hycesia.it
With 8 rooms and garden. €€€

Lisca Bianca
Via Lani 1
Tel: 0909 83004
www.liscabianca.it
With 25 rooms, beach and pool. Large garden and balconies to each room. Open Apr–end Oct. €€€

Tesoriero
Via Lani-San Pietro
Tel: 0909 83098
www.hoteltesoriero.it
Overlooks the sea. €€€

Raya
Via San Pietro
Tel: 090 983 013
www.hotelraya.it
At once contemporary and timeless, set on the most chic island in the Aeolians yet still laid-back and effortlessly charming. €€–€€€

Salina

Capofaro
Via Faro 3
Tel: 090 984 4330

www.capofaro.it
This feels like essence of Mediterranean in its "barefoot luxury" simplicity, matched by sea views, Malvasia vineyards and whitewashed interiors on the island where *Il Postino* was filmed. €€€–€€€€

Bellavista
Via Risorgimento 8, Santa Marina Salina
Tel: 0909 843 009
www.hotelbellavista.me.it
On the sea, with verandas and views. Open Apr–Oct. €€€

Signum
Via Scalo 15, at Malfa
Tel: 0909 844 222
www.hotelsignum.it
Sited near beautiful cliffs. €€€€

Mamma Santina
Via Sanità 40, Santa Marina Salina
Tel: 090 984 3054
www.mammasantina.it
Luxurious hotel in the centre of Salina. Pool. Open end Mar–mid-Sept. €€€

Strómboli

La Sciara Residence
Via Soldato Cincotta
Tel: 090 986 004
www.lasciara.it
A comfortable hotel, one of Strómboli's best. 62 rooms, friendly service. Open May–end Oct. €€€€

ABOVE: the pool at Capofaro in Salina.

La Sirenetta
Via Marina 33
Tel: 090 986 025
www.lasirenetta.it
Elegant, with its own nightclub and pool. 55 rooms. Open Mar–Oct. €€€

Miramare
Via Nunziante 3
Tel: 0909 86047
www.miramarestromboli.it
Basic but smart. Open Apr–Oct. €€

Vulcano

Les Sables Noirs
Loc. Porto Ponente
Tel: 090 9850
Luxury seafront hotel near the black-sand beach. Restaurant. Open Easter–end Oct. €€€€

Garden Vulcano
Località Porto Ponente
Tel: 0909 985 2106
www.hotelgardenvulcano.com
Old-fashioned hotel in exotic gardens, owned by a retired sea-captain who has decorated the rooms with his "treasures". Open Apr–Oct. €€

PRICE CATEGORIES
For a double room in high season:
€ = under €100
€€ = €100–180
€€€ = €180–250
€€€€ = €250–400
€€€€€ = over €400

A CTIVITIES

THE ARTS, NIGHTLIFE, CALENDAR OF EVENTS, SHOPPING, CULTURAL ACTIVITIES AND SPORT

THE ARTS

Theatre and Music

Catania and Palermo have their own companies and present complete seasons of opera and ballet as well as classical music. In summer, most major cities and smaller resorts stage vibrant festivals involving anything from music to folklore or classical theatre.

Palermo

Teatro Massimo Piazza Giuseppe Verdi. Tel: 091 605 3111; www.teatromassimo.it. The city opera house. Opera, ballet and classical music.
Politeama Piazza Ruggero. Tel: 091 605 3421; www.orchestras infonicasiciliana.eu. Opera and ballet.

Catania

Teatro Massimo Bellini Via Perrotta 12. Tel: 095 730 6111; www. teatromassimobellini.it. Opera, classical music and ballet.
Villa Bellini Concerts and other open-air events in the gardens.

Classical Drama

Sicily's classical theatres often return to their original function as great settings for ancient Greek drama. Between May and June different dramatic cycles are performed in the Greek amphitheatres, from Siracusa and Segesta to Selinunte, Agrigento and Morgantina. **Siracusa** is home to the Institute of Classical Drama, so has home-grown talent to display in the great Greek tragedies (tel: 0931 487 200; www.indafondazione. org). **Segesta** also stages classical and contemporary dramas in its Greek theatre from May to June.

In **Taormina**, the Greco-Roman theatre is the setting for an annual summer arts festival in July and August which includes classical drama as well as opera, dance and music. (Book through the archaeological sites.)

Puppet Theatre

Traditional plays featuring puppets can be seen in Acireale, Catania, Palermo and Siracusa.

Palermo

Laboratorio Cuticchio Via Bara all'Olivella 95. Tel: 091 323 400; www.figliedartecuticchio.com. Perhaps the last generation of an old puppeteering family, with reinterpreted versions of traditional puppet theatre. Mimmo Cuticchio is one of the few remaining amazing recitors of the *cuntastorie*.
Opera dei Pupi Via Collegio di Maria 17. Tel: 091 814 6971. Two or three shows weekly at 5.30pm.

Museo delle Marionette Via Butera 1. Tel: 091 328 060; www. museomarionettepalermo.it. Free shows in summer: check with museum for details.

Acireale

Cooperativa E. Magri Corso Umberto 113. Tel: 095 604 521; www.teatropupimacri.it.
Turi Grasso Via Nazionale 95. Tel: 095 764 8035.

Siracusa

Piccolo Teatro dei Pupi Via della Giudecca 17. Tel: 0931 465 540; www.pupari.com. Traditional puppet shows are staged here several times a week.

NIGHTLIFE

From a visitor's point of view, Taormina, Cefalù and Mondello offer the most sophisticated summer nightlife, revolving around sedate piano bars and mellow clubs. Even so, these are now interspersed with trendy design cafés. On summer nights, the offshore islands come alive, with Ustica, the Egadi Islands (especially Lévanzo) and the Aeolian Islands (notably Lípari) awash with strollers, but Panarea popular with a celebrity crowd.

Beyond the coastal resorts,

Sicilian nightlife is surprisingly inward-looking. Even in Palermo and Catania, the nightlife scene can be a magical mystery tour. As ample compensation, visitors will be fully embraced by Sicilians during any festivity, so leap in and cast inhibitions aside *(see Calendar of Events).* Catania is definitely cooler for a younger crowd, while Palermitan nightlife can feel like a bewilderingly insider experience. The city empties on summer evenings, when the locals decamp to the beach resort of Mondello.

Outside the festivals, romance takes the form of a *passeggiata* (stroll), an Italian institution that finds favour in Sicily. Mondello and Taormina witness a nightly fashion parade, but in cities such as Siracusa, the Ortigia waterfront turns any walk into a moody melodrama. Much Sicilian "nightlife" actually revolves around food, including grazing on street food, artisanal *gelati* and refreshing *granite.*

City Nightspots

Palermo

Nightlife can feel unfathomable, but Palermo plays with the rough and the smooth. Cocktail hour in the upmarket quarter around Viale della Libertà is definitely smooth, with a *passeggiata* and chic cafès, such as **Antico Caffè Spinnato** (Via Principe Belmonte). Palermo fuses styles and moods to perfection in **Kursaal Kalhesa** (Foro Italico 21; tel: 091 616 2282; www.kursaalkalhesa.it). This eclectic café, restaurant, arty wine bar and mellow club is set within ancient stone walls. On the edge of town is **Tonnara Bordonaro** (via Bordonaro; tel: 091 637 2267; www.kursaaltonnara.it), a 16th-century tuna fishery which comes alive as a summery, waterside venue, with bars, gardens, a restaurant and live music.

Catania

Nightlife is cool and youthful, revolving around bars and clubs.

The **Mercati Generali** (SS 417 Caltagirone to Gela; tel: 095 571 458) a cult music venue, including summer partying in the courtyard (May–Oct).

Siracusa

Siracusa's nightlife is mostly café life on the island of **Ortigia,** especially around Fontana Aretusa and the Lungomare Alfeo. **Tinkitè** (Via della Giudecca 63; www.tinkite.it) is a bohemian bar for *aperitivi* and mingling over Nero d'Avola and nibbles. For magical live entertainment, the **Greek theatre** is the stage for classical drama.

Taormina

Seize the opportunity to attend a live event at the **Greek theatre**. A sophisticated evening is guaranteed in the elegant bars in Taormina's top hotels, from San Domenico to the Metropole. Among the more enduring bars is Wunderbar, on Piazza IX Aprile, where the view is truly *wunderbar.*

CALENDAR OF EVENTS

January–March

Carnival (pre-Lenten): the best are in Sciacca and Acireale.
Catania: Feast of Sant'Agata, the patron saint (3–5 Feb).
Easter festivals: Sicily-wide, including Trápani and Prizzi.

Agrigento: Almond Fair (Jan–Mar), www.mandorliinfiore.net.
Palermo: Opera season, Teatro Massimo, www.teatromasimo.it

May–June

Siracusa and Segesta: classical comedies and tragedies in the Greek theatres. The season runs until end of summer. Part of Circuito del Mito, www.ilcircuitodelmito.it
Taormina: Taormina Arte: cinema, music, opera, ballet in the Greek theatre (June until end Aug) www.taormina-arte.com

July–August

Summer festivals in Catania, Cefalù, Enna, Erice, Siracusa, Ragusa and Taormina.
Caltagirone: Scala Illuminata (Staircase of Light, July) www.comune.caltagirone.ct.it
Palermo: Feast of Santa Rosalia (patron saint, July)
Enna: Estate Ennese. Summer concerts in the city castle.
Erice: Festival of Medieval Music, held in town churches.
Piazza Armerina: Palio dei Normanni (medieval pageantry, Aug) www.comunepiazzaarmerina.en.it
Madonie mountains: Tradizioni Nobiliari (food and folklore, Aug) www.comune.geracisiculo.pa.it
Castelbuono: Jazz Festival (Aug), www.castelbuonojazzfestival.it
Trápani: Luglio Musicale. Summer Music. www.lugliomusicale.it

BELOW: Allesandro Amorosso concert at the Teatro Greco, Taormina.

September–December

Etna villages: food and wine harvest festivals.
San Vito lo Capo: Couscous Festival in Sept, www.couscousfest.it
Ragusa: Ibla Buskers Festival (Oct, www.iblabuskers.it)
Catania: Concert season in Teatro Bellini.
Monreale: Sacred organ music in the cathedral, www.settimanamusica sacra.it
Módica: Chocobarocco (chocolate festival, Dec), www.chocobarocco.it
Siracusa: Feast of Santa Lucia (patron saint, Dec)
Palermo: opera season (Teatro Massimo) runs until May.

SHOPPING

Sicily is not always as sophisticated as mainland Italy, but that is part of the island's charm, and the markets feel like a force of nature, especially in Palermo and Catania. Even so, designer shopping is readily available in the resorts. **Sicilia Fashion Village**, in Agira, just east of Enna, is Sicily's first luxury designer shopping mall, with all the big names (www.siciliafashionvillage.it). It's a big deal in Sicily, and there's a free shuttle from Agrigento, Catania, Messina, Palermo, Siracusa and Trápani.

Pottery, puppets and coral jewellery represent the best of traditional Sicilian handicrafts, while art books or special foodstuffs make excellent souvenirs.

Shopping Hours

Weekday hours are 9am–1pm and 4–7.30pm, but many non-food shops close on Monday, with food shops generally closed on Wednesday (supermarkets excepted). In Taormina the shops are open daily.

Antiques

Siracusa is renowned for its reproductions of classical Greek

SICILY'S FINEST FOODS AND PRODUCE

Many of the island's delicacies make lovely souvenirs or, more likely, will be devoured en route, whether pistachios from Bronte on Mount Etna, Módica chocolate or pastries from Noto.

These are a few foodie suggestions. Near **Alcamo**, **Azienda Agricola Saverio Adamo** (Contrada Fico; tel: 0924 506 970; email: saverio.adamo@yahoo.it; contact beforehand in English) can supply (including for export) olive oil, wine and typical Sicilian produce.

In Módica, **Palazzo Failla** (5 Via Blandini) is a celebrity chef-owned delicatessen in the town's best hotel, with gourmet Sicilian produce – from olive oil, capers and oregano to Módica chocolate and saffron from Enna. Try the ingredients in his simple inn next door or his superb restaurant nearby, La Gazza Ladra. In **Chiaramonte**,

request the Percorsi dell'Olio oil route map from the town hall (or olive oil museum) and visit producers such as Gulfi (www.gulfi.it), which produce some of the best oil in Sicily. Near Sciacca, **Villareale** (Campo d'Oro; www.villareale.net) produces the finest Sicilian gourmet preserves and vegetable pâtés, including almond spreads, *caponata*, spicy pesto, honey and oils (for export too).

In Palermo, buy "**Mafia free**" **foodstuffs** and tasteful souvenirs (caps, ceramics, books) from producers fighting the Mafia (**Emporio Pizzofree**, Via V. Emanuele 172; www.puntopizzofree.com). Or choose **Libera Terre produce** in Palermo, grown on lands confiscated from the Mafia (**Bottega dei Sapori**; Piazza Castelnuovo 13; www.liberaterre.it). There are other outlets in Erice and Corleone.

coins. In Palermo a number of shops around Corso Umberto sell a mixture of antiques and bric-a-brac. Near the Cappuccini Catacombs Palermo's daily antiques market also contains fakes and junk.

Books

In Palermo, for second-hand books (including lavish books on art and history), try the Quattro Canti area along Via Roma. For stylish, Sicilian-produced books on the island's culture, visit Libreria Sellerio, Viale Regina Elena 59, Palermo. Feltrinelli is a reliable generalist bookshop (Via Maqueda 395).

Clothes

For fashionable clothes, the best bets are Viale della Libertà and Via Ruggero Settimo in Palermo, Via Etnea in Catania, and Corso Umberto in Taormina. Here you will find designer clothes from

Valentino, Coveri, Gucci and Armani, as you will at Sicilia Fashion Village *(see above)*. For cheaper shopping, in Palermo try Via Maqueda or Via Roma. In Catania opt for the side streets off Via Etnea.

Jewellery

Special coral and gold jewellery is obtainable from jewellers in Palermo, Catania and Taormina. Arty jewellery is sold in Cefalù, while coral pieces can be bought from many shops in resorts. Around Etna, glittering (or garish) lavastone necklaces and bracelets have novelty value.

Painted Carts

Models of traditional Sicilian carts *(see pages 200–1)* are sold all over the island. In Catania, Alice Valente paints carts (www.alicevalenti.it), while craftsmen in Aci Sant'Antonio will actually make them.

Papyrus

Papermaking and writing and drawing on papyrus are traditional crafts around Siracusa. Stalls and shops sell inexpensive examples, ranging from copies of Egyptian designs to portraits of you while you wait.

Pottery and Ceramics

Sicily's main centres for ceramics are **Caltagirone**, **Santo Stefano di Camastra** and **Sciacca**, with Caltagirone the most prestigious in historical terms. Pottery, one of Sicily's glories, has been around for a long time. Kilns from the 3rd century BC have been found around Siracusa, Catania and Mózia. When the Arabs arrived in Sicily in 827, they introduced glazing techniques used in Persia, Syria and Egypt. Tin-glazed pottery, or majolica, appeared in the Trápani area in 1309.

Caltagirone ceramics boast instantly recognisable animal and floral motifs in dark blue and copper green with splashes of yellow. Look out for the tall *alberelli*, jars with nipped-in waists once used for storing dry drugs, and the vast selection of heads depicting characters from Sicilian history that are used as ornaments of flower pots. Snap up some painted tiles, sturdy vases and chunky little stoups.

The devastating 1693 earthquake destroyed much of eastern Sicily as well as razing the ceramics workshops of Caltagirone, but there was a revival. At the end of the 19th century the Sicilian market, led by the Bourbons, became flooded with imported Neapolitan wares. To stem the flow, a pottery factory was set up in Santo Stefano di Camastra.

Santo Stefano ceramics. This ceramics centre comes into sight behind a jumble of crockery on the Messina–Palermo road. Tiers of dishes, soup tureens and fruit bowls rise at ever-increasing heights on each bend in the road, while cracked platters along the roadside testify to cars that have

come a cropper among the cauldrons and cake stands. High-quality local clay and fine workmanship have ensured the town's fame. Styles are very mixed, but the authentic ware has a rustic look and feel. Look out, too, for lovely wall tiles decorated with smiling suns and local saints, also seen in **Monreale**.

Sciacca: the charm of Sciacca is that the styles are so varied, and that the workshops are happy for you to watch them create, with the best being **Salvatore Sabella** (Corso Vittorio Emanuele 3).

Puppets *(Pupi)*

Puppetry's main traditions are in Palermo, and some of the best models are still made there. Vincenzo Argento (Corso Vittorio Emanuele 445, Palermo; tel: 091 611 3680) continues a 160-year-old family tradition. He will make you a *paladino* (paladin or knight) to order in his tiny workshop. After carving the wooden body, he solders on the copper armour and creates the costume with the help of his wife.

CULTURAL ACTIVITIES

Sicily is, above all, a cultural destination, and much of it is readily accessible by following this guide. However, if you have a special passion, consider a specialist tour, focusing, perhaps, on the classical heritage, the Baroque treasures, the archaeological sites, or on Palermo's palaces.

In Sicily, booking through a specialist operator often ensures a fascinating insight into the area of specialisation. In many cases, it will also ensure that you visit places, and palaces, normally closed to the public (such as Palazzo Biscari in Catania or a number of the fabulous aristocratic homes in Palermo).

However, another way of seeing the palaces is simply to stay there, usually in atmospheric

apartments, still called B&Bs. This is the case in or around Palermo, where you can stay with Conte Federico or the Tomasi Lampedusa dynasty, or in a villa, wine estate or island resort belonging to the noble Tasca d'Almerita family. Elsewhere, you can stay in upmarket wine resorts, many of which are owned by entrepreneurial aristocratic winemakers, such as the Marchese de Gregorio *(see page 286).*

Alternatively, to follow a folkloric tour of the island, choose a festival with particular resonance and time your visit to coincide with that *(see pages 283–4).* Folkloric festivals that stand out are the feast of Sant'Agata in Catania, the almond blossom in Agrigento, or Easter in Trápani.

Specialist Tour Operators

The following are recommended UK specialists:

ABTOI, the Association of British Tour Operators to Italy (www.love italy.co.uk), is a good place to start when planning holidays to Italy and booking unusual itineraries, ranging from art trails to adventures, including foodie, wine and walking trails.

ACE Cultural Tours, tel:+44 01223 835 055, www.acecultural tours.co.uk

Martin Randall, tel: +44 020 8742 3355, www.martinrandall.com

Film and Literary Trails

Sicily has a fascinating cinematic and literary heritage, with cultural trails attached. The most gripping recent trail is **"in the footsteps of Montalbano"**, which visits beguiling towns around Ragusa that are linked to the books written by Italy's bestselling author *(see page 171).*

In the footsteps of *The Godfather*. This is one of the most popular tours from Taormina, and can be done independently, with a visit to the villages of Forza d'Agro and Savoca, where *The Godfather* was fimed *(see page 248)*. Concierges at the top hotels (such as Grand Hotel Timeo) will set up a customised tour. In Palermo, book a tour of Teatro Massimo, where the melodramatic massacre in *Godfather III* was filmed.

In the footsteps of *The Leopard*. Tomasi di Lampedusa's *The Leopard* is Italy's greatest novel and breathes old-school Sicily in every sentence. The novelist was linked to both Palermo and the Agrigento hinterland. You can book a Palermo walking tour, do the walk independently or stay in his palace. In the case of the Agrigento sites, these are best seen on an organised tour *(see page 131)*.

Mafia-free tours. If you want an ethical holiday in a good cause, patronise shops, wine estates and farmstays that are standing up to the Mafia *(see page 33)*. These you can do through Addiopizzo Travel (tel: 380 154 4995; www.addiopizzotravel. it) or Libera Terre (www.liberaterre.it).

ABOVE: hikers on Vulcano in the Aeolian Islands.

FOOD AND WINE ACTIVITIES

Cookery Courses

One of the best known is **Anna Tasca Lanza**, run by the daughter of the cookery doyenne, Fabrizia, in the dynastic wine estate of Regaleali *(see page 144*; tel: 380 754 1365; www.annatascalanza.com). For another noble experience try **"In the Leopard's kitchen"**: a culinary and cultural experience. Spend a day shopping, cooking and dining with the Duchess of Palma, Lampedusa's daughter-in-law (www.butera28.it). At the other end of the scale, get a taste for "peasant cuisine" with **Giovanna Giglio** in Chiaramonte, in the Monte Iblei area (tel. +39 3655 1822). Courses featuring food and wine pairing are best done in Wine Resorts such as Sirignano *(see right).*

Wine Estates

The following wine estates (known as *tenute*) do guided tastings and vineyard visits, but best to call to arrange a visit beforehand, and check directions:

Azienda Agricola Pollara, Contrada Malvello, SP4 bis for 2km, Monreale, Palermo Province, tel: 091 846 2922, www.principedicor leone.it

Donnafugata, Via Sebastiano Lipari 18, Marsala, Trápani Province, tel: 0923 724245, www.donnafugata.it. (Donnafugata also has estates that can be visited in Pantelleria and Contessa Entellina, in Palermo Province, with full details on the website).

Duca di Salaparuta, Via Nazionale, SS113, Casteldaccia Palermo Province, tel: 091 945201, www.duca.it

Gulfi, Contrada da. Patrìa, Chiaramonte Gulfi, Ragusa Province, tel: 0932 921 654 and 0932 928 081, www.gulfi.it

Planeta, Contrada Dispensa, Menfi, Agrigento Province, tel: 091 327 965, www.planeta.it

Tasca d'Almerita, Contrada da Regaleali, Sclafani Bagni, Palermo Province, tel: 091 645 9711 and 0921 544 011, www.tascadalmerita.it (also cooking courses and estate accommodation).

Marsala producers: Known as *stabilmenti*, these producers provide some of the slickest tours, with wine-tasting, cellar tours and

a film. Florio (now owned by Martini) leads the market in sales, while De Bartoli is a rare independent producer.

De Bartoli, Contrada Fornara Samperi 292, Marsala, Trápani Province, tel: 0923 962 093, www. marcodebartoli.com

Stabilmento Florio, Via Vincenzo Florio 1, Marsala, Trápani Province, tel: 0923 781 111, www.can tineflorio.com (Mon–Fri 9am–5pm, Sat 9am–3pm). The Florio staff are particularly amenable to visits and offer an interesting and enjoyable tour of the cellars. Their Vergine Marsala is best.

Pellegrino, 39 Via del Fante, Marsala, Trápani Province, tel: 0923 719 911, www.carlopellegrino.it

Wine Resorts

Proper wine estates where you can usually stay, dine, or do a cookery or wine-tasting course. For more information, *see page 45*.

Baglio San Vincenzo, Contrada San Vincenzo Menfi, Agrigento Province, tel: 0925 75065, www. bagliosanvincenzo.it

Capofaro Malvasia & Resort, Isola di Salina, Aeolian Islands, tel: 090 9844 33301, www.capo faro.it (a chic spot owned by the Tasca d'Almerita dynasty).

La Foresteria dell'Azienda Planeta, Contrada Passo di Gurra ex SS115 SP79, Menfi, Agrigento Province, tel: 0925 195 5460, www.planeta.it

Sirignano Wine Resort, Contrada Sirignano, Monreale, Palermo Province (but in reality outside Alcamo), tel: 091 781 680, www.marchesidegrigorio.it. Guided tastings, cookery courses, archaeological tours.

OUTDOOR ACTIVITIES

Beaches and Watersports

It is not a problem to find somewhere to swim, whether in the sea, lakes or rivers. The smaller islands offer the cleanest and clearest water *(see Diving, below)*. Patches of the sea are severely polluted (the coasts around Augusta, Gela and Termini Imerese). *For information on Sicily's best beaches, see page 173.*

Diving

Sicily's coasts are rich in flora and fauna. Both snorkelling and scuba-diving are popular. The island of **Ustica** is the haunt of scuba fans. Its coastline is protected and offers spectacular diving in deep water, including sightings of wrecks. The Egadi Islands, particularly **Maréttimo**, are also a favourite with divers: they have crystal-clear, clean, deep water. Tanks can be filled on most islands, and several, including Ustica, also have decompression chambers available.

Snorkelling gives instant access to an exciting world, particularly wherever there are rocky shorelines, meaning the north and the islands. The area around **Isola Bella**, Taormina, is good for snorkellers. *(For more on diving and snorkelling, see pages 92 and 113.)*

Sailing

Palermo Province has lovely beaches not too far from the city of Palermo. Many have exclusive yacht clubs as well as a sophisticated nightlife. West of Palermo, the stretch of coast from Mondello and Capo Gallo to Isole delle Femmine is a standard yacht excursion. East of Palermo, the stretch of coast from Romagnolo to Capo Zafferano makes a pleasant boat trip. The wild stretch of northern coastline from Capo d'Orlando to Cefalù is one of the loveliest.

Windsurfing

Surfboards can be hired locally. The south coast is the best place for surfing because of the strong, dry wind, but conditions in Mondello's bay are also adequate, particularly near the lagoons below Tindari.

Hiking and Cycling

Hiking

The "wild west" feel is part of the appeal of walking in Sicily. However, in the case of both hiking and cycling this same wildness means that many trails are poorly marked or maintained. For this reason it's a great idea to book a guide, or join a guided excursion. The guides are generally very knowledgeable about history, botany and geology, and drop in fascinating facts about the cave-dwellings that you had barely noticed or the ancient Greek quarry that you mistook for a pile of rubble.

Walks range from peaceful coastal strolls through the nature reserve of **Lo Zíngaro** on Capo San Vito to treks in the **Nebrodi** and **Madonie mountains**. Walks through Sicily's volcanic landscapes are always popular. The **Aeolian Islands** offer magnificent unspoilt coastal walks *(see pages 46–9)*.

The excitement of walking on Mount Etna exerts an obvious pull, but it is not wise to do so without a guide *(see page 222)*. **Etna Trekking**, Via Roma 334, Linguaglossa (tel: 095 647 877; www.etnatrekking.com) is an agency that organises hikes, or call the information office in Linguaglossa, tel: 095 643 094.

Cycling

The round Etna bicycle race is held in April. It is an interesting event to take part in, but perhaps more fun is to be had standing on the sidelines watching and enjoying the scenery.

Unfortunately urban leisure cycling has yet to take off in Sicily, not just because the traffic is so chaotic. A few years ago, a promising public cycle scheme in Siracusa succumbed to Sicilian torpor, so the public bikes, either stolen or broken, lie abandoned in Ortigia. But there are Sicilians devoted to cycling, and demand has risen from visitors in recent years. Typical tours include Etna, the Val di Noto, the Marsala coast and Favignana. Many of the agencies along Taormina's Corso Umberto offer cycling trips, whether on the "mainland" or the offshore islands, where cycling is particularly popular, and reflects the slower pace of life on the islands. Concierges in the grander hotels will also be happy to organise a day's cycling. However, given the steep gradients in much of Sicily, it's important to be clear about your ability.

The foolproof option is to book a cycling holiday with a specialist *(see below)*, but you could also consider joining a Sicilian-run bike tour, for instance through Sole&Bike (www.solebike.it). The company offers a "Bike Tour Barocco" (Baroque Bike Tour) through the rugged Val di Noto area.

Specialist Tour Operators

In Sicily, whether self-guided or in a guided group, booking through a specialist operator often ensures a better deal, along with tried and tested routes, not subject to the vagaries of "lost in translation" itineraries. The following are recommended UK specialists:
Collett's (tel: +44 01763 289 660, www.colletts.co.uk)
Inntravel (tel: +44 01653 617 001, wwww.inntravel.co.uk)
Headwater (tel: +44 01606 720

199, www.headwater.com)
Hedonistic Hiking (tel: +44 0845
680 1948, www.hedonistichiking.com)
Sunvil (+44 020 8568 4499,
www.sunvil.co.uk) for farmstays with
great walks nearby.

SPORT

Golf, Riding and Skiing

Golf

Golf resorts are popping up all
over Sicily to cater to demand.
The most luxurious one is **Verdura Golf and Spa Resort**, near
Sciacca, with golf courses
designed by American Kyle Phil-
lips (www.verduraresort.it; *see page
273*). Instead, closer to Ragusa,
the Donnafugata Resort *(see
page 275)* boasts two courses set
amongst the carob trees, making
the most of the undulating terrain
and dry-stone walls of this patch
of southeastern Sicily: the Gary
Player-designed Parkland Course
is extremely popular. Also try the
swish Kempinski **Giardino di
Costanza Golf Resort** near Mazara del Vallo *(see page 270)*. The
most established golf club, **Il Pic-
ciolo**, is an 18-hole, par-72
course on the slopes of the ever-
present Mount Etna, so a smoking volcano can enliven any
game. Given occasional lava
flows that reach the course, the

terrain proves more challenging
than most golfers expect. The
clubhouse used to be a family
farmhouse. www.ilpicciologolfclub.
com

Le Madonie Golf Club, near
Cefalù, is an 18-hole, par-72
course overlooking the sea and
offshore islands on one side and
the Madonie Hills nature reserve
on the other, with views of olive
and citrus groves. Villas can be
rented. www.lemadoniegolfclub.com.

Facilities at the main courses
include a driving range, pitching
and chipping green. For more
information: www.sicilygolf.com

Gyms and Tennis

Gyms and fitness centres have
become part of the urban lifestyle, especially in wealthier cities
or in the luxury golf and spa
resorts. Most city gyms will accept
guest visitors. Many large (or
business-oriented) hotels also
have a fitness centre, especially
in newer resorts. Ask your hotel
for additional information.

Tennis clubs are open only to
members and their guests, so
choose a hotel or resort that
offers tennis.

Riding

Horse-riding is not really traditional
in Sicily; mules rather than horses
have always been used to carry
loads across the mountains. Nevertheless, riding is catching on,
including in the Nebrodi and

Madonie mountains. Stables near
Palermo include **Monaco di
Mezzo** (tel: 0934 673 949, www.
monacodimezzo.com) and **Portella
della Ginestra** (Piana degli
Albanesi, tel: 091 213 4597, www.
liberaterre.it). The latter, including the
stables of Centro Ippico di Matteo,
form part of a rural estate confiscated from the Mafia but now run
for the common good, including an
agriturismo (farmstay).

Skiing

Ski on Etna, on black snow with a
view of orange trees? Not quite.
You would need a very strong tele-
scope to see the orange trees, but
they are there. Etna is frequently
snowcapped all summer, and the
skiing season normally runs from
December to March. The snow
really is black, at least in patches,
where ash, dust and lava from
minor eruptions have blown
across it. In places, "hot" rocks,
those which are still cooling, melt
the snow and then stand out
through it like lumps of coal.

The views are spectacular, and
perhaps there is an element of
bravado in the idea of skiing on a
live volcano. Every now and then,
Etna really does come to life again,
and the skiing areas have to close
because of the danger from ash or
lava flows. Check that your insurance covers you for this risk.

Ski Resorts

Linguaglossa is on the northern
side of Etna. The Autobus della
Neve (snow bus) runs every Sunday between January and April
from Piano Provenzano, organised
by the **Ferrovia Circumetnea**
(see page 215). General information from Catania or Taormina
tourist offices *(page 293)*.

Nicolosi (**Rifugio Sapienza**) is
on the southern side of Etna,
above Zafferana Etnea; the altitude
is slightly higher than the northern
side. For information on the pistes,
Etna Guide, tel: 095 791 4755.

Both resorts are suitable for
intermediate and expert skiers;
Linguaglossa is the better choice
for beginners.

BELOW: Verdura Golf and Spa Resort.

A – Z

A SUMMARY OF PRACTICAL INFORMATION

A dmission Charges

Museum and gallery charges vary, but the average is between €5 and €15, while some churches now charge too. Most state and civic galleries offer free entrance or special rates to EU citizens under 18 or over 65. A document of proof of age is often asked for.

B udgeting for Your Trip

Prices generally match those in Italy; the island is not much cheaper except, perhaps, for eating out and shopping in food markets. Food, wine and clothes remain good value.

Mid-range hotels charge around €140 a night for a double room, and you can pay more than €400 at a luxury hotel. But there are good bed and breakfast establishments, and the spread of *agriturismo* provides inexpensive farmstay accommodation (but only accessible by car).

In touristy areas you'll find a three-course dinner with wine will set you back €40 a head, but simple trattorie with equally delicious food and wine charge much less.

Fuel costs have risen in line with rising costs across Europe, but public transport remains comfortably inexpensive, even if train travel is painfully slow.

C limate

Sicily is renowned for its sunshine, with July to August hottest (averaging 28°C/85°F) when high temperatures are intensified by a rise in humidity and lack of rain.

CLIMATE CHART

Palermo

Maximum temperature
Minimum temperature
Rainfall

The coldest month is February (10°C/50°F). Along the coasts, winters are short and generally mild. The Etna ski resorts are usually open December to March. Temperatures remain comfortable into May or June, but the landscape begins to brown.

Clothes to Bring

You will need light clothing during the hot summer months. But remember that many churches and cathedrals will not admit visitors with bare legs (i.e. no short skirts or shorts) or bare shoulders (cover with a scarf or shawl). In spring (April and May) and autumn (October and November), you will need light clothes but also a summer jacket or sweater for evenings. Between December and March, bring warmer clothes since winter, particularly in the mountainous central areas, can be cold. Hotels and houses tend to be less well heated than is usual in northern climates: indoors is sometimes chillier than out. Mount Etna is often snow-covered in winter, and its lava-based rock requires strong footwear in any season.

Crime and Safety

The main problem for tourists is petty crime: pickpocketing and bag-snatching (by young criminals known as *scippatori* or *scippi*), together with theft from cars in Palermo, Catania and the historic centre of Siracusa. The resorts of Taormina and Cefalù are normally very safe. Elsewhere, use common sense and don't flaunt valuables.

Expect the police to have a casual attitude to petty crime and a slightly suspect attitude to a woman on her own. Expect, also, to have to prove who you are and where you are staying before even beginning to embark on your tale of woe. In the event of a serious crime, contact your consulate or embassy as well as the Carabinieri. Following that, try the Sicilian approach: summon the most influential Sicilian you know and request advice. Having friends in the right places helps.

If you are robbed, report it as soon as possible to the local police. You will need a copy of the declaration in order to claim on your insurance.

Danger Zones: Palermo, Catania and big-city backstreets are the most likely places for *scippi*. Avoid the station areas of Palermo and Catania, and also the myriad unlit backstreets of Palermo's historic centre after dark. La Kalsa in Palermo is fairly safe during the day, but should be avoided by night. Be wary of the San Cristoforo area of Catania (behind the castle) and in the portside fish markets. In Siracusa, by all means visit the characteristic restaurants, but steer clear of the Via Nizza port area late at night unless there are plenty of people about. In Mazara del Vallo, explore the Moorish Kasbah, but ideally in company (with a local guide) and not at night.

Driving: Always lock car doors when driving, and keep valuables hidden. Unfortunately, roads are often poorly signposted, especially in Palermo, Marsala and Mazara del Vallo, as well as in much of inland Sicily. If you're lost, stop and ask someone, and don't be surprised if they offer to escort you to your destination: that's Sicilian hospitality.

Driving tips: To save time on long journeys across the island, take the A19 *autostrada* between Palermo and Catania, or use the A20 which runs along the Messina coast. The A18 Messina to Siracusa is another fast route. In the Catania area, take the RA15 (Tangenziale Catania) to bypass the centre of Catania.

Customs Regulations

For European Union citizens: provided goods obtained in the EU are for your personal use there is no further tax to be paid.

For non-EU citizens: the duty-free allowances are 200 cigarettes, 50 cigars, or 3lb (1,360g) of tobacco; 1 US quart of alcoholic beverages and duty-free gifts worth up to $175.

If you plan to import or export large quantities of goods, or goods of exceptionally high value, contact the Italian Consulate and your own customs authorities

beforehand to check on any special regulations which may apply.

The customs authorities are quite active in Sicily, partly to combat smuggling from North Africa, and partly because of the level of Mafia activity and the associated movements of goods and money.

D isabled Facilities

Sicily remains a challenging holiday destination. Most churches, museums and sites have steps, inside and out. Little has been done to create wheelchair access. Some trains have access arrangements (but check first) and seats reserved for disabled passengers.

Given the challenges in Sicily, it is wisest to book through a specialised tour operator or travel agency. These will offer customised tours and itineraries for those with disabilities.

Recommended tour operators are **Flying Wheels Travel** (www.flyingwheelstravel.com) and **Accessible Journeys** (www.disabilitytravel.com). In the UK travellers can contact **Holiday Care** (Tel: 0845 124 9971; www.holidaycare.org.uk) to access travel resources for disabled and elderly people. **Access-Able Travel Source** (www.access-able.com) is a database of travel agents from around the world with experience in accessible travel. **Flying with Disability** (www.flying-with-disability.org) provides comprehensive information on just that theme.

E lectricity

Standard: 220 volts AC, 50 cycles. Connections are either two or three round-pins. Adaptors can be found locally, but it is wiser to carry an international adaptor.

Embassies & Consulates

In Rome

Australian Embassy
Via A. Bosio 5
Tel: 06 852 721
www.italy.embassy.gov.au

TRANSPORT

Open Mon–Fri 9am–5pm.
Canadian Embassy
Via Zara 30
Tel: 06 0544 43937
www.canada.it
Open Mon–Fri 8.30am–12.30pm
and 1.30–4pm.
Irish Embassy
Piazza Campitelli 3
Tel: 06 697 9121
www.ambasciata-irlanda.it
Open Mon–Fri 10am–12.30pm
and 3–4.30pm.
New Zealand Embassy
Via Clitunno 44
Tel: 06 853 7501
Open Mon–Fri 8.30am–
12.45pm and 1.45–5pm.
www.nzembassy.com
UK Embassy
Via XX Settembre 80a
Tel: 06 4220 0001
www.britain.it
Open Mon–Fri 9.30am–1.30pm.
US Embassy
Via Vittorio Veneto 121
Tel: 06 46741
www.usembassy.it
Open Mon–Fri 8.30am–noon.

In Naples

UK Consulate
Via dei Mille 40
Tel: 081 423 8911
Open Mon–Fri 9.30am–12.30pm
and 2–4.30pm.
US Consulate
Piazza della Repubblica
Tel: 081 583 8111
Open Mon–Fri 8am–noon
(8–10am for visas).

Emergency Numbers

Police: 113
Carabinieri: 112
Fire: (*Vigili del fuoco* is the fire brigade) 115
Ambulance/Medical emergencies: 118
Breakdown/road assistance: 116

Entry Requirements

Visas are not required by visitors from EU countries. A current passport or valid Identification Card is sufficient documentation for entry. For visitors from the US, Canada, Australia or New Zealand a visa is not required, but a valid passport is essential for entry to be granted for a stay of up to three months.

Nationals of most other countries require a visa. This must be obtained in advance from an Italian Embassy or Consulate.

Animal Quarantine: If you want to take a pet you need to have a Pet Passport, or the pet must be microchipped and have a vaccination certificate for rabies and an official document stating that the pet is healthy.

G ays and Lesbians

There is little of an organised gay scene in Sicily, but attitudes are fairly relaxed and gay magazines are sold at most newsstands. Taormina is still the focus for the native and foreign gay community. Its gay bars come and go. Consult Arci-gay, a gay national organisation (www.arcigay.it), or contact the Palermo branch (tel: 349 884 5809; email: palermo@arcigay.it). To accesss bars and clubs, you need to join the association, with a special membership card for foreigners.

H ealth & Medical Care

European Union residents are entitled to the same medical treatment as Italians, as long as they obtain a European Health Insurance Card (EHIC) before they travel. This covers medical treatment and medicines, although you will have to pay a percentage of the costs. Note that the EHIC does not provide for repatriation in case of illness.

In many areas in summer, there is a *Guardia Medica Turistica* (tourist emergency medical service), which functions 24 hours a day. Telephone numbers are available from hotels, chemists, tourist offices and local papers.

The *Guardia Medica* or *Pronto Soccorso* (first aid) for the area can also help in an emergency.

Lists of duty pharmacists are published in the daily papers (*Giornale di Sicilia* for Palermo and the west or *La Sicilia* for Catania and the east). In Palermo and Catania some are open late at night. The duty pharmacists will often speak some English.

General emergencies: 113.
Mosquitoes: If you are bothered by them, buy the small electrical devices which plug into a standard socket. Mosquito repellents are available in supermarkets.

Thermal spas: Many islands and resorts offer the chance to wallow in mud baths or take water cures. These are available at Sciacca (Agrigento Province), Castellammare del Golfo (Trápani Province) or on the Egadi and Aeolian Islands.

Water supply: Tap water is safe to drink in most places, but Italians generally prefer to drink mineral water, and this will usually be offered in restaurants. In some places the water supply becomes erratic in summer. Water supplies marked *Non Potabile* should never be used for drinking.

I nternet

Internet cafés are slowly opening up, but Sicily is behind the times, including with regard to WiFi hotspots. The best option is generally your (upmarket, modern, or business) hotel or a smartphone. Because of Italian anti-terrorism laws, to use an internet café you will need to show a passport or EU Identity Card.

Palermo: Internet Café, Via Candelai, tel: 091 327 151. Others come and go in the Via Maqueda/Quattro Canti area. There is a WiFi hotspot on Mondello beachfront and in the Alitalia VIP lounge at the airport.
Taormina: Internet Café, Corso Umberto 214.
Enna: Stupor Mundi, Via Roma 264.
Tourist information: Sicilian websites are improving and many are very good, though often still only in Italian (*see Useful Websites, page 294*).

ACCOMMODATION

ACTIVITIES

A – Z

LANGUAGE

M aps

The Sicilian tourist offices can supply maps which may be adequate if you are staying in one place. For touring, detailed maps are produced by the Touring Club Italia (TCI). One of their maps covers the whole of Sicily together with the islands. For general purposes, *Insight FlexiMap Sicily* is laminated for ease of use and durability and contains useful facts and travel information as well as clear cartography.

Money

The currency in Italy is the euro, written as €. A euro is divided into 100 cents, with 1, 2, 5, 20 and 50 cent coins. The euro notes are 5, 10, 20, 50, 100, 200 and 500. **Credit cards:** Except in the smaller villages, major credit cards are accepted by shops, hotels and restaurants. They can also be used to pay *autostrada* tolls. ATMs, the automated cash dispensers (known here as *Bancomat*) are widespread.

N ewspapers & Magazines

The main Italian papers *(Corriere della Sera, La Repubblica)* publish southern editions, but the local dailies are more popular. *Il Giornale di Sicilia*, Palermo's morning paper, includes practical listings (timetables, etc). *La Sicilia*, Catania's main paper, also has provincial supplements for Siracusa, Ragusa and Enna.

The following are Sicilian publications that may interest visitors: *Sicilia Magazine* – a glossy, highly illustrated art and culture magazine in Italian and English, published in Catania four times a year. *Sicilia Illustrata* – this glossy monthly covers Sicilian current affairs, politics and culture.

O pening Hours

Shops are generally open 9am– 1pm and 4–7.30pm. Except for those in tourist resorts, shops are

closed on Sundays. Food shops and fuel stations may also close on Wednesday afternoons. In cities, other shops are closed on Monday mornings. **Bars and restaurants** close one day a week: a notice indicates which day.

Banks are open Mon–Fri 8.30am–1.20pm. Some also open from 2.45pm–4pm. Changing money can be a slow operation. ATMs are widespread, but often only in towns.

Post offices open Mon–Fri 8.30am–1.15pm, Sat 8.30– 11.20am. The following open in the afternoon: **Palermo**: Corso Pisani 246; Piazza Verdi 7; Via Danimarca 54; Via Roma (Palazzo Poste). **Catania**: Corso Italia 33/35.

P ostal Services

Post offices in the big towns and cities are generally open all day, with offices in smaller towns closing around 1pm. In Palermo, the main post office in Via Roma (near Piazza Domenico) is open Mon– Sat 8am–6.30pm *(see above)*.

Stamps *(francobolli)* are also available from tobacconists *(tabacchi)* and bars that also sell cigarettes. Letters and postcards within the EU cost €0.41; outside the EU it is €0.52 (for less than 20g). The postal service is not renowned for its speed. If you need to send an urgent letter, send it by *Posta Prioritaria* (ask for the special stamps at the tobacconists, and the mail should be posted in the blue pillar boxes, not the red ones).

Public Holidays

Banks and most shops are closed on the following holidays:
1 January: New Year's Day *(Capodanno)*
6 January: Epiphany *(Befana)*
Easter Monday *(Lunedì di Pasqua)*: variable
25 April: Liberation Day *(Anniversario della Liberazione)*
1 May: May Day *(Festa del Lavoro)*
2 June: Republic Day *(Giorno della Repubblica)*

15 August: August holiday *(Ferragosto)*
1 November: All Saints' Day *(Ognissanti)*
8 December: Feast of the Immaculate Conception *(Immacolata Concezione)*
25 December: Christmas Day *(Natale)*
26 December: Boxing Day *(Santo Stefano)*

R eligious Services

Italy is a Catholic country. The hours of Mass and services vary from city to country village, but Masses are usually held on Saturday afternoon and Sunday.

Each church has its own Mass timetable pinned inside its main door. Other denominations may practise their faith without hindrance and have their own services in Palermo and Catania.

T elephones

Telephone boxes have been phased out, as Italians have the highest use of mobile phones in Europe. In big cities, however, there are often combined call and internet centres.

For calls within Italy, telephone numbers must be preceded by the area code, even if the call is made within the same district. Mobile phones work well in Sicily.

Enquiries: 4176 for international directory enquiries; 170 for operator assisted calls.

International dialling codes: To make international calls, dial 00, then the country code
Australia: 61
Canada and US: 1
Ireland: 353
UK: 44

Telephone offices
In Palermo, phone from: Piazza Giulio Cesare (24 hours); Via P. Belmonte 92 (8am–8pm); at the airport (8am–10pm).
In Catania, phone from: Via A. Longo (24 hours); Piazza Giovanni XXIII (8am–8pm); the airport (8am–8pm).

Television and Radio

There are dozens of private radio and TV stations, most of them awful. The commercial radio stations provide a mix of pop and phone-ins. The national radio stations (RAI) include news, current affairs and documentaries.

Time Zones

Italy and Sicily follow Central European Time (GMT + 1) but, from the last Sunday in March to the last Sunday in October, the clocks advance one addition hour to become GMT + 2. This means in summer when it is noon in Sicily it will be 11am in London, 6am in New York and 8pm in Sydney.

Toilets

Bars, cafés, restaurants and *autostrada* service stations have facilities. In a bar it is best to consume something first before heading for a toilet. Major sites now have reasonable facilities.

Tourist Information

The Sicilian tourism scene is still rather confusing, and information is hard to come by. On the other hand, Sicilian websites are improving, and many are very good, though often still only in Italian.

Tourism is now run by the Provinces, with varying degrees of success, and written material in short supply in many cases. Although the tourist office listings below are currently valid, addresses (and telephone numbers) change on a regular basis. Your first stop for information on the island is the Sicilian Tourist Board, although it functions better for general background than for precise requests for information. Brochures can be downloaded from their website:
Sicilian Tourist Board
Via Notarbartolo 9, Palermo 90141, tel: 091 707 8100 or extensions 707 8230/707 8258/707 8276. www.yourwaytosicilia.com; email: urp.dipturismo@regione.sicilia.it

In addition to tourist offices, a number of **tourism consortia**, either backed by local hoteliers, local interest groups or by the Chamber of Commerce, are beginning to take the place of some tourist offices.

In the absence of a visible tourist office, call in to **a travel agency or local tour operator** as these can be good sources of advice. In the more entrepreneurial resorts, especially in Taormina, Cefalù, Catania and Enna, some tour operators offer excellent, often adventurous day trips to anywhere from Mount Etna (explored in a 4x4) or a day trip to the Egadi or Aeolian islands. In Taormina, the Corso (the main street) is full of agencies offering such services.

Sicilian Tourist Offices

Official tourist offices are generally known as **IAT (Informazione Assistenza Turistica)**. Most big tourist offices will have staff who speak foreign languages, but this is far less true of smaller offices. When looking for the office, ask for *l'ufficio informazioni turistiche*. Tourist offices that can be singled out for their helpfulness include Palermo, Piazza Armerina and Taormina (which doubles as a tourist office for the Etna national park and Alcántara Gorge).
The main offices are listed below; note that opening times tend to be unpredictable in many cases.
Acireale Via Oreste Scionti 15, tel: 095 891 999
Agrigento Via Empédocle 73, tel: 0922 20391
Caltanissetta Corso Vittorio Emanuele 109, tel: 0934 534 826
Catania (city centre): Herborium, Via Crociferi (daily Mon – Fri 9am – 1pm, 2 – 6pm).
New tourist office with tearooms and museum combined.
Via Etnea 63, tel: 095 414 070
Catania airport tel: 095 093 7023
Cefalù Corso Ruggero 77, tel: 0921 421 458
Enna Piazza Napoleone Colajanni 6, tel: 0935 500 875
Erice Viale Conte Agostino Pepoli,

11, tel: 0923 869 388/869 173
Lípari Corso Vittorio Emanuele 202, tel: 090 988 0095
Messina Piazza Cairoli 45, tel: 090 293 5292
Milazzo Piazza C. Duilio 20, tel: 090 922 2865
Palermo Salita Belmonte 1, Villa Igiea, tel: 091 639 8011
Palermo airport tel: 091 591698.
Palermo train station tel: 091 616 5914
Piazza Armerina Via C. Cavour 15, tel: 0935 982 2462
Ragusa Giordano Bruno 3, tel: 0932 675 837
Sciacca Via Vittorio Emanuele 84, tel: 0925 22744/21182
Siracusa (Ortigia) Via Maestranza 33, tel: 0931 464 255
Taormina Piazza Santa Caterina (Palazzo Corvaja), tel: 0942 23243, www.gate2taormina.com and www.taormina-ol.it
Trápani Via San Francesco d'Assisi 27, tel: 0923 806 8008

Tourist Information Abroad

Canada: Office National Italien de Tourisme, 110 Yonge Street, Suite 503, Toronto (Ontario) M5C 1T4 Tel: 416 925 4882
UK and Ireland: Italian State Tourist Board, 1 Princes Street, London W1B 2AY.
Tel: 020 7408 1254
USA: Italian Government Tourist Office, 630 5th Avenue, Suite 1565, New York, NY 10111. Tel: 212 245 5618
The official website is www.enit.it

Tipping

In restaurants, a service charge is included in the bill unless the menu indicates otherwise. It is customary to leave a few euros (€3 – 5), rather than a percentage of the total bill, if the service has been good. Taxi drivers will expect a passenger to round up the fare. For small services, including to guides, around €5 per person is fine. In many small villages, a custodian nearby may open closed churches and should be tipped around €5 per person with many *grazie*.

U seful Websites

Sicilian tourism (themes)
Assessore al Turismo della
Regione Sicilia:
www.regione.sicilia.it/turismo
www.yourwaytosicilia.com
www.iat.it (tourist offices)
Sicilian heritage sites
Dipartmento dei Beni Culturali
www.regione.sicilia.it/beniculturali/
dirbenicult
Palermo tourism
www.palermotourism.com

Parks and nature reserves
www.parks.it
Riserva Naturale dello Zíngaro
www.riservaZíngaro.it
Oasi di Vendicari
www.oasivendicari.net
Parco Regionale dei Nebrodi
www.parcodeinebrodi.it

Sicilian Transport
Airports
Trápani-Birgi airport: www.aeropor
toTrápani.com
Palermo (Falcone-Borsellino) air-
port: www.gesap.it:
Catania (Fontanarossa) Airport:
www.aeroporto.catania.it
Pantelleria airport: www.pantelleriair
port.it
Trains
Services: www.trenitalia.it
Train timetables: www.ferroviedel
lostato.it
Shipping lines
Ferry comparison: www.traghettion
line.net
Grimaldi Ferries: www.grimaldi-fer
ries.com
Siremar: www.siremar.it
Snav: www.snav.it
Tirrenia: www.tirrenia.it
Ustica Lines: www.usticalines.it

W eights and Measures

All weights and measurements
are in the metric system. As a
rough but approximate guide:
A kilometre (1km) is five-eighths of
a mile. So 80km equals 50 miles.
2.5cm = 1 inch
1 metre = approximately 1 yard
100 grams = 4oz
1 kilo = 2lb 2oz

What to Read

History and Culture

The Leopard, Giuseppe Tomasi di
Lampedusa (Vintage). This is both
the classic Sicilian novel and Italy's greatest novel. A timeless
masterpiece.
*The Last Leopard: A Life of
Giuseppe Tomasi di Lampedusa*,
David Gilmour (Quartet). This is a
sensitive literary biography and
companion to *The Leopard* itself,
based on interviews with the
author's adopted son and full
access to the family archives.
The Normans in Sicily, John
Julius Norwich (Penguin/Barnes
& Noble). This remains the best
introduction to the "other" Norman Conquest, including of
Southern Italy and Sicily – led by
the great Euro-adventurers.

Crime and Society

The Shape of Water, *The Terracotta Dog*, *The Voice of the Vio-
lin* and *The Snack Thief*, Andrea
Camilleri. These detective stories/
thrillers are worldwide best-sellers,
helped by the Montalbano films.
All are available in English paper-
back editions (Picador).
Boss of Bosses, Clare Longrigg
(John Murray). This account covers the role and importance of
Bernardo Provenzano, the Mafia
boss *(capo di tutti capi)* who was
finally arrested in 2006 near his
home in Corleone.
The Day of the Owl, Leonardo
Sciascia (Granta/Jonathan Cape).
This novel about the Mafia was
written by a rigorous writer and
politician (1921–83) often known
as 'the conscience of Sicily'.
Midnight in Sicily, Peter Robb
(Panther). Personal insights and
trenchant observations on Sicilian society, customs, relationships, art, food, history and the
Mafia, especially centred on Palermo and western Sicily.
No Questions Asked, Clare
Longrigg (Miramax Books). Subti-
tled "The Secret Life of Women in
the Mob", this account covers the
varied role of women in the Cosa

Nostra, whom the author persuaded to talk.

Travel and General

Bagheria, Dacia Maraini (Rizzoli).
The author, the daughter of a
Sicilian princess, revisits the family's ancestral villa in Bagheria, in
an attempt to come to terms with
her past and with the desecration
of this once glorious town close to
Palermo.
Bitter Almonds, Mary Taylor
Simeti and Maria Grammatico
(Bantam). This foodie memoir is
inspired by a disappearing Sicily,
linked to the convents producing
pastries, notably the almond pastries in Erice.
Clay Ghosts in Sicily, Angie Voluti
(Bank House Books). Set in post-
war Palermo, this quirky new
novel features a lovelorn young
Sicilian sculptress haunted by
memories conjured up by visits to
the capital, with its secret tunnels
and dilapidated palaces.
Good Girls Don't Wear Trousers,
Lara Cardella (Arcade Publishing).
Living in a stifling Sicilian town in
the early 1960s, teenage Annetta,
the narrator, dreams that wearing
trousers will give her freedom, but
is told that "only two kinds of people in Sicily wear trousers: men
and *puttane* (sluts)."
A House in Sicily, Daphne Phelps
(Virago Press). An affectionate
travel memoir centred on Casa
Cuseni, a Taormina *pensione* that
welcomed artists and writers
such as Tennessee Williams, Ber-
trand Russell and Roald Dahl.
Made in Sicily, Giorgio Locatelli
(Fourth Estate). This new gastronomic tour of Sicily presents the
celebrity chef's simplest yet most
authentic island recipes. As Locatelli says, "In a Sicilian village,
you don't go out with a list, you
just go out and see what there is."
The Silent Duchess, Dacia
Maraini (Flamingo, also on Kindle).
Set in the mid-18th century, this
novel tells of a noble family, seen
through the eyes of the deaf-mute
duchess who strives for fulfilment
in a society in which women's lives
were circumscribed.

L ANGUAGE

UNDERSTANDING THE SICILIANS

The language of Sicily is Italian, supplemented by Sicilian dialects. Dialects may differ enormously within a few villages, and are an essential part of Sicilian culture.

In large cities and tourist centres you will find many people who speak English, French or German. In fact, given the number of returning immigrants – descendants of the families that were part of the massive emigration over the past 100 years – you may meet fluent speakers of these languages, often with a New York, Melbourne, Brussels or Bavarian accent.

One dialect with a difference is that of Piana degli Albanesi in Palermo Province: here Albanian is spoken. The population is descended from Albanians who arrived in the 15th century.

Pronunciation

A few important rules for English speakers: c before e or i is pronounced ch, e.g. *ciao* ("chow"), *mi dispiace* ("mee dispyache"). Then ch before i or e is pronounced as k, e.g. *la chiesa* ("la kyesa"). Z is pronounced as ts, e.g. *la coincidenza* ("la coinchidentsa"), and *gli* is pronounced ly, e.g. *biglietto* ("bilyetto").

The stress is usually on the penultimate syllable of a word. In this book, where the stress falls elsewhere, we have indicated this with an accent (e.g. Trápani, Cefalù), although Italians often do not bother to use one (and, if they do, they may disagree about their direction).

Nouns are either masculine (*il*, plural *i*) or feminine (*la*, plural *le*). Plurals of nouns are most often formed by changing an o to an i and an a to an e, e.g. *il panino – i panini; la chiesa – le chiese*.

Like many languages, Italian has formal and informal words for "you". In the singular, *Tu* is informal while *Lei* is more polite. For visitors, it is simplest and most respectful to use the formal form unless invited to do otherwise. To supplement the phrases below, we recommend the handy *Berlitz Italian Phrasebook & Dictionary*.

Numbers

1 Uno		**14** Quattordici	
2 Due		**15** Quindici	
3 Tre		**16** Sedici	
4 Quattro		**17** Diciassette	
5 Cinque		**18** Diciotto	
6 Sei		**19** Diciannove	
7 Sette		**20** Venti	
8 Otto		**30** Trenta	
9 Nove		**40** Quaranta	
10 Dieci		**50** Cinquanta	
11 Undici		**60** Sessanta	
12 Dodici		**70** Settanta	
13 Tredici		**80** Ottanta	

90 Novanta	**200** Duecento
100 Cento	**1,000** Mille

Basic Phrases

Hello (Good day) Buon giorno
Good evening Buona sera
Good night Buona notte
Goodbye Arrivederci
Hi/Goodbye (familiar) Ciao
Yes Sì
No No
Thank you Grazie
You're welcome Prego
All right (OK) Va bene
Please Per favore/per piacere
Excuse me (to get attention) Scusi (singular)/Scusate (plural)
Excuse me (in a crowd) Permesso
Can you show me...? Puo indicarmi..?
Can you help me, please? Puo aiutarmi, per piacere?
I'm lost Mi sono perso
Sorry Mi dispiace
I don't understand Non capisco
I am English/American Sono inglese/americano
Do you speak English? Parla inglese?
Do you like Sicily? (you will often be asked) Le piace la Sicilia?
I love it Mi piace moltissimo (correct answer)

Questions and Answers

I would like... Vorrei...
I would like that one, please

Vorrei quello li, per favore
Is there …? C'è (un) …?
Do you have …? Avete …?
Yes, of course Si, certo/Ma certo
No, we don't No, non c'è (also
used to mean: S/he is not here)
Where is the lavatory? Dov'è il
bagno?
Gentlemen Signori or Uomini
Ladies Signore or Donne

Transport

airport l'aeroporto
aeroplane l'aereo
arrivals arrivi
boat la barca
bus il autobus/il pullman
bus station autostazione
connection la coincidenza
departures le partenze
ferry il traghetto
ferry terminal stazione marittima
flight il volo
hydrofoil l'aliscafo
left luggage il deposito
bagaglio
no smoking vietato fumare
platform il binario
port il porto
railway station la stazione
ferroviaria
return ticket un biglietto di
andata e ritorno
single ticket un biglietto di
andata sola
station la stazione
stop la fermata
train il treno
What time does the train leave?
Quando parte il treno?
**What time does the train
arrive?** Quando arriva il treno?
**What time does the bus leave
for Monreale?** Quando parte
l'autobus per Monreale?
**How long will it take to get
there?** Quanto tempo ci vuole per
arrivare?
Can you tell me when to get off?
Mi può dire di scendere alla fermata giusta?
The train is late Il treno è in
ritardo

Directions

right a destra
left a sinistra

straight on sempre diritto
far away lontano
nearby vicino
opposite di fronte
next to accanto a
traffic lights il semaforo
junction l'incrocio, il bivio
Turn left Gira a sinistra
Where is …? Dov'è …?
Where are …? Dove sono…?
**Where is the nearest bank/
petrol station/bus stop/hotel/
garage?** Dov'è la banca/il benzi-
naio/la fermata di autobus/
l'albergo/ l'officina più vicino?
**Can you show me where I am on
the map?** Potrebbe indicarmi
sulla cartina dove mi trovo?
How do I get there? Come si può
andare?
You're on the wrong road E sulla
strada sbagliata

Road Signs

Alt Stop
Attenzione Caution
Caduta massi Danger of falling
rocks
Deviazione Diversion
Divieto di campeggio No camp-
ing allowed
Divieto di passaggio No entry
Divieto di sosta, Sosta vietata
No parking
Galleria Tunnel
Incrocio Crossroads
Limite di velocità Speed limit
Passaggio a livello Railway
crossing
Parcheggio Parking
Pericolo Danger
Pericolo di incendio Danger of
fire
Rallentare Slow down
Rimozione forzata Parked cars
will be towed away (Tow Zone)
Semaforo Traffic lights
Senso unico One way street
Sentiero Footpath
Strada interrotta Road blocked
Strada senza uscita Dead end
Vietato il sorpasso No overtaking

Shopping

How much does it cost? Quanto
costa?
(half) a kilo un (mezzo) kilo

100 grams un etto
200 grams due etti
a little un pochino
That's enough Basta così
That's too expensive E troppo
caro
It's too small E troppo piccolo
It's too big E troppo grande
I like it Mi piace
I don't like it Non mi piace
I'll take it Lo prendo

In the Hotel

I would like Vorrei
**a single/double room (with a
double bed)** una camera
singola/doppia (con letto matrimoniale)
with bath/shower con bagno/
doccia
for one night per una notte
How much is it? Quanto costa?
Is breakfast included? E com-
presa la colazione?
half/full board mezza pensione/
pensione completa
key la chiave
towel un asciugamano
toilet paper la carta igienica
**Do you have a room with a
balcony/view of the sea?**
C'è una camera con balcone/una
vista del mare?
Can I see the room? Posso
vedere la camera?
Is it a quiet room? E una stanza
tranquilla?
We have one with a double bed
Ne abbiamo una matrimoniale
Can I have the bill, please?
Posso avere il conto, per favore?

Finding the Sights

Custode Custodian
Suonare il campanello Ring the
bell
Abbazia Abbey
Aperto Open
Chiuso Closed
Chiesa Church
Entrata Entrance
Museo Museum
Ruderi Ruins
Scavi Excavations/archaeologi-
cal site
Spiaggia Beach
Tempio Temple

ART AND PHOTO CREDITS

akg-images 30, 35T, 87T, 235
Alamy 87, 141, 208, 216, 218, 225, 245
Neil Buchan-Grant/APA 2/3, 4T, 5, 6B, 7TL, CL, CR&BR, 8T&B, 9T, CL&BL, 10(all), 11, 12/13, 14/15, 16, 17, 18, 19, 20, 21, 22, 33, 34B, 42, 43R, 44, 46, 47, 49, 50/51, 52/53, 54, 55, 60, 61, 62&T, 63, 64, 65&T, 66, 67(all), 68, 69(all), 70, 71&T, 72&T, 73, 74&T, 75, 76, 77, 79, 82, 83, 84, 85, 90&T, 91, 92, 96, 97, 98, 99, 100&T, 101, 102, 103(all), 104, 105&T, 106, 108, 113T, 118, 121, 122&T, 123, 124, 125&T, 128, 132, 133(all), 134T, 135, 140, 145, 146, 148, 149, 151, 153, 156&T, 157, 158&T, 160, 161, 163(all), 164, 165&T, 169, 170L&R, 171T, 172&T, 173, 177, 178, 179T, 180, 181T, 183, 184, 185&T, 186L&R, 187, 190, 191, 192, 193, 194L&R, 195&T, 196, 197&T, 198, 202, 203(all), 205&T, 206&T, 207, 210, 211(all), 212, 213&T, 214L&R, 215, 219L&R, 221, 223L&R, 228, 229, 231, 232&T, 233, 234&T, 238, 239, 241, 242, 244, 247, 248, 250, 251, 252, 253, 254&T, 255, 256, 257&T, 258, 260, 262, 263, 265, 279, 280, 282, 283, 286, 289, 295
Caol Ishka 277
Capofaro 281

Contrasto/eyevine 126
Corbis 27, 31, 48, 86, 114T
Eremo della Giubiliana 174, 266, 274
Fotolia 3BR, 4B, 43L, 112, 113B, 115, 116, 136, 179, 225T, 230, 246, 271
Patrick Frilet/Rex Features 7C
Alessandro Fucarini/AP/Empics 40
Glyn Genin/APA 9BR, 66T, 88, 107, 108T, 126T, 129, 134, 168T, 181, 248T
Getty Images 154
Grand Hotel Timeo 237
Ronald Grant Archive 41
Hilton Hotels & Resorts 269
International Mathematical Union 182
iStockphoto.com 3C, 6TR, 111, 119, 136T, 142, 144B, 222
Michael Jenner 4C
Lyle Lawson 1, 23, 24, 25, 26, 28, 29, 76T, 92T, 130, 223T, 245T
Locanda Don Serafino 175
Magnum 38, 39
NASA 35B
Nni Lausta 259
Photoshot 7TR&BL, 45, 110, 114, 143, 152, 171, 217, 220, 243
SuperStock 6TL, 224
Verdura Golf and Spa Resort 137, 288
Villa Athena 272

Gregory Wrona/APA 88T, 89, 117, 120, 144T, 153T, 155T, 166, 167, 168, 189, 199, 209, 214T, 226, 227, 240, 249, 273
Zafferano 188

PHOTO FEATURES

36/37: all images **Neil Buchan-Grant/APA** except 36CR **iStock-photo.com** and 36BR **SuperStock**
80/81: all images **Neil Buchan-Grant/APA**
94/95: all images **Neil Buchan-Grant/APA** except 95BR **Photoshot**
138/139: Neil Buchan-Grant/APA 139TR; **Corbis** 138/139; **Getty Images** 139BL; **Robert Harding** 138BL; **Photoshot** 138CR, 139BR
200/201: all images **Neil Buchan-Grant/APA**

Map Production: original cartography Berndtson & Berndtson, updated by Apa Cartography Department

© 2012 Apa Publications (UK) Ltd

Production: Tynan Dean, Linton Donaldson and Rebeka Ellam

Index